The Winc
Makes Dust

The Wind Makes Dust

Four centuries of travel in southern Africa

Ben Maclennan

Tafelberg

This book is for David Calum Maclennan.

Tafelberg Publishers Limited
40 Heerengracht, Cape Town 8001
© 2003 author

Cover design by Michiel Botha
Author photograph by Simon Maclennan
Map by Abdul Amin
Book design by Etienne van Duyker,
Alinea Studio, Cape Town
Set in 10.25 on 12 pt Palatino

Printed and bound by Paarl Print, Oosterland Street,
Paarl, South Africa
First edition, first printing 2003

ISBN 0 624 04165 4

The wind does thus when we die, our own wind blows; for we, who are human beings, we possess wind; we make clouds, when we die. Therefore, the wind does thus when we die, the wind makes dust, because it intends to blow, taking away our footprints, with which we had walked about while we still had nothing the matter with us; and our footprints, which the wind intends to blow away, would otherwise still lie plainly visible. For, the thing would seem as if we still lived. Therefore, the wind intends to blow, taking away our footprints.

Dia!kwain, of the /Xam San, about 1875

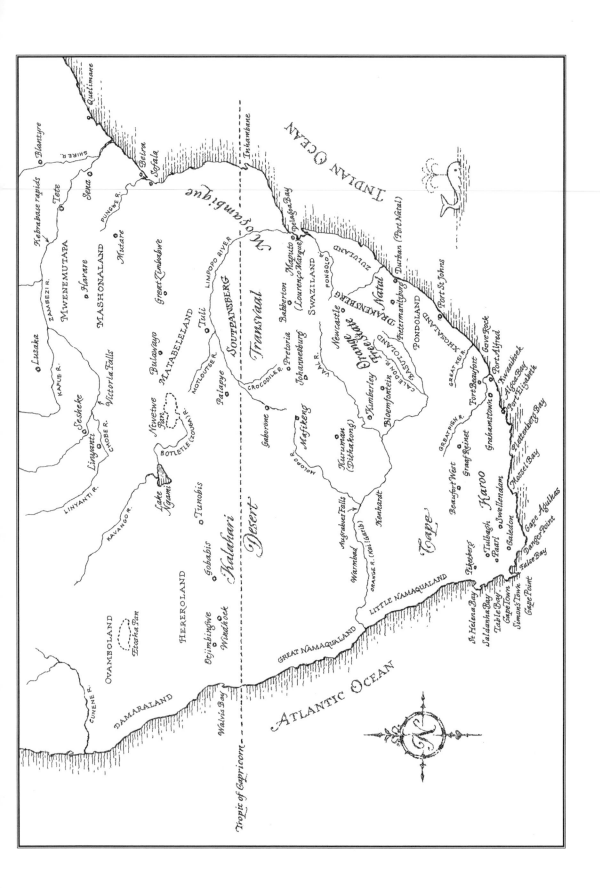

CONTENTS

Cloud Effects   Saldanha Bay   18..94

PREFACE

This anthology spans four centuries of travel in and around the southern tip of Africa. It begins with the sagas of early European seafarers making sometimes bloody contact with Khoikhoi at the Cape, and ends in an era of railways, barbed-wire fences and pass laws. In between, it parades a cast that includes soldiers and statesmen, cannibals both black and white, missionaries, elephant hunters, escaping slaves, circus showmen, fossil hunters, a shipwrecked Siamese mandarin and a homesick San shaman. It also contains directions for cooking elephant's foot, some truly awful poetry, a quest for the unicorn, and a sprinkling of discreet references to sex.

The collection has its genesis, in a negative sort of way, in my experiences at a government school in Grahamstown in the late 1960s. There, history lessons ran along the lines of: "When was the Great Trek, and name five contributing factors." Mess up badly enough, and you got a thrashing. Now, in middle age, I do remember that date: 1838 is seared into my memory like a cattle brand, along with sundry other milestones in the Steady Advance of European Civilisation. So when I discovered, well after leaving school, that southern Africa's past is made of more than just dates and contributing factors, it was a delightful revelation. I discovered a drama, alive with human beings who love and hate, who grieve and rejoice, who lie shamelessly or thunder out the truth, who are content just to get by in the world, or who proudly celebrate existence. Above all, who have voices, and voices that deserve to be heard. This anthology is an attempt to share that discovery, and to make some of those voices accessible to a wider audience.

Of course it has limitations, the most glaring being that the overwhelming majority of writers are Europeans. Think on this: the Swedish traveller Anders Sparrman, with his laboriously assembled wagon, oxen, and tons of equipment, tells how a Khoikhoi youth he has just recruited to his service stands up in his skin cloak, pauses to sling a tobacco pouch over one arm, and is ready to go. We have two volumes on Sparrman's travels, but nothing on what the journey meant to the youngster.

Another difficulty is that the European view of Africa was not always an attractive one. "Twenty-five lashes would kill an average Toro native," wrote Cape-to-Cairo swashbuckler Ewart Grogan in his tips for subsequent travellers. "But a hundred lashes barely make the dust fly off a Manyema porter." At worst, this view denied that black people were even human; in more benevolent form it saw them as a resource that needed to be carefully managed and exploited. However, there were also a few Europeans – just a few – who showed that they understood what their presence in Africa meant. One of these was an officer's wife, known now only as Mrs Hutchinson, who spent nine months in South Africa just before the outbreak of the 1879 war that the British engineered against the Zulu. "One must hope," she wrote, "… that the Kafirs will accept our apparently violent methods of civilizing them in the spirit in which they are meant, and will cheerfully suffer themselves to be missionized, shot, and bayonetted into tail-coats, monogamy, and trial by jury. They must see – that is, they must be made to see – that it is better to be improved, even if needs be off the face of the earth, than to remain in their present condition of barbarous, if blissful, ignorance." This collection is not meant as a history lesson. But I hope that here and there, it does give some indication of the processes, so devastatingly articulated by Mrs Hutchinson, that these writers were part of.

For those who are curious: I used the end of the nineteenth century as a cut-off simply because by then moving around southern Africa was appreciably less of an adventure. In 1894 Alice Balfour made a five-month overland journey from the Cape to Moçambique, and lamented at the end that she had seen neither lion, crocodile nor hippopotamus. I have also generally avoided accounts from military campaigns, even though they could easily come under my loose definition of travel, simply because they deserve a separate book.

About the click symbols used in the text: "!" as in Dia!kwain's name is a click off the palate, the noise used to imitate the clop of a horse's hoof. The "//" in //Kabbo is made at the side of the mouth, as if urging the horse to go faster. For /Han≠kass'o, the "/" is pronounced with the tip of the tongue against the back of the upper front teeth; "≠" is sounded with the front part of the tongue against the alveolar ridge. Although I talk of the "Khoikhoi", lexicographers prefer the spelling "Khoekoe".

I have not altered the sometimes unconventional spelling and punctuation of the original sources.

My thanks to the Foundation for Creative Arts, which gave me research funding at a very early stage in this project; to the endlessly patient and accommodating staffs of the Cape Town branch of the National Library of South Africa and of the Library of Parliament, and especially Maryke Jooste, my guide to the Mendelssohn collection before it was subjected to bar-coding; to Jackie Loos, Jean Jordaan, Peter Coates and Patrick Cullinan for advice on sources; to Hester Waher, Jean again, Louis Nel and Alfred Schaffer for help with translations; to Janette Deacon and Stephen Volz for help with matters of fact and terminology; to Dan Wylie for making me think a little more carefully about what I was doing; and to Gillian Warren-Brown for help with everything.

CHAPTER ONE

1497 to 1700

*In which a noble lady is stripped naked, shipwrecked
sailors eat frogs, dogs, local residents and their dead
comrades, Jan Verdonk surrenders his hat to a rhinoceros
and we are told of a nation with eyes in their feet.*

ANONYMOUS

*In a voyage that stretched over two full years, Vasco da Gama opened a sea route
from Portugal to India. An extraordinary feat of seamanship, it ensured that the
Cape and its inhabitants would become pivotal to European interests. At their first
landfall, at St Helena Bay on the West Coast in November 1497, Da Gama's men
discovered that the local dogs barked just like their Portuguese counterparts, and
Da Gama himself was wounded in a clash with Khoikhoi. This extract from the
journal kept by one of his subordinates describes their second venture on shore, at
Mossel Bay. A contemporary described Da Gama as irritable and "very disdain-
ful": he must have been in an atypically good mood here.*

MAKING A PRETTY HARMONY

On Saturday about two hundred negroes came, both young and old. They
brought with them about a dozen oxen and cows and four
or five sheep. As soon as we saw them we went ashore.
They forthwith began to play on four or five flutes, some
producing high notes and others low ones, thus making a
pretty harmony for negroes who are not expected to be
musicians; and they danced in the style of negroes. The
captain-major [Da Gama] then ordered the trumpets to be
sounded, and we, in the boats, danced, and the captain-
major did so likewise when he rejoined us. This festivity
ended, we landed where we had landed before, and bought
a black ox for three bracelets. This ox we dined off on
Sunday. We found him very fat, and his meat as toothsome
as the beef of Portugal.

FERNÃO LOPES DE CASTANHEDA

*Following in Da Gama's footsteps came Francisco d'Almeida, the
first viceroy of India, and one of the most formidable of the
Portuguese empire-makers. A man of "grave and majestic coun-*

3

tenance", he set out from Lisbon in 1505 with an armada of 21 vessels and orders to shut down the Arab spice trade in the Indian Ocean. His bloody victories, including the sack of Mombasa, ensured that for nearly a century the commerce of the East was as much a monopoly of the Portuguese as it had previously been of the Muslims. On the return voyage in 1510, D'Almeida's fleet put in at Table Bay for fresh water and raided a Khoikhoi settlement. Though each of three contemporary versions of the encounter gives a different reason for the clash, all agree the Portuguese were to blame. Castanheda says a group of Portuguese tried to kidnap one of the Khoikhoi, who stoned them in retaliation. They reported this to D'Almeida as an unprovoked attack, and without much difficulty, the viceroy was persuaded to launch a retaliatory expedition. So confident were the Portuguese that most of them did not carry any weapons, "that they might be unencumbered and walk more freely".

THE VICEROY IS DEAD

They reached the village at dawn on the 1st of March 1510, and Pedro Barreto and Jorge Barreto with the men divided into two companies attacked it, each on his own side, as had been arranged. The negroes heard them, and sallied out very readily with their stones, which they carried in pouches of undressed hide slung round them, and also many irons like our harpoons about a span in length, and these were set in rods of fire-hardened wood of the length of assagais, with a socket into which the irons were inserted, and these they carried on their shoulders in bundles. They seemed confident from the experience of the day before, for without any fear of the lances and cross-bows of our men, they attacked them immediately with stones and assagais, and one of their first shots killed the brother of Manuel de Lacerda, whose surname was Pereira.

Notwithstanding all, our men seized a quantity of their cattle which was behind the village, and the captains, seeing this, ordered them to retreat. They retired towards the spot where the viceroy was with the royal standard, who had disembarked and was stationed within two cross-bow shots of the village, to wait for our men and take them in when they arrived with the cattle, for he had left the boats meaning to return to them. Our men coming with the cattle towards the place where the viceroy was, he, seeing them, thought all was safely concluded, and went towards the boats, but they were no longer there, for Diogo d'Unhos, master of the flag-ship, had taken them back to the watering place, although, as I have said, the viceroy left them with the intention of returning to them. Not seeing the boats, he went in the direction of the watering place. He walked in front, to avoid the dust raised by the cattle, which were driven by three men in front of the rest of the company, who went a little behind to resist the negroes if they should appear.

As they were marching thus, the negroes ran very lightly straight among

The death of D'Almeida.

4

the cattle, and made them stand still by speaking to them; and they killed the three men who were driving them. Upon this the body of our men who were in the rear came up and began to spread themselves out, and the negroes also spread themselves out and began to fight with them very bravely; and some of those who were with the cattle began to move on with them. By this time they had overtaken the viceroy, who, seeing the strength of the negroes and their mode of fighting, and that our men were without arms, and the great peril which they ran, would not turn back, but continued to retreat, and he took no notice of the cattle which the negroes were driving off. But Lourenço de Brito, thinking that he did not see it, said to him three times, "My lord, they are carrying off the cattle," which annoyed the viceroy, and he answered "To the devil with the cattle, they will carry them off and us with them." Thereupon he turned and faced the negroes, and made them draw off.

Seeing how things were going, our men again assembled in a body and pursued their way; and the negroes again followed them, molesting them severely with stones and assagais, taking the cattle with them, with which they defended themselves, for they had taught them to move or stand still as they required, and thus they had a better opportunity of wounding our men. As our men were in a band, they never missed them, and so many were wounded that they began to fall, especially those who had no servants to help them along, and those who fell were trodden under foot by the others and suffocated, for they could not assist them, having no weapons of defence. They were so fatigued by the close pursuit that they were almost routed, which the negroes plainly perceived, and as men whom they despised they made grimaces and frightful gestures at them to terrify them more. Seeing this, Pedro Barreto could not endure it, and attacked one who annoyed them most with these grimaces. The negro fled, and he pursued and overtook him, and pierced him through with his lance, but immediately fell dead himself under the shower of stones and assagais which rained upon him; at which the viceroy was deeply grieved, the more so that he was unable to succour him.

Pursuing their way under these difficulties, it would seem that the viceroy foresaw what would happen, for he said to Jorge de Mello that he delivered the royal standard of the king, his master, to him, bidding him die upon it rather than leave it to these negroes. And near the watering place there was thrown from amongst them a headless lance, which pierced the throat of the viceroy, who wore no gorgelet, and he fell upon his knees with his hands upon the lance, and feeling that he was choking, he took his hands from the lance and raised them to heaven, as one who commends himself to our Lord, and thus fell dead.

As the viceroy fell, one of our men said to Lourenço de Brito, who, being fatigued, was carried on the shoulders of a page: "Sir, the viceroy is dead." He, seeing that it was true, being struck with grief, bade his page put him down; and he let himself fall, saying that since the viceroy was dead, he did not wish to reach Portugal alive. And so said Martim Coelho also, who was wounded, and he let himself fall, saying with great sorrow "O gentlemen what excuse will you make in Portugal for not dying, since it is only to embark, and what matter if it be this afternoon or tomorrow?"

The negroes charging our men, as there was none to encourage or direct them to unite and support each other against the enemy's charge, they were routed, and fled, each as fast as he could, towards the watering place, leaving the two aforesaid captains alive in the hands of the enemy, who promptly put them to death. And the royal standard was also left behind, there being no one to defend it. The negroes pursued them so closely as far as the watering place, that they were obliged to enter the water to reach the boats, which were so far out that the water came up to some of their necks. The negroes, seeing them embark, returned, leaving sixty-five dead, among whom were eleven captains with the viceroy, whose death caused great consternation, being so unfortunate, and in a place where it was so little expected, after escaping from the perilous battles which I have related.

A presumably better-armed force which returned to the shore that afternoon found D'Almeida stripped of his crimson velvet doublet, and his body cut open at chest and stomach. He was buried on the beach.

JOÃO DE BARROS

When the Portuguese learned there was gold in the region they knew as Monomotapa – the kingdom of Mwenemutapa, which dominated central Moçambique and stretched into the Zimbabwe highlands – they decided this was the biblical Ophir where the Queen of Sheba got her riches. Gold, it was reported, was not only found among stones "but grows up within the bark of several trees". Mwenemutapa, or "Benomotapa", as the contemporary chronicler Barros spells it, was also the title of the ruler of this territory. The "square fortress" here would have been Great Zimbabwe, a complex constructed of close on a million granite blocks. At the height of its prosperity in the late 14th century, before the rise of Mwenemutapa, it was the focus of a community of some 18,000 people.

STONES OF MARVELLOUS SIZE

There are other mines in a district called Toróa, which by another name is

known as the kingdom of Butua, which is ruled by a prince called Burrom, a vassal of Benomotapa, which land adjoins that aforesaid consisting of vast plains, and these mines are the most ancient known in the country, and they are all in the plain, in the midst of which there is a square fortress, of masonry within and without, built of stones of marvellous size, and there appears to be no mortar joining them. The wall is more than twenty-five spans in width, and the height is not so great considering the width. Above the door of this edifice is an inscription, which some Moorish merchants, learned men, who went thither, could not read, neither could they tell what the character might be. This edifice is almost surrounded by hills, upon which are others resembling it in the fashioning of the stone and the absence of mortar, and one of them is a tower more than twelve fathoms high.

The natives of the country call all these edifices Symbaoe, which according to their language signifies court, for every place where Benomotapa may be is so called; and they say that being royal property all the king's other dwellings have this name. It is guarded by a nobleman, who has charge of it after the manner of a chief alcaide, and they call this officer Symbacáyo, as we should say keeper of the Symbaoe; and there are always some of Benomotapa's wives therein, of whom this Symbacáyo takes care. When, and by whom, these edifices were raised, as the people of the land are ignorant of the art of writing, there is no record, but they say they are the work of the devil, for in comparison with their power and knowledge it does not seem possible to them that they should be the work of man. Some Moors who saw it, to whom Vicente Pegado, who was captain of Sofala, showed our fortress there and the work of the windows and arches, that they might compare it with the stone work of the said edifice, said that they could not be compared with it for smoothness and perfection.

ANONYMOUS

Even without natural hazards, a voyage on the Portuguese merchantmen that began regularly making the run to the East was risky enough. The owners, seeking to wring the last cruzado of profit from the run, jammed as much cargo as they could into vessels often already rotting at the seams. One of these was the galleon
São João, *which on her return journey in 1552 was laden with more than 600 people and the richest cargo that had ever left India on a Portuguese vessel. Her decayed rudder was carried away by the sea, her tattered sails could not take the strain, and she ran aground, probably in the vicinity of the Mtamvuna River on the KwaZulu-Natal south coast. A hundred people perished in the surf; the survivors began walking northwards along the coast, led by the ship's captain, Manoel de Sousa de Sepulveda. Only seven Europeans and 14 slaves reached Moçambique; Sepulveda was not one of them. We pick up the story northeast of present-day Maputo, after the Portuguese had been separated and robbed by a chief (the "king" in the text) who secured their confidence with promises of help.*

RELAÇAõ
DA MUY NOTAVEL PERDA
DO
GALEAõ GRANDE S. JOAõ
Em que se contaõ os grandes trabalhos, e
lastimosas cousas que acontecèraõ
AO CAPITAõ
MANOEL DE SOUSA
SEPULVEDA,

E O LAMENTAVEL FIM, QUE ELLE,
e sua mulher, e filhos, e toda a mais gente
houveraõ na Terra do Natal, onde se perdè-
raõ a 24. de Junho de 1552.

SHE MADE A HOLE

They now no longer looked like men; they had no one to lead them, and, in their disorder, they travelled quite out of the right path. No council was held any more, nor was there any one capable of calling one together. Some went through the jungle; others went over the mountains; they spread hither and thither and at last each of them only cared for finding some way of preserving his life, either amongst the Kaffirs or amongst the Moors. But, as they were now completely lost, I shall speak of them no more, but return to Manoel de Sousa, and his unfortunate wife, and his children.

When Manoel de Sousa found he had been robbed and then sent away by the king to look for his company, and that he had no money, arms, or people that could have wielded them, he felt the wrong which had been done him deeply; and that despite the fact that his head had been disordered for some days. But if he did so, can we imagine what a most delicate woman would feel brought face to face with such trials and such need, above all, when she saw her husband in that state, unable either to command any more or to take thought for his children. But she, being a woman of intelligence, took the advice of the men she still had with her, and they began to go through the jungle with no help and stay but God. At this time, André Vaz the pilot was still in her company, and the boatswain, who never left her, and one or two Portuguese women, and some female slaves. Whilst they went along they decided it would be best to follow the track of the ninety despoiled men who were two days' journey on ahead. By now Dona Leonor was very weak, sad, and disconsolate, because she saw how ill her husband was, and because she found the others were so far off that she thought it impossible ever to join them. To think of it is a thing to break one's heart. As they went along thus the Kaffirs again came upon the captain, his wife, and the few people who were in their company and stripped them there without leaving anything on them. When they were both left like that, with two very young children with them, they commended themselves finally to the Lord.

Here they say that Dona Leonor would not let herself be stripped, but defended herself with buffets and blows, for she was of a nature to prefer being killed by the Kaffirs to being left naked before all the people. There is no doubt, even, but that her life would have been over if Manoel de Sousa had not begged her to let herself be stripped, reminding her that all were born naked, and, as it was God's will, she should not now refuse to be so, too. One of their great trials was seeing those two little children of theirs there crying and asking for food whilst they, the parents, were unable to help them. When Dona Leonor was left without clothes, she flung herself on the ground immediately and covered herself completely with her hair, which was very long. She made a hole in the sand in which she buried herself up to the waist and never arose from it again. Manoel de Sousa then turned to an old nurse of hers who had been left with a torn shawl and asked her for it to cover Dona Leonor with, and she gave it to him. For all that, Dona Leonor never again consented to arise from the spot on which she had flung herself down when she had been left naked.

Truly I do not know who could consider this without great pity and sadness. Here was a most noble woman, the daughter and the wife of very honourable gentlemen, most cruelly and ignominiously used! When the men who were still in their company saw Manoel de Sousa and his wife naked they moved away a little, being ashamed to see their captain and

Dona Leonor so. Then she said to André Vaz the pilot: "You see the state we are in and that we cannot go on any further and that we must end our lives here, for our sins. Go on your way, save yourselves, and commend us to God. If you reach India or Portugal at some future time, tell them how you left Manoel de Sousa and myself and our children." They, seeing it was not in their power to alleviate their captain's exhaustion, nor the poverty and misery of his wife and children, went off through the jungle to save their lives as best they might.

After André Vaz had left Manoel de Sousa and his wife, Duarte Fernandes the boatswain of the galleon stayed with them, as did some female slaves; three of these were afterwards saved and went to Goa where they told how they had seen Dona Leonor die. Though Manoel de Sousa was not in his right mind he did not forget the great need of eating his wife and children were in. He was limping from a wound the Kaffirs had given him in his leg, but, nevertheless, he went out wounded as he was into the jungle to find fruit for them to eat. On his return he found Dona Leonor very weak with hunger and weeping, for, after the Kaffirs had stripped her, she had never arisen from that place, nor ceased weeping. And he found one of the children dead, and buried him in the sand with his own hands. The next day, Manoel de Sousa again went out into the jungle to look for fruit, and, when he returned, Dona Leonor had died, and the other child, and the five slaves were weeping over her with violent cries.

They say that when he found her dead he did nothing but make the slaves retire and sit down near her with his head in his hands for the space of half an hour, without weeping or saying anything. His eyes were fixed on her, and he paid little heed to the child. When that space of time was over, he arose and began to dig a hole in the sand with the help of the slaves. Still not speaking a word, he buried her and his son with her. When this was ended, he again took the same path which he had taken when he had gone to look for the fruits, saying nothing to the slaves. He went into the jungle and they never saw him again.

MAKING A LITTLE MUD

Pantaleão de Sá is recorded as being Sepulveda's brother-in-law – possibly then Dona Leonor's brother. After the Portuguese were separated and robbed, he struggled on by himself. The "palace" here is not identified: perhaps it was at Sofala, a trading port south of present-day Beira.

Pantaleão de Sá wandered for a long time through the lands of the Kaffirs. He reached the palace almost exhausted by hunger, nakedness, and the trials of so long a journey. When he reached the door of the palace he begged the people of the palace to obtain some relief from the king for him. They refused to ask him, but excused themselves on account of the great illness the king had long been suffering. The illustrious Portuguese asked them what illness that was, and they replied, a sore on his leg which was so beyond treatment and so festered that they expected his death at any time. He listened attentively and asked them to let the king know of his coming, for he said he was a doctor and that he could perhaps restore him to health. They were very glad to hear it and went in at once to tell the news to the king. The king instantly asked them to bring Pantaleão de Sá in. He, when he saw the wound, said to the king: "Take good heart. You will easily recover your health." He went out and began to think over the task he had undertaken. He could not even escape from that situation alive, for he knew of no sort of treatment to apply to the king, seeing that he had learned rather to take lives than to cure complaints and save people. Thinking thus, despairing of life, and preferring to die once than many times, he pissed on the ground, thus making a little mud, and went in to put it on the almost incurable sore. That day went by; on the following the illustrious Sá expected to receive his own death sentence and saw no hope of life either for himself or for the king. But the courtiers came out with a huge commotion, wishing to carry him around on their shoulders. He asked them the cause of their unexpected gaiety, and they replied that all the suppuration of the sore had disappeared because of the medicament which had been put on it, and that only the flesh now showed, in a good, healthy state. The supposed doctor went in, and, when he saw that it was as they had related, he ordered the treatment to be continued. In this manner the king recovered his perfect health in a few days' time. In view of this, besides other honours, they placed Pantaleão de Sá on an altar, and the king, worshipping him like a divinity, asked him to stay in his palace; and he offered him the half of his kingdom, and, if not that, he would do whatever he wished. Pantaleão de Sá refused his offer, and told him he had to return to his own people. The king ordered a great quantity of gold and precious stones to be brought, with which he plentifully rewarded him, and ordered his men to accompany him to Mozambique.

MANUEL DE MESQUITA PERESTRELLO

The São Bento, *damaged by heavy seas on the run back to Portugal and in danger of sinking, was deliberately run onto the Pondoland coast in 1554. The 224 slaves and 98 Portuguese who survived and were able to walk, Mesquita Perestrello among them, battled hostile tribesmen and starvation as they headed north along the coast. At one point they bartered a cow for an astrolabe; they ate shoes and shield-straps and fought over locusts and beetles. Only 21 Portuguese and four slaves reached Delagoa Bay, the site of present-day Maputo; the author's brother was one of those who died on the way.*

The wreck of the São Bento.

THEY SEIZED A KAFFIR
On the southern approaches to Delagoa Bay the survivors met a "multitude of Kaffirs" who were arguing among themselves whether to attack or not, but in the end decided on a show of friendship.

These Kaffirs told us that the four men whom we sent on before with a message to Lourenço Marques were dead, and they killed them close to that spot because, constrained by hunger, they seized a Kaffir whom they found on the sea-shore, and carrying him into a wood they cut him up and roasted him to furnish their wallets; but the inhabitants of that place found that he was missing, and the ground being dry and sandy, they followed their track and came upon them in the act; and then carrying our men to the shore, and thinking it proper to be revenged upon them, they slew the poor wretches with cruel butchery.

Several days later the Portuguese slew one of the "Kaffirs" who were harrassing them, and some suggested eating the corpse. "But the captain would not consent to it, saying that if it was noised about that we ate human beings they would flee from us to the ends of the earth, and would endeavour to persecute us with still greater hatred."

WRIGGLING DOWN OUR THROATS
We proceeded on our way that day and the next, always along the shore, where we found large shoals of white crabs in the surf, which were left uncovered when the waves receded. We killed some while the daylight permitted, and as it was not a time for daintiness, this was done in such a hurry that often when we put them in our mouths they held on to our lips with their claws and stuck fast, while the rest of them half-masticated was wriggling down our throats. Though this fish was to cost some of the party dear, because in collecting them they took no heed of the waves which sometimes swept them back in confusion, we continued catching them till night, when we took shelter among some shrubs which were close by.

ANDRÉ FERNANDES

Fernandes was one of the first Jesuit missionaries to work in the country south of the Zambesi, where he arrived in 1560. He later became gravely ill and returned to Goa in India, then was assigned to a Comorin mission, where he died about 1568.

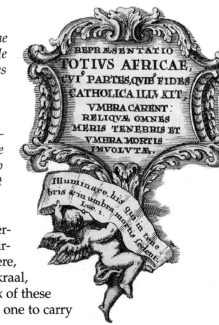

NOT ONE OF US CAN MOVE
Though he talks here of travel by litter, he mentioned undertaking a major journey on foot "which is not usual for the Portuguese", and feeling that it was a matter of honour to keep up with his black companions "as otherwise they would not acknowledge my authority".

… not one of us can move without taking at least eight persons with us, who must be fed during the twelve days journey there and back and during the time we remain there, besides a piece of cloth to each worth a cruzado in each kraal, besides other gratuities which amount to a good deal. Six of these men are required to carry us in litters on their shoulders, one to carry the bed, and another the provisions.

SOME SORT OF A PRISON
Here Fernandes is sharing Christian thoughts about the locals with his Father Provincial in India.

Many of them like very much to hear and understand the Christian doctrine, and are easily reclaimed from their errors. All the women show great devotion to the picture of our Lady, and many visit the church to see it. These things which appeal to their eyes make a great impression upon them, and it pleases them very much to have the meaning of the pictures explained to them, for which reason I have sent to ask for a picture of the Judgment, which seems to me most suitable for them, as we give beginners the exercise of the first week.

They are more domesticated and friendly than you would think; if we had sufficient people here and they persevered, there is no doubt but that an excellent republic could be formed. I greatly desire to introduce justice among them, and have some sort of a prison, and afterwards introduce such slight penalties as we can, and for this reason I greatly long to have the aforesaid picture of the judgment here, with which to commence the work.

FRANCISCO DE MONCLAROS

Monclaros was a Jesuit priest and a favourite in the Portuguese court. He was sent as adviser on a 1569 military expedition to subjugate Mwenemutapa, with the optimistic goal of securing for newly crowned boy king Sebastião a dominion comparable to Spain's American possessions. The voyage to Moçambique, which included a six-month stopover in Brazil, took 13 months. This is an incident from that sea journey.

WITHOUT THE LEAST DISGUST
At this time we began to catch fish, and some days took more than a hundred albacores. There was also a great fishing for sharks, a very ugly fish like a large sea-lamprey, with three rows of teeth, very greedy, and easy to catch. One soldier caught more than a hundred to his own share. In the stomach of one which was cut open they found a pewter plate, a gimlet, and a shoe. It happened that a ham which lay with others in the sun fell overboard, and a shark came immediately and swallowed it. The owner arranged with a soldier, who caught the shark with the ham in its stomach, still fresh and entire. The owner gave it to the soldier when he saw it, through abhorrence of the shark, and the soldier and his companions ate it without the least disgust.

DIOGO DO COUTO

Francisco Barreto, a "notable cavalier", had once been governor of what the Portuguese called India, a territory which included all its claims on Africa's east coast. Since then he had been having difficulty with his finances, so when King Sebastião offered him the governorship of Mwenemutapa alone, he accepted. His task was more accurately described by his additional title of Conqueror of the Mines, to accomplish which he was given a force of 1,000 men, plus the Jesuit adviser Monclaros, whom we have already met. In 1572 Barreto marched his force up the Zambezi to attack a chief named Mongas, who after the Mwenemutapa was the most powerful ruler in the region. He met Mongas' army not far from the fort of Sena, and with his cannon, arquebuses and muskets, slaughtered by the official chronicler Do Couto's account more than 6,000 tribesmen. Despite the bold front Barreto puts on in this extract, by the time Mongas decided to sue for peace, the Portuguese were in dire straits, reduced to eating forest vegetation boiled with salt. The terrifying camels, we are told, came from "the shores of the Bedouins".

Diogo do Couto

NOTHING TO EAT

When our men were preparing to encamp and to rest themselves, a Kaffir appeared with a white flag, and came with great confidence to our army. The governor sent a fifer to ask what he wanted, and he answered that his king wished for peace. The governor then commanded him to be brought before him, and awaited his coming seated on a velvet-covered chair, with all the companies drawn up in order with their firelocks and their matches in readiness, the artillery placed in front, and the gunners with their linstocks in their hands.

The governor wore a strong coat of mail with sleeves, with a sword ornamented with silver slung crossways, and a page stood near him with a shield of shining steel. When the Kaffir was brought before him he was so overcome with amazement that he could not speak or answer any of the questions put to him, but trembled from head to foot. The governor commanded some sweetmeats and a cup of wine to be given to him, after which he recovered himself a little and said that his king, Mongas, sent to ask for peace and was very anxious to be friends with him. To which the governor caused a reply to be made to him that he was travelling onward, and that within two or three days he could send to treat of what he desired. With this the Kaffir took leave.

Our cavalry followed him to reconnoitre the country, but discovered nothing. They rested that night, and at dawn the next day the army set out, and continued marching until close on nightfall, when they encamped in a very convenient place, where there was an abundance of water. Shortly afterwards two Kaffirs approached and informed the governor that Mongas sent to ask for leave to treat of peace, and that if he was in need of provisions he would supply him with them. The governor sent him word that peace would be established in due time, and that he had provisions in abundance.

While they were thus conversing a camel broke loose and came running towards the governor's tent, pursued by the man who had charge of it, who endeavoured to put a halter upon it. The camel stopped and commenced to snort and raise his neck, which was very long, and to extend his nostrils. Mongas's Kaffirs, upon seeing this huge animal, as there were no camels in Kaffraria, were so alarmed

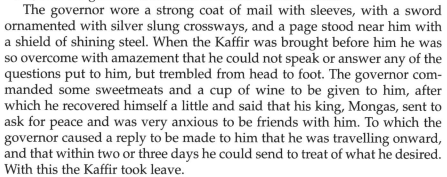

13

that they took refuge in the governor's tent, and throwing themselves on the ground they gazed at it from under the tent with amazement. The governor rose, and, going towards the camel, which waited for him very tamely, he commanded a halter to be put upon it, and returning to his seat he sent to summon the Kaffirs, who came as if stupefied, and asked the interpreter what animal it was. The governor told him to say that he had a great number of these animals, that they only ate human flesh, and that this one had come to ask him on the part of the others on no account to make peace with Mongas, as they would then have nothing to eat, and that all the Kaffirs who were killed by our men in the past battles had been eaten by these animals, which were waiting to eat all the others. The Kaffirs beat their hands together two or three times, which is their manner of showing great amazement, and begged the governor to ask these animals not to eat any more of Mongas's people, as they would bring them many cows for their maintenance. This was a gift from heaven to our men, as they were already without provisions for their sustenance. The governor replied that he would beg the animals to maintain themselves and be content only with cows, and not eat any more of Mongas's men; and with this he took leave of them, saying that he was going towards the town of their king, where he would see them. The Kaffirs sprang away in amazement, and went to Mongas and related everything to him, and he was no less astounded than they were.

Though Mongas sent a token tribute of cattle, sheep, a little gold and a few tusks of ivory, no peace terms were arranged, and the expedition retreated, worn down by malaria and other diseases, hunger and exhaustion. Barreto clashed repeatedly with Monclaros, who reproved him for not ending his campaign sooner, and said God would hold him to account for the lives lost. After one particularly unpleasant exchange, Barreto was so affected that he retired to bed and died "without any other sickness, breathing out his soul in sighs". The gold and silver mines of Mwenemutapa proved a disappointment to the Portuguese: they were difficult to reach, and the output was modest by South American standards. From the mid-1700s, first ivory and then slaves replaced precious metals as the mainstay of Moçambique's commerce with the outside world.

JOÃO DOS SANTOS

A Dominican priest sent as missionary to Sofala in 1586, Dos Santos left an entertainingly vivid account of the country on subjects ranging from politics to fireflies. "The country is very hot, unhealthy, and prejudicial to foreigners, especially the Portuguese, who generally fall sick and die of fever; but this is not sufficient to restrain their avarice and the eagerness with which they go thither in search of the mines and riches of the county." He was at Sofala for four years, during which he and a colleague baptised 1,694 local people, then was moved to the town of Moçambique.

THEY KILLED THEMSELVES
Quiteve, about which Santos is writing here, was a province of Mwenemutapa, and also the title of its ruler.

It was formerly the custom of the kings of this land to commit suicide by taking poison when any disaster or natural physical defect fell upon them, such as impotence, infectious disease, the loss of their front teeth by which they were disfigured, or any other deformity or affliction. To put an end to such defects they killed themselves, saying that the king should be free from any blemish, and if not it was better for his honour that he should die and seek another life where he would be made whole, for there everything was perfect. But the Quiteve who reigned when I was in those parts would not imitate his predecessors in this, being discreet and dreaded as he was; for having lost a front tooth he caused it to be proclaimed throughout the kingdom that all should be aware that he had lost a tooth and should recognise him when they saw him without it, and if his predecessors killed themselves for such things they were very foolish, and he would not do so; on the contrary he would be very sorry when the time came for him to die a natural death, for his life was very necessary to preserve his kingdom and defend it from his enemies; and he recommended his successors to follow his example.

A 1538 map of Moçambique settlement.

THE EVIL SMELL
The musimos *were festivals for the dead.*

A Portuguese resident of Sofala went with his merchandise to Zimbaoe, where Quiteve dwells, in order to proceed thence to Manica where there are many gold mines; and being in the city of Quiteve he ordered a cow to be killed in his house, in order to feed his slaves and the other men whom he had with him to help him in the sale of his merchandise. On the day this cow was killed one of these said *musimos* feasts was being held, and the intelligence was immediately carried to Quiteve by his spies, of whom he has an infinite number to report to him all that goes on in the city and even in the whole kingdom. Quiteve immediately sent word to the Portuguese that they had done very ill in breaking his saint's day by killing a cow, but since it was done they must not lay hands upon it, but must cover it with branches and the *musimo* of the day would eat it. The dead cow remained thus in the house of the Portuguese, and the king would not allow it to be touched, and it grew putrid and smelt so badly that the Portuguese wished to leave that house and take another. But Quiteve would not consent, insisting that as a penalty for killing the cow on the day of his *musimo*, he should endure the evil smell, or pay the *empofia* which he demanded. The Portuguese, moved by the inconvenience which he was forced to endure, came to an agreement with the king and paid him fifty pieces of cloth for the *empofia* laid upon him, and did not eat the cow, but endured the smell of it for many days. This thief of a Quiteve exacted this strict observance of that holy day more as a pretext for robbing the Portuguese than from zeal for the observance of such a day.

15

HORNS ALL OVER THEIR HEADS

Most of these Kaffirs are as black as jet, with woolly hair; they are handsome men, especially the Macarangas, who dwell in the lands of Quiteve. All wear their hair made into horns all over their heads for finery. Their hair is made to stand up as straight as an arrow by being twisted round a thin piece of wood, so that it cannot bend, and outside it is bound with the outer covering of a certain herb like that of spurge laurel, which when it is fresh sticks like glue, and when it is dry becomes as hard as wood. With this they tie their hair in twists from the root to the point, making each twist into a very well shaped horn, and this is all their finery and show, which they arrange for each other. They make great sport of a man who wears no horns, saying that he is like a woman, because a man being the male should have horns, thus comparing themselves to the wild animals among which the female has no horns, such as stags, gnus, zebras, paraparas, and nondos.

No Kaffir may wear his horns in the same fashion as Quiteve; he wears four horns: one a palm in length above his forehead like a unicorn, and three half a palm in length, one at the back of the head, and one over each ear; each horn standing very straight up in its place. Because of these horns they all go bareheaded, and use no hats.

A STRONGER MOOR

Long before the Portuguese arrived, there was a strong presence of Muslim Arab and Swahili traders on the Moçambique coast and on the trade route up the Zambezi Valley.

In many places upon this coast of Eastern Ethiopia dwell certain dark-skinned Moors, almost resembling Kaffirs in their customs, and still more given to many barbarous superstitions.

When one of these Moors gets married, on the day of the wedding he procures another strong and healthy Moor to carry him on his shoulders to the house of the bride without resting on the way, even though the distance be half a league, as very often happens, for these Moors of Sofala live scattered in the palm groves around the fortress, which are like farms in Portugal, and are sometimes almost a league distant from each other. If it happens that the Moor who carries the bridegroom on his shoulders gets tired upon the road, and cannot reach the house of the bride, in such a case the wedding does not take place that day, for the Moors consider it a very ill omen for the bridegroom not to reach the house of the woman who is to be his wife without the one who carries him resting on the way. They therefore choose another day and a stronger Moor, who is able to carry him the whole distance without resting on the way. This ceremony is so common among them that no Moor is married without it.

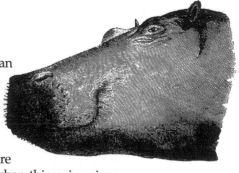

ATTACKS OF MELANCHOLY

These hippopotami have a very much thicker hide than that of an ox. They are all of an ash grey colour, and have very coarse hair; nearly all of them, or the greater number, have a very white mark running from the middle of their foreheads to the nostrils and a very fine white star on the forehead. They have a very short and scanty mane, and have no tuft or long hairs on the tail. They are very subject to epilepsy or attacks of melancholy, and when this pain seizes them they press their left fore foot very tightly against the breast, doubling it back, and let themselves fall to the ground upon it, their hoofs coming under the breast, by virtue of which the Kaffirs say the attacks pass off more quickly, by which nature's providence never failing in necessary things may be seen. For this reason the Kaffirs and Moors assert that the hoofs of the left fore foot of the hippopotamus have great virtue against melancholy. God knows the truth of this, but it is a fact that these animals suffer from the attacks I speak of, and that they press themselves tightly with the hoofs of their left fore foot, as the Kaffirs have frequently found them on land in this position, and some of them so weakened and senseless from the pain they were suffering that they have killed several without their being able to rise or to escape.

And crocodiles, he said, produce a large quantity of farts, "the bad smell of which no living thing can tolerate".

THE BOATS BECOME LAZY
Cape das Correntes is just south of Inhambane.

All the vessels employed in navigation along this coast from Cape das Correntes to the straits of Mecca are made of wood, which the Moors cut down in the forests. They split the log down the middle with an axe, and then dress the pieces with an adze held in both hands after the manner of a pickaxe. Thus from each log they make only two planks, whereas they might make a good many if they were to use a saw, but this is an implement not used on this coast. With the planks they make vessels fastened with coir cord and nailed with wooden pins, and with coir they make all the cordage and the cables. The big vessels are called navetas, the medium-sized pangayos, and the small ones luzios or almadias. The sails of all of these are mats made of the leaves of palm or wild date trees.

The sailors of all these vessels are Moors, most of them black. They are barbarians, and very fond of wine; and are only Moors in name and in the practice of circumcision, as they neither know nor keep the creed of Mohamed that they profess. The principal observance in which they are most exact is in celebrating with great feasting every new moon, upon which occasions they usually all get intoxicated, though their creed forbids them to take wine.

They are very superstitious when at sea. In a storm, although the boat may be overladen they will not lighten it, saying that the sea swallows up all that is thrown into it and is never satiated, and the more one throws into it the rougher it becomes, and its waves never subside until everything in the boat has been cast out.

In navigating, when the wind fails these sailors flog their vessels with cords on the poop and on the sides until they themselves are tired and perspire, shouting all the time and abusing them as though they had intelligence to understand what they say and do to them, or stopped sailing through their own fault, which is what they attribute to them, as they say that even the boats become lazy and are tired of sailing, and that the wind seeing them thus takes pity on them and ceases blowing to let them repose, and when they are rested it blows again as before. Some of these sailors believe so firmly in this superstition that there is no dissuading them from it.

THIS EXCESS OF ZEAL

Santos got the Portuguese captain of Tete to arrest, humiliate, publicly whip and banish two diviners in the area that he labelled witches. The indigenous religious practices were not the only ones to suffer. He is talking here about a wealthy Muslim at Sofala named Muynhe Mohamed, who despite his faith had been fond of Portuguese wine, ham and pork sausages.

When this Moor [Mohamed] died, the Moors of Sofala made him a mosque in the island of Inhansato, in which they held his tomb in great veneration and respect, simply because he was a rich and honoured Moor, and these barbarous Moors considered these qualities sufficient ground for holding and honouring him as a saint, he being a Moor in name only. This mosque was all hung with painted calico, the stones of the sepulchre were anointed with fragrant sandal, and around it were many braziers in which they threw incense to perfume the mosque. Above his grave quantities of rice and millet were strewn by the Moors, who petitioned him for prosperous harvests in return for this offering. Opposite the door of the mosque was a half mast fixed in the ground. In this were many nails, upon which the Moorish sailors before undertaking any voyage hung pieces of oars, pulleys, or any cordage from their vessel, that this Moor might grant them a prosperous voyage, so that they offered him petitions and prayed to him as though he were a saint.

Knowing this, I ardently desired to see this mosque, in order to do it the honours which it deserved. I did in fact see it when I went one day pleasuring to the said island with the owner thereof, who was then a noble and honourable Portuguese named Pedro Lobo, and when we were on the

island I called two of our young men in secret and one of Pedro Lobo's who knew where the mosque was, and asked him to lead me to it, because I wished to see it very much. They led me about a quarter of a league into the island to the spot where the mosque stood in a large open space, surrounded by thick woods.

After examining it well, I set fire to it with a piece of gun-match which I bade one of the young men bring with him alight, not telling him for what purpose it was required, for had I done so, or had they imagined what I was about, they would not have accompanied me, as they have a great fear of offending the dead, and much more such a one as this, whom the Moors regarded as a saint. As soon as I set fire to the mosque, which was of wood, thatched with straw, as are all the houses in Sofala, it burned with all the hangings which were in it, and nothing escaped. The fire was so great that it brought to the spot most of the Moors on the island, and seeing the mosque burnt to the ground and reduced to glowing embers (a good picture of the fire in which Mohamed was burning), they were amazed and grieved, and would have taken vengeance on me if it had not been for their fear of the Portuguese and their veneration and respect for our religious [ecclesiastics], but one and all called down a thousand curses upon me among themselves, and augured that a thousand evils and punishments would fall upon me from the hand of Mohamed, because of the insult I had offered to his tomb. This was said not only by the Moors, but also by some of the Christians of the country, who thought me rash, and the least they expected was that I should die for this excess of zeal.

A few days after this it happened that I had a running from one of my eyes, and the Moors on hearing of it held great rejoicings, saying that Mohamed had already begun to punish me and I would lose my eyes. But it pleased God whom I served to give me perfect health, by which the hopes of the Moors were frustrated.

DIOGO DO COUTO

The carrack São Thomé *left Cochin in January 1589, and began taking water badly off the coast of southern Moçambique. The pepper in the hold swelled as it got wet, burst from the bales, and blocked the pumps. Even though the crew cast into the sea "all the riches and luxury-goods with which the ship was so richly laden", the water kept rising. There was only one boat, and preference was given to the priests, the gentlemen and their ladies. Do Couto, who compiled his account from the stories of survivors, says the nurse of Dona Joanna de Mendoça's one-year-old daughter was one of those left on board. Despite the tears and pleadings of the mother, she refused to hand the child down unless she was also taken into the already overcrowded boat. "Because this caused some delay, and the girl was hard-hearted, and the ship was rolling most terribly, they were forced to put off the boat that it might not be swamped, which they did with great pity for the wretched mother, whose eyes were fixed upon her child with that tenderness which all are wont to show when they look upon those they dearly love." But this was not the end of the drama.*

The end of the *São Thomé*.

THIS ABOMINABLE CRUELTY
As soon as it set out, the officers found it so over-burdened, being so heavily laden that it was nearly under water, that they insisted that some persons should be thrown into the sea to save the rest. To this those gentlemen consented, leaving the selection of them to the officers, who at once threw six people into the sea. These were lifted into the air and thrown overboard, where they were swallowed by

the cruel waves and never reappeared. This pitiful sacrifice so horrified those who witnessed it that they were in a maze, not realizing what they saw, or regarding it as something seen in a dream. And even after these six persons had been thrown overboard, there were still one hundred and four people left in the boat.

Continuing on their course, they could not make any progress, for the current drove them from the land out to sea, the men being unable to row, from exhaustion after their labours, and the boat being unmanageable from its weight. At midnight they found themselves out at sea a good distance from the ship, and taking to their oars they rowed towards it. They saw many lights in it, which were burning candles, for those in the ship passed the whole night in processions and litanies, commending themselves to God Our Lord with such loud cries and clamours that they could be heard in the boat.

When day dawned the boat drew near to the ship, and they spoke with those on board, encouraging them to make rafts, and offering to wait and accompany them. Those in the ship replied with loud cries and wails, begging for mercy in voices so heartfelt and pitiful as to inspire fear and terror, for the half-light of early dawn made the scene more awful and appalling. When it was broad daylight, several persons tried to reach the ship to get some matchlocks and provisions, for which purpose three or four sailors swam out to her. On climbing aboard, they found the deck already under water, and all the people as if out of their minds with fear of the death which they expected. Withal they had placed on the top-gallant-poop a beautiful altar-picture of Our Lady, round which were gathered all the slave-women, who with dishevelled hair were piteously wailing and begging that Lady for mercy.

The nurse of Dona Joanna was standing in front of them all with the baby in her arms, which she never put down, the child's tender age not allowing her to realize her danger; and even had she done so, in her innocence it would have troubled her little, for there is nothing which makes death seem so terrible as doubt of salvation. The sailors threw into the sea some kegs of water and biscuit, and one of wine, that were taken into the boat, which tried to approach the ship, to be lightened of still more persons, as it was not fit for navigation. The sailors returned without bringing Dona Joanna's baby, for most of these men are inhuman and cruel by nature.

As those in the boat could not get near enough to the ship to send away more people, they drew off, and let the officers have their way. These threw overboard some more persons, including Diogo Fernandes, a good man but a very timid one, who had just relinquished the post of Factor of Ceylon; a soldier named Diogo de Seixas; Diogo Duarte, a merchant; and Diogo Lopes Bayão, who was for many years in the Balagate, where the Idalxà gave him an income of three thousand *cruzados*, since he was a clever and scheming man who exported horses from Goa to that place, and who kept him informed of everything. He was even suspected of being doubtful in the faith, for which reason he was sent to Portugal (of which we gave a lengthy account in our tenth Decade), for it was he who contrived the plot to lure Çufucão to the mainland, whom the Idalxà wished to have in his power in order to kill him, because the kingdom was rightly his; and on this occasion [the Adil Shah] succeeded through the machinations of this Diogo Lopes, and commanded his eyes to be put out. This Diogo Lopes, when he was seized to be thrown overboard, handed to Friar Nicolau a little bag of jewels, said to be worth ten or twelve thousand *cruzados*, asking him, if he were saved, to deliver it to his agents at Goa if he went thither, or to his heirs at home if God should bring him to Portugal. Several slaves were thrown overboard with these men, all of whom were at once swallowed by those cruel waves. This abominable cruelty was done by the hands of the sea-officers, which God permitted that they should pay for very shortly, since all or most of them died very miserably on shore in the bush.

The boat now began to row towards the land, and when they were some distance from the ship at ten o'clock in the morning, they saw it give a great lurch, and then founder immediately afterwards, disappearing under the water in sight of all as quick as a flash of lightning. They were left astounded, like men in a dream, at thus seeing a great ship, in which they had so recently been voyaging, so heavily laden with riches and merchandise almost beyond computation, now devoured by the waves and sunk under the water, heaping up riches in the depths of the sea from all those things which belonged to those in her and to others in India, acquired by such means as God knows, for which reason He often permits as little enjoyment of them as He did of these.

Although this sight was a very terrible one for them all, it was even more painful and fearful for the wretched Dona Joanna de Mendoça, for she saw that her beloved baby daughter and tender darling would be the prey of some sea-monster that might perhaps devour her while she was still alive; but as she had already offered everything in sacrifice to God, she spoke with Him in her heart about her sorrows, nor could He have failed to help her with some spiritual consolation, as could be gathered from the exemplary patience, virtue, and resignation which she showed on this occasion.

About 375 of the São Thomé's *passengers and crew drowned; probably one in five of those who initially reached land made it home.*

JOHN DAVIS

Davis was one of the most noted seamen of his age, a skilled pilot and fearless explorer. He searched for the North-West Passage, discovered the Falkland Islands, and was killed in a scuffle with Japanese pirates on his third voyage to the East in 1605. This is from the 1598 journal of his first, as pilot in one of the early Dutch merchant fleets taking advantage of the route opened up by the Portuguese. Saldanha was the name originally given to Table Bay; it was later transferred to an anchorage 140 kilometres to the north.

Belegered with Canibals and Cowes
The eleventh we anchored in the Bay of Saldania, in thirtie foure degrees of the South Pole, ten leagues short of Cape Bono Esperanza,

where there are three fresh Rivers. The people came to us with Oxen and Sheep in great plentie, which they sold for peices of old Iron and spike Nailes. The best of that we bought, cost not more then the value of one penie in old Iron. Their Cattell are large, and under severall markes, having upon the backe by the fore shoulders a great lumpe of flesh like a Camels backe. Their Sheepe have exceeding great tailes only of fat, weighing twelve or four-teene pounds: they have no wooll but a long shag haire. The people are not circumcised, their colour is Olive blacke, blacker then the Brasilians, their haire curled and blacke as the Negroes of Angola, their words are for the most part inarticulate, and, in speaking, they clocke with the Tongue like a brood Hen, which clocking and the word are both pronounced together, verie strangely.

They goe all naked, having only a short Cloke of Skinnes, and Sandals tyed to their feet, they paint their faces with divers colours, they are a strong active people, and runne exceedingly, and are subject to the King of Monomotapa, who is reported to be a mightie King, their weapons are only hard Darts. The Flemmings [Davis' shipmates] offering them some rude wrong, they absent-ed themselves three dayes, in which time they made great fires upon the Mountaines in the Countrey. The nineteenth hereof there came great troups of them to us, bringing much cattell with them, and in the time of bartering, suddenly taking their advantage, they set upon us, and slue thirteene of our people with hand Darts, which at foure Pikes length could not offend.

Notwithstanding, the Flemmings fled before them like Mice before Cats, throwing away their weapons most basely. And our Baase to save himselfe stayed aboord, and sent us Corslets, Two-hand-swords, Pikes, Muskets, and Targets, so we were armed and laden with weapons, but there was nei-ther courage nor discretion. For we stayed by our Tents being belegered with Canibals and Cowes; we were in Muster Giants, with great armed bodies, but in action Babes, with Wrens hearts. Hereupon Master Tomkins and my selfe undertooke to order these Fellowes, from that excellent methode which we had seene in your Lordships most honorable Actions. Some consented to us, but the most part unwilling, and divers ranne to the Pottage Pot, for they swore it was dinner time. This night we went all aboord, only leaving our great Mastive Dogge behind us, who by no meanes would come to us. For I thinke he was ashamed of our Companie.

ANONYMOUS

Portuguese domination of the spice trade crumbled in the face of the well-armed Dutch fleets. Sapped by political and economic stagnation the Portuguese, as the colonial historian George McCall Theal quaintly put it, "ceased to be participants in the great progressive movement of the Caucasian race". Cornelis Matelief, admiral of a 1605 Dutch fleet, was also a director of the newly constituted Dutch East India Company (DEIC), and one of the architects of its policy in the East. He

*stopped over at the Cape on his return in 1608, and went
ashore to barter with the Khoikhoi for livestock. The first
time he tried to trade, the natives took his proffered hoop
iron and beads and ran away without surrendering the
animals. Matelief was more careful the next time. From
the journal of his voyage.*

A REAL MONKEY-BUSINESS

Then they brought a Sheep along, which they held
fast by the forelegs. At this the Admiral showed
them a copper arm-ring, and they agreed to the bargain, so he grasped the Sheep by the leg and
reached out the ring to them, and when they let loose the sheep he also let
the ring loose; he held onto the Sheep and they onto the ring. As soon as
they had this they ran all together about a ship's length without looking
back, and then looked behind them to see if anyone followed them, thinking that we should have regretted the bargain. In somma, we bartered in
this manner thirty-eight Sheep and two Cows; for each Cow we gave an old
iron hoop from a meat barrel, and for each Sheep a hoop a span in length
with a ring, so that for the forty animals we gave about the value of one
guilder, the Blacks thinking that they had swindled us, and we that they
had been truly taken for a ride. The Admiral had with him a Pistol: they
asked what it was, and he replied that it made a great noise, and shouted
dou dou. They asked that he should let it cry out once, and went back fully
a hundred paces. He fired it, and they all fell flat on their backs with a great
shriek, and then ran off. But we went to them and again calmed them, and
gave them some biscuit, which they ate with great pleasure. This business
lasted till midday. We loaded the beasts into the longboat and the shallop,
as also the wood we had cut, which the Blacks helped to carry. Thus everything turned out well, though it would be hard to tell all the game we had
before they would be brought to trade. They whistled, the Admiral joining
in; they danced, so did he; and in short it was a real monkey-business.

EDWARD TERRY

*Terry, a plump and high-minded chaplain with the English East India Company,
described the Khoikhoi he saw at the Cape in 1615 as "beasts in the skins of men".
The locals were, however, sophisticated enough to trick the visitors by bartering
oxen for brass, then recalling the animals from a distance and trading them a second or even a third time. Coree, whose 1613 kidnapping Terry describes here, was
probably a chief of the Gorachouqua.*

COREE HOME GO

Methinks, when I have seriously considered the dresses, the habitations,
and the diet of these people, with other things, and how the beasts of
mankind live like brutes, nay worse, I have thought that if they had the
accommodations we enjoy, (to make our lives more comfortable) by good
dwelling, warm cloathing, sweet lodging, and wholsome food, they would

be abundantly pleased with such a change of their condition: For as love proceeds from knowledge and liking, and we can neither love nor like any thing we cannot know; so when we come to a sensible understanding of things we knew not before; when the belly teaches, and the back instructs, a man would believe that these should work some strong convictions. But I shall here insert a short story. About three years before I went to India, it happened, that one of the company's ships returning thence, and arriving at this harbour, after a little stay, when she was ready to set sail for England, and having then two of those savages aboard, her commander resolved to bring them both home with him; thinking, that when they had got some English here, they might discover something of their country which we could not know before. These poor wretches being thus brought away, very much against both their minds, one of them (merely out of extreme sullenness, though he was very well used) died shortly after they put to sea; the other, who call'd himself Cooree, (whom I mentioned before) lived, and was brought to London, and there kept, for the space of six months, in Sir Thomas Smith's house, (then governor of the East-India company) where he had good diet, good cloaths, good lodging, with all other fitting accommodations. Now one would think that this wretch might have conceived his present, compared with his former condition, an Heaven upon Earth; but he did not so, though he had to his good entertainment made for him a chain of bright brass, an armour, breast, back, and head-piece, with a buckler, all of brass, his beloved metal; yet all this contented him not, for never any seemed to be more weary of ill usage, than he was of courtesies; none ever more desirous to return home to his country, than he; for when he had learned a little of our language, he would daily lie upon the ground, and cry very often thus in broken English, "Coree home go, Souldania go, home go;" and not long after, when he had his desire, and was returned home, he had no sooner set footing on his own shore, but presently he threw away his cloaths, his linen, with all other covering, and got his sheeps skins upon his back, guts about his neck, and such a perfum'd [stinking] cap, as before we named, upon his head; by whom that proverb mentioned, 2 Pet. 2, v.22, was literally fulfill'd, *Canis ad vomitum*; "the dog is return'd to his vomit, and the swine to his wallowing in the mire." From all which we may draw this conclusion, that a continued custom may make many things that seems strange and loathsome to some, even natural to others; and that the most brutish life may seem civil, and best to a most brutish man; and he thus pleading for it.

FRANCISCO VAZ D'ALMADA

The Portuguese ship São João Baptista *was abandoned near the Fish River in 1622, dismasted and leaking badly after being mauled in a fight with two Dutch vessels. Only 31 of the 279 castaways made it to Sofala: those too weak to walk, including women and children, were abandoned on the way. It was the longest journey ever undertaken by Portuguese survivors on this coast. Vaz d'Almada, who had served as a soldier in India, was one of those who lived to tell the tale.*

THE SORROWFUL THINGS

As our people were growing steadily weaker, especially those who were carrying the litters, and the provisions were virtually finished, and we were now somewhat rested, we resolved to push on; since we gathered from what the Kaffir had told us, that the country ahead was well provided. Next day we went and slept near a swamp that had no frogs in it, which was a great disappointment to us. Our hunger was now intolerable, and all the dogs in the camp that could be killed were eaten. They make very good food (not speaking of times of famine) for often when I had cow's flesh and there was a fat dog to be had, I chose the latter in preference to the beef, and so did many others. The men who carried the litters now declined to do so any longer, as they were utterly exhausted, and when the captain tried to force some of them to do so, a sailor named Rezão fled from this place to the Kaffirs.

Journeying on for a few days we came to a river, where there was a village of fisher-folk upon a height on the side in the direction of the Cape [of Good Hope], and we pitched our camp on the other bank. They brought us for sale a small quantity of dough made from some seeds smaller than mustard which come from a herb that sticks to one's clothes. It tasted very good to those who were able to get any of it.

Here all the men who carried the litters assembled in a body, saying that if no one in the camp could take a step for want of food, and many had already died from starvation, what could they do who carried the litters on their shoulders? They might well be ordered to be put to death, but they could carry them no further, even though they were given all the treasures in the world; and it seemed to them that they had done enough in carrying them for a month and a half, up hill and down dale, and they were ready to forego all that had been promised them for their past labours – all this being said with a loud outcry and tears. Then the Religious intervened, telling the captain that he had no right to force anyone to undertake such deadly labour, that one man had already fled to the Kaffirs, and that each one of these poor men looked like a picture of death. The captain then assembled all the people, and in a loud voice ordered a proclamation to be made that he would give eight thousand *cruzados* to any four men who would carry Lopo de Sousa on their shoulders, and the same for any of the women who were in the litters, and he would immediately pay the money into their hands, each according to his share. But no one came forward to volunteer.

In this place, for my sins, I witnessed the greatest cruelties and the most grievous sights which ever occurred or can be imagined. For the women who were in the litters were asked if they could accompany us on foot, since there was no alternative, and for their sakes we had come very slowly and were very backward in our journey, and many of our company had died of pure hunger, and there was no one willing to carry them for any money. Moreover, in order to avoid greater evils, and upon the advice of a qualified Religious theologian, it had been decided not to wait for anyone who could not walk, for our numbers were decreasing. Therefore those who had strength to walk were given until next day to decide, and those who were to remain would be left, together with

25

many others in the camp who were weak and ill, in the fishing-village which was opposite us.

Your worship can now imagine what this news meant to Beatriz Alvarez, who had with her four children, three of tender age, and to Dona Ursula, who had three little children, the eldest eleven years old, and her old mother, who would necessarily be left behind, her husband and father both being already dead – to say nothing of Lopo de Sousa, that honourable and valiant gentleman, who had fought as such on board the ship, and whose wounds were still open and who was suffering from dysentery. This to me was the greatest pain and sorrow of all, for we were brought up together in Lisbon and we had served in India at the same time.

All this night was passed wholly in tears and lamentations, those who were to go on taking leave of those who were to be left behind. It was the most pitiful sight ever witnessed, and whenever I think of it I cannot restrain my tears. It was learnt next day that Beatriz Alvarez would remain with two of her three boys and a girl of two years old, a lovely little creature. We took her youngest son with us, though against her will, that a whole generation might not perish there. There remained also the mother of Dona Ursula, Maria Colaça, and Lopo de Sousa, and three or four persons who were too weak to accompany us. They all confessed themselves with great sorrow and tears, so that really it seemed a cruel thing that we did not remain with them rather than suffer such a parting.

On the one hand we saw Beatriz Alvarez, a delicate and gently nurtured lady, with a little girl of two years on the breast of a Kaffir woman who remained with her and would never consent to abandon her, a little son of five years old, and another of seventeen. The latter showed the greatest courage and love, behaving in the noblest manner possible in such a situation; for his mother told him many times that she was half-dead, her old disease of the liver having made great progress, so that she could not live many days longer even if she had been surrounded with every comfort, and that his father had gone in one of those ships which had fought against us and might very well be dead, and that he was a youth and should go with us. All the Religious likewise urged him with many arguments, telling him that he was not only risking his body but his soul by remaining in this heathen land, where he might be perverted by their evil customs and ceremonies. To all this he replied very courageously that Our Lord would have mercy on his soul, and that hitherto he had always regarded them as his friends, but now he thought differently about them, for what excuse could he subsequently make to men if he left his mother in the hands of savage Kaffirs?

On the other hand we saw Dona Ursula taking leave of her mother who was to remain. Your worship can imagine the sorrowful things that they said to each other, and the grief which they caused us. Everyone went to take leave of Lopo de Sousa, and he, seeing that I did not do so, ordered his litter to be carried to the tent where I was, and he spoke these words to me in a loud voice and with great spirit: "How now, Senhor Francisco Vaz d'Almada! Are you not that friend who was brought up with me at school, and were we not always together in India? Why don't you speak to me now?" Your worship can imagine how I felt on seeing a gentleman whose particular servant I was in that sad state. I rose up and embraced him, saying:

"I confess my weakness, your worship, for I had not the courage to see one whom I love so much in such straits," asking him to pardon me if I had offended him in this. He, whose face had hitherto been dry, could not restrain his tears at this, and he bade those who carried him go forward. I would have gone with him to the Kaffir kraal where he was to stay, but he would not suffer it, and covering his eyes with his hands he said: "Go in peace, my friend, and remember my soul, if God brings you to a land where you can do so." I confess that this was for me the greatest sorrow and grief that I had hitherto endured.

LIKE MOST SAVOURY PORK
Rough justice administered to slaves who murdered a group of Portuguese in a dispute over food.

The captain ordered them to be hanged that very day, though they did not remain on the gallows until morning, because of the fearful hunger we then suffered, but they were secretly eaten by Negroes (and by others who were none such) of our camp, which was overlooked and allowed to pass. Often in the camp at night I saw many spit-fulls of meat, which smelt like most savoury pork; so that one day when I got up to go on guard-duty, my comrade Gregorio de Vidanha told me to go and see what meat our servants were roasting that smelt so appetizing. I went to look, and asking one of them what it was, he asked if I would like to eat some, for it was excellent and very strengthening. But realizing that it was human flesh, I went away, pretending not to understand. By this your worship can see to what straits we were reduced, all for my sins.

Two days later, while we were still in this same place, the captain ordered a Portuguese lad who was a servant of the boatswain to be hanged, because he had been detected bartering for some food with a piece of an iron hoop which he had taken from the wallet of the second pilot, and also because he had fled to the Kaffirs. He was a sturdy youth, who could have been useful to the company, and truly these excessive cruelties finished us off in the midst of so many hardships – for although great rigour is requisite in whoever controls seamen, it should not be carried to such excess. This poor wretch begged for burial, that he might not be eaten; but his petition availed him little, for the captain gave an opportunity to our servants, who were weak with hunger, by ordering them to throw him into the bush, and they took good care to give him the same burial as they had usually given to those who died.

ARSES TO THE OCEAN
These people had lured us out of our way simply in order to see us, and they showed great surprise at the sight of us. They asked us the reason why we came through strange lands with our women and children, and when our Kaffirs told them, they twisted their fingers as if invoking curses upon whoever had caused our shipwreck.

Thence we travelled over a flat country inhabited by very poor people who nevertheless received us hospitably. After two days we reached a kraal near the shore, in which we found some fish, and the people showed themselves more compassionate than any we had yet met. For the women and children went down to the beach and threw many stones into the sea, uttering certain words which seemed like curses; and then turning their backs upon it they lifted up the skins which covered their backsides and exhibited their arses to the ocean. This is the worst form of insult which they have, and they did this because they had been told that the sea was the cause of our suffering so many hardships and of our wandering for five months through strange lands.

JOSEPH DE CABREYA

The Nossa Senhora de Belem *was already leaking badly when she left Goa in February 1635; Cabreya and his crew ran the waterlogged hulk aground on the Natal coast, built another boat, and sailed to the Portuguese settlement at Luanda. Their relationship with the local people at Natal got off to a rocky start, as we see here, but improved to the extent that Cabreya was once asked by a chief to make rain. He did so by delaying his prediction until the weather became threatening.*

AN UNGRATEFUL RACE

In the beginning, before we could go about safely among these people, it happened that a few of them came to the other side of the river where some timber had been thrown ashore by the tide, and they burnt it and carried off the nails, though we tried to prevent them; and as it was on the other bank it was not possible always to keep guard there. One morning some of the ship's boys were on the shore and fired several arquebuses at them from our side, hitting a negro, who fell among the stones. I sent for him, as he was calling to the rest to come and help him or we would devour him. But I treated him well, dressing his wound, for he was shot through the leg, and in a few days the wound healed, but he was lame, the shinbone being broken. I hung some nails round his neck, and sent him back to his people, that he might publish the benefit he had received, and they might come to us and bring what they could, as I told him when he left us; but he never returned, for they are an ungrateful race and to be dealt with by injuries rather than affection.

LEENDERT JANSZEN

The Dutch Indiaman Nieuwe Haerlem *foundered on a sandbank on the eastern shore of Table Bay in 1647. Though the rest of her fleet carried on homewards, Janszen, an assistant merchant, was instructed to stay on shore with some of the crew to salvage the cargo of spices. They built a fort among the dunes, and spent 375 days at the Cape before being picked up by the 1648 home-bound fleet.*

ALWAYS LEFT UNSPOKEN

Others will say that the natives are brutish and cannibals, from whom nothing good is to be expected, and that we shall have to be on our guard continually; but this is only a sailors' yarn as shall be more closely shown and denied. It is not to be denied that they are without laws or government like many Indians, and it is indeed true, that also some sailors and soldiers have been killed by them; but the reason for this is always left unspoken by our folk, to excuse themselves for having been the cause of it, since we firmly believe that the peasants of this country [Holland], if their cattle were to be shot down and taken off without payment, would not show themselves a whit better than these natives, had they not to fear the law.

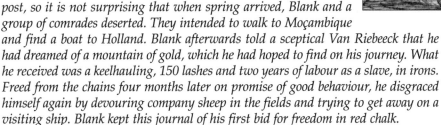

JAN BLANK

One of the passengers on the fleet that picked up Janszen was Jan van Riebeeck, a DEIC merchant who returned to the Cape in April 1652 as commander of the first permanent Dutch establishment there. Life was harsh that first winter for the poorly provisioned outpost, so it is not surprising that when spring arrived, Blank and a group of comrades deserted. They intended to walk to Moçambique and find a boat to Holland. Blank afterwards told a sceptical Van Riebeeck that he had dreamed of a mountain of gold, which he had hoped to find on his journey. What he received was a keelhauling, 150 lashes and two years of labour as a slave, in irons. Freed from the chains four months later on promise of good behaviour, he disgraced himself again by devouring company sheep in the fields and trying to get away on a visiting ship. Blank kept this journal of his first bid for freedom in red chalk.

INTENDING TO DESTROY US
In the name of the Lord Jesus Christ.

Sept. 24. In the evening set out from the *Kaap de Boa Esperance*, directing our course to Mozambique, four of us, Jan Verdonk, of Vlaanderen, Willem Huytgens, of Maastricht, Gerrit Dirkse, of Maastricht, and Jan Blank, of Mechelen, having with us four biscuits and fish, God grant us success on the journey, also four swords, two pistols, and the dog.

Sept. 25. This evening marched seven *mylen*; saw two rhinoceroses, which advanced upon us intending to destroy us, Jan Verdonk was obliged to leave behind his hat and sword; a little before our dog ran at a porcupine, by which he was so wounded in the neck that we thought he would die; took our rest to-night by a rivulet, in God's name; saw also two ostriches; obliged to leave *ditto* again because of two rhinoceroses that came towards us, then we chose the beach; after we had gone two *mylen* we made our camp in the first of the sand hills.

Sept. 26. This morning again set out on our journey, chose the coast to the *Kaap Aquillas*, marched about seven *mylen*, our first food was four young birds who lay in the nest, and three eggs; encamped on the beach where we got some limpets.

Sept. 27. Went along the beach about seven *mylen*, came in the evening to a very high mountain close to the sea, which we must over, therefore rested at the foot until –

Sept. 28. And provided ourselves with limpets to take with us over the mountain, which we prepared, strung on lines and dried, and also with calabashes to carry water.

Sept. 29. Setting out in the morning intending to get over this corner, but not being well able to do so, Jan Verdonk and Willem Huytgens begun to repent, but went on –

Sept. 30. – notwithstanding until the afternoon of next day, when Gerrit also was knocked up, and, for me, I could not make a dance of it alone, therefore resolved to return to the Fort, in hopes of mercy and grace in God's name.

WILLEM MULLER

In September 1655 Corporal Muller and a party of eight men, accompanied by a duplicitous Khoikhoi interpreter named Autshumato, trekked across the Cape Flats to the area of present-day Stellenbosch to barter for cattle. The expedition was not a success, despite Autshumato's claim that he wanted to please the commander so he would be invited to "eet hollantse kaes ende boter, ende drinckt spaense wijn".

ON THEIR BELLIES

The 13th ditto again got under way, after we made ourselves ready, began to march and took our course to the S.E., and having marched half a mile, we saw a strange thing of the Hottentot women, below the pass where we were going, where a large rock, lay; these women together took a green branch in the hand and went to lie on their bellies on the same rock, saying some words, which we did not understand: we asked them what they meant, on which they said "Hette Hie", and pointed to on high as if they wished to say, it is an offering to God.

ALBRECHT HERPORT

Crossing the Equator on the voyage to the Cape in 1659, a soldier on the Indiaman carrying Herport "forgetfully lay by night in the moonlight, by which for about a month his mouth and eyes were twisted to the side, but after this returned as they had been". Herport, a Swiss who also enlisted as a soldier with the DEIC, managed to avoid the ravages of lunar exposure, as well as the more serious illnesses – including, presumably, scurvy – that at one point in the voyage were carrying off three or four people a day. By the end of the four-month journey biscuit and water were being strictly rationed.

WITH LEAVES AND STALKS

On the 21st of September we saw a Nord-Capper, this being a small kind of whale, and also some sea-dogs, from which the Master and the Mates could see that we must not be far from the coast of Africa, as also they had found at noon from the altitude of the sun. Therefore the Master ordered, that diligent watch for land be kept by day and night, and at the same time promised 6 rixdollars and 4 cans of Spanish wine to him who should first sight the same.

On the 25th in the early morning there was a glad shout from the foremast of Land! Land! which caused no little joy among us all. About an hour later we could all see the land, and recognised it for the coast of Africa and for the Promontory Caput bonae Spei whither we were bound. About 3 in the afternoon we passed between the Roben and Taxen [Dassen] Islands, and came safely into the harbour and dropped anchor there: that same night we must strike our yard and topmast because of the heavy winds. Also water was now issued freely, which caused so great a joy among us, that it cannot duly be described in words, and would appear incredible to any who had not himself experienced it, since before this many had only one desire, once again to drink his fill of water before his death, which desire however he could not fulfil until now. Next day the longboat and the two shallops were launched and rowed to the land, where our Master was very well received by the Commandeur at the Fort, who also at once sent us 2 cows and 6 sheep, as also all sorts of green vegetables such as cabbage; and among these also radishes, which we, from our great longing and hankering for fresh food, ate with leaves and stalks, and drank the lovely fresh water as if it had been good new wine.

In this harbour there lay at anchor also another ship, named the *Erasmus*, of Rotterdam, which the year previous had sailed with the fleet from Batavia on the island of Java, but had been driven away from the fleet by a storm, and came here only after 9 months. During this time they suffered great lack of food and drink, so that most of the crew died therefrom, and as a result the ship could hardly be handled. Also she was so damaged that she must be bound around thrice with iron chains, so that she should not completely fall apart.

PIETER VAN MEERHOFF

Van Meerhoff, a Dane serving as surgeon with the DEIC, accompanied or led several expeditions north from the settlement. On this one, in 1661, he and his companions made the first contact with the Nama, who mined and worked copper and who promised to trade sheep and cattle. Van Meerhoff, who as a medical man ought to have known better, taught the Nama how to use tobacco. "They were eager enough to smoke, but most of them did not know how. The king, instead of inhaling, blew the smoke away from him. I took his pipe 4 or 5 times and demonstrated how he should inhale. He began to get the knack of it."

MANY BEAUTIFUL MOVEMENTS

In the evening the king's son brought another sheep and a young goat, which we were to accept, so we again gave each one another present of a rod of copper and a piece of tobacco. Most of the afternoon the king spent sitting with us and we treated them to bread, mutton and tobacco. In the evening the king had a fanfare blown in my presence. This is the way in

which it was done: Between 100 and 200 fine persons arranged themselves in a circle, each holding a hollowed reed in the hand, some long, some short, some thick, some thin. In the middle stood one with a long staff, and he sang while the others blew into their reeds and danced in a circle, making many beautiful movements with their feet. The women danced around the circle. It brought forth a sound like that of trumpets blowing. At some distance sat the king on his chair, which was circular and made of wood, 3 or 4 fingers thick, magnificently studded with copper beads. This chair they usually carry along wherever they go.

This game continued with all sorts of dances and lasted for about 2 hours, after which they stopped. The king accompanied me to our camp, where he, too, smoked a pipe or two of tobacco, but when it grew dark he left us and went home. They began to blow on their instruments again and it continued into the night for 3 or 4 hours, after which they settled down to sleep.

Wouter Schouten

WOUTER SCHOUTEN

Impelled by "the combined longings for travel and for learning", Schouten signed on as an under-surgeon with the DEIC. He passed through the Cape in 1658 on his way to India, where he remained six years, and stopped over again on the return journey in 1665. His account of his travels includes some information on the Khoikhoi "who because of their beastliness bear no resemblance to mankind".

ITS WONDERFUL HEIGHT

Two high hills are to be seen in the Table Bay, namely the Lion Hill and the Table Mountain, which are indeed thus called on account of their shapes. We had visited the Lion Hill in 1658, and we were told wonderful things of the Table Mountain; but it was mighty high, and therefore I had difficulty in finding companions to satisfy my curiosity by making a trip thither. But at last, having won over to my proposal the Mate and a Carpenter, on the aforesaid first of *April* we three wanderers left the ship early in the morning, after we had watched the jolly whale [which had appeared that morning next to the ship] to our content, and went ashore, to climb (if it were possible) the very high Table Mountain. Having

32

walked thither we found ourselves at seven o'clock at the foot of this mountain, and then set our course upwards, climbing over a narrow ridge of the hill, which running upwards came to an end at about half the height, against the vertically-rising steep of the Table Mountain. On each side of the ridge we had a downwards slope, and to the right also a stream flowing rapidly downwards in a valley set everywhere with rocks, caves and thick groves, which could make most convenient hiding-places for wild beasts such as lions, tigers, leopards and wolves. Nevertheless we must at times descend into this low valley, because the multitude of rocks made our path impassable, and after going somewhat further in it, again climb up, which indeed was pretty toilsome for us. So we passed many rocks and cliffs, which we must sometimes climb through, sometimes over; but we had come barely half-way up the height of the Table Mountain, when the Mate suddenly lost the courage to go higher. We therefore left him there after giving him a part of the food we had brought, on his promise to await us there for two hours, and then, if he had no news of us, he could be free to return down again, naming to each other a lodging in the town where we hoped to meet in the evening. So we left the Mate half-way up the hill, where he took his place of rest under a shady tree.

We two then climbed upwards from thence, coming to a passage which we found to be barely 4 feet wide, set and walled on the left with an overhanging precipice which because of its vertical upwards slope seemed to reach the sky, and on the right falling very steeply downwards from this dangerous path to a terrifying abyss. Also on this narrow footpath we found that we must continually secure ourselves by our hands in the grass or other scrub in our climb, so steeply did it ascend, or else we could readily have fallen into this dangerous abyss and broken neck and limbs. We found the path beset everywhere with vertical cliffs and rocks, but we climbed and clambered upwards with hands and feet, and thereby came between the two huge rocky overhanging steeps into the ascending gorge of this wonderful Table Mountain, which here presents a narrow cleft from above to below. This narrow gorge was enjoyably set with sweet-smelling flowers and herbs, as also with pleasant grass; and this now formed our path upwards. Here we found an exceptionally clear echo, and could still hear the calling of the Mate whom we had left half-way up the hill because of the triple and quadruple resounding of this echo, although we could no longer see each other owing to the wonderful height. We had brought some *Batavian* home-made arrack with us, as also biscuit and Dutch cheese, which served us well, since because of our mighty thirst (no fresh water being found) we sometimes took a little of this arrack, and partook of some biscuit therewith, which greatly served to our refreshment. We climbed on thence between steep and overhanging cliffs on both sides, and sometimes over large stony cliffs, finding here rocks as large as whole buildings which hung out from the precipices in such a manner that they seemed nowhere to be fastened, so that we were amazed that these suspended rocks did not fall down by their great weight. Also once we heard a terrifying noise and wonderful din not far from us on this steep mountain, and perceived that a huge rock had begun to roll, and came crashing down from above. But we climbed onwards up this narrow gorge of the Table Mountain, which higher up became so narrow that we found it only six or seven feet wide, with steep

or overhanging walls rising upwards on both sides. Thus steadily going onwards, we at last reached the top of the flat Table Mountain, where by the clear sunlight we found that it was already fully one o'clock in the afternoon, we having been busied since 7 in the morning with climbing upwards.

The first thing that occupied us on this mountain was the search for fresh water, to quench our thirst (which was mighty great): this also we soon found in the hollows of some flat rocks with which this hill was as if floored, which water seemed to have gathered from the abundant dew of the thick clouds (which so often cover the whole upper surface of the mountain) in the said hollow rocks. We found it quite sweet and exceptionally pleasant in taste, the more so from our almost unbearable thirst, of which I can truly say that it was never greater in all my travels. Our heavenly liquid now tasted better than ordinarily does the most exquisite drink of the world. Having carefully cooled, refreshed and entertained our very heated entrails with this clear liquid, we went on further, to the front of this mountain, to look at the surrounding country from its wonderful height as if from the air; but it is impossible to describe in words in what a small compass all the nearest landscapes and hills now showed themselves to us: the large Table Bay and all the mighty hills that descend to it from the inland North seemed to be of small extent and importance; we could hardly recognise the Dutch ships lying at anchor within this Table Bay, these looking only like little dots; also in the same way the Dutch Castle of Good Hope and all the houses, farms and green meadows lying around it were, because of the distant and down-sloping depth, seen as if they were in the extreme distance, few details being

properly distinguishable. Even the high Lion Hill and the other hills showed themselves to us from here (except for their most highest tops) as nothing more than uniform flats. Further off, we could see the very high *African* hills to the north, at a guess fully 40 miles away.

JOHANN SCHREYER

Although apparently trained as a surgeon, Schreyer was compelled by financial necessity to enlist as a soldier with the DEIC. He arrived at the Cape in 1669 and spent eight years there, during which he made more than one journey to the interior. His prejudices against the Khoikhoi were no different from those of many of his contemporaries, but he at least relied largely on his own observations of their daily life, customs and beliefs when he compiled his Neue Ost-Indiansche Reis-Beschreibung. *The book includes a reference to the Khoikhoi use of a dried herb "called by them Tagga, which they chew, and become very drunken therefrom".*

FROM THE HEAD DOWNWARDS
Of the Cure and Healing of Wounds by the Hottentots.

They are very unskilled in healing wounds. If a wound is deeper than they can see into, they at once cut it open, and indeed make it 3 or 4 times larger, without regarding whether some member or other may be damaged thereby. If a large vein or artery is cut they do not know how to staunch the blood, and thus must let the man die, because blood-letting is not customary among them. Their plasters and salves are nothing but the fat of the beasts, wherewith they over-diligently smear the wound and all the body. If they fall or are bruised, and see that the place has blood below it, they cut open the skin, suck out the blood, and rub the charcoal of a certain wood therein. For internal sicknesses they use no remedy other than that the surgeon smears the sick person with fat, and rubs it well in, besides doing also some superstitious actions thereby. This is proved by the following history.

A Wonderful Cure Done to a Sick Man.

When once I must travel 30 to 40 miles inland with some soldiers, on business of the Company, we had some Hottentots with us as guides, among whom was one whose testicle was swollen as large as a fist, so that he could hardly walk for the pain. (N.B. These folk are semi-castrated for the most part, which is done in childhood, perhaps to prevent the too-great breeding of children, since they must see that they themselves and their children are in very bad conditions.)

The sun was setting when they made a small fire, near which none of us might come, to which end also they built a separate fire for us. Around this fire they sat in a ring. The surgeon, after he had turned towards the sun with many movements and words, went to the patient, who sat quite naked on the ground, and began to pass his urine on him, from the head downwards and around the body, until he

had no more, in which task 7 or 8 of the other Hottentots then duly followed the surgeon. The sick man, after he was thus thoroughly bathed, went to sleep in his cloak, and next day was fit to continue the journey with us.

I have also seen how for adder- and snake-bites they also use this method, and have the same superstitions regarding them. Also I saw how they attribute great powers to a piece of wood an inch thick and four fingers wide, cut by the surgeon from a certain bush and burned at one end: it is thought to help the sick to regain their health, and turn away the weapons of enemies, for which reason they always carry it on their necks as something holy, and if they fear any danger, they blacken their face with the burned end, and according to their fancy are thus freed therefrom.

Incidentally, Schreyer says later that the Khoikhoi cut away one testicle when a boy turned eight, not only as a birth control measure, but also "so that they may run the better", though a visitor at the end of the 18th century said they in fact pushed their testicles up into the cavity above the scrotum to keep them out of the way when they ran. Other early writers suggested women insisted on partial emasculation for fear of twins. Captain Daniel Beeckman wrote after a 1714 visit that it was the left testicle that they "bruise to pieces" possibly because they hoped for male children, "perhaps being of the opinion of some Naturalists, who hold that the Male Semen comes from the right Testicle, and the Female from the left".

GERRIT RIDDER MUYS

In 1670 Captain Muys was ordered to take the hooker Grundel north from the Cape as far as the Tropic of Capricorn. He was to survey rivers and bays on the way, to look for "een natie caffres", and buy one as a slave. Off the Namibian coast his crew saw only penguins, the odd Khoikhoi and lots of fog. The encounter here took place just south of Walvis Bay; they turned back a few days later, not having located any "caffres". It was only in 1677 that another vessel, the Bode, reached southern Angola where "the Kaffirs commenced and the Hottentots came to an end". A goteling is a small cannon.

WE TOOK TO FLIGHT
... coming on shore, I and two men with me on the beach that sloped upwards somewhat steeply saw five men with a dog as well coming to us, they on seeing us remained standing, however I made a sign, that they should come to us, they ran off again, then I and the other people with me went a little way down the beach, and saw three or four huts standing in a valley between some small sand dunes, which had a little green stuff growing on them, there, being all together on a rise, we remained standing one goteling shot from them, and I again made the same sign, though this time they were 8 or 10 in number, they gestured with a stick that was bound at the end with the tail of some animal, as we later saw, that we should go to them, we could see from here roundabout no greenery other than already mentioned, indeed, the high hills were made of nothing but sand, but eventually I was so desirous to know what nation that was, that with two other men, the one with a musket, and I and the other each with a broadsword

in our clothing, we went halfway to them, and again made the previous sign, and they the same, yet they came hopping and dancing with arrow bow and hassegaey with them in 3 or 4 groups and about 10 or 12 strong, to us, and close by us whistled and shouted to each other and showed they would shoot us, yet we remained standing until one of them was not ten paces from us and was still threatening to shoot, the man then took aim with his musket while the other stood directly in front of it, so that he could have touched the barrel with his hand, and the powder in the pan not wanting to catch, he got an hasegaey in his left breast between the ribs, so he had to drop the musket to escape death and with both hands pulled the hasegay out again, and took it with him. Because we had nothing but two broadswords, we took to flight and were severely pelted by them with many hassegays, sticks and stones, we came to our other people, who now and then held them back a bit, and we running with great difficulty and sometimes falling on our faces, got ahead of them and, exhausted, eventually got into the water and then to the sloop, we saw that this nation were very fat and yellow of colour, they were easily 30 or 40 strong, still pursuing us through the water with their arms full of stones, and still more coming from behind the aforementioned sand dunes, they appeared to be not the proper but nevertheless a sort of Hottentoo, they had skins for their shame and greased hair, yet the words did not come from their throats like proper Hottentoos they also had various dogs with them, there was no indication that they had ever seen any people other than their own, we lifted our grapnel and headed towards the ship, where we arrived shortly after midday, as the wounded man was extremely weak, and we did not know if the hasegay was poisoned or not, we found in the mouth of the river at high water it was $4^1/_2$ or five feet deep, but heavy surf came in. The afternoon we found we had reached 23 deg. 44 min., the wind as above.

CHRISTOPHER SCHWEITZER

Schweitzer, apparently also suffering pecuniary embarrassment, signed up in Amsterdam as a steward on an Indiaman. The fleet weighed anchor in January 1676; south of the Canaries his ship lost 12 men in repulsing a Turkish pirate. By the end of March they had been at sea three and a half months.

I OPEN'D MY EYES
From the 6th to the 24th of *March*, we had very blustering Winds, and a dreadful violent Storm, so that we often thought our selves at the very brink of Death.

The 25th, While that Tempestuous Weather still lasted, the Mate and his Boy were catch'd together acting the abominable Sin of Sodomy. A Council was held upon it, and Sentence was given that they should be tied back to back, (which was done by the Boatswain), and tied in a Sack, and thrown alive into the Sea. As the Minister was doing his Duty towards these Malefactors, representing to them the hainousness of their Crime, and directing them to prepare for Death, the Boy, about 14 years of Age, wept bitterly; But the Mate, being an Italian, about 40 years old, shew'd himself mighty ready to Die, saying; 'Twas better he should be punish'd alone for his horrid Sin, then that the whole Ship should suffer for his sake.

The 26th, the Wind ceased; But we hardly knew where we were, nor had known it for 20 days time, having not been able to make an Observation since the 6th day: And,

On the 27th, it being very fine Weather, we found that the Storm had carried us under the Equinoctial Line. Here it is extream unhealthy, and a certain Distemper seized most of our Men, which made them raving mad: In one day five Persons died, one of which was our Chaplain, the other four Soldiers. These Dead Men, were (according to the Custom of our Dutch Ships) sew'd, each Corps by it self, in a sheet, and after our usual Morning or Evening Prayer, (with a Psalm sung at the end of it) thrown into the Sea.

The 28th, we had no Wind: On this day, one of our Barbers, and two Seamen died; and two Soldiers, in their raving Fit, (caused by the intollerable Heat) leapt into the Sea; which two of our best Swimmers perceiving, leap'd in after them, and brought 'em into the Ship again: But one of 'em after all this, hang'd himself that very Night by his Bed-side.

On the 29th, The other Soldier that had leapt into the Sea, died, having no regard to any good Advice that was given him, and could not be made to Pray. We had not a Breath of Wind this day, nor

The 30th and 31th: These two days we threw over-board our late Chaplain's 4 Children, 4 Chirurgions and Barbers, a Carpenter, and 10 Soldiers.

The 1st, 2d, 3d, and 4th of *April*, the Calm held us still; And in those four days we lost a Steersman, two Carpenters, the Serjeant, and 30 Soldiers and Seamen; so that we expected every Soul should Die out of the Ship.

The 5th *Ditto*, it pleased God to deliver us from that fatal place by a favourable Wind at West and by-South. We had still a great many sick Men, and not enough in health to be able to Brace our Main-Sail, tho' the Mortality ceased; so we were forced to make shift with our small Sails. That day we caught with a Hook one of the great Fishes called Sharks, that rowl'd and toss'd about our Ship. We design'd to dress him, and refresh our selves with it; but when we cut it open, we found in the Belly of it our Serjeant that we had thrown over-board, not yet digested. The sight of this so turn'd our Stomachs, that none could find in their Heart to Eat of the Fish; so that we threw Man and Fish into the Sea again. It is observable, That these great Fish have always some small ones to go before 'em, that are called by the name of Pilot-Fishes, and swim in and out of the Shark's Mouth. And when a Shark is catch'd, they cleave to his Back like a Burr.

But I must not omit what happen'd to my self. As I fell Ill and was in a Swoun, he that look'd after the sick, took me for Dead, and fetch'd a new Shirt out of my Chest, and was putting it upon me; The Sail-maker too was a going to sew me up; and he handling me a little roughly, after all his pushing and tossing of me, I open'd my Eyes: Those that were about me were not a little startled; and said, it was high time for me to open 'em; for if I had winck'd but a little longer, over I had gone. Our chief Merchant gave me a Glass of Sack, which refreshed me very much.

They arrived at the Cape two weeks later.

OLOF BERGH

This encounter took place during Ensign Bergh's unsuccessful 1682 expedition up the West Coast to find the source of the copper that the Nama were bringing to the fort at the Cape.

EYES ON THEIR FEET

The Ensign asked the Amacquas all particulars as to the road and its condition; they spun us many yarns and told us there was no chance of getting further. They said we must pass all the undermentioned nations ere we arrived at the Bri[quas] and Gri[quas] and firstly we should encounter the Cobicijqua beyond the Amacquas. They lived twelve days' journey from them and were a small nation; the Caminge ad idem, Noecqua a great nation, Quinonqui a small nation, Nimpey a great ditto, Keijgij a small ditto, Goeachij a small ditto, Goegouckij a small, Ket Sarkeij a great; Chaliesbri were Kaffirs who wear made clothes; Alabriqua white folk who wear skins and are Hottentots; Aart Eyck Gamoere a people having eyes on their feet. When the Ensign caused them to be asked if they had in truth seen such and if a single one of them had been there, they replied, "No", they had only repeated what other Hottentots had told them.

DAVID TAPPE

Like Herport and Schreyer, Tappe was a DEIC soldier. He was at the Cape twice – in 1668, as a stopover on a tour of duty that took him as far as China – and again in 1682. He records going out with his shipmates into the country "to amuse ourselves" among the Khoikhoi. "If one wishes them to dance, one needs only give them a pipeful of tobacco, and then they stiffen their legs and continually leap up and down, and meanwhile sing Hottentot Brukwa, *and this is the beginning and end of their continual song. If one says to them* Karos op Zey *they push the scrap of sheep skin from before their privities to the back, and let the whole gear be seen, and laugh therewith." Europeans were fascinated by the elongated labia of Khoikhoi women.*

UP TO HER NAVEL

A Dutch woman of our ship had heard that the Hottentot women had over their privities a piece of flesh hanging, such as the turkeys have in front of the head, and that this covered the vulva. She wished to examine a Hottentot woman, but this was quicker, and lifted the Dutch woman's skirt up to her navel, and we watched this with amusement through a window; and when we could not contain our laughter the woman heard it and perceived us and went off, but the Hottentot woman laughed.

NOT TO BE TRUSTED

… on April 29, 1682 we set sail in God's Name, taking with us 2 ostriches for H.M. the Prince of Orange, and other ships took also 8 such; also the Admiral took along 2 Hottentots. And when the other savages learned in advance that two of them were kept in the Fortress and should be taken to Holland, there came some 100 from inland. When now the time came to embark, and since the savages were not to be trusted too much, soldiers fully armed and with burning linstocks were set from the Fortress to the seashore, between which the General marched down, and after him the Hottentots, and all the cannon of the Fortress were fired thrice. And since these savages who were come from inland stood close below the cannon and were not accustomed to the roar of the cannon-royal, they set up a great shrieking and made off inland, and did not return to see the Hottentots depart.

GUI TACHARD

In early 1685 the French king Louis XIV dispatched an embassy to Siam. He did this partly out of scientific curiosity, partly to make converts to Christianity, but also in hopes – never realised – of turning the kingdom into a French dependency. The delegation included four ecclesiastics for mission work in Siam, and six Jesuit mathematicians destined for China, which it was hoped they would reach with Siamese help. Father Tachard was one of the six, though he was to return to France rather than carry on to China. They arrived in Table Bay in May that year, and were received civilly enough, despite dark Dutch suspicions of French popery. During their three-month stay the Jesuits set up an astronomical observatory in a pavilion near the entrance to the company gardens.

THE FORT FIRED NONE AT ALL
Here they have anchored in the roadstead off Cape Town, where there is already a fleet of "four great Ships" from Holland under the command of an admiral.

No sooner were we come to an Anchor, but two Boats came on Board of us, to know who we were, and next Morning about seven a Clock the [Dutch] Commissary General sent and complimented my Lord Ambassador, who on his Part ordered the *Chevaler de Forbin*, Lieutenant of the Ship, and three other Officers to go ashoar and salute him, and withal, to desire leave of him that we might take in fresh Water and necessary Provisions. He very civilly gave his Consent, and being informed that there were several Gentlemen in the Ambassadors Retinue, he invited them to come and hunt ashoar. He inquired if there were any Jesuits on board our Ship, and it is probable that they who came the day before had taken notice of us, and talked of it upon their Return.

Monsieur de Forbin made answer, that there were six of us going to *China*, and that there were other Church men on board also bound for *Siam*.

Then they came to speak of the Salutes, and it was agreed upon that the Fort should render Gun for Gun when our Ship saluted it. This Article was ill explained, or ill understood by these Gentlemen, for about ten of the Clock my Lord Ambassador having ordered seven Guns to be fired, the Admiral answered only with five Guns, and the Fort fired none at all. Immediately the Ambassador sent ashoar again, and it was determined that the Admirals Salute should pass for nothing, and so the

Fort fired seven Guns, the Admiral seven Guns, and the other Ships five, to salute the Kings Ship, which returned them their Salutation, for which the Fort and Ships gave their Thanks. After that we made ready our Boats, and thought of nothing now but of going ashoar to refresh our selves.

MASTERS OF THE EARTH

The *Hotentots* being perswaded that there is no other life after this, labour as little and take as much ease as they can in this World. To hear them talk even when they are serving the Dutch, for a little Bread, Tobacco, or Brandy, they look upon them as slaves who labour the Land of their Country, and as People of no Courage who shut themselves up within Houses and Forts to secure them from their Enemies, whilst their people Encamp securely in the open Fields without stooping so low as to labour Land. By that way of living they pretend to demonstrate that they are Masters of the Earth, and the happiest People of the World, because they alone live in liberty and repose, wherein they place their felicity. Whilst we were in the Companies Garden, a leading Man amongst them seeing how civilly we were used by the chief of the Dutch there; came to the Observatory, and there meeting Father *Fontenay*, he presented him with two Oranges, saying to him in Portuguese, *Reverendo Padre, Géral dos Ottentots á vossa Senhoria* [Reverend Father, Hottentot General to your Highness]; thereby intimating that his Captain and Nation congratulated our arrival.

Whatever good Opinion they may have of themselves, they lead a wretched life. They are nasty even to excess, and it would seem that they study to make themselves hideous. When they would deck themselves, they rub over their heads, face, and hands, with the sutt of their kettles, and when that is wanting, they have recourse to a certain kind of black grease, that makes them stink and look so horridly that there is no enduring of them. Hence it is that their hair which is naturally almost as woolly as the hair of *Negroes*, runs into little round knots, to which they fasten pieces of Copper or Glass. Those amongst them of greatest note to these Ornaments add great Ivory Rings which they wear about their Arms above and below the Elbows. Their food is far more surprising than all the rest for they make a delicious dish of the Vermin that breeds in the skins wherewith they are clad. We have seen this oftener than once, otherwise we could never have believed it. The Women besides this Apparel, encompass their legs with the guts of Beasts, or small skins which they cut for this use: they do it to preserve them from the prickings of Thorns, when they go through the woods, and to have always a present remedy against hunger if they should be put to a pinch. Their Attire consists of several strings of Beads made of Shells or Bones of different colours, whereof they make themselves Neck-laces and Girdles, and some thicker Rings which they wear about their Arms.

However Barbarity has not so totally effaced all the Tracts of Humanity in those People, but that there remains still some footsteps of Virtue: they are trusty, and the Dutch allow them free access into their houses without any fear of being Robbed by them. Nevertheless it is said, that they are not so reserved as to Strangers, or to the Dutch who are new comers, who know them not so well as to get them punished for it. They are beneficent and helpful, and keep nothing wholly for themselves. When they have any thing given them, if it can be divided, they give a share of it to the first of their acquaintance they meet, nay they'll hunt about for them for that purpose, and commonly keep the least share of what they have to themselves.

OK-KHUN CHAMNAN

Returning from Siam in 1686 the French, including Tachard, passed through Table Bay with a reciprocal Siamese embassy to the French court. Coincidentally another Siamese delegation – this one to the king of Portugal – was following close behind in the Nossa Senhora dos Milagros. *It consisted of nine mandarins, including Chamnan, and their attendants. A misjudgment put the* Milagros *on the rocks just east of Cape Agulhas, and the survivors had to make a gruelling month-long trek to Cape Town. The lot of the Siamese was not made any easier when the Portuguese deserted them early on. Chamnan's story of the ordeal was recorded by Tachard during a subsequent, less hazardous, voyage which took the Siamese to France and Rome, where his portrait was painted by the Vatican court painter.*

TRIED TO EAT THE HAT

After much trouble we reached the foot of a mountain, which was hollow at its base, as if nature had intended it to serve as a lodging for passers-by. It was large enough for all of us altogether, and we passed a very cold and miserable night there. For some days my legs and feet had been so swollen that I could wear neither shoes nor stockings; but this inconvenience was greatly increased by the extreme cold which I endured this night, and the dampness of the rock. On waking in the morning, I perceived a considerable space covered with the water which had run from my feet. But weak as I was, I found strength on the morrow, when the others were preparing to start. It appeared that the more I suffered pain, the more care I took to preserve my life; I really hoped more than ever to preserve it, after having suffered so cruelly and having run so much risk of death. The whole of the morrow we continued along the river's bank in the expectation of discovering the Portuguese, whom we believed not far distant. From time to time we found traces of them. A quarter of a league from the rock where we had slept one of our men saw a gun a little aside, with a flask full of powder, which a Portuguese had no doubt left from inability to carry it further. This discovery was of very great use to us. We separated the stock from the barrel, and took with us the lock and the powder flask for the purpose of striking fire. It was indeed very fortunate; for since we had gone along the river, we had found absolutely nothing, and were nearly dead of hunger. We immediately made a fire; and seeing that my shoes were not only useless to me, as I could not put them on, but had become an encumbrance, – for I continued to carry them in my hand in the hope that the swelling of the feet would go down, – I yielded at length to necessity; I separated the different pieces, and having had them well roasted, we ate them with a very good appetite. Not that they tasted remarkably well, for the leather was so dry that there was no moisture whatever left in it; but it was enough that they were not bitter, and that it was possible to swallow them, so great was the hunger that tormented us. We then tried to eat the hat of one of our servants, after having roasted it well; but this we could not manage. In order to masticate it at all we were compelled to burn several pieces to a cinder, and in this state it was so bitter and loathsome that, famished as we were, we could not swallow it.

MARCEL LE BLANC

Le Blanc was one of 15 Jesuits – again including Tachard – who passed through the Cape in 1687 headed for Siam. During the two-and-a-half-week stopover Le Blanc got dragged up Table Mountain by a fellow priest, Father De Béze. De Béze enthusiastically collected plants and a soil sample from the top, and recorded views in several directions; Le Blanc was less passionate.

You need to be a goat
The day before yesterday, I went up Table Mountain from whence I saw *omnia regna mundi*. This expedition is a silly idea because it is necessary to climb from rock to rock through bushes and by the steepest road in the world. You need to be a goat to get up this dreadful mountain properly.

The Protestant chaplain Francois Valentyn, a contemporary of Le Blanc's, sensibly pieced together his description of the "toilsome and dangerous" mountain from the accounts of other people who made the climb. "I have never spoken with anyone who had once gone up there and had a desire to go up again," he said.

GUILLAUME CHENU DE CHALEZAC

Chalezac was a 14-year-old cabin boy on an English vessel headed for the Indies in 1687. Unsure of his position off the Cape east coast, the captain sent eight men, including Chalezac, ashore in a small boat to find out where they were. The Xhosa they met on the beach killed the youngster's companions, and he received a terrible beating. However, he was taken in by the local chief, who showed a tenderness "that was not that of a barbarian" and treated the boy as if he was his own son. During the year he stayed there – in the area of present-day East London – Chalezac learned to speak Xhosa, took part in a military expedition against Khoikhoi raiders, built up a small herd of cattle, and turned down an offer of marriage. Living in the same area was a handful of survivors of the Stavenisse, *a Dutch vessel wrecked near Port St Johns higher up the coast a year earlier. They had tried unsuccessfully to walk to Cape Town. Another group of survivors stayed at the wreck site, painstakingly built a boat from the wreckage and sailed to the Cape. This boat, the* Centaur, *returned in February 1688 to pick up 18* Stavenisse *men, and the French boy, who later penned these memoirs.*

Decency and decorum
I would not have believed, that among these people [the Xhosa], so brutal and rough, decency and decorum would have been so

43

strongly adhered to. If by misfortune or otherwise a man broke wind in the presence of others, above all if they happened to be women, his behaviour would be considered infamous and he would have difficulty thereafter in being received in company again.

WET WITH TEARS

One day when I was going out to visit one of the Dutchmen who was living separately from the rest in another dwelling place, I met a woman on my journey, who said to me: "Where are you off to – and why are you still here? All your comrades left here yesterday: a little ship has come to look for them, and they have already embarked." This news caused me great alarm. With great impatience I found out as quickly as I could where the ship was lying. She showed me the place, which was four leagues away. I took my leave from this woman and asked her to take my excuses to my host for not returning to see him. After that I set off on the road at top speed so that I arrived before midday at the place of embarkation.

I found there our party, who had not yet sailed. After waiting for two days, while the rest of our comrades gathered at the ship, we went on board, numbering 19 in all. There were a further six of us who had not found the rendezvous. Before leaving, however, I received the farewells of my host. This man, when he heard about my departure from the woman I have spoken of, came next day to find me and stayed with me until the day of my embarkation. As the ship could not come close up to the land, it was necessary to wade out into the sea. He sat me on his neck and carried me out to the ship, albeit against my will. During this journey his face was no less wet with tears at my parting from him than his body was with sea water. Until we parted he rent the air with his cries, and I in turn could not refuse the love of a man to whom I owed so much.

CREW OF THE *STAVENISSE*

Back in Cape Town, the Stavenisse *men reported that they had been well treated by the Xhosa, a people who loved one another "with a most remarkable affection".*

WITHOUT ANY CAUSE OF FEAR

In their intercourse with each other, they are very civil, polite, and talkative, saluting each other, whether male or female, young or old, whenever they meet; asking whence they come, and whither they are going, what is their news, and whether they have learned any new dances or tunes; they are, however, thievish and lying, though hospitable.

Revenge has little or no sway among them, as they are obliged to submit their disputes to the king, who, after hearing the parties, gives sentence on the spot, to which all parties submit without a murmur; but should the matter in dispute be of great importance, and when he cannot rely upon his own judgment, he refers the parties to an older king in his neigbourhood.

When a father beats his son so as to draw blood, and complaint is made to the king, he must pay the king a cow, as a fine.

The kings are much respected and beloved by their subjects. Their houses are like hay-cocks in Europe, and merely a little larger than the common huts, and they (the chiefs) wear the skins of the deer or tiger, but in other respects they are quite like the common people. Of their courage little can be said, as during the stay of the Netherlanders amongst them they had no wars.

One may travel 200 or 300 *mylen* through the country, without any cause of fear from men, provided you go naked (*blood*), and without any iron or copper, for these things give inducement to the murder of those who have them.

Neither need one be in any apprehension about meat and drink, as they have in every village or kraal a house of entertainment for travellers, where these are not only lodged, but fed also; care must only be taken, towards night fall, when one cannot get any further, to put up there, and not to go on before morning.

In an extent of 150 *mylen* travelled by your servants along the coast, to the depth of about 30 *mylen* inland, and through five kingdoms, namely: the *Magoses*, *Makriggas*, the *Matimbes*, *Mapontes*, and *Emboas*, they found no standing waters, but many rivers with plenty of fish and full of sea cows.

There are many dense forests, with short stemmed trees; but at the bay of Natal are two forests, each fully a *myl* square, with tall, straight, and thick trees, fit for house or ship timber, in which is abundance of honey and wax; but no wax is to be had from the natives, as they eat the wax as well as the honey.

In all the time of their stay in that country, or of travelling through it, they found but one European; an old Portuguese, in the country of the Mapontes; he had been shipwrecked there about 40 years before, while returning from India. The wreck, built of teak, is still to be seen on the shore, and, as the Africans state, several brass and iron cannon are still to be found there. This Portuguese had been circumcised, and had a wife, children, cattle and land, he spoke only the African language, having forgotten every thing, his God included.

CORNELIS HEEREMANS

After the Centaur *came the galliot* Noord, *despatched from Cape Town in October 1688 to survey the east coast and pick up the remaining* Stavenisse *survivors. Chalezac, who since his own rescue had signed on with the DEIC, was one of the crew. Heeremans was mate and likely keeper of this journal. The* Noord *was also instructed to sound out possibilities for trade with the locals at Delagoa Bay – which proved easier said than done.*

Dry bread with water
At Delagoa Bay, with the Noord *at anchor, a delegation bearing gifts headed upriver in a boat for the place of the king.*

... that afternoon it rained so heavily that we could not continue, and the boat was continually filling with water, so that we were obliged to head for the bank and make a large fire, which we did, in this way again drying out our goods and guns; here we decided to cook some rice and while we were busy chopping wood and drying our things, the inhabitants came to us displaying extreme courtesy and in pretence of friendship helping us gather wood and while our kettle with rice was standing to cook on the fire and we were laying out the grapnel, and one was busy with this, and another with that, it was already about 8 o'clock in the evening when we were intending to eat and then the inhabitants had stolen our kettle, we ran after them but because they were much quicker in running than we were we could not catch up with them, and this obliged us that evening to eat dry bread with water of which there was no lack and the rain continued until the morning.

THE GIFTS OF THE ENGLISHMAN
The Hollanders' misery did not end when they found the king, who was well over two metres tall and apparently named Jan Jacques. He was already being courted by a visiting English captain, who was seeking ivory.

... in the evening the great king came home with the English capt. and told us that he had been on board our ship and that our skipper gave him one $^1/_2$ piece of guinea linen cloth, he seemed to laugh at this, and we honoured him with one of our neck-rings for one of his children, being a son of about 7 or 8 years, but the English capt. gave him a pistol with a flintlock together with 6 pieces of cloth each of about 12 ells long, so that the gifts of the Englishman were considerably more acceptable to him, and the Englishman in that way impressed him, so that our herring did not fry on that fire at all ...

WITH TEARS IN HIS EYES
On the return journey, the Noord *picked up two men at the spot the* Stavenisse *was wrecked. One of them was the boatswain Adrian Jansz Kind, the "Arij Kint" in this extract. Then they headed for the distinctive Cove Rock, west of the Buffalo River, where the* Centaur *had rescued the 18 crewmen and Chalezac. They arrived there at the end of January 1689, and approached it from the southwest.*

Friday the 28 do. this morning fair weather and a S.W. wind; we passed the said rock about the third glass of the morning watch, and anchored about $1^1/_2$ miles to the east of it before a great river, where the surf broke heavily, so that we saw no chance of entering; when we anchored we instantly put the boat out to fetch the people, they pulled towards the shore with 6 men. On approaching the surf we dropped a grapnel and the boatswain Arij Kint (whom we had delivered from Terra de Natal on the 4th) swam through the surf with a letter to be given to the Dutch, this was instantly undertaken by the natives (on the request of the boatswain), on which the boatswain swam back to the boat, and immediately returned on board to make his report to the captain, saying that the people would come soon, as they lived about three hours from there and upon their arrival about 2 hours after midday, the boat was again sent to the shore; but before reaching the surf one of the men swam out through the surf and met them, he was an old man named Paij Isak, but the other stood on the shore, not daring to go through the surf, and desired that we would come and take him from the great rock where he could better get through the surf, on this the boat returned on board with the old man, who, as soon as he got on board, thanked God, and reported to us that two of the men who had been with them had on 1 January set out for the lodging whence we had brought the boatswain and the boy [i.e. back to the Stavenisse wreck site]. Meanwhile the wind began to freshen, and we were obliged to weigh anchor and head for the open sea so that the next day we could come to the rock; that night it began to blow hard, and we had to lie to in order not to be pushed too far from our position; by mid[night] we turned again towards the shore and at sunrise we came to our old place again.

Saturday the 29 do. came to our old place again at sunrise, we could not go beyond the rock because the strong wind still raged from the S.W., and we had to lie off again; towards evening we came again to the shoreline below the aforementioned rock, having it S.W. of us, we again had to lie off-shore until the next morning because of the rough sea.

Sunday the 30 do. this morning at sunrise, the wind from the eastward, stood in for the shore; about the third glass of the morning watch, we saw the rock, steered for it, got there about the 6th glass of the morning watch, hove to: remained there head to wind, put out the boat, on reaching the breakers they dropped anchor, and the said boatswain swam to meet him with a lead line, he seeing this also took to the water and swam until they were 2 boat lengths from each other and in the worst part of the surf which just then was breaking very heavily, the shipwrecked man turned for the shore, not daring to venture further; the boatswain on seeing this called to him that he only had to come a little nearer but he to the contrary turned again to the rock and on reaching it waved to them to go away, at which the said boatswain swam back to the boat, coming soon after back on board where with tears in his eyes, he gave us these particulars; we could not stay here any longer in consequence of the strong easterly wind and the current, set our sails again and put the vessel before the wind, saw no means of getting him off, as all along the coast was a rocky reef over which the sea broke with violence …

FRANÇOIS LEGUAT

Leguat was a French Huguenot who for two years led a Crusoe-like existence as a settler on the Indian Ocean island of Rodriguez – an "earthly paradise", where he feasted on turtles, dugongs and the solitaire, a stately bird destined to become extinct in the 1700s. He passed through the Cape on his outward journey in 1691, and on his way back seven years later.

THE BEARD OF THE SERJEANT
We found four Ships there [in Table Bay], two *Dutch* (the *Black Lion* and the *Mountain* of *China*), one *English*, and one *Danish*. Our Guns being still in the *Hold*, we cou'd not Salute them at first according to Custom. 'Twas the next day before they were ready, and when fir'd, it had been better we had let it alone, unless we cou'd have come off more luckily; though as it happen'd, 'twas well it was no worse; for one of our Guns which was loaden with Ball ever since we came from the *Texel*, and had not been discharg'd, was for-

47

gotten to be loaden, and being fir'd struck the Wall of the Fort, after having past through the middle of thirty Persons, and brush'd a little the Beard of the Serjeant, who return'd us our Bullet: We were chid for our Negligence and that was all.

FINEST WOMEN IN THE WORLD
Like earlier writers, Leguat saw the Khoikhoi as brutish and debased, but to his credit he did record their own opinion as well.

But what is yet more frightful, is their Necks; they seem to have two long, half-dry'd, and half-fill'd Hoggs Bladders hanging at them. These nasty Dugs, whose Flesh is black, wrinkled and rough as Shagreen, come down as low as their Navels, and have Fillemot Teats as large as those of a Cow. In truth these swinging Udders have this commodious in them, that you may lead a Woman by them to the Right or Left, forwards or backwards as you please. For the most part they throw them behind their Shoulders to suckle their Child, who is slung upon their Backs. Notwithstanding all this, the vanity of these ugly Witches is incredible. They fancy themselves the finest Women in the World, and look on us from top to bottom with their Hands to their Sides disdainfully.

DANIEL SILLEMAN

The Gouden Buys *sailed from the DEIC's home port of Texel in May 1693. By the time she limped to a landfall on the West Coast just north of St Helena Bay five months later, 160 of her crew of 190 had died, most of them victims of scurvy. Half the survivors were also stricken with the disease. A party of seven, including Silleman, whose job on board ship was to distil seawater into drinking water, landed to seek help. They spent several days wandering in the bush, eating tortoises and whatever else they could find; as their number dwindled, they became more desperate.*

TORTURED BY HUNGER
Meanwhile, our Water had once again run out/we looked mournfully at each other/and out of desperation we once again went into the bushes; to look for food for ourselves; eventually we found some of the blue Berries, which were mentioned before/ate some of them and remained there for 14 Days, drinking our own Water, as we had done several times before/ then we lost the steward, this being around 26 or 27 December/and having removed a small way from the corpse/the Commander said to me Daniel Silleman; Jan Crist or Christiaansz (as his Name was) is Dead now/ and we are suffering extreme hunger/let us go back and cut off a piece of the thick Flesh/and then let us roast it and eat it/God will not hold us to account for that as a sin; I was terrified at such a suggestion/and said No/nonetheless, after much arguing/he said tortured by hunger/he said then I

The wreck of the *Gouden Buys.*

will go and cut a piece off for myself; and as my hunger was no less than his, I said to him/should you cut some of that off and roast it/I will help you eat it; This was around Nightfall, I collected Wood and made a Fire, while he went ahead and cut from the thick part of the Leg a piece about the size of a Hand; and roasted it; but when it was roasted/we could not eat any of it, because of its dry, tough texture; however, we did eat one or two mouthfuls of it/and then placed the remainder in our sack, wanting to see whether the following Day we would be able to make ourselves eat some of it/then we lay down to sleep approximately 20 paces from the dead Body (being without strength or courage)/until the following Day.

Khoikhoi came to their aid, but by the time Silleman managed to attract the attention of the Dageraat, *sent from the Cape to salvage the* Gouden Buys, *he and a companion were the only ones of the entire crew still alive. Their ship, foetid with the stench of rotting corpses, was abandoned. Making her way back into Table Bay, the* Dageraat *ran aground in fog on the western side of Robben Island, and 16 of her crew were drowned. Silleman was washed ashore, stark naked but alive.*

CHRISTOFFEL LANGHANSZ

When the East Indies fleets approached Texel at the end of often horrendous voyages, the sailors embarked on low-key anarchy, says Langhansz. They would break up kitchen equipment and toss empty brandy-kegs overboard, "and if the Skipper has not treated them well on the journey he had better lock himself away safely". Once on shore, their pay was soon spent; there they were known as "six-week lords", and Langhansz tells the delightful story of one sailor who hired three coaches, the first to carry his hat, the second his pipe and tobacco, and the third himself. A German, Langhansz passed through the Cape in 1694, on his way to the Indies as a DEIC soldier. He picked up enough seafaring experience to sign on as a mate on later voyages to Spain and Portugal, the Ionian Islands and Greenland. Here he describes Cape Town.

ALL THEIR MONEY

About 100 paces from the Castle towards the Lion Hill is a town of some 70 houses, most of them inhabited by Dutch and Germans, who have all their living from the ships that touch, by taking as boarders those who come ashore, these paying $1/8$ Rxd. for a meal. They also do a secret trade with the "Bahren", as those coming out from Holland are called, whereas those coming from the Indies are called "Orlammi". From the former they get especially brandy and tobacco, since these are declared contraband here by the Company, and a Fiscal is set here who keeps a sharp eye on this through his servants, called Caffers – but nevertheless this trade is practised ashore secretly to an extent that can scarcely be imagined, nor in what ways they trick the Fiscal and his inspectors.

When the wind is at S.E. it often blows so strongly and for so long that for several days no one can go from shore to ship nor

from ship to shore, so that those who are ashore and have spent all their money must give to these folk for their lodging the clothes that they have brought from Holland, and often go aboard in a linen shirt and linen trousers. These clothes are sold again pretty dear by the inhabitants to those who come from the Indies and are bound for Holland, so that they get a double profit on them.

SUCH DISHONEST DANCING

When ships come into the harbour they [the Khoikhoi] do their best to come aboard with one boat or another, and when this succeeds, they go at once to the galley and beg the cook for grease or fat, however black and stinking it may be, and smear and anoint themselves quite openly with this from top to toe, including even that which God has made it natural to be kept hidden. Such smearing is indeed a habit among all East-Indian peoples, but not all use such stinking fat as these: in India they smear themselves with the oil of the coconut, especially their long hair, which thereby becomes as thick and strong as horsehair, and this oil keeps them as black as pitch, the colour which they prefer above all others. The first day when we were come into the harbour three came aboard with our shallop, two men and a woman, and filled the whole ship with their stink. If one gave the men a scrap of tobacco they danced and leapt and called therewith Hot: Hot: Hot:, and both men and woman pushed their Carotzes aside and let their privities be seen, and called out repeatedly "de Dieber hal de Domine van Hammerfoort, Hammerfoort", "The Devil take the Dominee of Hammerfort", which no doubt they had learned from the sailors. For such dishonest dancing they got tobacco enough, and put it in a little bag which they had hanging on the front of their necks.

AT LAST BOTH DIE
The Khoikhoi again.

As to their religion, they have none, but live like the unreasoning brutes from day to day. Although some say of them that they reverence the moon this is not so, although it is true that by night, especially at the New Moon, they dance, or better said leap before it, and thereby howl rather than sing. But this dancing is done only for their pleasure, since leaping against their shadows and clapping their hands delights them especially, in that they see their shadows also do this; and this they continue so long as the moon shines on them, so that this dancing is thus to be considered as solely and entirely for their pleasure and amusement. Also although all the peoples of the Indies much like dancing by night, yet these most especially, since they take no heed of work: after they have lain asleep all the day in the sun, and sought for something to eat which they themselves produce, all their task is then thus to tire themselves by night with leaping and dancing; and also they take little thought for clothing. If it rains, and they are asked Whence it comes? they say "Groot Captain pissem", which in their opinion is as much as to say, "The Captain of the folk who live above is passing his water"; since in their opinion very large folk live above there. They wish to know nothing of God, but make do with the following excuse which they bring out in broken Dutch "Hollaender arbeitem sterbem dem Hottentot sterbem is storbem krup der als ock Hollaender mann", which is to say "The Dutch work and toil but not the Hottentots, and at last both die and one is buried in the earth like the other". If they are told of a Resurrection to a better life they shake their heads like the atheists, and say that they and their cattle have one and the same burial, and that one will rise again as little as the other. And let this be enough concerning the Hottentots.

JOHANNES DE GREVENBROEK

The Dutchman and company servant Grevenbroek served as secretary to the Council of Policy at the Cape. He resigned in 1694 to live at Stellenbosch as a free burgher, where he penned – in clumsy Latin – a manuscript titled An Elegant *and* Accurate Account of The African Race. *It contains both his own observations on the Khoikhoi, and descriptions of the way of life of the Xhosa drawn in part from the accounts of the survivors of the* Stavenisse, *which he himself had copied into the official records. The traveller Peter Kolb said he was a man of "remarkable industry, understanding and knowledge".*

A PIECE OF SKIN
Grevenbroek is here describing Khoikhoi customs. Early in the 20th century the skin taken warm off a living goat was still used by their descendants as an application against severe pain, while poultices were made of the entrails of a goat disembowelled alive.

When a soothsayer or priest is about to make a sacrifice he first whets the knife; he then places the cow with its feet tied and its head to the North three or four paces from the door of the hut in which the sick man lies, and gives it a light blow with his fist on the left side. It falls to the right on to green branches lying ready for it; and forthwith he cuts away with his right hand from near the navel a piece of skin the size of his palm, as much as he can hold in his left hand; then he immediately binds this on the right wrist of the patient. His next business is to skin the animal alive. I have heard a disembowelled cow lowing, and have seen the Hottentots eating the badly roasted side of another cow in the same condition and still alive. After this he washes the face of the sick man in a little blood which he catches in a pot, or dish, or tortoise shell; and making libation of the gall of the victim, he puts the gall-bladder on the roof of the sick man's house.

FRAGRANT AND AGREEABLE
Like all Africans and Asiatics they rub their limbs with any sort of fat, just as if it was olive oil, anointing themselves copiously as a protection against the danger of sun, cold or disease. The noisome stench of which our people accuse them is to be ascribed not to dirt but rather to a plant known to European botanists and called Bochu by the natives. This they crush with stones and reduce to a powder, and then sprinkle or rub on their heads as a sweet fumigatory, potent charm, or disinfectant scent. Strangers find the smell of this plant unpleasant, heavy, and offensive, but to those who have had time to become accustomed to it, it seems choice, fragrant and agreeable.

CHAPTER TWO

1700 to 1800

Containing accounts of the most farting animal
under the sun, some extraordinary smoking,
stockings and gloves that grow on bushes,
the order of precedence in love, the Right Honourable
Lord Governor Baron Joachim van Plettenberg's
return to the Castle, a star like a porcupine,
and the effect of tobacco oil on a snake.

PETER KOLB

*Kolb, a German scientist and theologian, came to the Cape in 1705 to make astro-
nomical observations, and remained for almost a decade. During the last few years
of his stay he was the DEIC's secretary at Stellenbosch. This posting enabled him
to gather material for an account of the Khoikhoi which, even though he castigated
them as lazy and drunken, was more sympathetic than anything earlier writers had
produced. "Numbers of 'em [Khoikhoi] have told me," he said, "that the Vices they
saw prevail among Christians; their Avarice, their Envy and Hatred of one another, their restless discontented Tempers, their Lasciviousness and Injustice were the
Things that principally kept the* Hottentots *from Hearkening to Christianity."*

Peter Kolb

A VERY HIGH MOUNTAIN

[Governor Simon Van Der Stel] took an infinite Pleasure in imposing
all the Fictions and Sotteries he could upon everyone. Having the
Honour, forsooth, to be once in his Company at his Seat, call'd
Constantia, he took it in his Head, among other extravagant
Assertions, to assure me very gravely, that in a Journey from
the *Cape* towards *Monomotapa* he reach'd, at the Distance of
200 Miles, a very high Mountain, where passing the Night,
he ascended to the Top, and discover'd from thence very
plainly, that the Moon was not so far from the Earth as the
Astronomers asserted; for that as that Planet, said he, pass'd
at that Time over my Head, the Night being very still and
clear, I could plainly perceive the Grass there to wave to and
again, and had the Noise of its Motion in my Ears. You set up
for a Philosopher and Astronomer, said he: What do you think
of this Matter? Think, Sir! I replied (seeing him very grave, and
knowing his Temper) I think, that your Excellency's Eyes and
Ears are as good as other Peoples; and that it would be very ill
Manners for me to dispute their Evidence. And so the Matter dropt.

WITH SO GREAT A FORCE

The Sense of Smelling is wonderful in the Rhinoceros. He catches immediately, and at a considerable Distance, the Scent of any Creature that is to Windward of him. And as soon as he catches it, if the Creature is of his Prey, he marches towards it in a right Line, tearing his Way very furiously through all Opposition of Trees and Bushes. He grunts like a Hog; but his Grunting is not heard far. But when he is upon the March, he is heard at a great Distance, forcing his way through thick Bushes and snapping of Trees. His Throwing of Stones likewise, if he meets with any in his Way, gives fair Warning of him; for he flings 'em over  his Head with so great a Force, that they are heard to bounce and trundle upon the Ground a great Way, or else to fall with a mighty Clattering upon the next Rocks.

If he is not provok'd, he attacks not a Man; unless the Man is in a red Coat, for then he attacks him very furiously, without any Manner of Provocation, and is all in a Flame for his Destruction, rending and destroying every Thing that stands in the Way to the Gratification of his Rage. If he seizes a Man, he flings him over his Head with so great a Force, that the Man is kill'd by the Fall. The Beast then feeds upon him by Licking, with his rough and prickly Tongue, the Flesh from the Bones.

The Eyes of the Rhinoceros are very small, and vastly short of Proportion to his Body, which is very large. He sees only right forward; and, as I have said, he travels and pursues ever in a right Line, forcing his Way through all Opposition of Trees and Bushes. He is pretty swift of Foot, but very slow and awkward in Turning. If he makes at you, the Way to avoid him is to suffer him to come within 8 or 10 Paces of you; and then to whip a few Paces aside; for then he loses Sight of you; and it costs him a great Deal of awkward Trouble to get you in his Eye again. This I have experienc'd my self; for he has more than once made with all his Fury towards me.

He is not fond of Feeding on Grass, chusing rather Shrubs, Broom and Thistles. But the Delight of his Tooth is a Shrub, not much unlike the *Juniper*, but not of so fine a Scent, nor quite so prickly.

The *Cape-Europeans* call it the *Rhinoceros*-Bush. The Heathy Parts of the *Hottentot* Countries abound with those Bushes. Great Numbers of 'em are seen on the *Tiger*-Hills and the *Moshel*-Bank; the Inhabitants of which Places cut 'em for Firing.

The Rhinoceros is in perpetual Enmity with the Elephant; and, whenever he discovers him, makes at him with all his Rage. The Elephant knows him to be his mortal Enemy; and therefore, when he 'spies him, gets out of his Way as fast as he can. If a Rhinoceros surprises an Elephant, he rips up the Elephant's Belly with the Horn on his Snout; by which Means the Elephant's Entrails tumble out and he quickly expires.

Kolb added that dried rhinoceros blood was prized by Europeans at the Cape, who took it in a glass of wine, or in a dish of coffee or tea, for the "Opening of Obstructions, and the Healing of inward Sores".

53

Top: Baboons robbing an orchard.

Above: Kolb: "A wild Goat in the Cape Countries."

SO HORRID A STENCH

In the *Hottentot* Countries there is an Animal the *Dutch* call *Stinkbingsem*, i.e. *Stink-box* or *Stink-breeches*. 'Tis the most farting, fizzling, stinking Animal under the Sun. Stinking is the grand Defence Nature has given this Creature against all its Enemies; and, for the most Part, it farts and stinks 'em out of the Field. 'Tis shap'd like a Ferret; and is of the Size of a midling Dog. When his Pursuer, whether Man or Beast, is come pretty near him, he pours out from his Tail so horrid a Stench, that neither Man nor Beast can endure it. A Man that is surpris'd with this Stench, is almost knock'd down by it before he can get out of it. And a Dog, or any other Animal that runs into it, is strangely confounded and madded by it, and ever starts aside to relieve himself by Rubbing his Nose in the Grass or against a Tree. The *Stinkbingsem*, having thus stop't his Pursuer, gets a great Way a Head of him before the Chace can be renew'd. And when his Pursuer comes up with him a second Time, he gives him a second Dose, and by that Means escapes again, If his Pursuer comes up with him a Third Time, he administers a Third Dose, and so on, 'till his Pursuer is tir'd, or farted and stunk out of the Field.

The CAPE-*Europeans* sometimes shoot the *Stinkbingsem*. And where he falls, there he lies till he rots away, for No body cares to touch him. His Body, as soon as the Life is out of it, contracts all over it so horrible and tenacious a Stink, that if you do but barely touch the Carcass with your Fingers, you catch a Stench upon 'em which you can neither endure nor easily get off by any Sort of Washing.

MUTTERING SOMETHING TO THEMSELVES

It is a Custom of the *Hottentots*, of a religious Kind without Doubt, that when they are to pass over a rapid River, they first sprinkle some of the Water upon their Bodies, and daub their Foreheads with a little of the Mud. This Ceremony they perform with great Sedateness and Composure of Mind, sighing now and then, and muttering Something to themselves. At this I have seen them many a Time. But whatever Pains I took to know the Reason of it, I could never draw any Thing from them but this, "Do you not see the Current is strong and dangerous?"

ANONYMOUS

Govert Cnoll, the DEIC commander on the east coast of Java, had been ill for almost a decade with an indisposition that manifested as a "heavy and depressing hoarseness ... accompanied by a hard feeling on both the left and right sides and also in the belly below the navel". He eventually obtained leave to go to the Cape to seek treatment at the hot springs above present-day Caledon. On the voyage out the pain and difficulty in breathing became so much worse that "his Honour was obliged to have recourse to an emetic every two or three days in order to complete the voyage in safety". He and his entourage, including the anonymous author of this graphic account, arrived at the springs in late January 1710.

It was amazing

We were welcomed there by five Europeans, who stated that they had left the Cape of Good Hope for this place about fourteen days ago, suffering from bodily ailments, and had made the journey in order to cure themselves. They were, by God's blessing, so far advanced that they intended returning home the following morning, since they were now completely cured. We were most eager to learn from these good friends what ailments they had been cured of, and were given the following accounts. First, by Sergeant Cornelis that he had suffered from a sort of stiffness and lameness of all his limbs, and had, in addition a large ulceration on the skin, which had been treated by doctors during the last two years, but without success; whereupon he showed us his leg, which we found to be entirely healed with firm, healthy flesh. The baker, Hans Caspers, had been subject to a heavy headache, rheumy eyes, and a palsy in his legs; Andries Muller had had gravel; Hans Casparse, bad eyes; from Jan Smeetman we could extract no information, except that his sickness was a very old one; apparently he was too ashamed to give any further clue to the real cause of his illness. Through the sergeant, we also examined a small negro, who had, on this occasion, been healed of a bad scurvy. We greatly rejoiced that our former impressions of the hot springs had been confirmed by actual living patients, and we were more than ever strengthened in our desire to hasten forward, and to complete all that was necessary for our sojourn and for effecting our own cures.

Our first task was to erect a tent and to arrange our kitchen, no easy task, as the materials here for making a fireplace were only collected with difficulty. When our preparations were complete, we partook of supper, with the sweet milk which we had obtained from the post of our guide Appel, and then retired early to bed.

The 23rd ditto. – When we awoke at daybreak, we found that a heavy north-west wind was blowing, accompanied by rain and extreme cold, on which account we postponed our intention of taking the baths for the first time until better conditions prevailed. We found that they had been left in good order by our friends.

In the meantime, we did not sit doing nothing, but explored the mountain on all sides, and noted the numerous baths dug out in the various springs, and in this way discovered streams which poured their water into these dugout baths with a jet like that of a handpump. In some places, this water flows out at a temperature not much below boiling point. By flowing into the dug-out baths, the water is rendered fit for use, and the temperature is reduced. The streams along which the water runs are continually covered with a cloud of steam, and their course has a deposit of some substance resembling yellow ochre. When the water is left standing, it becomes coated with a film, of a fatty or oily appearance. This low mountain, which has the appearance of a tortoise, lies at the foot of a high rocky stony mountain, opposite a level stretch about 200 paces in extent. The ground, which below is covered with broken stones, is loose, fine, and in colour very like brown ochre. On and about this mountain there are also many loose black stones, which look as if they were pieces of burnt-out smithy's coal. This gives one the impression that there must be minerals in these mountains which probably in the past had been subject to volcanic eruptions. There are no trees here, nor in the neighbourhood, but, as along the entire route, there are only dry stony moors.

We saw spotted wild buck in troops, numerous partridges and pheasants, now and then hartebeest and rhebuck, and the wolf was sometimes heard at night giving his unearthly cry. Lions and tigers were not far distant, for three of our draught horses were attacked one night during our stay by these beasts, and severely mauled. Having completed all we wished to do to-day, we had a hearty meal and retired to rest.

The 24th ditto. – Very early this morning Commissary Cnoll was the first member of our party to try the effects of the hot spring. When his Honour stepped into the water for the second time it was amazing to the bystanders to hear how strongly the water affected his Honour's body. He was barely in for as long as it takes to count 100, when a noise was heard in his chest, like the sound of a pot of stew or starch boiling on a fire. After this his Honour retired for a short time into a field tent, sweating from head to foot, where he lay between two cotton blankets. Shortly afterwards he began to cough continuously, and for ten days he was troubled with this, accompanied by frequent stooling, and the discomfort of quantities of loose phlegm, mostly from the throat. So that for the first five days he was barely in a condition to find a means of sleeping for more than a short period at a time. His Honour's body was, on that account, and through a daily application of the waters, very much fatigued at first. The bath was used very assiduously and with great enjoyment every day by his Honour and the entire company, and the Commissary's ailment daily diminished, while his bodily strength was gradually built up by his extraordinary appetite. After we had made use of the bath for about fifteen days, we all, with his Honour, had reason to thank God that He had, in His divine mercy, restored our health to us once again.

In addition, we bathed every other morning after breakfast, but this did not in any way hasten on the cure, which progressed at the same rate as if we had bathed once daily, early in the morning before breakfast.

On first entering the water, and when it flows into the bath, the heat is almost unbearable, but when once one is immersed up to the neck, the heat does not seem quite as great, as long as one remains seated without moving very much. It must, however, be added that after a little less or a little more than a quarter of an hour, one is forced to leave the bath, not on account of the heat, but because of a stifling pulsation, which gradually oppresses one. Some say that the sweating commences at the same time as the stifling feeling; but those who have taken the waters will remember that the sweating commences before that, and after one has sat in the bath for as long as it takes to count 100, until the entire body, from head to foot, is bathed in perspiration, which trickles down in large drops, and first comes out on the head and face. On leaving the bath, one should lie down under one or two blankets in order to increase the sweating, and a pint of the spring water should also be taken hot. This increases the perspiring considerably, so that the sweat runs off the body. The choking sensation is not felt at this stage. After an hour or longer has been spent under the blankets, and when the patient has had a rub down and got dressed, a most invigorated feeling is experienced, and the body seems capable of performing any physical exercises, while after about an hour one feels disposed for a good meal.

JAKOB DE BUCQUOI

De Bucquoi was sent to Delagoa Bay in 1721 as engineer for a fort the Dutch were building there. However, the garrison was decimated by disease, and offered only token resistance to a trio of English pirate ships that overran the fort the following year. The pirates took De Bucquoi and several companions to Madagascar and abandoned them there. The castaways spent three years building a boat in which they eventually sailed back across the straits to the settlement of Moçambique. There they fell victim to blindness and severe diarrhoea, which De Bucquoi blamed on eating fruit and drinking unhealthy water, and were admitted to a hospital run by priests.

I SCREAMED LIKE A PIG
It was on the first night that I, being asleep, was woken by a Father, and therefore being still half asleep, was astonished at the flickering of a Fire, which burned in full flame at my side: but the consternation increased greatly when three or four strong slaves then and there laid hands on my body, vigorously pulled out one leg, and the Father pressed a glowing Iron under the ball of the foot, not unlike a Smith brands the hooves of a Horse: when I saw it and still only half felt it, I screamed like a Pig that is being pulled by the ears, but the Father carried on. The one leg having been done, the slaves beat it thoroughly with the soles of old slippers, until it appeared enough to the Father; then the other leg was treated like the first, and this done, the Father went to another, and so on to all those whose sight had been affected, and who appeared to need this cure. I suppose it [was a cure] because I became better, as did the others. The whole night I was still in a state of fear, that the Father might make another visit; when the day arrived, I sought to get out of the hospital, and crawled as well as I could to the door, but I found it locked against me, and discovered that one could well enter without asking, but could not again go out without permission.

Slaves.

BAATJOE OF SAMBOUA

In early 1746 Baatjoe and eight other slaves at the Cape stole a boat in Hout Bay, hoping to sail to "Cafferland" and liberty. Leaks and bad weather forced them ashore, and, hungry and demoralised, they were captured by a farmer east of Onrust. This account is Baatjoe's confession, part of the record of his trial. It is not particularly dramatic, being an official's pre-cis of what the captive said, rather than his own words. But it is still poignant tes-timony to the nine slaves' desperate bid for freedom. Baatjoe, together with Isak of Fernaten, Damon of Batavia, Jafta of Batavia, Thomas of Samboua, January of Bugis, January of Macassar, Jason of Macassar, and Arlequijn of Bengal, were all sentenced to be hanged, their bodies to swing on the gibbet until they rotted. Samboua is Sumbawa, one of a chain of islands making up present-day Indonesia.

INTENDING TO PRESS ON

[Baatjoe confesses that] … after they were at sea four days and four nights in fine weather, they were struck by a storm off the Hang Lip, causing leaks in the boat, as a result they stopped over there for two days.

That January did as much patching-up on the boat as he could, they again took to sea, but heavy weather returned, and the boat leaked so badly that it could barely stay afloat. This forced them to land again on this sec-ond journey, with the confessant unable to say what the place was called, where they abandoned the vessel, and stayed a few days.

That the nine of them subsequently walked along the beach, intending to press on with the journey to Cafferland. In the morning they came to the top of a mountain, from which they saw from afar the place called Uyle Craal, where driven by pressing hunger they ate the fruit of a tree standing there, on which they became drunk, and accordingly lay there until the afternoon, when they again came to realise, when they consulted one other, that they had a great need to seek food; confessant to this end made his way to the place of the farmer Jan Swart, where he was taken prisoner by the same and was brought in captivity to the Cape.

AUGUST BEUTLER

Beutler was an ensign with the DEIC who in 1752 led 71 men on an expedition as far as present-day Butterworth in the Eastern Cape, erecting beacons along the coast to warn off potential French colonisers. His journey, says one old-school South African historian, was the first serious attempt to get the measure of the region, "and therefore laid the foundation for the history of the Eastern Province".

THIS EXTRAORDINARY SMOKING

The 1st ditto we left this resting place in the morning before seven o' clock, set our course to the S. over a great plain from where we saw the sea below the mouth of the Kromme river an estimated 4 miles to the S.S.E of us and to the Leeuwenboschriver and having crossed a dry stream, we took our route S.S.E, saw here 2 Hottentots hunt-ing, who came to welcome us, they were of the Gamtous nation, one of them who spoke Dutch told us they were poor Hottentots and had no stock or anything so that they had to go seek their livelihood in the veld, we gave them tobacco at which they thanked us pro-fusely, those people use an eland horn to smoke, into which they have stuck a reed with a piece of wood made like a pipe, they intro-duce water inside the horn, through which the smoke must first be drawn to take out the bitterness before it comes into the mouth, if there is no water they use their own; instead of blowing the smoke out of the mouth they suck it in, which causes such a violent coughing that the blood spurts from the nose, having seen this extraordinary smoking the ensign took the Hottentots with him and arrived in the afternoon at a Yellow wood forest …

THE DEVIL HAD MADE THEM

The 2 ditto we trekked on an easterly course over heights from which the Cafferland mountains appeared as a high prominent peak in the N. East and the sea visible in the south we then came upon a rocky height where we found 2 stone heaps on which Capt Claas tossed a green branch while he mumbled some words, we who saw it first thought, that they were Hottentot burial grounds and that this was some sort of ceremony among their folk, but when we saw Capt ruijter did the same to the two heaps, we asked him what the structures meant and why his people did that he gave us no other answer to that than the devil had made them and he threw the branches on to pray to him to look on them with favour, to grant long life and good fortune, we crossed various difficult heights and arrived at 3 o'clock in the afternoon at the Fish river …

WILLIAM WEBB

The Doddington, *an English Indiaman carrying 270 people and a substantial quantity of silver, ran onto rocks in Algoa Bay in dirty weather in July 1755. Third mate Webb was one of the 23 who survived to find themselves trapped on tiny guano-encrusted Bird Island, where the only resources were those washed ashore from the wreck. With tools they found or crafted, including a saw fashioned from a sword blade, they built a nine-metre sloop, and sailed into Delagoa Bay 61 days after being wrecked. Here they are taking stock of the island.*

A MOST TENDER AFFECTION

Saturday, July 19, Wind westerly. Early this Morning mustered all the Strength we could in order to secure the Water we discovered yesterday, and

succeeded so well, as safely to get up four Butts before Dinner; and afterwards one Cask of Flour and a Hogshead of Brandy, with some other Necessaries. In the Mean Time every Body was very diligent in Search of Tools, but found none except a Scraper. In great Hopes of being more successful to-morrow, having had a prodigious Surf rolling in all Day. Found one of our little Boats, very much damaged. At low Water went on the Rocks to gather Limpits and Muscles, of which there is great Plenty, tho' they are very bad eating.

Sunday 20, Wind and Weather much as yesterday. Found myself, by God's Blessing, much better, and able to walk out; went with our People in

Search of more Necessaries, and had the good Fortune to find two of *Hadley*'s Sea-quadrants, which gave us fresh Spirits, as we took it for a kind of Earnest, that we were once more to use them to good Purpose. We also discovered a Hamper, in which were Files, Sail-needles, Gimblets, and an Azimuth Compass-card. We also found a Chest of Treasure, a Carpenter's Adze, a Chisel, three Sword-blades, and two or three Books of Navigation; all of which contributed still more to enliven us. But our next Discovery had a quite contrary Effect; it was a Female Corps, the Body of poor Mrs. *Collet*, ou[r] second Mate's Wife, who happened to be at some Distance; Mr. *Jones*, our first Mate, in order to conceal from him a Sight which he knew would most sensibly and perhaps fatally affect him, went to Mr. *Collet*, and, under Pretence of Business, took him to the other Side of the Rock, whilst I, and the other Mate, with the Carpenter and three others, digged a Grave in the Birds Dung, and buried her, reading the Burial Service out of a French Common-Prayer Book that was drove on Shore from the Wreck. Some Days after we by degrees disclosed the Matter to Mr. *Collet*, which, however he hardly could believe, till Mr. *Jones* gave him her Wedding-Ring, taken off her Finger. After this, Mr. *Collet*, who had ever a most tender Affection for his Wife, spent many Days in raising a Monument over her, by piling up the squarest Stones he could meet with, and throwing in the Birds Dung by way of Cement. On the Top he laid an Elm Plank, and thereon with a Chissel cut her Name, Age, and the Time of her Death, with some Account of the unhappy Catastrophe.

JACOB FRANCKEN

Francken held the office of sick-comforter on the Dutch Indiaman De Naar-stigheid *on its return journey from Batavia, now Jakarta, in 1757. The ship made slow progress to a point southeast of Madagascar, where on the afternoon of April 7 there was a large circle around the sun, and the air became "very thick, and blood red". The wind rose, and the sea was running high …*

BATTERED BETWEEN THESE WAVES

We Sailed with reefs in the Topsails, and sometimes with them lowered, until the 9th following, coming to the Southern latitude of 28 *deg.* 45 *min.*

longitude 69 *deg.* 52 *min.*, which day was for us a sorrowful Scene of all disasters, and calamity; because that morning we encountered a high, wrathful, and clashing Sea, which was such that one could not distinguish between water and air. When we looked ahead, we saw nothing but pitiful prospects, turning our gaze backwards, we feared nothing other than being overwhelmed by the tall Sea, so that the Ship lay battered between these Waves, and laboured in a fearful manner; along with this the wind began to strengthen violently from the SE, so that we were forced to furl the Topsails, and to let it run under the Foresail alone. This continued to the evening at half past five, when the wind suddenly blasting from the South with a heavy Hurricane, at once blew the Foresail from its sheets; soon after this the Foremast broke into three pieces; the main topmast, which without sail was bent like a hoop, came down with it from above, and the main Yard followed swiftly. Had this been the only misfortune, we could have still saved ourselves, but that evening at half past eight we also lost the Mizzenmast and the Bowsprit, the latter taking with it the Lion which was positioned at the front of our Ship, so that within a short time we were deprived of all our Masts, excepting the Mainmast, which according to what the people said, and with God's help, was the preservation of the Ship. Our Sun Awning, which was fastened with iron stays to the rail and quarter-deck, ripped to pieces, and went over the side, along with the chicken runs, with poultry, and everything that was on the Poop. With the tremendous lurching of the Ship the Boat became loose, and was going, though it was noticed just in time, and secured, otherwise it could have taken the whole rail with it, and we would have been sunk by it. The binnacle, table and benches, indeed everything that was on the quarter-deck, and between decks, was battered to pieces. Our Stock, all the Cows, Pigs and Goats, lay drowned in the waist; and the poor Folk saw themselves being robbed of the few things they had by the water that came between the decks. We exerted all effort to chop down the Net of the Fore-rigging, which would otherwise have brought us even more problems, which, even though it was very dark, fortunately was accomplished. We suffered in this misfortune however no dead, though a few wounded, who found themselves on the deck when the Foremast broke. Yet it is quite remarkable, and who must not see with me here God's extraordinary protection, that three Sailors, who were busy lowering the Mizzen arm, went overboard when the Mizzenmast broke, and were tossed in again by the Sea, without coming to any harm at all.

With these tall seas, and through the labouring of the Ship, so much water came aboard, we found it two feet high between decks, and thirty inches at the pump. The Officers, who in these circumstances still had faith, at least by outward appearances, gave the Sailors good courage, and themselves were pleased to pump, yet one of the passengers made so free as to say, *rather wish to die, than to pump*: this found little accord, and everyone set to work. That night the wind dropped a great deal, and the Sea also began to die down by degrees; but when the dawn broke, we saw with pain our precious and richly-laden vessel, for it was in a wretched and disastrous state, several Cannon lay out of their carriages, seven of them had gone over the side, with three anchors, which had also taken the railing, up to the forecastle head; the Forechains, on the starboard side, were completely gone, the main chains badly damaged. The Glass at the back of the Ship suffered so much from the Sea, that almost all the panes of the Cabin were smashed to pieces.

The wretched circumstances in which we found ourselves, made us at first despair of our preservation, but finding no better course than trust in the power of the Almighty, and seeking our refuge in that alone, we harnessed all our strength, that could serve to preserve us …

JACOBUS COETSÉ

Coetsé, who had a farm at Piketberg north of Cape Town, secured the governor's permission in 1760 to hunt elephants in the territory to the north. With two wagons and 12 Khoikhoi servants he travelled as far as the Warmbad area of southern Namibia before turning back. He was probably not the first European to cross the Orange River, but he was the first to report on the region. Coetsé bagged only two elephants on the trip.

A SORT OF CAMEL

Further, there was found in the Land of the Great Amacquas, a great number of Lions and Rhinoceros, along with another Animal, thus far unknown in this country, which was not so heavy as an elephant, but considerably taller in Body, the Deponent accordingly supposes, And also on account of the long neck, humped back and long legs, that if it was not the real camel it must indeed be a sort of camel; these Animals appeared Extremely Heavy and Slow of pace, so that Deponent, being on horseback at a certain Time, and chasing them, caught up with two of them with little difficulty and shot them dead; they were both female, of which one had a Young One with her, which Deponent took with him, and kept Alive for about 14 days with bran soaked in water, however it died for lack of Milk or other good food, the Deponent brought the skin with him from thence, however the appearance of the adult Animals can not be well imagined from this Skin, because the Young One was spotted, and Without a hump on the back, the big one however without spots, reddish in appearance and with Heavy humps, just like on the front of the head of the Young Animal, two horn-like outgrowths are found, those of the large ones Actually only stubby Knobs; the flesh of these Animals, especially the Young Ones, serve the Amacquas as an exceptional Delicacy.

JEMIMA KINDERSLEY

Kindersley stayed over at the Cape for six months in 1764-65, en route to Bengal with her officer husband. Her book, Letters from the Island of Teneriffe, Brazil, The Cape of Good Hope, and the East Indies, *is the first published account of the Cape by a woman, but is extraordinarily impersonal.*

SO MUCH COMFORT

I never was in a place where people seemed to enjoy so much comfort; few are very rich, none miserably poor; great riches would be useless, as they have no means of spending; those who have just the necessaries of life are therewith content, because they never expected more; their ideas and wants are few, and there is that happy constitutional dulness in the Dutch, which keeps them perfectly satisfied without either business or pleasures to occupy their mind.

The Khoikhoi language, she said, consisted "chiefly in signs, nodding the head, and an indistinct rattling in the throat". Her account of their childrearing practices suffers from a similar lack of understanding.

I have purposely deferred giving you any account of the natives of this country, the Hottentots, till I could be assured that the strange accounts I heard of them were true; my eyes have convinced me, that some of them are, and others I have from good authority.

They are by nature tolerably white, and not unhandsome, but as soon as a child is born, they rub it all over with oil, and lay it in the sun; this they repeat till it becomes brown: and always break the infant's nose, so that it lays close to its face; as they grow up, they continue constantly to rub themselves with oil or grease, and by degrees become almost a jet black; this it seems they do to strengthen themselves.

RICHARD COLLINS

A near-victory for victims of the slave trade. The incident, in 1766, is recorded here by a British officer, Colonel Richard Collins, in a report to the governor of the Cape 43 years later. Incidentally, logs of the Meermin *from the 1780s are in the National Library in Cape Town: she was still running slaves from Moçambique and Madagascar then. A trip in 1784 seems to have been particularly horrendous, for day after day on the return leg, small skulls and crossbones are penned in the margin alongside entries such as "Obiit een Caffer", or "Obiit 2 Negriens".*

THEY TESTIFIED THEIR JOY

This vessel [the hooker *De Meermin*] belonged to the Dutch East India Company, and was commanded by a man named Muller; she sailed about 40 years ago from the Cape for the island of Madagascar, to exchange copper and merchandise for slaves. Having arrived at her destination, a chief and party of natives were invited on board, and having been lulled to security, were bound and carried off.

The ship having made Cape Point on her return, the captain supposed all danger past, and released his prisoners; they instantly seized the ship and put all their kidnappers to death, except the captain and a few persons whom they spared for the purpose of navigating the vessel back to Madagascar.

Bottled message from the sailors on the *Meermin*.

The savages knew that they had come from the point where the sun rises, and could not be much deceived during the day respecting the proper course to be taken; but in the night the ship was always steered in a contrary direction. At length they arrived off Point Aiguillas, and the vessel was anchored at Schoonberg; the mate, who was the only person who had any influence over the minds of the late captives, having persuaded them that this country was part of their own, and that they should proceed on their voyage as soon as some repairs were performed to the vessel.

Letters descriptive of their situation were inclosed by the captain in bottles, and committed to the sea, and were both received by some inhabitants who happened to be fishing near the spot. The affair was reported to the landdrost, who assembled a party immediately, and placed them in ambush at a short distance, directing some slaves and Hottentots to light a fire. This was the signal of friendship, and aid requested to be made by the captain, who ran the ship on shore as soon as he observed it. The savages supposing the people they perceived were unconnected with any nation like their base betrayers, swam in a body to the beach, where they testified their joy by dancing and acclamations. Their festivity was not of long duration. Those who did not fall by a discharge of musquetry, or prefer a watery grave to slavery, were again secured.

The author of this infamous transaction, fearing that his conduct in liberating the prisoners, which was done against the advice of his officers, might subject him to punishment when known in Holland, or else unable to bear the stings of conscience, put a period soon afterwards to his criminal existence.

JACOB HAAFNER

Haafner's father sailed for Batavia in 1766 to take up an appointment as surgeon, bringing his 11-year-old son with him. Typhoid broke out on board, carrying off passengers and crew by the score. The voyage to the Cape, which should have taken a mere three months, dragged on to six, and as land came into sight, young Jacob's father was also claimed by the disease. Left to fend for himself, Jacob became first a seaman, then a self-taught accountant for the DEIC.

THEY ROLLED CANNONBALLS
From the early days of the 1766 voyage.

Our Under Merchant H…, a proud and ambitious person, had his wife and daughter with him; on a certain night, when a fresh coolness had eventually come up at evening time, we were woken by a great tumult and stormy exchange of words. The angry shouting of the Under Merchant, – the shrill voice of his wife, – the crude argument between the first and second mates, – and the roars of laughter of others, made such an inexplicable and confused scene, that for a considerable time we could not understand, what could have given rise to it. Eventually we gathered that the Second Mate, who had found himself on deck because of a pressing need, was just in time to wake the third watch, who had fallen asleep at the helm, and with his help to turn the ship, before it ran with its bow onto another great vessel, which was coming down on us under full sail. This danger was no sooner past, and the course resumed, than the Second Mate went in search of the Officer of the watch, who was the first Mate, who ought not have stirred from his post; – they found him in his cabin, sleeping in the arms of Miss H…

This incident would have given rise to no more than amusement, had we not been exposed by it to great danger and almost certain disaster. The Captain therefore ordered the wife and daughter of the Under Merchant not to step from their room after ten at night, and punished the first Mate and the third watch for their carelessness. The family H... believed themselves insulted by this, and they developed a bitter hatred not only against the Captain and the Second Mate, but also against my father, who together with the Surgeon, had scolded them for their scandalous conduct. Allied to them was the first Mate, who knew how to find ways of reconciling himself with the father, in addition to the third watch and the Commander of the soldiers; each of these parties had in turn a portion of the people on their side, and they appeared to think of nothing but than that each should try to cause as much sorrow and unpleasantness to the others as possible. The order of the Captain to the family of the Under Merchant, not to stir from their room after ten, they not only disobeyed when an Officer, one of their friends, had the watch, but they did everything possible that could aggravate their opponents; they rolled cannonballs against the cabins of the Captain and of my father and the Surgeon, danced above their compartments, and invented a thousand other similar things, to torment them.

Another ship's Commander would have maintained better order; but ours, an elderly and otherwise brave man, had neither the courage nor the competence, to act in these circumstances with the proper vigour, which was his duty; possibly he feared also the strength of his opponents, which consisted of the most prominent Officers and the greatest portion of the sailors and soldiers; at any rate he bore everything patiently, and hardly dared show his displeasure.

MY SWEATING BREAST
On his return from the East in 1769, Jacob was of course in his lusty teens. He sought to oblige his Cape Town landlady by climbing the slopes of Lion's Head to collect branches of the fragrant koekoemakranka bush, used to protect stored clothes from moths.

I had already collected a few plants, when I saw, on the other side of the mountain, a young Hottentot girl of an extraordinary beauty; she belonged to a community of independent Hottentots, of which a few tribes exist on the furthermost borders of the colony, who had come to the *Cape* with the intention of complaining to the Government about the arbitrary actions of the tyrannical farmers and to ask for justice in their desperate suffering.

She appeared to have sat herself down there, to enjoy the wide view and see the flag, which just then announced the approach of a ship in the sea.

When she saw me, and saw what I was busy with, she stood up of her own accord, and helped me search; having collected a sufficient quantity, and tired from the heat and clambering about, I went to sit and rest, on which she immediately, and without the least fear, placed herself at my side, took my kerchief, with which I was drying my sweating breast, from my hand, and with apparent pleasure stroked it over my face. Apart from the nauseous mixture of fat and soot, with which she, just like all the others of her nation, was smeared, and that did not really detract from her appearance, she was the most charming and beautifully formed figure of a woman, that one can in truth imagine; in place of the flat nose and jutting jaw, which is the general characteristic of those of her nation who groan under oppression and slavery, she had on the contrary, a full face with the most endearing expressions, a row of sparkling white teeth and a fiery well-open eye. The neatest-proportioned limbs and the well-formed bosom concentrated the beauties so scarce in Hottentots, in one creature, in which Nature appeared to have collected all her art, to redeem the general hideousness of her race.

I addressed her in Dutch, which she understood as little as I did Hottentot, in which she answered me. After some space of time was spent trying to converse with each other through signs, I eventually made myself ready to go back; she followed me halfway down the mountain, where she stopped me, and showed me the camp of the group of her people on a flat, and at the same time made me understand that early the following morning she would expect to find me again at the same place. After a brief moment, in which her former playfulness seemed to change to sadness, she stroked her hand over my face, and with that raced, with an inconceivable swiftness, down the mountain, where she soon disappeared behind some bushes.

I did not know what to think of this meeting. Captain HANSSEN and his wife, to whom I related this, laughed heartily and wished me luck with my Hottentot conquest. The next day I nonetheless went early to the same place – yet, – how great was my regret – Hottentots, camp, all had vanished; they had already gone at daybreak, as I heard shortly after, indignant that people had, as was their disagreeable custom, sought to satisfy them with simple promises and nice words.

When I came to the place where I had sat with the girl the previous day, I found there a string of the beads she had worn around her arms, legs and neck; probably she had laid them there, when she realised she had to leave suddenly, with the aim that I would find and keep them; at any rate I took them with me, and that was the only memento which I had of my Hottentot love.

JACOB WALLENBERG

A university dropout and one-time tutor, Wallenberg signed on in 1769 as chaplain on a Swedish East Indiaman. The voyage provided material for a book, My son has gone gallavanting, *which gained him a place in Swedish literature as a humorist. Despite the acerbic comments here on the Dutch at the Cape, he did appreciate their hospitality, and noted they were "very courteous to strangers". Wallenberg's later works included a biblical drama in five acts, and some spirited drinking songs.*

SOME BLACK-EYED MAID

The slaves, of whom the majority are bought in Madagascar, are the inhabitants' most valuable household effects. When a property is alienated, they go with it, like other cattle. They do all the work inside and outside the house, for the mistress and her daughters appear to be inseparably

Young Jacob and his "Hottentot love".

attached to the tea-table, and undertake nothing themselves. The slaves as a whole are short in stature and weak of limb. I have seen four of them round a load which one boy from Dalarna at home would shoulder alone, slaves included. This I reckon to be a consequence of their irregular sexual connections; for both sexes huddle together in one bunk, pairing like brute beasts, as opportunity offers, often at the age of no more than twelve or thirteen. And thus their masters most culpably leave them to the mire of paganism: so much for the Dutch conscience! If there is to be any vigorous progeny, a European must have a hand in it. For this reason the host considers it as a particular attention to his humble house if his guest is pleased to fall in love with some black-eyed maid; for he who increases the size of his slave-girls increases also the size of his fortune. The Englishman sometimes takes to himself "a dear black sweetheart" *(sic)*, and the lively Frenchman never neglects to prostrate himself "aux pieds de sa belle brune"; but my simple-minded countrymen commonly account this as bestiality.

Which, think you, is the blacker, her skin, or their actions?

LAYING SIEGE TO BEAUTY

But apart from these promenades the Cape has no public pleasures. Assembly-Rooms, Opera, Masquerade, are here not known even by name; and (what must appear yet more incomprehensible) there is no tavern either, no coffee-house, no billiards-saloon, no news-club. I disregard some few alehouses for sailors. All this gives the town the aspect of a desert to one coming from gay and busy Europe. After two days all novelty is exhausted. The dreary monotony of the surroundings induces emptiness and boredom. Nobody with any ideas above eating and drinking can be happy here for long. The poverty of topics of discussion, the dreary pedestrian manner in which they are discussed, or their limitation to a circle of plaguey scandal-mongers, puts it out of the power of a foreigner to venture upon a gallant or polite conversation. The Dutchman's vocabulary is too limited for that. If I visit *Myn Heer*, I get an invariable: "Smoke a pipe, have a drink"; should I venture to *Mefrowe*, who sits in decorative immobility with her hands folded and her useless legs resting on a foot-warmer (for idleness is always chilly) – then she whines her eternal *koppie the, Myn Heer*! And when I accept this offer, she hands me a fragment of flint-hard candy-sugar, as small as one of her own eyes, which must serve me (since cour-

tesy demands that I follow her own frugal example) not only for this cup, but for the three following. If she offers me coffee, it is no better than her tea. If I make her a compliment, she answers with a banality, or bawls for the spittoon. If I should happen to have a neat snuff-box, or some other pleasant trifle, with vulgar importunity she demands to look at it, ogles me with a pair of covetous eyes, turns it over and over between her fingers, and wishes she had one like it – and, on occasion, is capable of stuffing it into her skirts and laughing, as though her gracious grimaces were sufficient recompense. In a word, the women were the most intolerable things I saw at the Cape; and therefore I kept myself for choice at the man's end of the room where at least I could conceal my surly countenance in a billowing cloud of tobacco-smoke.

The Dutchman, though sufficiently ceremonious, has no manners. With his pipe in his mouth, and his hat on his head – a hat which seems not so much to cover as to engulf his unbrushed pate – he is to be found in the middle of a circle of females emitting a succession of Frenchified compliments. The smoke, which belches from either corner of his mouth in great spreading clouds, might easily lead you to suppose that he was laying siege to Beauty with twelve-pounders; and if it were not that their kindling eyes, like stars in the darkness, illumined this beclouded firmament, you would be constrained to find your way by groping.

ANDERS SPARRMAN

In spite of a reputation for prudishness, the Swedish naturalist Sparrman had an engaging sense of humour. He recorded how the ladies on a farm on the eastern frontier ate a dish of calves' testicles "without blushing", and was one of the few European travellers to admit that he was drawn to the Khoikhoi women. Sparrman was a disciple of his celebrated countryman and naturalist Carl Linnaeus, and one of a number of Linnaeus' pupils who scoured the globe for botanical specimens. Sparrman's A Voyage to the Cape of Good Hope, *based on two visits between 1772 and 1776, was the first detailed account of travel in the interior. Between those visits he served on Captain James Cook's* Resolution *on a round-the-world voyage that dipped below the Antarctic Circle and included the South Sea Islands where, he said, "a nail was the price of love making".*

PRECEDENCE IN LOVE
Losing the way between Paarl and Cape Town.

But I must not omit to tell you, how puzzled and undetermined we frequently were on our return homewards, particularly once on a large plain. After wandering about it for a considerable time, we met with seven of the Company's servants or soldiers, but by no means to our advantage; for these my fellow-Christians, intoxicated with the wine which they carried about them in leathern bottles or calabasses, were at variance among themselves, and seemingly did not wish to give us any information, as every one of them pointed out to us an almost entirely different way. Jabbering to me all at once in High Dutch, Low Dutch, Hanoverian, &c. they all endeavoured to make me believe, that I should meet with rivers, mountains, deserts, and the like, if, according to their sea dialect, I did not steer my course right. Another asked me whither I was bound? and then told me how I should follow the way right and left. I thanked them, and got away from them as well as I could; on which they formed a ring round my servant, and chattered to him about the road till his head was quite turned. At length they got into a dispute themselves about the same subject, by which means we both got loose from them. What was now to be done? Being without chart or compass, I endeavored to direct my course by the sun, till I overtook a black heathen, who was tending sheep; and in consequence of whose sober and sensible directions, I arrived in the evening at a farmhouse, the bailiff of which, a Hanoverian, welcomed me in the most friendly manner, with a hearty slap of the hand, in the African style. He entertained me with milk, and an account of the love affairs and intrigues he had when he was a soldier in England. He also gave me a list (which, by his desire, I took down in my pocket-book, as the result of his own experience) of the constant order of precedence in love, which ought to be observed among the fair sex in Africa: this was as follows. First the *Madagascar* women, who are the blackest and best; next to these the *Malabars*, then the *Bugunese* or *Malays*, after these the Hottentots, and last and worst of all, the white Dutch women. The excessively nice stewed cabbage we had for supper, he supposed to be the best in the world ...

IN THE HEART
The tale of a resilient, but unlucky leguan.

One of this species, of the middle size, which, together with its two young ones, I brought home with me from *Agter Bruintjes-hoogte,* was about two feet long in the body, and three in the tail; having caught her by the neck, so that she could not bite me, and finding that it required some strength to hold her fast, I got a large worsted needle, and gave her several punctures with it, not only in the heart, but in every part of the cranium which was in contact with the brain. This, however, was so far from answering my purpose, which was to kill her in the most speedy and least painful manner, without mangling or mutilating her, that she seemed still to have life enough left to be able to run away. After this my host undertook to put an end to her, and after having given her several hard squeezes about the chest, and tied her feet together, hung her up by the neck in a noose, which he drew as close as he possibly could. From this situation she was found in the space of 48 hours to have extricated herself, though she still remained near the farm, appearing at the same time to be almost entirely exhausted. Upon this, we tied her feet close behind her, so that with her long and sharp claws, of which she had five upon each foot, she could not damage the serpents and other animals which I kept in a cask of brandy, and among which I put her with my own hands, holding her a long time under the surface of the liquor; yet she was so far from being suffocated immediately by the strength of the liquor, that she flounced about a good deal in it; and even a quarter of an hour afterwards, convinced us by her motions that she still had some life remaining in her.

CARL THUNBERG

Sparrman's fellow Swede Thunberg was another of Linnaeus' gifted botanical pupils. Thunberg took up a surgeon's post with the DEIC, and was fortunate to make it all the way to the Cape in 1772 after the ship's cook mistook a container of white lead for flour, and mixed it into the officers' pancakes. Despite a shortage of money, Thunberg made several trips to the interior during his three-year stay. He assembled more than 3,000 species of plants, of which over a third were new to science. On his return to Sweden he was appointed professor of botany at the University of Uppsala.

THESE MARVELLOUS PRODUCTS
Roodezand is the Tulbagh area.

A report that was very general at Roode-zand, struck me with the greatest astonishment, and excited my curiosity in the highest degree. The inhabitants all assured me with one voice, that there was a bush to be found on the mountains, on which grew various wonderful products, such as caps, gloves, worsted stockings, &c. of a substance resembling a fine plush. I importuned almost every body in the neighbourhood, to procure me, if possible, some of these marvellous products, and I resolved not to leave the place till I should have unriddled this mystery. In the course of a few days, I had several of the leaves brought me down from the mountains, which were covered with a very thick shag or down (*tomentum*) and very much resembled white velvet. The girls, who were used to the management of these leaves, began immediately, with singular dexterity and nicety, to strip off this downy coat, whole and entire as it was, without rending it. After it had been taken off in this manner, it was turned inside outwards; when the green veins of the leaf appeared on one side. Accordingly as the leaf was more or less round or oval, divers of the above-mentioned articles were formed out of it, the shape being now and then assisted a little by the scissars. The stalks of the leaves furnished stockings, and ladies fingered gloves; the smaller leaves, caps. So that the matter was not quite so wonderful, as it was wonderfully related.

A GIBBET WAS ERECTED
Thunberg was on hand to witness the Indiaman De Jonge Thomas *driven ashore in Table Bay by a winter gale in 1773. Wolraad Woltemade's heroics, which he describes here, became the stuff of school history textbooks; less well known is that the 25 sailors left on board were able to wade ashore the next day.*

The ship had scarcely struck, which happened just at day-break, when the most efficacious expedients were used to save as much as possible of the company's property that might chance to be thrown on shore, though I could not perceive that the least care was taken to deliver a single soul of the crew from their forlorn and miserable situation. Thirty men were instantly ordered out, with a stripling of a lieutenant, from the citadel, to the place where the ship lay, in order to keep a strict look-out, and prevent any of the company's effects from being stolen; and a gibbet was erected, and at the same time an edict issued, importing that whoever should come near that spot, should be hanged up immediately, without trial or sentence of judgment being passed upon him. This was the cause that the compassionate inhabitants, who had gone out on horseback to afford the wretched sufferers some assistance, were obliged to turn back without being able to do them the least service; but on the contrary were, together with me, ocular witnesses of the brutality and want of feeling shewn by certain persons on this occasion, who did not bestow a thought on affording their fellow-creatures, that sat on the wreck perishing with cold, hunger, and thirst, and were almost in the arms of death, the least assistance or relief.

Another circumstance contributed to render this otherwise distressing scene still more afflicting. Among the few, who were lucky enough to be able to save their lives by swimming from the wreck, was the gunner, a man with whom I was acquainted, and met with several times afterwards in the town: he had stript himself quite naked, in order that he might swim the easier, and had the good luck to come alive to shore, which was not the case with every one that could swim; for many were either dashed to pieces against the rocks, or else by the violence of the surf carried back again to sea. When he arrived on shore, he found his chest landed before him; but just as he was going to open it, and take out his great coat, the lieutenant, who commanded the party, drove him away from it: and though he earnestly begged for leave to take out the clothes necessary for covering his naked and shivering body, and could also prove by the key, fastened, according to the sailors custom, to his girdle, as well as by his name cut out on the lid of the chest, that it was actually his property, he was, nevertheless, forced to retreat without effecting his purpose, by this unmerciful hero, who gave him several smart blows with a cane on his bare back. After he had passed the whole day naked and hungry, and exposed to the cold winds, and was going to be taken in the evening to town along with the others who had been saved from the wreck, he again asked leave to take a coat out of his chest to cover himself with; but this having been previously plundered, he found empty. On entering the town, where he arrived stark naked, he met with a burgher, who took compassion on him, and lent him his great coat. Afterwards he, as well as the

other unfortunate wretches, was forced to run about the town for several days together, begging for victuals, clothes, and money, till at length they were supported at the company's expence, and taken back again into its service.

Another action that does greater honour to humanity, deserves the more to be recorded here, as it shews that at all times, and in all places, there are both good and considerate people, as well as such as have nothing human but the shape. An old man, of the name of WOLTEMAD, by birth an European, who was at this time the keeper of the beasts in the menagerie near the garden, had a son in the citadel, who was a corporal, and among the first who had been ordered out to *Paarden Island* (Horse Island) where a guard was to be set for the preservation of the wrecked goods. This worthy veteran borrowed a horse, and rode out in the morning, with a bottle of wine and a loaf of bread for his son's breakfast. This happened so early, that the gibbet had not yet been erected, nor the edict posted up, to point to the traveller the nearest road to eternity. This hoary sire had no sooner delivered to his son the refreshments he had brought him, and heard the lamentations of the distressed crew from the wreck, than he resolved to ride his horse, which was a good swimmer, to the wreck, with a view of saving some of them. He repeated this dangerous trip six times more, bringing each time two men alive on shore, and thus saved in all fourteen persons. The horse was by this time so much fatigued, that he did not think it prudent to venture out again; but the cries and intreaties of the poor wretches on the wreck increasing, he ventured to take one trip more, which proved so unfortunate, that he lost his own life, as on this occasion too many from the wreck rushed upon him at once, some of them catching hold of the horse's tail, and others of the bridle, by which means the horse, both wearied out, and now too heavily laden, turned head over heels, and all were drowned together. This noble and heroic action of a superannuated old man, sufficiently shews that a great many lives might probably have been saved, if a strong rope had been fastened by one end to the wreck, and by the other to the shore. Along this rope, either a basket or a large copper vessel might have been hawled to and from the ship, with a man in it each time. When the storm and waves had subsided, the ship was found to lie at so small a distance from the land, that one might have almost leaped from it on shore.

The vigorous measures taken to preserve the company's effects and merchandize, were not, however, so efficacious, as to prevent certain persons in office from enriching themselves considerably on this occasion. For when whole horse-loads of iron from the wreck could be sold to the smiths in town, it is easy to conceive that their consciences would not stand greatly in their way, if they could lay their hands upon portable and valuable commodities. The soldiers also were so careful, when on guard, that nothing should be pillaged from the wreck, that they themselves every night, when relieved, marched into town with their musket-barrels stuffed full of solid gold lace, which, though somewhat damaged by the salt water, answered very well when thrown into the melting pot.

I AM ALIVE STILL
A variation of Christopher Schweitzer's tale. There was, incidentally, a tradition that the last stitch of the dead man's hammock would be through his nose, to make certain there was no life in him.

A ship from Holland, the *Bekvliet*, arrived here, after a long and unfortunate voyage. Through the captain's neglect and ignorance, the ship had got so much under the African coast as to lose its proper winds, and to be obliged to make *Angola*, after first making *Waalvisch* bay, with only nine men in health on board. During this long voyage the scurvy had raged among the crew, which was said to have been very generally as well as plentifully bled, so that the greatest part of it had died. Complaint was made both against the surgeon and the captain for not having understood their business. The former died on the passage, and the latter received the punishment he richly deserved. The sick had not only been supplied with improper medicines, but also, in other respects been treated with great negligence. One morning four men were reported as dead; one of whom, just as they were going to sew him up in his hammock, was found alive by the sail-maker, although he soon after breathed his last. Another morning five men had been reported dead, all of them had been sewed up in their hammocks, and two had already been thrown overboard, when the third, the instant he was put on the plank, called out, *"Master Boatswain, I am alive still!"* to which the Boatswain, with unseasonable jocularity, replied, – "You alive, indeed! what, do you pretend to know better than the surgeon?"

To get a dead dog
When the people of the [Cape] town planted trees before their houses, they were very solicitous to get a dead dog to put in the hole, by which means they thought the growth of the tree would be much accelerated.

KARL VON WURMB

Little is known about Von Wurmb other than that he was German, that he was at the Cape in 1775, and that he went on to travel in the Far East.

Which way to walk
In the interior up to 50 or 60 hours away are Europeans ... as farmers. They bring their products on large waggons often with a span of 12 or more oxen, some of which they slaughter on the way for food. Because of the difficult journey over the high mountains from their settlements to the Cape, they are said to be often more than a month on the way. They control the long line of oxen with a whip, which is over six feet long. They carry these whips in their hands and despite their length one smack is like a pistol shot. Some people of the Cape consider it unseemly when these farmers, or peasants as they are called at the Cape, crack their whips in front of the Cape burghers. While I was at the Cape a law was passed that any cracking in town would be subject to a fine of 50 thalers. Therefore the peasants took the riems off their whips – much to their regret – and tried to guide the oxen just by sticks as laid down by law. The oxen did not realise that the whip had been stopped by law and did not understand their silence and they could not decide which way to walk. They wandered to the left or the right of the way and demolished with their waggons staircases, steps and stoeps in front of the doors of the burghers. A burgher considers himself, generally, as in all other places, above the peasant.

HENDRIK WIKAR

Wikar, yet another Swede, deserted the service of the DEIC at the Cape in 1775 to escape the embarrassment of gambling debts. He spent an extraordinary four and a half years in the interior, living with Khoikhoi and San (Bushman) groups and becoming a spiritual brother to a San chief named Ouga. He was the first recorded European to travel along the Orange River, which he would have known as the Kai !Garib or Great River. Wikar says that when he asked his companions where the source of the river was "they replied by asking me if I could explain where the sky ended". The mass of knowledge he accumulated gained him a pardon and reinstatement in the company's service. These pieces are from his account.

74

IN THIS BRUTAL MANNER

The killing of the animals at all ceremonial slaughtering is done by cutting open the abdominal covering, thrusting the hand inside and severing the pulmonary vessels.

Their enemies captured in war are treated in a similar way; while still alive they are cut open, a hand is thrust in and the pulmonary vessels are severed. Sometimes when the prisoner will not beg for mercy, his private parts are cut off and with this he is struck over the mouth. I know this happened between the Kamingou and the Naningais while I was among them. These tribes fought for two days during December last and 13 of the Naningais were killed, while nearly 30 of them were wounded; but the Naningais captured only one of the Great Namaquoas or Kamingou, and in chagrin at their great loss they treated him in this brutal manner.

LYING ON HER BED

When a Hottentot courts a woman in marriage he never addresses her, nor does he ask her, but *ouas* or looks for her, and this is the way it is done: The Hottentot carefully notes beforehand where this particular woman goes to lie down at night; if he is not too shy and his intentions are sincere, then he enters, while the fire is still burning in the evening, his father-in-law's house, and, when all have gone to bed and the fire is out, he also goes and lies down next to his future bride; then the girl, if she is not in too great a hurry, gets up and goes to lie elsewhere. The suitor just remains lying on her bed until the morning at daybreak, when he rises and goes away without saying a word. The next evening exactly the same thing happens. If his sweetheart's bed is in the same place as on the previous evening, it is a sign that his suit will be successful. Even should the girl he is courting leave him on several successive nights, that would not make any difference; it is only to test the suitor's constancy, and if he perseveres, he gains the day. When at last she remains with him, the lover does not get up till broad daylight and leaves behind him on the bed a string of beads to be worn round the body. This is for his mother-in-law in return for the use of the bed. Now he again goes away without saying a word, this time in the broad daylight, after having, in silence, given his bride his karos; and she gives him scented buchu with which he powders his head and rubs himself under the arms.

EXCHANGING WIVES

Among the Nomacquoa and also among the Eynikkoa they have the custom of exchanging wives with one another. This is regarded by both sides as merely an excuse for slaughtering and

75

merry-making. If at night a married Hottentot comes upon another Hottentot cohabiting with his wife, he goes to lie with that man's wife. The woman's husband makes way for the other and goes to lie somewhere else. The next night the other has to make way for him in the same way; but if the wife of the one who started the game is ugly, then this exchange of wives is not quite such a success.

CLEANED WITH FAT

A young Hottentot must be initiated to manhood, otherwise, be he ever so old, he may not join in discussion. Among the Eynikkoas this is the procedure: first he is washed clean with water; that, they say, is to cleanse him of the uncleanliness of his childhood or of his shepherd days; then he is cleaned with fat; and then the old men urinate on him for three successive days; next he is cleansed with the blood of an animal killed for that purpose; and lastly he is again washed and rubbed with fat, and all the cattle he owns are also besprinkled with fat; thus he attains manhood.

ITS FEET ARE BURNT THROUGH

In the months of December, January, February and March the climate here is exceptionally hot so that you cannot leave a skin or leather thong lying outside for an hour without its being shrivelled up, with the result that you can pull it to pieces. The sun is so fierce here that you cannot walk barefoot in the dust or the sand for 20 yards without getting your feet blistered. On the plains of the Great River at this time of the year you can catch even a steenbuck with your hand (of course, that is when it has not rained), for when it jumps up you just let it go its way. You now remain sitting in the shade under a bush for as long as it takes to smoke a pipe, then you take the spoor of the steenbuck and follow it; after you have driven it up again you sit down once more for 7 or 8 minutes as before. The third or fourth time you do this you can catch it with the hand as it jumps up – then its feet are burnt through. This is the regular custom of the Bushmen of the plain in the hot season.

THE STRONGEST POISON

The two kinds of tree poison they [the San] use on their arrows are the most remarkable of all. The tree producing the first, the strongest poison, grows in the mountains along the Great River and has a very powerful scent, so different from that of all other trees that one can find it by its scent alone without knowing anything more about it; its foliage is green. In July the poison worms, which during the time that the tree is dry live at the bottom in the grey-brown bark of the stem, begin to appear on the leaves. These worms are exactly the same colour as the leaves they eat. The Hottentots take only the worms which are tightly tied up in a piece of leather and kept until they rot. Then they are ground to a fine powder which is rubbed all round the arrows with spit. No one wounded with this mixture, when the gall of the big rock lizard has been added, has any chance of recovery, unless he is immediately given the urine of a poison drinker. When a twig of this tree is broken off a strong-smelling sap or oil oozes out. You must be careful that this does not get into your eyes, for if it should you would become stone blind.

I had an extraordinary personal experience with this tree which I cannot help relating. One day my brother companion Ouga brought me some honey which he said we might make beer of, but which he forbade me to eat. I did not quite understand why, and I did not take much heed, but I had hardly eaten a spoonful when my throat began to burn like fire, and not two minutes later my whole body became affected, and, by your leave, with apologies, I began to purge and got rid of worms looking like tape quite three fathom long, and even longer, whereupon I fainted and the Hottentots poured water on me until I recovered consciousness; then I began vomiting so much that I had to lie down all that afternoon from weakness and faintness. I had been troubled with worms from childhood, so that sometimes I did not know which way to turn for the pain in my body, but since this occurrence, the Lord God be thanked, I have felt no pain. When it was all over, the Hottentots told me that the bees had sucked the flowers of the tree I have mentioned, and that was why the honey was so poisonous.

A RESTFUL NIGHT
It was bitterly cold, and, clad as I was only in shirt and trousers, I thought I should have to spend the night just sitting by the fire; but the Bushmen made me a warm bed, so that I was able to sleep.

First they made a huge fire in the sand, and when that had burnt out, they dug a trench in the warm sand just long enough for me. They placed grass and bushes in the trench and then I went to lie in it, covering myself with more grass and bushes. The warmth coming from the ground on which I lay made me feel so comfortable that I soon fell asleep and spent a restful night. A bed like this they call "eykaro".

Governor Van
Plettenberg

ANONYMOUS

In 1778 governor of the Cape Baron Joachim van Plettenberg made a journey of inspection to the limits of the colony, setting up a stone marker inscribed with the DEIC monogram on the northeast boundary, near present-day Colesberg. One of his companions was Robert Gordon, whom we will meet in the next entry. The baron arrived back in Cape Town after a three-month absence: the welcome described here is recorded in the official journal of his expedition.

THE SALUTE WAS FIRED
The Right Honourable Lord Governor was awaited at the Salt River by some of the foremost of the Company's Servants; and the Burgher Cavalry rode across the same River to meet his Right Honourable self and escorted his Honour: he crossed in a Coach which already stood there, up to the Barrier: At the entry of the Barrier the Salute was fired with Seventeen shots from

77

Fort Imhof, and followed by the simultaneous firing of the ordnance of the Dutch and French ships riding at anchor: the Burgher Infantry stood waiting on the further side of the Watch Patrol, under the Coat of Arms were crowded certain Officers, as well as those of the Militia who were under the Arms in the Castle, who Saluted the procession with their Spontoons and Banners: on our arrival in the Castle, which occurred in the forenoon at a quarter to Ten, on his descent from the Coach the Right Honourable Lord Governor was welcomed by the Lord Secunde and the other gentlemen of the Government, followed at the same time by the Members of the respective Colleges of Justice, Church Councils, Masters of Orphans, and Commissioners of Civil and Marriage affairs, in addition to all who further qualified among the Company's Servants and the Burghers to gather on the Kat, who also paid compliments: the Militia and the Burghers loosed Three Salvos from their Guns, and the Inhabitants collectively showed their joy at his Honour's fortunate return ...

Van Plettenberg's marker.

ROBERT GORDON

A military officer by profession and explorer by inclination, Gordon in 1779 renamed the Kai !Garib the Orange, after the Dutch royal house, and followed it to its mouth. He was the first person to record finding fossils in South Africa, was capable of devoting the best part of a day to examining a hippo's entrails, and sent back to Holland the hide of the last giraffe shot south of the Orange. Born of a Dutch mother and a father of Scots descent, he was intelligent and accomplished, spoke several European languages including Gaelic, and could converse with Xhosa and Khoikhoi in their own tongues. Controversial commander of the Cape garrison when the British invaded in 1795, he committed suicide after the Dutch forces capitulated.

RUN TO ME
The celebrated French philosopher Denis Diderot met Gordon at The Hague in 1774, after Gordon had completed his first journey into the interior of South Africa. Diderot recorded Gordon's translation of this Khoikhoi song.

Robert Gordon

Run to me, my women; sing, I return from far away. Your song will delight me.

WHERE THE SUN SETS
From a 1777 journey that has here taken Gordon over the Sneeuwberg, north of the yet-to-be-established Graaff-Reinet, into "the land of the wild Bushmen".

I found everything peaceful here as far as the Bushmen are concerned, but further W[est], it is said, they stole sheep from a certain Villier and killed the shepherd. These so-called Bushmen or Chinese have a famous chief called "Koeríkei", or "escaper from bullets". This Koerikei called to the *veldtwagtmeester* Van Der Merwe, so he told me, after an action he commanded, while standing on a cliff out of range: "What are you doing in my territory? You occupy all the

78

places where eland and game are. Why do you not remain where the sun sets, where you first were?" Van der Werwe [sic] called back, asking why he did not remain in peace as before, and go on hunts and live with them (he had lived with the farmers), and whether he did not have sufficient territory. He replied that he did not wish to leave the area of his birth, and that he would kill their shepherds and drive them all away and, withdrawing further, he said people would see who would win.

SINGING FURIOUSLY
Near present-day Worcester, 1778. Goideni *is honey beer.*

Saw an old Hottentot witchdoctor (though he did not want to admit it) making *goideni*. Sometimes he strikes the big Hottentots, and they dare not defend themselves. He was afraid of me. Everything he asked of the others they did not dare to refuse. In the evening I saw him healing and doctoring, and practising magic on a youth after their fashion, which he did after a great deal of refusing, and mostly out of fear of me, for I had let him look at the sun through a smoked glass. He thought that I would bewitch him otherwise. He made the youth come naked into his hut in the twilight. My Hottentot, Iteki, also feared him greatly and sat in rapt attention beside the doctor's wife and a young Hottentot woman at the fireside. I had a candle lit in order to see better, whereupon we went to sit beside the youth, who had a pain in his foot. He rubbed his thigh and his leg, and, holding his foot against his head, roared and growled like a lion and tiger. He then held his hands against the youth's head and heart and did this a few times, after which he sneezed three or four times in succession and, opening his hand, displayed some beetles which he said he had taken from the leg. First he rubbed some sheep fat on his leg, and rubbed himself with the rest. After that he fetched some thorn-tree or mimosa roots, bound togeth-er, which were hollow and in which were little stones rattling, and began his magic song, always sitting, but with many con-tortions of the body, beating on the ground with the bushes, often singing furiously and shaking his head, while his wife accompanied him, clapping her hands. We could not under-stand him, not even Iteki, who said that it was the language of Bushman magicians. When he stopped, wet with perspiration, I asked him several questions, but all I could get out of him was that Tuiqua (God) had taught him in a dream. Joubert said he must have been very afraid of me to have practised magic in my presence, since they say that things do not go well when a white skin is present, and that they had never been willing to do magic in front of him. I also pretended to be very serious, although I often almost burst out laughing at his cures and the fear of my Hottentots. They are said to have jackal and other animals in their service who take messages for them to other magicians. I bought his magic rattle for a tinder-box.

A painting by Gordon of himself hunting giraffe.

BACK TO HIS COUNTRY

Cabas, which means "red", was a San boy given to Gordon's Boer companions by a woman in northern Namaqualand. Courageous and tough, Cabas stuck close to Gordon during more than a month of travelling, but ran away repeatedly when they got back near his home. He was brought back silent and fearful by his father, who explained, said Gordon, that "they did not have much food at the village, and that Cabas was therefore better off with me than with him". "I told him I would take him [Cabas] to the Cape and let him see everything, and that if he wanted to return to his country, I would have him brought there," Gordon wrote. But the boy still tried to escape.

Little Cabas, my young [companion], seeing us now leaving the river and his region, did everything he could to run away (even though he would now have to go across an unknown veld which had little water; for the rest he could live off lizards, mice and other veld foods). However, I watched him very closely, because I first wanted to let him see the Cape. But now, at this place, he must have known that the mountains [he could see were those] of the Great River. Therefore, while I was busy taking bearings, and seeing no other opportunity, he ran down the rocks as fast as he could and would have got away, but the Baster Klaas, who was with me, ran after him and, as he ran up the next rise like a klipspringer, prevented him from crossing it. He therefore crept into a dassie hole and another Hottentot, who came from the farm at our call, fetched him out of it, whereupon Claas gave him a few blows with a riem. However, as soon as he escaped from his grasp, he ran to me and attached himself to me with hands and legs around my body, after which I released him to sleep and again told him that I only wanted him to see the Cape and that I would then send him back to his country.

Cabas did go to the Cape, but Gordon is silent on whether he was ever sent home.

IT RESEMBLED A PORCUPINE

When I came to the village I saw a Hottentot who was missing an eye. I asked him how he had lost it, and he told me in the presence of the entire village that a star had fallen from the sky onto his head and in that way had treated him so harshly. On enquiring more closely I found that there was superstition mixed with this story, and that he must have had a sort of stroke. When I asked him what the star looked like, he and an old woman said it resembled a porcupine, and that three women had caught the thing. He said that although he had already slaughtered many cattle – since he had been very rich – (being "made different"), he had not yet been able to get strong and healthy again.

DEFINITELY NOT

This morning Nieuwenhuisen, who was like an old Jewish patriarch in many respects, wanted to show me how lions were shot in front of the trap which he had set for the purpose. When we arrived there he wanted to walk against it to show me how it went off. I asked him whether the gun was not loaded, to which he replied, "No." When I asked him again, he said, "Definitely not." Thereupon he went against the rope and the shot went off with a loud report. At first I thought he wanted to surprise me and I laughed at him, but having heard the bullet whistling past and seeing him looking bewildered, I saw that the gun had indeed been loaded with a bullet. When I examined him I found that the bullet had passed through his overcoat a hand's breadth from his thighs. In this way his stupidity almost cost him his life.

IN MORTAL PANIC

On the Orange near its confluence with what is today the Caledon, although Gordon named it Wilhelmina's River, after the Princess of Orange.

This beautiful river and [the] foliage made it most enchanting here, for in this country one is accustomed to nothing but rivulets and brooks – which people call "rivers". I rode alone along the river to the wagon, and since I had fired my musket I wanted to wash it out, so I gave it to the artist. After riding for some time, and seeing various beautiful birds and guineafowl – the same as a *polipentade* in almost all respects – I sought to ride to a reef stretching from one bank to the other in the shape of a half-moon, over which the water rushed noisily, to see whether I could cross this river on my horse. After looking for some time and finding the crossing to be impossible on horseback, I had a mind to ride down the river again. Following a hippopotamus path between some reeds on the ridge I fell quite unexpectedly with my horse into a pit which had been dug by the wild Bushmen for the hippopotamus. As I fell I jerked the horse's bit hard, so that in the main it was his hindquarters which descended to the bottom. Dust and sticks fell on me from all sides, so that I struck out with both hands to avoid being suffocated. When I had made an opening I grabbed the horse, which had begun to kick and struggle violently, by both ears, and held them closed – which I had heard to be effective. The poor creature lay still for a little, and sweated in mortal panic and from the constriction of this pit. Keeping my head and not having been injured, I saw that the pit was more than eight feet high above my head. I realized that I would quickly have to make an attempt, for breathing was very difficult there. I therefore leapt up as high as I could, and fortunately remained hanging in the pit by my shoulders and feet, above the horse, which began to struggle furiously. I now summoned all my strength and, having worked myself upwards like a chimney-sweep three or four times, I grasped with one hand one of the remaining sticks at the edge of the pit, where it was firm enough to support me. In this way I most fortunately escaped from danger. I spoke to my poor horse, and the creature again became still. I thereupon ran as fast as I could to the wagon and fetched servants with a shovel to save the beast, but when we reached the pit we found that the animal had died of suffocation. The sweat was like water on its body. We would not

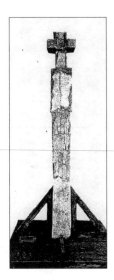

have been able to dig it out in half a day, for the pit was sixteen feet deep. It seemed incomprehensible to my companions and to me how I escaped from this pit without assistance. We lowered a Hottentot to bring the saddle and bridle out, but his claustrophobia would not allow him to endure it [long enough] for the saddle to be loosened. At last we retrieved the saddle and bridle, with nothing broken. Even my pistols, which had been under the horse, were undamaged, though one had become cocked. We left the poor creature lying there and went to the wagon.

TO MAKE WOMEN FERTILE
With the aid of a centuries-old Portuguese text, and probably information from local farmers and Khoikhoi, Gordon managed on a 1786 trip to the Eastern Cape to pinpoint the site of the padrão, *or stone cross, erected in 1488 at Kwaaihoek by Bartolomeu Dias. Dias was the first European to round the Cape; Kwaaihoek was where he turned back.*

The reconstructed
padrão.

On a hill jutting out into the sea – a ruined monument. From it I carried away three stones which are covered with inscriptions. On one side there are Roman letters, like those on our old tombs, and on the other side there are Arabic ones. These stones, which I took with me on my wagon to the Cape, have the appearance of being truly [?] old ... The stone is a kind of marble and I have not found [?] like it. Some Hottentots have told me that the Caffers who lived in these parts a while ago, but who are now living more to the east, believed that this monument served to make women fertile when they rubbed themselves against it.

The Portuguese erected a padrão *at the mouth of the Congo River in 1483: in the 1880s its remains too were revered as a fetish by local people.*

LUGUBU KA MANGALISO

Lugubu was a Thembu chief in the Weenen area of Natal. James Stuart, the civil servant and historian who recorded this interview in 1909, describes him as being tall, about 61 years old, with a grey beard: a "very intelligent, clear-headed man", splendid at throwing light on the meaning of izibongo, or praise poems. Stuart, incidentally, was a fluent Zulu speaker, who filled more than 100 notebooks with the oral testimony he so patiently gathered.

IT CAME TRUE
There used to be a folk tale which said that there were white people living, and that they would one day come. The old women of former times, those who bore our fathers and [Zulu king] Tshaka, would say, "There are white people who wear clothes. They will one day come to this country." Our forefathers would ask, "Where will they come from?" The answer was, "They are on the other side of the sea."

Our people would query this, saying, "How could they cross the sea?" But indeed there came white people who wore clothes.

They had simply been telling stories. It was only a tale, but when they talked about it they would say, "It came true." But I no longer remember these stories well.

NZUNZU

Another Stuart informant, whose full name is not recorded. The wreck he describes here has not been identified. One of the men present while he was relating this to Stuart was a direct descendant of the woman from the wreck.

SHE HAD BREASTS

My father's mother says two men and one girl got out of this wreck. They came out on a piece of the wreckage. They rolled a safe or chest of money along and buried it. They then wrote on a rock, saying that the two of them and a girl had escaped. The two men lived on wild plums (*amatungule*), and afterwards died of fever. Black men came along to gather mussels, and found the girl and tended her. They reported this. "We saw a white person with long hair, a wanderer or waif." They said they had come out of an *uqwembe*, not knowing what a ship was. The chief, whose name I forget, then told them to go and "catch her" on the beach. The girl cried. They escorted her back to the chief. They saw she had breasts and was a woman. She lived on fowl's eggs chiefly. She then saw that no harm was intended and was happy. The chief then looked out for an *umnumzana* who had much property. In those days the practice was to send to a man of importance to ask him to give the daughter of the man asking a snuff-spoon. The chief could not find a sufficiently wealthy man in his own tribe, so the application for a snuff-spoon was made to Mbukwe. This custom meant an offer to marry a daughter to the man of whom the request was made. She was then married off and made a wife. I do not know how many children she had, but Mntengwane was her son.

JOHN HENDERSON SOGA

Soga was a Xhosa missionary and author, who trained in Glasgow and Edinburgh and spent most of his working life spreading the Presbyterian gospel in the Transkei. His South Eastern Bantu, *the first complete history of the Xhosa, was published in 1930.*

A PECULIAR TRIBE

There is in Pondoland a peculiar tribe, the descendants of an alien race. Its tribal name is Ama-Mholo or Ama-Molo (the first *o* is pronounced with an aspirate). The progenitors of

this tribe are described as men of a black race, having long black hair, and features of a different cast from those of the Bantu. Though these features are still evident in some members of the tribe, they are, as the writer saw them in 1924, gradually merging into those of the Bantu. The progenitors were three in number, two males and a female, who had been cast ashore on the Pondoland coast, from some wreck. Their names, according to Native pronunciation, were Bhayi, and Mera; the name of the female, however, was not given. They were probably Malay or Indian, possibly natives of Madagascar. The story concerning them, as handed down by tradition, is as follows. On a certain day, in their own country, Bhayi, his wife, and two others named Tulwana and Pita, walked down to the shore near their home to bathe. While in the water, they were suddenly surrounded by white men, captured, and placed on board of a ship. In the course of the voyage the ship was wrecked on the coast of Pondoland, and the three mentioned were cast ashore. Two of the original party must have been lost, but another man, Mera, was washed ashore with them. Imagining that they could reach their own country by following the coast line eastwards, they walked for many days but lost all hope in the end and turned south. Reaching Pondoland they determined to settle among the Pondos. Bhayi's wife being childless he married a Pondo woman, by whom he had six sons, named Poto, Mngcolwana, Mnyuli, Mgareni and Falteni, the last two being twins, and finally, Nyango.

WILLIAM HUBBERLY

Hubberly was a seaman on the Indiaman Grosvenor, *which ran onto the Pondoland coast in 1782 with 141 people on board. The survivors set off on what was to be an arduous five-month overland journey south. They ate sorrel, wild celery, limpets, berries, frogs and crabs, dead whales and seals found on the beach, and even the rawhide they had bound around their feet in place of shoes. At one point they dismembered a passing dog with mussel shells. Hubberly, skin blackened by scurvy, was one of 18 men who reached Cape Town. A rescue expedition found only groups of skeletons and scraps of clothing along the coast. He dictated his 225-page journal from memory when he returned to England, a feat almost as remarkable as his trek down the coast.*

SOME DEGREE OF PITY
Monday the 11th of November. It was late in the day before I stirred out and, casting my eyes along the beach, not a rock was to be seen, and of course no shell-fish to be had. Being at a loss what track I should now take I sat myself down quite careless of what became of me, and had not rested long before I observed some cattle grazing inland, when, after a little consideration, I was determined to find out the inhabitants, being easy as to what reception I might meet with, for if they should kill me then my sufferings would be over. [I] therefore was fully bent to proceed up the country, which was clear, but was often obliged to rest. I, however, soon came in sight of some calves, with three boys attending them. When they perceived me they drove the cattle away, and as I advanced towards them they retreated. After following some time I came in view of a village, and as I descended into the

valley, I could see the villagers in great confusion. As soon as the boys arrived at it, the women and children left the huts, all making a great noise and running off. Therefore on seeing the disturbance I had occasioned, and not knowing what way to take, I halted; but my mind being made up with respect to how I might be received, I therefore entered the village, where in the centre of it was a large hut in which an old man and woman resided. Before this hut I took courage and sat myself down, making every motion I could think for them not to be alarmed at me, and gave them to understand how much I wanted provisions. The old man then put a basket of milk out of the hut, but would not suffer me to take it from his hands, and there left it for me. As I sat, some of the women came and gazed at me, with as much fear as if I was some dangerous monster. I must acknowledge the appearance I made was enough to affright them, my dress being a pair of trousers cut off half-way up the thighs, part of a shawl next my body, a waist-coat without sleeves, and the thigh part of a pair of breeches for a cap. When I attempted to move they instantly ran off. One of them in running dropped a young child, and being so terrified at me would not return to take it up. So I went and, carefully picking it up, brought it to the old people at the hut. The child making a noise the mother came back, but not near enough to receive it; so I got up and walked away, and made motions for her to take it which she did. I then resumed my station as before. The old woman gave me a small earthen pot full of boiled meat, the broth of which I was thankful for, and some of the women produced pieces of meat, which they laid down for me not daring to give it me themselves. The woman whose child I had picked up fetched me some milk, and was bold enough to give it me herself. After this their fears subsided a little, and they came and sat down by me. Just before sunset I heard a great noise which alarmed me so much as to make me tremble, and soon after was surrounded by a number of dogs which came running into the village, and was followed by about twenty men, with lances and targets in their hands, who immediately came up; which greatly terrified me, not knowing what treatment I might experience from them. It appeared they had been a-hunting, and brought home some deer's and baboon's flesh, with their skins on. They were not seemingly the least surprised at seeing me. The old man and woman discoursed some time with them about me, for I could observe them look and that cheered up my spirits, as I thought they seemed to notice me with some degree of pity, which was contrary to what I expected. An old man, chief of the village as I afterwards found him to be, made signs for me to follow him, which I instantly did, into the enclosure where the cattle was kept. He then sat down, and made motions for me to do the same, and talked a great deal but of which I could not comprehend. When they milked the cows he gave me some of the new milk, and just as it was dark they brought him a large earthen pot, full of boiled meat, of which he likewise offered me as much as I could eat. As soon as they had finished their meal, they retired to their huts, and there being a little fire left where I was under a large tree, I laid myself down well satisfied with the entertainment I had met with. One of the natives again returned, and brought me some wood to replenish my fire with. Having eagerly overfilled myself, prevented my sleeping much in the night, for I thought really I should have bursted; but fortunately for me nature eased itself and I went some distance for that purpose from the village. My situation was so different to what it was the night before, that I often fancied myself in a dream.

FRANCOIS LE VAILLANT

As a youngster in Dutch Guiana, Le Vaillant was a keen naturalist, although his endeavours received a setback when his pet monkey ate much of his collection of insects – including the pins on which they were mounted – and died. In 1781 he went to the Cape to build up a collection of birds from a region that had never been systematically studied before. The vessel in which he was travelling, together with most of his possessions, was blown up after an engagement with the British fleet at Saldanha Bay, but Le Vaillant recovered from this misfortune to make one journey through the Eastern Cape and Karoo, and a second, lasting over a year, through Namaqualand, Damaraland and the Kalahari desert. He returned to France with thousands of specimens and produced five entertaining volumes of travels. Modern scholars – and his contemporaries – have shown that Le Vaillant was creative with the truth, and have raised doubts whether he travelled as far as he claimed. However, the books became bestsellers, and within a few years had been translated into seven languages. Like Anders Sparrman, Le Vaillant admired the Khoikhoi women, although we are assured he never did anything ungentlemanly about it.

AN ABSURD CUSTOM
I know not whether I ought here to relate an asburd custom practised by the Nimiquas, which, like many others, arises solely from their ignorance; which is tying up the prepuce when they have a river to cross. This is performed with a thread of gut; and, as their ideas of modesty differ from ours on certain points, they do it before their daughters without any scruple.

When I asked them the reason of this custom, they told me, like true savages, that it was to close an opening by which the water might enter their bodies. Yet, as a proof how extravagant and even contradictory the prejudices of ignorance are, the women on such occasions neither tie nor stop up any part of the body, whatever access it may appear to offer to the fluid element.

Le Vaillant crossing the Olifants River.

IT WAS ALWAYS SATURDAY
The opportunistic "Hottentots" here were his travelling servants.

On leaving the Cape I had forgot to procure an almanack, but wishing to reckon how time went, I computed each month at thirty days, and as I never passed one without an exact distinction of weeks, the omission was not very material.

Every Saturday it was my custom to deliver the *Hottentots* their weekly portion of tobacco: if the name of the day had slipped my memory, and I did not choose to take the trouble of consulting my book (which was sometimes the case) on referring to them, the answer may easily be devined, it was always Saturday according to their calculation; and on my return to the Cape, computing my register, after fifteen months travel, I found several weeks had contained two of these Saturdays.

SUCH INSUPPPORTABLE PAIN
The "horde" were Nama.

The eagerness with which I was observed to seek and catch insects, which are very plentiful in the country, had engaged several persons of the horde in contributing to my collection. A woman, who had made herself of the party, brought me a superb beetle, which I believe is to be found in no cabinet in Europe, at least it is not in any one that I have seen.

While I was examining this beautiful insect with attention, I felt my face suddenly wetted by a caustic liquor, of a very strong alkaline smell. The sprinkling was accompanied by a sort of explosion, loud enough to be heard at some distance. Unfortunately some of the liquor entered one of my eyes, and occasioned such insuppportable pain, that I thought I should have lost the sight of it. I was obliged to keep it covered for several days, and bathe it from time to time with milk. In every part of my face that the alkaline liquor had touched, I felt the pain of a burn; and every where the skin changed to a deep brown, which wore out only by degrees and a long time after.

AN INTRACTABLE ANIMAL
Le Vaillant discovered that something was stealing the eggs of his travelling hen. Kees was his pet baboon, who ran freely around the camp, and hitched rides on the explorer's dogs while on the march.

It was possible, that a weasel or some such animal had come unknown to us, and devoured the produce of my hen; but there was a culprit nearer at hand that might be suspected with more appearance of probability. This was my ape. Such is the effect of a reputation deservedly lost. If any crime was committed to which gluttony was the incentive, if any theft of eatables was discovered, Kees was instantly accused, and the accusation was seldom unfounded.

On this occasion I was desirous of satisfying myself whether I was right in my conjecture: and the next morning I kept on the watch, till the hen should inform me by her cries of having laid. Kees was then on my waggon: but no sooner did he hear the first cackle of the hen, than he leaped upon the ground, and was running to the egg. Stopped unexpectedly by my presence, he affected a careless attitude, balanced himself awhile on his hind-legs, and, winking his eyes with a silly air, walked backward and forward several times before me; in short, he employed all his cunning to take off my attention, and deceive me respecting his design. These hypocritical maneouvres confirmed me in my suspicions; and presently I was convinced of the truth, when, to deceive him in my turn, pretending to turn my

87

back on the bush, I saw him dart towards it and bear away the egg. I ran after him, and arrived just at the moment when, having broken the shell, he was swallowing its contents. It will readily be presumed, that the knave did not escape unpunished for his crime. Yet, so incorrigible is a perverse disposition, that my correction, severe as it was, had no effect in curing him of the practice.

An ape is in reality an intractable animal. It is true he possesses such powers of instinct, that he can often render important services; as mine did to me on more than one occasion. But if he has invention, and becomes useful, it is always for himself and not for you that he labours. Certainly no animal upon earth is so dexterous, or perhaps so artful. Yet if you attempt to employ him in any exercise or any work which is not voluntary, you will find him dull and awkward. It is only by dint of hunger and blows that you can discipline him to certain tricks: and of some faults that are natural to him it is impossible to correct him. He is lascivious, gluttonous, thievish, revengeful, and passionate; and if he has not the vice of lying, the savages say it is because he does not choose to talk.

Persuaded that I should never change the nature of mine, and never get an egg, unless I kept him chained up all the morning, I endeavoured to beat him at his own weapons. For this purpose I trained one of my dogs to run to the nest the moment the hen gave notice of having laid, and bring me the egg without breaking it. This was done in a few days: but Kees, when the signal was given, ran as well as he to the nest. A contest then arose, and often it was not the dog, though the stronger of the two, that carried the day. If the dog was successful, he ran with joy to bring me his prize, while the ape followed growling and threatening with his teeth, till I had taken the egg; when he appeared to be consoled for the loss of his prize, by finding that his antagonist did not enjoy it. If Kees was the victor, he ran up into a tree, and, having swallowed the egg, threw the shell at the dog, as if by way of defiance, who returned with a look of shame that informed me of his misadventure.

From Le Vaillant's *Histoire Naturelle*: a fiscal shrike.

Le Fiscal.

AN EXTRAORDINARY SHOT

At sun-rise, when every one retired to sleep, I took my gun, and went to try my success in the neighbourhood. I found nothing to add to my collection; but chance afforded me an extraordinary shot, such as perhaps no other sportsman can boast.

I was sitting at the foot of a tree, with my double-barrelled gun between my legs straight before me, the butt-end resting on the ground, and my finger on the trigger. In the other hand I held a leaf, on the edge of which I was whistling in the manner of fowlers when they wish to draw round them small birds. A species of red-breast came and pitched boldly on my hat, thence hopped to the mouth of my fusee, and, setting one foot on each barrel, remained motionless, listening to the music of my leaf, which was altogether new to him.

In desert countries, an animal that has never beheld a human being sees one for the first time without alarm, particularly if the individual it perceives be in a state of rest and do not move.

Whatever might have been the motive of the bird's familiarity, its boldness so suprised me, that, mechanically and without reflection, I pulled the trigger, and the gun went off. I supposed the bird would have been torn in a thousand pieces: but, to my great astonishment, I saw it carried up thirty feet above my head, in an almost perpendicular direction, and fall a few paces from me.

I ran to pick it up. The ends of its quill feathers were a little scorched, and it appeared panting and extremely frightened; but by degrees it recovered, and, after I had satisfied myself that it had received no wound, I gave it its liberty, and it flew away without appearing to be in the least injured. It is probable that the column of air which filled the barrel, being driven out by the explosion, first struck the bird, which, by a single motion of its wings, was thrown out of the line of direction of the shot, which passed in a body without touching it, while the fire, occupying a larger space, scorched the ends of its wings and tail.

WITHOUT WASTING TIME
One of Le Vaillant's guns was discharged by mistake in a Nama encampment. Three men standing a hundred yards away, who received a few pellets of lead in their legs, collapsed on the ground "howling in a most frightful manner, and exhibiting every symptom of despair". The Klaas here is one of Le Vaillant's servants.

I was astonished at their consternation, and could not conceive how men inured to sufferings should be so much affected by a few small punctures, the pain of which could have scarcely drawn tears from an infant. They at length told me the cause of their wailings. These savages, accustomed to poison their arrows, imagined that I had in like manner poisoned the lead with which they were wounded. They had, therefore, given themselves up as lost, and expected in a few moments to expire.

It was with great difficulty I could cause to be explained to them that they had nothing to fear. To convince them, in a manner still more satisfactory, I pulled down one of my stockings, and showed them, in the flesh of my leg, a dozen shots of lead, for which I was indebted to M. Papillon de la Ferté, who, when hunting in the plains of Gennevilliers, had fired at me instead of a rabbit.

Klaas approached the wounded savages also; and, without wasting time in words which they would not have understood, took from his shot-bag a few grains of lead, and, having shown them to the three men, immediately swallowed them. This conclusive proof, which I had never thought of, produced a most wonderful effect. Their cries instantly ceased; serenity again appeared in their faces; and their wounds were no more mentioned.

THIS FAITHFUL SERVANT
In the northern Cape, and desperately short of water.

During the night two of my oxen had died, and three of my dogs had deserted me. I lost also one of my horses, which I saw expire before my eyes. Thus was I losing one by one my whole stock of cattle; and I beheld them perish with the more regret, because, having shared in my fatigues, I had become attached to them as so many servants of my household. They approached slowly indeed to their last moments, but these moments were singularly painful. They were first seized with convulsions, which ended in a long and dreadful agony. Scarcely was one deprived of life than another became a sacri[f]ice. Next after my horse, this unhappy lot fell upon the very best of my oxen; and of all my losses, this in particular occasioned me the greatest affliction. The reader will pardon me if I digress for a moment to tell him the reason.

I had given to this faithful servant the name of Ingland. He was the oldest and strongest beast I possessed: accordingly he had successfully encountered the fatigue of my first journey, though, during the whole route, he had constantly occupied the thill to my heaviest and principal waggon. Distinguished by an instinct superior to the other animals of his species, my people, when they unharnessed him, gave themselves no concern to prevent him from escaping; he wandered at will in the pasture, and was committed, if I may so express myself, to the guidance of his own understanding; there was no fear that he would wander from the place. When it was time to travel another stage, it was unnecessary to fetch him from the pasture, and bring him to the waggon, as was requisite for the rest: three smacks of the whip was our signal for march, and as soon as he heard them he came to his post. He was always first to present himself to the traces, as if he had been afraid to lose his priority in a place which he had constantly been employed to occupy.

If I went out for exercise, or to hunt, at my return Ingland, as far as he could see me, quitted his pasture, and ran towards me with a particular sort of bellowing, expressive of his joy. He rubbed his head against my body in different directions, and caressed me after his manner. Frequently he licked my hands; and I was constrained to stop long enough to receive his civilities, which sometimes lasted for a quarter of an hour. At length, when I had replied by my endearments and by a kiss, he led the way to my tent, and walked quietly before me.

The evening before he died, Ingland laid down near the shaft of his waggon; and it was in this place he expired. I saw his last agonies, but was unable to render him the slightest assistance. Ah! how frequently, when friendship has misled me, when seducing appearances have allured my confidence, have I thought of poor Ingland, and involuntarily cast my eye upon the hand he had so often licked!

JACOB VAN REENEN

Van Reenen was one of the members of an expedition commissioned in 1790 to search for female survivors of the Grosvenor *reportedly still languishing among the tribes along the coast. With the added incentive of permission to hunt and trade ivory, the expedition advanced further than any of its predecessors, but did not find anyone from the* Grosvenor. *However, on the northern Natal coast they did find an entire village of "baastard Christians" descended from people shipwrecked in that area, and three old white women whom a local chief had taken as his wives. They women said they were sisters, and had been children when they were cast ashore. They did not know where they had come from. The expedition stopped at the village again on the way back.*

WITH THEIR WHOLE RACE

I would now have taken the three old women with us; to which they seemed well inclined, as appearing much to wish to live amongst Christians; but mentioned their desire, before they could accomplish such a plan, of waiting till their harvest, to gather in their crops: adding that, for this reason, they would at present rather remain with their children and grandchildren; after which, with their whole race, to the amount of four hundred, they would be happy to depart from their present settlement. I concluded by promising that I would give a full account of them to the government of the Cape, in order that they might be removed from their present situation. It is to be observed, that on our visit to these women, they appeared to be exceedingly agitated at seeing people of their own complexion and description.

CORNELIUS DE JONG

Valiant commander of a Dutch frigate, on his first visit to the Cape in 1792 he praised the "soft humour, the faithfulness and the extraordinary sensibility" of the ladies there. On his second voyage two years later, he married one of them.

INNUMERABLE SMALL STARS

Here De Jong is describing the Magellanic clouds, visible only in the southern hemisphere, and seen by European eyes only when the first seafarers ventured below the Equator.

In these clear still nights south of the Line one also sees another phenomenon, which you do not have where you are, and which is known to seafarers as the Cape clouds. They consist of two small, round, white patches, close by one another, and a small blue patch in the middle of the Milky Way, which indeed have the appearance of clouds yet, just like the stars, rise and set regularly. Because one sees them at the Cape above the Table-mountain, people have given them the name of Cape clouds, but, to my mind, quite unjustly, for through my spyglass, which is reasonably good, I can see that the white patches, just like the Milky Way itself, are made up of a collection of innumerable small stars, and that the blue one is an empty space in the Milky Way, or rather a place, where infinitely fewer stars are, than in the remaining part.

DUST AND SAND

The south-easterly wind, which first announces itself by certain clouds, mainly on the Table Mountain, whose top they cover completely, and plunge down the mountain with rushing violence, forces sand and dust through the most tightly shut windows, and even carries small stones onto the ships lying some distance from the quay. A cloud of dust, sand and gravel make breathing difficult; one can neither go for walks, nor look up in the wind; it closes the pores, interferes with exhalation, and has an influence on the temper, for though the air is shaken and stirred, it is not cooled. Several days of a strong south-easterly wind makes people uncomfortable; without being ill one is out of sorts, listless, languid. Along with the unpleasantnesses of red eyes, difficult breathing and bad temper, comes one which is no less; the dust and sand which has penetrated the houses in defiance of windows and doors, settles on clothing in trunks and cabinets; all household items and furniture are covered; one eats or drinks nothing that does not contain at least some sand; the bread, the cooking spices, everything one puts in the mouth, has some in it. The most stringent precautions, even sandbags before the doors, are here in vain; the wind is too violent. Add to this a quantity of flies, which come sit in hordes on dishes, tables and even on the face, which is the most annoying, when one is awake, and which wake one when one is asleep.

A TERRIFYING VIOLENCE
The Chief Commissioner SLUISKEN was sitting with Mrs CLOETE in a coach, drawn by six horses; her husband PIETER LAURENS CLOETE, and I followed in a chaise with two horses; it blew strong from the South-east; we came from outside, and were already in the Town, on the road from the castle to the garden, just past, but not far from the Court of Justice, when a blast raged down from the *Table-Mountain* with such a terrifying violence, that the coach could not move forward, and the chaise, despite the horses, was actually blown backwards. We had eyes, nose and mouth full of sand, and for fear of accident we had to get the slave, who stood at the back, to climb down to hold the horses; he did, but could not move forward without clinging to the vehicle, along which he pulled himself.

ROBERT PERCIVAL

Captain Percival arrived at the Cape soon after the British captured it from the Dutch in 1795. He was generally unimpressed by the "unsocial, inhospitable and boorish" colonists, and believed Britain should take permanent possession of the territory.

LEFT TO HIS PROTECTION
By a law long in existence when a planter or farmer, ever so remote from the Cape, wishes to marry, he must bring the object of his affections with him to town, and be there joined in wedlock by a particular licence from the

Governor, in the presence of the Fiscal, at the same time paying handsomely for that privilege, and for leave to enter into the state of matrimony. The instances of the pernicious effects of this law have been many, and ought long since to have opened their eyes to its impolicy; for it often happens when the lovers and their parents agree about the match, that the young woman is intrusted to the care of her future husband, as probably her parents cannot accompany her on such a distant journey. She is in consequence left to his protection to take to town; when as a natural consequence arising from two young people, with perhaps no other attendants but the slaves, being so long together and almost looking on each other as already united, the consummation frequently takes place before they arrive at their destination; and when that happens, the lover's passion being cooled by enjoyment, he frequently refuses to marry the unfortunate young woman, who must consequently return the best way she can to her parents, whilst her deceiver only pays a certain fine for his breach of faith. Luckily for the poor deluded female she is not considered in much the worse light for such a misadventure, but often meets with another lover, who makes no great account for the loss she has sustained: the colonists indeed are seldom over nice in those matters.

RICHARD RENSHAW

An artilleryman who also arrived at the Cape soon after its 1795 capture, Renshaw tells how some Xhosa made the journey from the eastern frontier specially to meet the new possessors of the colony.

So completely docile
A few of the Caffrees travelled the distance of near four hundred miles to see us, and pay their respects to the General, among whom was one of their chiefs or princes. Their caravan consisted of two tame bullocks and several sheep, which were so completely docile, as to follow them like dogs, and were carefully attended by their owners, who appeared extremely fond of those useful and peaceable animals.

BENJAMIN STOUT

Captain Stout, an American, deliberately ran his badly leaking ship, the Hercules, *onto a beach near the Bira River mouth in the Eastern Cape in 1796. She was carrying 9,000 bags of rice on charter for the English East India Company. In his account of the wreck and the subsequent overland journey to Cape Town, Stout praised the Xhosa as "liberal benefactors" and recommended that the United States establish a colony in their territory.*

The pleasure of the Almighty
In the general search on the shore, one of the Caffrees had picked up the ship's compass. Not knowing what it was, yet pleased with its formation, he delivered it to the *chief*, who immediately took it to pieces; and after

contemplating the various parts, took the copper-ring in which it hung, and suspended it from his neck. He appeared highly pleased with the ornament; and this circumstance, induced me to present him with one still more *glittering*, and of course, in his estimation, more *valuable*. Recollecting that I wore a pair of paste knee-buckles, I took them out, and after having prepared two loops, I hung one upon each of his ears. The moment this was done, the chief stalked about with an air of uncommon dignity. His people seemed to pay him greater reverence than before, and they were employed for some time in gazing at the brilliancy of the ornaments, and contemplating the *august* deportment of their *chief magistrate*. The EUROPEAN may smile at this recital; the exhibition of my *knee-buckles* may indeed provoke his risibility; but when he treats the feelings of the *savage* on this occasion with contempt, let him bestow a thought on the *star*, the *garter* or the *coronet*, and then make a sensible distinction if he can.

As this donation gave me a powerful interest with the chief, I resolved, during my stay with the Caffrees, to procure every possible information respecting the customs, manners and opinions of these people. Some travellers have reported, that the natives of Caffraria are the only Savages on the southern continent of Africa who entertain any idea of a Supreme Being. Others have asserted, that *all* the inhabitants of these regions are totally ignorant not only of such an existence, but are also strangers to any opinion respecting a future state.

To be convinced how the matter really stood, I embraced the present opportunity, and entered into conversation on this subject with the chief, through the medium of our interpreters. After giving him a further description of the tempest, and the miseries we had so recently endured, I added, "that, as it was the pleasure of the *Almighty* to afflict his creatures, it would be impious in us to repine at his will." – The *savage*, after some consideration, declared, he did not understand what I meant by the *Almighty*. I explained to him my ideas of the Divinity. That he was a Being of such transcendent power, as to create the *world* on which we lived, the *sun, moon* and *stars*; and that they all moved and were directed by his hand. His countenance on this occasion demonstrated that his mind was a perfect void respecting such opinions; but after a few moments of reflection, he asked, if the Being I had described possessed a power sufficient to controul the *seas* and the *winds*? I answered immediately in the affirmative. Then, said he, "can you tell me his reasons for suffering the tempest to throw you and your people on our coast?" I replied, that his reasons for so doing were above our comprehensions; but that, as he was not only all powerful but just, we should remain satisfied that all his acts were good and beneficent. When this was explained to the chief, I observed a *smile* on his countenance; but starting, as if a sudden and hostile thought had seized his mind, he desired to know, "if *my Almighty* could tame the *wild animals* of the deserts?" I replied, that he certainly could. "If this be true! exclaimed the *savage*, "he must be a very wicked Being, for he suffered a LION to *kill* and *eat* my FATHER." As I had obtained the information I wanted, and observing the passions of the man highly agitated at the recollection of his father's melancholy fate, I thought it necessary to change the conversation …

JOHN SHIPP

Shipp joined the British army as a bandsman at the age of ten and rose to the rank of lieutenant, a formidable achievement in the days when class and hard cash, rather than merit, usually determined advancement. The 1797 voyage he describes here took him first to the Cape, where he served on the eastern frontier, then to India and action in a series of campaigns that extended Britain's hold over the subcontinent. He emerged with the scars of six bullet wounds, including one through the forehead. After more than 30 years' service, he was court-martialled over a shady deal involving racehorses, and returned to England. There he became a police superintendent in Liverpool and wrote melodramas, including The Maniac of the Pyrenees; or, the Heroic Soldier's Wife, *and his memoirs.*

The dying were burying the dead

Some three weeks after this we were again visited by a most dreadful storm, that far exceeded the former one, and from which we suffered much external injury, our main top-mast, and other smaller masts, being carried away. But the interior of our poor bark exhibited a scene of far greater desolation. We were then far from land, and a pestilential disease was raging among us in all its terrific forms. Nought could be seen but the pallid cheek of disease, or the sunken eye of despair. The sea-gulls soared over the ship, and huge sharks hovered around it, watching for their prey. These creatures are sure indications of ships having some pestilential disease on board, and they have been known to follow a vessel so circumstanced to the most distant climes – to countries far from their native element. To add to our distresses, some ten barrels of ship's paint, or colour, got loose from their lashings, and rolled from side to side, and from head to stern, carrying everything before them by their enormous weight. From our inability to stop them in their destructive progress, they one and all were staved in, and the gun-deck soon became one mass of colours, in which lay the dead and the dying, both white and black.

It would be difficult for the reader to picture to himself a set of men

more deplorably situated than we now were; but our distresses were not yet at their height: for, as though our miseries still required aggravation, the scurvy broke out among us in a most frightful manner. Scarcely a single individual on board escaped this melancholy disorder, and the swoln legs, and gums protruding beyond the lips, attested the malignancy of the visitation. The dying were burying the dead, and the features of all on board wore the garb of mourning.

Every assistance and attention that humanity or generosity could dictate, was freely and liberally bestowed by the officers on board, who cheerfully gave up their fresh meats and many other comforts, for the benefit of the distressed; but the pestilence baffled the aid of medicine and the skill of the medical attendants. My poor legs were as big as drums; my gums swoln to an enormous size; my tongue too big for my mouth; and all I could eat was raw potatoes and vinegar. But my kind and affectionate officers sometimes brought me some tea and coffee, at which the languid eye would brighten, and the tear of gratitude would intuitively fall, in spite of my efforts to repress what was thought unmanly. Our spirits were so subdued by suffering, and our frames so much reduced and emaciated, that I have seen poor men weep bitterly, they knew not why. Thus passed the time; men dying in dozens, and, ere their blood was cold, hurled into the briny deep, there to become a prey to sharks. It was a dreadful sight to see the bodies of our comrades the bone of disputation with these voracious natives of the dreary deep; and the reflection that such might soon be our own fate would crush our best feelings, and with horror drive the eye from such a sight. Our muster-rolls were dreadfully thinned: indeed, almost every fourth man amongst the Europeans, and more than two-thirds of the natives, had fallen victims to the diseases on board; and it was by the mercy of Providence only, that the ship ever reached its destination, for we had scarcely a seaman fit for duty to work her. Never shall I forget the morning I saw the land. In the moment of joy I forgot all my miseries, and cast them into the deep, in the hope of future happiness. This is mortal man's career. Past scenes are drowned and forgotten, in the anticipation of happier events to come; and, by a cherished delusion, we allow ourselves to be transported into the fairy land of imagination, in quest of future joys – never, perhaps, to be realized, but the contemplation of which, in the distance, serves at least to soothe us under present suffering.

When the view of land first blessed our sight, the morning was foggy and dreary. We were close under the land, and were in the very act of standing from it, when the fog dispersed, the wind shifted fair, and we ran in close to the mouth of Simmon's Bay. The now agreeable breeze ravished our sickened souls, and the surrounding view delighted our dim and desponding eyes. Every one who could crawl was upon deck, to welcome the sight of land, and inhale the salubrious air. Every soul on board seemed elated with joy; and, when the anchor was let go, it was indeed an anchor to the broken hearts of poor creatures then stretched on the bed of sickness, who had not, during the whole voyage, seen the bright sun rising and setting – sights at sea that beggar the power of description. For myself, I jumped and danced about like a merry-andrew, and I found, or fancied I found, myself already a convalescent.

ANNE BARNARD

Married at the age of 42 to Andrew Barnard, 12 years her junior, Lady Anne Barnard used her society contacts to secure him the post of secretary of the civilian administration that the British were establishing in Cape Town. The wife of new governor Lord George Macartney decided not to accompany her husband on the posting, and Barnard took on the role of his official hostess. This put her at the top of Cape Town's social ladder, and gave her intimate knowledge of its foibles. Her journals speak of a witty and warm woman, with a generosity of spirit that embraced every-thing from her attempts to reconcile Dutch burghers with the alien administration, to smuggling oranges to imprisoned soldiers in the Castle.

Anne Barnard

SKIN AND ALL
The Barnards and Macartney made the four-month voyage to the Cape in early 1797. The couple's shipboard baggage included a post chaise; quantities of English beer, rasberry wine and "portable soups"; an apparatus for preserving flowers; all the crimson damask curtains Barnard could find for sale in London; a cow and a calf; and a number of strawberry plants, none of which survived the journey.

On the deck to day I saw a poor sick Lascar basking in the Sun, emaciated and apparently very miserable … I spoke to the Surgeon about him, his lit-tle Story was interesting … he is now along with four others of his Countrymen sent home by Government having been taken on board of an Enemies Ship. Those of his cast are permitted to eat certain meats if they kill the Animals themselves, but Hogs flesh is forbidden.

The Sailors in fun told this poor creature that he had eat of it in his soup, which I believe they had reason to *know*, his companions threatened to tell his cast of it when he got home, the horror and disgrace was more than he could bear so tying a rope round his neck he hanged himself in a corner where he hoped no one would see him. He was however found and cut down in time to save him, but his recovery was attended with fever and he was then crawling out for the first time … I gave him a couple of Oranges and some ginger bread … the first he eat up skin and all.

TO LICK HIS HAND
Still at sea. The Barnards took several dogs with them; Andrew's favourite was Fanny, a gentle and obedient white retriever "whom he said particularly resembled me", Barnard wrote.

Before we went to Bed, Pawell [a manservant] according to Mr. Barnard's orders took the dogs on deck for a short time … Fanny crept under my Sofa wagging her tail in gratitude but evidently declining the invitation, it was done in a manner "prophetic of her end" you will say, nor would she stir for Pawell, but the coaxing voice of her Master … "Fan – Fan" … she could not resist.

She followed him on deck, and in about ten minutes he passed hastily thro' my room to the quarter gallery sighing so deeply that I followed him to know what was the matter.

"Nothing ... nothing love, only, poor Fan has fallen over board" ... and poor Fans Master burst into tears of humanity, bile and weakness ...

"I am ashamed of myself" said he as he put my hand on his throbbing forehead ... "Oh had the poor Animal only been killed at once by some accident, I should not have minded it, but to think how much a poor dog in the water who swims well has to suffer for hours, struggling, swelling, till nature is exhausted!" ... I begged him to say no more, the subject unhinged him, and I own it had the same effect on me.

"Was there no saving her still?"

"Oh no, no Love! ... the wind is foul ... the waves run high & all of her own colour ... we are going obliquely at five knots an hour ... it would take half an hour to get down the boat ... there is only the watch on deck ... and when down how could we find her in the ocean? ... She could not howl poor thing to let us know where to find her ... we are already a mile from the place ... we might lose the Commodore ... the Captain was on deck when the accident happened and said that had it been day light he would have gladly attempted to save her, but in the dark the attempt must be fruitless."

I went on deck and found a Sea of foam ... and returned to my birth with a pain in my heart at the circumstance and at the manner it affected him I had never felt so instantaneously created before. I endeavoured to convince him that ere this time some Shark, of which hundreds played about, had abridged the life of poor Fan.

"I hope so" said he ... "I loved that creature my Anne!" ... (he did not *say* because she resembled me) but drew me to his heart.

I found afterwards that she had followed him on deck reluctantly but when there, jumped on the side of the Ship where he stood, and where some hammocks were placed, to lick his hand and slipped down between two of them into the ocean; ... this last act of affection and the thoughts of being accessary to her death quite demolished him ...

No business of mine
The "rather ... good looking" Mrs Baumgardt was the wife of the Collector of Land Revenue at the Cape, and one of the first to make a social call on Barnard after her arrival.

I had heard not a little of Mrs Baumgardt before I saw her, she has always been reckoned in a literal & figurative sense *attached to Government* ever since the taking of the Cape, for with the existing Government she has constantly passed, from Commander in Chief, varying only from army to Navy, and from Navy to Army. That matter however being entirely between her, her conscience and her Husband and neither of the two last making any objection, I thought it was no business of mine to have *any ears* for *idle* reports, indeed I predetermined to listen to nothing ...

Something very revolting
There is something very revolting at first to human Nature in ones *presuming* to *bid* for a fellow creature. I have not got over this feeling yet, never having been obliged to buy. I remember while at Mr. Stromboms he said he must go to a Sale that morning to purchase a Coachman ... "A *Coach*" said

I laughing, "you said a Coachman". "And I meant a Coachman" said he "my Lady, the goods of the deceased are to be sold, and him amongst the rest, he is warranted good and free from ailment, so I suppose he will go high" – he did so … the Coachman fetched 800 dollars.

He also bought a Woman and five Children for 300 dollars which was reckoned a good bargain – the youngest Child was but a few months old, the eldest Six years. I presumed she was a Widow by the Children accompanying her not being aware that in Africa (amongst the Slaves) there is no marrying or giving in marriage, tho' there is often constancy from choice, so the property of the Children is vested with the female Slaves master.

Before I knew this, I remember making a Dutch lady stare one day when I said, it must be difficult to preserve so many young Girls *correct*, amongst such a variety of lovers of their own complexion. She did not understand what I meant, and I found that Virtue in a female Slave was considered to be a most *unproductive* quality and as such it is discouraged by the Mistress, who boasts of the number of Children her Slaves have and encourages the addresses of those by whom they may be half cast. The effects of this want of principle in domestic life you may conceive to be very odious.

Ironically, Barnard discovered after Andrew's death in 1807 that he had fathered a daughter with a woman of colour at the Cape.

STINKS OF EVERY DESCRIPTION
In May 1798, after Andrew had been "screwed to his desk one whole twelvemonth" (Barnard's words), Macartney gave him a month's leave. The couple took two young relatives, Anne Elizabeth Barnard and John Dalrymple, on a wagon tour to the mouth of the Breede River, then up its valley and across to Saldanha Bay. During the trip they stayed with local officials such as landdrosts or farmers "who upon the whole we found hospitable and good humoured at least to travellers, but … in their persons and Houses slovenly and dirty a few excepted". This was perhaps the most trying of Barnard's farmhouse experiences on the journey.

Imprimis … The room we had all to sleep in was dirty … dirty past expression … every association of nastiness which fancy could form … appearing in every corner of it … the bed which Mr. Barnard and I were to occupy had curtains and very dirty blankets … two truckle Bed steads for Anne Elizabeth and Johnnie in the same room had nothing, a couple of old mattresses excepted. In this room, the unfortunate legs were seen by Anne Elizabeth repairing for the night, while I sat in the publick room doing the civilities to the people of the House. One of the old Men could talk a very little French … he smoked his pipe & went on talking to me and leaning on the back of the cane Chair I had raised my feet on to keep them from the floor where abominations of all kinds were to be found.

Elizabeth you know how far I would walk on some occasions to avoid what is to be met with on floors, particularly in France. I was not prepared for his spitting straight down thro' the cane of the Chair … it abridged my conversation … that is all I shall say. Supper being served we sat down amidst stinks of every description … by me was a dead Chicken which had paid the last debt to nature by some malady and was half boil'd, it was swimming in rice and water … some pieces of boil'd dried mutton, ditto of Beef putrid … A dish of terrible Spinage … a stew pan with a dogs mess in it of yellow pumkin, a Jar of a *different sort*, which I leave fancy to delineate with boil'd milk … and brown bread, which tho' bad was the only thing which could be tasted … I forgot to mention a pot of Sheeps tail grease for butter … One of the gentlemen was not blessed with very good teeth … the tough mutton of course incommoded him, but in his left hand he had a two pronged resource, and that when it rid him of the Grievance kindly helped him to distribute the Spinage to the Company from the publick dish.

The Madona I have already mentioned as a chilly cold faced Saint painted on wood, of course a woman of this sort must be expected at all seasons short of the very warmest, to have a nose Jewel of the purest water … An ornament however of this sort being inconvenient, the napkin which lay on her plate (for there is generally napkins put down), answered the purpose of withdrawing the diamond and afterwards of wiping a dirty plate to help a Friend to Pumkin … to the pumkin on the plate of that friend succeeded every other dish … sweet, sour or greasy.

I durst not look, but tried to float my eyes lightly over every thing … fixing them on nothing … Johnnie tugg'd away at boil'd mutton. Anne Elizabeth put on her plate a bit of the fowl which there remained. … Mr. Barnard knew not well where to apply and I declared that as I *never ate supper* I would beg permission of the Vrow to have some tea and bread and butter … that I had every thing with me and only requested boiling water. I perceived the countenances of two of my friends rise on this proposal which I carried into effect and certainly there never was a heartier meal made in the *nursery* than Mr. Barnard, Johnnie and I made of what my stores produced. Anne Elizabeth would not join us but retired to bed in silent despair.

LAUGH'D AT BY MY FRIENDS
The same expedition: at Saldanha Bay.

Cape Town and Table Bay: a painting by Barnard.

The day being a fine one, we proposed going to the Out Keck, or look out post, about four miles distant to see the Bay and adjacent country from the highest ground. Mynheer Stockberg took us with his Oxen, and we had to ascend some hearty pulls by their means. I saw great quantities of Oval pebbles of a blackish Colour but so uniformly alike in shape and size that I requested to have a few picked up, I suppose other collectors of curiosities are at moments of their researches not without their knowledge of *similar disgrace*, tho' perhaps they don't tell. I found my oval pebbles when cracked neither more nor less than Sheep or Goats dung, and was laugh'd at by my friends accordingly.

100

With two exotic gentlemen doing the social rounds at the Cape in mid-1799 – Seth Sam, a wealthy Armenian merchant who wore a black velvet hat, and the turbaned Persian Abū Tālib Ibn Muhammad Khān – the scene was set for some confusion. Charles was a young slave of the Barnards, and pilow *is Barnard's spelling of the rice and meat dish pilaff.*

Castle, Friday, July 12, 1799
Nineteen people to dinner, No cook but her Ladyship & the two black men [slaves], of course *She* had a good deal to do – a ridiculous mal entendue happened which disconcerted me much but which had by no means disconcerted the person I felt for – when *Seth Sam* the young Armenian merchant dined at Paradise he offerd to bring a pilow with him the first time he dined with us in town, on this occasion Mr Barnard reminded him of it and desired me to send him three fowls as he did not wish to put him to any expense in the making of it – I wrote a note with the fowls thanking him for the trouble he was taking to oblige us, & making an apology for sending *fowls only* to his cook, but that I knew not what were the other ingredients that were necessary.

I heard nothing further till seated at dinner with Khan Sayb at my left hand. Capt Richardson said he hoped I shoud find the pilow good … it stood before him … I said I was sure I shoud as Mr Seth Sam had sent it to me – Khan Sayb, replied he, it was him who sent you the pilow … No said I it was Mr Seth Sam – pardon me said the other – I know it was Khan Saijb as on my return home this morning I found him very busy & his sleeves turnd up with much importance & secrecy of manner, at last I discoverd that he had had a note from you requesting him to make you a pilow & sending him (said he laughing) 3 fowls – so to work he went directly.

The whole affair soon came out, little Charles supposing that the note wrote to an Armenian who wore an odd black velvet cap, coud not do amiss for the man who wore a Turban, & finding the last livd nearer to us than the first, left the note & fowls at the Persians instead of the Armenians … how I blushd blue & black, Scarlet & purple at the rudeness I Had been guilty of apparently, for I saw that they had all blunderingly supposed that I had mistaken the name & had asked the great man to dress me a pilow instead of the merchant … I begun a thousand apologys & implored the two gentlemen to explain it to the Persian, they promised they woud, but I soon found out that he woud be more mortified by my explanation than by the mistake as he had been most extremely flatterd by my having requested the pilow: it is the fashion it seems when very great men dine with other great men for the person giving the intertainment to request the guest to order his cook to dress & send some dish such as he is fond of to be placed on the table, & this Asiatic compliment had been duly felt by Khan Saijb. however the explanation was made, some one was necessary for the immoderate quantity of pilows & currys which appeard … Seth Sam who I supposed had forgot the pilow, so far from forgetting it had sent one which on its appearance lookd as large as a Mountain, but it was so choicely good! the fowls so tender – the rice firm, so delicate, the plumbs & other ingredients so well mixd – the eggs so well boild & as to the curry it was divine! his much surpassd Khan Saijbs … & Khan Saijb was a judge of all, for never did I see a man lodge such a dinner within a gold belt as he did … plates so heapd with rice & fowl, three breasts – two wings – legs uncountable, not a morsel was to be seen of 10 fowls all of which vanishd before the attacks of my nineteen friends as did a Springer – two Roman fish & a fourth plate of fried [omission] – I certainly never saw a good dinner better bestowd than on this company, & was glad Mrs Capt Campbell & Donald had part of it, as they watch such sort of things and think expensive articles bestowed marks the respect of the giver for the guest. the cake in the center of the table at the desert cost me a guinea, it was good, but a guinea I thought better, however it is not often I am so extravagant.

WILL YOU NOTHING TAKE?
Another dinner party, this time with the head of the military hospital at the Cape, Dr Edmund Somers, and his unfortunate wife.

Khan Saijb who was of the party & who had had enough of other things before was now oppressd by the civilitys of the poor Somers who thought that by an improper transposition of words she coud make the Asiatic nobleman understand better than he otherwise shoud – "Sir will you nothing take?" said she in a languishing tone – "D– on your nothing take said the doctor at the bottom of the table squinting at her thro his spectacles – he will take nothing Mrs Somers so let him alone."

A CLEAR GOOD HAND
Barnard is commenting here on the stream of young women who made the voyage from England to India in the hope of securing husbands.

But I have said nothing as yet of the numberless fair ones who go like lambs to the Indian Market, their fleeces of snowy muslin & their manners no longer the daring ones of former times. All must now carry out irreproachable Characters … As I am always disposed to pity those poor Girls who are from Necessity obliged to do what they cannot be doing from choice I allowed the gentlemen in whose Ships they sailed, to bring them to the Castle if they were amiable and well behaved, and if I chanced to have a Ball or a party while they staid, this was always gratefully received, and it sometimes produced me a singular trait of character, but of what degree of singularity is not honest John Bull capable.

I was surprised to see one of the Lambs who had passed on to India on my first arrival at the Cape now returned & making one of my Ball.

I expressed a fear that the Climate had disagreed with her … "No" … she was very well … but the Gentleman to whom she was married … (Mr. Best) … "pardon me" said she smiling & hesitating, "if I request this may be entirely between ourselves … he made it a stipulation when he proposed to me, that I should sail home in the first fleet after our marriage." "Home!" said I.

"Yes Ma'm – he said that all his life he had contemplated the happiness there must be in having a faithful constant correspondent to write every thing to him and to be interested in all he said and did … willing therefore to secure this he married me after he perceived that I wrote a clear good hand

and had a tolerable easy style, he has settled 15,00 pr annum on me for life happen what will, and the same to continue after his death. I am quite satisfied my Lady, he is a very good elderly gentleman of the law, quite a Man of abilities, so I shall go home to my relations and be as Independant as can be, always talking of going back but never failing in my compact by doing it."

MEN OF THE SEA
The Barnards regularly enjoyed the hospitality of Jacob van Reenen, the farmer who nine years earlier went in search of Grosvenor *survivors.*

Before I apply this to the present time I must mark down what he observd of the past, when he was in their [Xhosa] country endeavouring to ascertain if any of the crew of the Grosvenor still livd amongst them – when introduced to the company of their king He carried his interpreter along with him and thro him learnt that No such men existed, He believed that such people had been seen many years before on that coast but that all had left the country or were dead; he observd that answers to his questions from the kind were obtaind after much consultation amongst his nobles in sheepskin behind his throne where a wild but numerous throng of chiefs were placed, the reason of this He did not know till some months after when his interpreter won to be his friend from his civil treatment of him & from perceiving he had no view in this enquiry that was to prejudice any of them let him a little into the Caffre politics, together with their opinions respecting those people Van Renin & his friends were in search of – the King who receivd him in all sorts of featherd finery with beads, shells & brass ornaments was in reality not the King, but a person placed there to represent him while the real King eight rows behind perhaps was watching every muscle of the countinance of the strangers unperceived and with his chosen people was preparing the replys to the question which had been transmitted to him by the pageant.

They woud not at first believe that Humanity woud lead men so far to look for other men supposed to be in distress, & askd what good it woud do to them to find them, for they coud not be their friends as they were *men of the sea*, a little time explaind the meaning of this, accustomed to hear of the Dutch at the Cape, the Dutch troops – the Dutch government, something of awe connected itself with *their* idea but they extended it no farther than to those at the Cape – on the contrary the Europeans that had in the course of years unfortunately been wreckd on their coast had all been miserable, half drownd, needy & begging on their knees for mercy[,] the idea of feebleness, poverty born in ships and living on the Sea *only*, was all connected together & as they were only Men of the Sea Van Renin inquired after, they coud not imagine it was of any consequence what became of them.

TO LOOK AT THE STARS
Towards the end of 1800 Andrew received long-awaited permission to return to England on leave. Barnard believed it would be a poor reflection on the secretary of the colony to have to confess there that he had never made it to the top of Table Mountain, and Andrew agreed. They hired 11 porters to carry their marquee, camp tables, bed, chairs, hams, turkeys and fowls, and began a frontal assault on the mountain at three o'clock one afternoon. Mentor, their guide, was "corporal" of slaves of

The back of Table Mountain: painted by Barnard from the verandah of her home in Newlands.

Dirk van Reenen, the Barnards' Newlands neighbour, and elder brother of Jacob. The "camera" she mentions is a camera obscura, a device used for tracing images.

Up – and up – we proceeded – Mentor complimenting Mr Barnard on his Braave Vrow who walkd better than any Vrow in aal de Caap – ascending is to me far less fatiguing than descending, so without halting above a minute at a time we reachd the top in less than three hours – Mr B: remarking that the gully by which we ascended certainly must have once been solid ground & rock, uniting the two sides, as it to him evidently appeard that the immense Stones which lay in the Chasm had fallen down in consequence of some concussion of nature forced out [more] probably by water spouts as to any thing of the volcano sort – it was now about six oclock & we saw his Majesty the sun step into bed, but that was not enough for me, I wishd to see him rise & charged them to wake me for that purpose – our tent was pitchd & all our lugguage arrived except a soldiers tent for our people to sleep in, which Mr B., ever anxious for the accommodation of all around him & particularly of the lower ranks, thought necessary, but which I thought they woud rather forego & sleep round than have the trouble of carrying, & I was right for our slaves left it at the foot of the mountain prefering to walk up unencumbered by their conveniency.

I was so tired I lay down for the night supperless in my great coat, but not to sleep as the fleas, the real natives of this country, had contrived to pack themselves into the blanket we carried & bit my ladyship most devilishly where Ladyships had never been bit before, on the top of the Table Mountain – fatigued & plagued by them, I got up in the night time & went out of the tent to look at the stars, & certainly the moon appeard so near me that if I had longed for a piece of her & the civil Major Glegg had been beside me (who had intended climbing the mountain along with us) he coud have reachd her easily on tip toe – I felt myself terribly hungry thro having made no dinner to keep myself light, so I eat up 3 *cookies* & drank a glass of wine, got me half hours sleep after & was up before the sun who popd up his red nose from behind a mountain just as I have seen him do before – after walking a good deal about, I coud see no flowers except everlastings & a quantity of bulbs such as we have plenty of below, near our house – but I took up a few of each for the sake of the place they grew on – & after much search found a beautifull bush of red & chocklate such as I had seen the last time I was on the mountain but coud not get transplanted with earth around its roots, I luckily was able to tear a good piece of one from the surface of a rock & hope it will grow – as to the view & my eager wish to trace it accurately by the camera – I found myself so infinitely above any object that the camera in a strange manner doubled the objects & no true representation was conveyd in the small one of Dr Grants which

I had procured – how I have been vexed at the foolish Boy Cockburn for giving away those he had of which I was really fond & for which I woud have given him any price coud I have supposed them of no value to him wc his giving them Gratis to a stranger proved – after many fruitless attempts I was obliged to take in the old way to my pencil & did a some-thing, better than nothing.

Mr B had now returned from shooting with Mentor & a few curious bulbs which grow by water – but he found so little in bloom to judge of, & so little to shoot that we both determind to descend the mountain after din-ner instead of remaining another night which coud do no good – mean time the good clean air I breathd began to make me as hungry again as some of Homers Heroes – I applied to the cook who having boiled 32 quails in a pot to be ready for dinner, the only hot dish excepting pottatoes & boild rice we had, I dispatched three of the quails to my own share & finding them insuf-ficient added two more – five quails to a delicate womans dejeuner! we shall have all the puny appetites of Europe crossing the ocean to ascend & eat five quails on the top of the Table Mountain! at one oclock arrived a great curios-ity, Dirk Van Rhenin on Horseback – he had wound the back way amongst the mountains, & being well mounted very lazy very large & fat & fully per-swaded that if fatigue was to be sufferd it was better that his horse shoud bear it than himself, he tried & made this point & the Horse instantly Begun rolling & afterwards breakfasted on such flowers & heather as he coud find without waiting to botanize – after V: R & his two young men had made a most hearty meal on our cold provisions they bid us adieu & we after pack-ing up our goods began descending the mountain.

I had walkd a good deal in the course of the morning, my feet were ten-der, my shoes nearly worn out by the sharp stones, & the descent was very fatiguing indeed, however we avoided all immoderate heat by pursuing the sun down the mountain keeping always a few yards within his shadow & it appeard to us that the sun & we exactly marchd at the same pace, being I pre-sume equally fatigued after his days work with ourselves, tho his walk between the tropicks is but a short one.

Abū Tālib Ibn Mohammad Khān

ABŪ TĀLIB IBN MUHAMMAD KHĀN

Khān, Anne Barnard's "Persian chief", embarked on his travels in order to rid himself of a bout of depression. Leaving Calcutta in February 1799, he travelled to the Cape, London, Paris, Italy, Turkey, Baghdad and Bom-bay, arriving there near the end of 1803. His account of the journey was originally written in Persian and distributed in manuscript form to a few friends, but was later translated into English and published for a wider audience. Khān describes Barnard as having "all the dignified manners of a person of quality", and talks of the "many delightful evenings" he passed at her home, but makes no mention of pilaff. Thanks to her con-nections, he was received in the highest circles in London, and had every opportunity to examine the ways of the English. Their greatest defect, he decided, was their "want of faith in religion, and their great inclination to philosophy".

SALT FISH AND PUTRID EGGS
Khān had the misfortune to embark in a Danish – not English – vessel for the voyage from India to the Cape.

For the benefit of my countrymen who may be inclined to travel, I shall here relate a few of the hardships and mortifications which I endured on board this ship, in hopes that they will take warning by my sufferings, and derive some advantage from my experience. In the first place, I must advise them never to embark in any but an *English vessel*; and if they are not possessed of sufficient wealth to provide themselves with a number of articles, not to undertake the voyage.

I shall comprise the miseries of this ship under four classes:

The first is that to which every ship is liable; viz. the want of good bread, butter, milk, fruit, and vegetables; to which are to be added, drinking stinking water, and washing the mouth with salt water; also the impurity of being shut up with dogs and hogs, and the difficulty of getting to and from the quarter-gallery, with the danger of being wet, or drowned, while there. To these I should add, the state of suspense and agitation to which a person is constantly exposed, the confinement in one place, and the sickness caused by the motion of the ship.

The second class arose from want of wealth; viz. a small and dark cabin, and the consequent deprivation of air and light; the neglect of servants; the want of a ship cot, on account of the deficiency of room; and the tyranny or rudeness of my neighbours, who ever studied their own convenience at my expence.

The third class is confined to foreigners, by which, I mean persons who are not Europeans; viz. the difficulty of shaving oneself; the cutting of one's own beard and nails; not having any private place for ablution; the necessity of eating with a knife and fork; and the impossibility of purification. From the latter I suffered much inconvenience; for as it was only customary on board to draw up water in buckets early in the morning, at which time all the crew washed themselves and whatever else they required, I was frequently under the necessity of drawing it up when I wanted it, in one of my own copper vessels; but during the rough weather many of these were lost in the attempt, and I was at last reduced to one ewer. I therefore relinquished the practice of purification, and was consequently incapacitated from the other duties of our religion.

The fourth class is confined to ships *not* belonging to the *English*; viz. noise and tumult when any business is done; the abusive language made use of while heaving the anchor; the quantity of bilge-water allowed to remain in the ship; and the unnecessary destruction of every thing on board. To these may be added, the quantity of stinking salt fish and putrid eggs, of which the sea store is composed, and the absurd custom of the crew lying on the wet decks; with a total want of discipline in the sailors, and science in the officers.

WITHOUT ANY INTERRUPTION
... I will now take the liberty of describing the inhabitants. All the *European* Dutch women whom I saw, were very fat, gross, and insipid; but the girls

born at the Cape are well made, handsome, and sprightly; they are also good-natured, but require costly presents. Even the married women are suspected; and each of the Englishmen of rank had his particular lady, whom he visited without any interruption from the husband, who generally walked out when the admirer entered the house. The consequence was, that the English spent all the money they got; while the Hollanders became rich, and more affluent than when under their own government.

He wrote of one encounter with these well-made girls: "… in dancing they made use of so many wanton airs, and threw such significant looks towards me, that I was often put to the blush, and obliged to retire to the other side of the room."

JOHN BARROW

Anne Barnard praised Barrow as "one of the pleasantest, best-informed and most eager-minded men in the world about everything curious or worth attention". When in 1797 he accepted an appointment as private secretary to governor Macartney, he had already travelled to Greenland and China. At the Cape Macartney sent his secretary on several expeditions though the territory. Barrow produced a map that would be unmatched for decades, plus a book that has been described as being as much a travelogue as a complete survey, in every sense, of the new British possession. On his return to England he helped found the Royal Geographical Society, and became its president.

BIT OFF HIS EAR
At the landdrost's of Zwellendam I saw a male and female zebra that, while young and attended to, were said to have been mild and docile; but by neglect, and probably by teasing, had become exceedingly vicious. One of the English dragoons persisted in mounting the female. She kicked and plunged, and laid herself down, but to no purpose; the man kept his seat; till taking a leap from the high bank of the river, she threw him into the water; but, holding fast by the bridle, she had no sooner dragged him to the shore than, walking up quietly to him, she put her head down to his face and completely bit off his ear.

SEVERAL GASHES ACROSS THE RIBS
The "horrible chasm" here is the valley of the Kowie River in the Eastern Cape, which Barrow's party encountered near the coast. The oxen were exhausted by the descent, and despite the curses of their Boer owners and floggings from their drivers, proved incapable of moving the wagons more than a hundred yards up the opposite slope.

After an hour's trial, bruising and fatiguing the oxen to no purpose, they had recourse to the method that ought in the first instance to have been adopted.

The reserved oxen were yoked before the others, and thus, by double teams, the waggons were at last drawn out of this horrible chasm; not, however, without producing an instance of brutality and cruelty that will scarcely be supposed to exist in a civilized country. While the poor animals were struggling and tearing on their knees, and exerting their strength to the utmost to draw up the waggons, the owner of one of the teams, enraged at their want of success, drew out of its case a large crooked knife with a sharp point, and fixing on one of the oxen for the object on which he might give vent to his fury, cut him with several gashes across the ribs, in the flank, and in the fleshy part of the thigh, some of them from six to seven inches long, and so deep that when the animal walked they opened two inches in width. The size of the wounds is not mentioned loosely for the sake of exaggeration, but is given from actual measurement. The ribs were literally laid bare, and the blood ran down in streams, yet in this condition the poor beast was obliged to draw in the waggon for the space of three hours, after having received such brutal treatment. By two of the gashes a large piece of flesh was very nearly taken out of the thick part of the thigh; and had it not been for the irritable state of mind into which the savage conduct of the fellow had thrown me, but more particularly lest it should seem to give a kind of countenance to his brutality, I should have asked him to have cut it entirely out, as it could not materially have encreased the pain to the beast; not for the sake of proving the delicacy of an Abyssinian beef-steak, quivering with life, but to have observed the progress of the wound. In three or four days the gashes were skinned over, and appeared to give the animal little uneasiness, but the cicatrices would always remain; and from these sort of scars on the bodies of many of the oxen, it is to be feared that cutting is a practice but too common among them, notwithstanding that most of the peasantry of the party seemed to be shocked at it. This was the second instance of the kind that I had occasion to witness in the course of this tour; the other was perhaps the more cruel, as it was exercised on parts of the body more subsceptible of pain, the nose and the tongue. In this instance the animal bellowed most hideously, burst from the yoke, and plunging into the thickets, made his escape. Even in the neighbourhood of the Cape, where, from a more extended civilization, one would expect a greater degree of humanity, several atrocious acts of the kind are notorious. One of the inhabitants, better known from his wealth and his vulgarity than from any good quality he possesses, boasts that he can at any time start his team on a full gallop by whetting his knife only on the side of the waggon.

The German explorer Lichtenstein accused Barrow of "wronging the [Boers] much … to assert … that they delight in such barbarity". "He does not seem to see how very wrong it is to take solitary examples, and apply them as the character of a whole class," he wrote. Barnard, incidentally, also described the practice of goading oxen by cutting them.

A VERY EXTRAORDINARY EFFECT
Snakes of different sorts were seen and killed daily, all of them, according to the Hottentots' information, more or less venomous. These people are not unacquainted with several interesting particulars as to the nature and

habits of the animal, as well as the vegetable part of the creation. From one I learned a very extraordinary effect produced by the application of the oil of tobacco to the mouth of a snake. One of these reptiles, about two feet in length, and of a blueish color, had coiled itself five or six times round the body of a lizard. As I was endeavouring to set at liberty the captive animal, one of the Hottentots took out with the point of a stick, from the short stem of his wooden tobacco pipe, a small quantity of a thick black matter which he called tobacco oil. This he applied to the mouth of the snake while darting out its tongue, as these creatures usually do when enraged. The effect of the application was instantaneous almost as that of an electric shock. With a convulsed motion, that was momentary, the snake half untwisted itself, and never stirred more; and the muscles were so contracted that the whole animal felt hard and rigid as if dried in the sun. The Hottentots consider the oil of tobacco among the most active of poisonous substances; but it is never applied to the points of their arrows, being probably of too volatile a nature to retain its deleterious quality for any length of time.

LIKE TRUE SPORTSMEN
Barrow accompanied a party of Sneeuwberg Boers on an expedition in search of alleged San stock thieves, but made the commandant promise beforehand not to fire on them except in self-defence. Fortified by brandy and a hymn-singing session, the farmers moved into position under cover of darkness.

Having halted here a couple of hours, in order to arrive at the mouth of the defile, in which the kraal was situated, just at the first dawn of day, the march was continued in solemn silence. As we entered the defile it was perceived that at the opposite extremity a hill stretched across, admitting a pass on either side; the party therefore divided into three companies in order to possess all the passes; and they again closed together slowly towards the hill, at the foot of which the horde was supposed to lie. A Hottentot, having ascended one of the heights, waved his hat as a signal of discovery, and then pointed to the spot where the horde was situated. We instantly set off on full gallop, and in a moment found ourselves in the middle of the kraal. Day was but just beginning to break; and by the faint light I could discover only a few straw-mats, bent each between two sticks, into a semicircular form; but our ears were stunned with a horrid scream like the war-hoop of savages; the shrieking of women and the cries of children proceeded from every side. I rode up with the commandant and another farmer, both of whom fired upon the kraal. I immediately expressed to the former my very great surprise that he, of all others, should have been the first to break a condition which he had solemnly promised to observe, and that I had expected from him a very different kind of conduct. "Good God!" he exclaimed, "have you not seen a shower of arrows falling among us?" I certainly had seen neither arrows nor people, but had heard enough to pierce the hardest heart; and I peremptorily insisted that neither he nor any of his party should fire another shot. In justification of their conduct they began to search on the ground for the arrows, a search in which they were encouraged to continue, in order to give the poor wretches a little time to scramble away among the detached fragments of rocks and the shrubbery that stood on the side of the heights. On their promises I could place no sort of dependance, knowing that, like true sportsmen when game was sprung, they could not withold their fire. Of this I was presently convinced by the report of a musquet on the opposite side of the hill; and, on riding round the point, I perceived a Bosjesman lying dead upon the ground. It appeared that as one of our party, who could speak their language, was endeavouring to prevail upon the savages to come down from the heights, this Bosjesman had stolen close to him behind a rock, and was taking deliberate aim with his drawn bow, which another of the colonists perceiving, levelled his musquet and shot him dead. It had been hoped the affair would happily have been accomplished without the shedding of human blood, and that the views of the expedition would have met with no interruption from an accident of such a nature. They soon perceived, however, that there was no attempt to pursue them up the heights, which could easily have been done; but that on the contrary the party had laid down their arms and turned their horses out to graze. Upon this, in a short space of time, several little children came down upon the plain. Among these we distributed some biscuits and other trifles, and then suffered them to return: presently afterwards the women and young girls, to the number of thirty or forty, came towards us, not without symptoms of fear. These being treated in the same manner, were sent back to desire their husbands would also come down in order to receive a present of tobacco. The men, however, had less confidence in the Christians than the women. They hovered a long time round the summit of the hill, doubting what step they should take; and the women had gone and returned, at least a dozen times, before they were able to prevail upon one man to descend; and when at last he ventured to come down, he approached us half-laughing, half-crying, trembled and acted just like a frightened child. A large piece of tobacco was immediately given to him, and he was sent back to his companions to let them know there was also a present for each of them. Three others mustered resolution to come down to us, but no more chose to venture themselves. The manner indeed in which their village was attacked was certainly not calculated to inspire them with much confidence. On the contrary, it was so directly hostile as perfectly to justify their shooting a volley of arrows among us, which was afterwards found to be the case, as the commandant had asserted. The conclusion of the business, however, must have appeared to them very different from what, on former occasions, they had always experienced, when those who escaped from immediate death were incessantly pursued and fired upon, and their wives and children seized and carried away into slavery. In this instance they were well treated, and left at full liberty to remain with us or to depart. The women all staid behind; but three of the men accompanied us to the waggons, where they continued for several days. We had wished to speak with the captain or chief of the horde, but they assured us there was no such person; that every one was master of his own family, and acted entirely without control, being at liberty to remain with, or quit, the society as it might best suit them.

WITH A SINGLE HORN

We still continued our search in the kloofs of the mountains, in the hope of meeting with the figure of the unicorn, the peasantry being equally sanguine to convince me of truth of their assertions as I was to gratify curiosity. We came, at length, to a very high and concealed kloof, at the head of which was a deep cave covered in front by thick shrubbery. One of the party mounted up the steep ascent, and having made his way through the close brushwood, he gave us notice that the sides of the cavern were covered with drawings. After clearing away the bushes to let in the light, and examining the numerous drawings, some of which were tolerably well executed, and others caricatures, part of a figure was discovered that was certainly intended as the representation of a beast with a single horn projecting from the forehead. Of that part of it which distinctly appeared, the following is a *fac simile*.

The body and legs had been erased to give place to the figure of an elephant that stood directly before it.

Nothing could be more mortifying than such an accident; but the peasantry, who could form no idea of the consequence I attached to the drawing of such an animal, seemed to enjoy my chagrin. On being told, however, that a thousand, or even five thousand, rixdollars would be given to any one who would produce an original, they stood gaping with open mouths, and were ready to enlist for an expedition behind the Bambos-berg, where some of them were quite certain the animal was to be found. Imperfect as the figure was, it was sufficient to convince me that the Bosjesmans are in the practice of including, among their representations of animals, that of an unicorn; and it also offered a strong argument for the existence of a living original.

In 1851 San on the western edge of the Kalahari told Francis Galton about an animal the size of a gemsbok, with spoor like a zebra and a single horn in the middle of its forehead. "They spoke of it as though they knew of it, but were not at all familiar with it," he said. "It will indeed be strange if, after all, the creature has a real existence."

WILLIAM NOAH

In April 1797 the 43-year-old Noah, a Shropshire carpenter, was condemned to death at the Old Bailey for burglary. The sentence was commuted to transportation for life. He and 299 fellow convicts were embarked on the Hillsborough, ironed sometimes two together on the dark and airless bottom deck, bound for Australia's Botany Bay. The deaths began even before the vessel set sail; at one point on the horrific voyage the despairing prisoners even considered drilling a hole in the bottom of the boat and sinking her. A third of them never made it to Sydney, where the governor described the survivors as "the most miserable and wretched convicts I ever beheld". Extraordinarily enough, Noah managed to keep a journal; he recorded

111

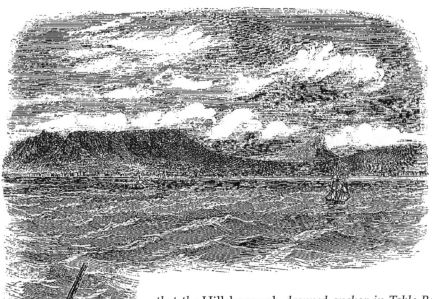

that the Hillsborough *dropped anchor in Table Bay at the end of March 1799, and within days was ordered round to Simon's Town "upon account of the sickness of the convicts". Here the vessel has just arrived in False Bay.*

DEPARTED THIS LIFE

14th April. Fresh mutton came on board. The *Camel*, of 44 guns, came in from England, loaded with bricks, tiles and timber for this place. Saw several fires at the top of the mountains, but could only imagine that they were made by Hottentots.

15th April. Captain on shore. Departed this life William Scofield and James Martin. This convict had been in the Guards. He was a gentle young man and was cast for death for burglarious breaking open a house in Tothill Street, and had permission from the Duke of Portland's office for his wife to accompany him to Botany Bay, and was left to bemoan his loss.

16th April. The Commandant gave permission to take the two corpses ashore and interred as decent as could be. Convicts received fresh mutton and beef, a happy relief having upwards of a hundred ill and some very bad. They now began to die very fast for want of nourishment, and are so far exhausted that care was now too late. Before we left we lost upwards of seventy poor souls, most of them fine hearty young men.

17th April. Unloading coals brought from England. Several convicts single-ironed. Captain surprised at seeing so many of us out of irons, and ordered the Doctor to get us ironed as fast as possible.

19th April. Departed this life John Craig and Edward Bailey, who were taken on shore and buried.

20th April. Employed on coals as before. Departed this life Edward Friend. Doctor ashore burying the dead, for which they charge 3/- a man with a strict order to dig the graves 6 foot deep from the wolves that ravage the graves.

21st April. Getting coals out. Arrived two Danish East Indiamen, one with 600 troops on board.

23rd April. Departed this life Thos. Smith and Richard Little, alias James.

24th April. Mrs Martin, wife of the convict lately deceased went ashore with the Captain, having liberty to return to England as servant with a lady going home. Doctor on shore burying dead, and on his return several convicts unshackled being sick.

25th April. Employed as before. Departed this life John Blundell and Robert Wiltshire. In the evening we had a desperate gale.

26th April. Departed this life John King. Doctor ashore burying the dead.

27th April. Captain Collins the Commandant came on board to look into the state of the sick. So many men dying alarmed this small town. The poop was cleaned, and the men ordered to walk it as long as they could, not having 50 convicts well. Departed this life John Billinghurst.

28th April. Getting ready for sea, 20 seamen having liberty. Departed this life W.G. Gascoyne. This convict was a gentleman officer, and relation to some great man of that name. Was transported at Bath with a Note to a great amount being found in his possession, belonging to a gentleman who was playing him at cards. He died in his 34th year, and was taken out to the mouth of the harbour, then thrown overboard for fear of the Captain being further interrogated. Not long after his body was thrown up on shore. Such is the uncertainty of our existence when doomed by offending the laws of our Mother Country.

CHAPTER THREE

1800 to 1830

With descriptions of a pretty good breakfast,
a display of bare bums, a strange method
of getting rid of flies, Kleinveld's loss of
his trousers, a loving father's reunion
with his son, the marital problems of a Xhosa king,
and men who change into jackals and lions.

WILLEM PARAVICINI DI CAPELLI

Following the Peace of Amiens in 1802 the Cape was handed back to the Dutch, and the administration at The Hague, now styling itself the Batavian Republic, appointed Jan Willem Janssens as governor. One of his first acts was a tour of the interior, which had been unsettled by armed clashes with and among the Xhosa, a Khoikhoi rebellion, and discontent among the farmers. His aide-de-camp, a young artillery captain named Willem Paravicini di Capelli, kept both the official journal of the expedition – quoted here – and his own personal diary. Paravicini di Capelli, the son and grandson of artillery generals in the Dutch army, was intelligent and lively, with a sense of humour – the ideal foil for the melancholic Janssens. As reflected in his writing, the young man also took a keen interest in his surroundings. "Our journal is becoming so long that I think it will never be read," the governor noted in a letter during the journey. They travelled through the southern and Eastern Cape as far as the Kat River, then north through Graaff-Reinet to the Orange River. Paravicini di Capelli was recalled to Holland before the British recaptured the Cape in 1806. As a lieutenant-colonel in Napoleon's Grand Army, he led a battalion in the disastrous 1812 invasion of Russia, surviving frostbite and capture by the enemy. By the time he retired in 1834, he was a major-general in the Dutch army and chief of staff of artillery – with a son following in his footsteps.

Governor Janssens

THE MAJESTY OF THE THUNDER
Emerging from the Langkloof.

After resting here for two hours we pursued our way, the sky promised us a speedy change in the weather that had so far been so good to us, the sky became overcast with dark clouds and before we had ridden half an hour, one of the heaviest thundershowers overtook us, accompanied by torrents of rain and hail; the high mountain tops being covered and obscured by the approaching weather were completely black, the light sombre and grey, heavy thunder-claps made the earth under us shake tremendously, while swift sulphurous lightning bolts lit the dark summits of the rocks with fire, the massive and immeasurably high crags gave a heavy roaring echo of the falling thunder-claps, the sky around and above us had the purple glow and heat of a coal fire, and was lit at 4, 5 places simultaneously by long shooting bolts; every one of the company saying he had never seen such weather in Europe, and that it defied imagination. The rain made us almost wet through, when the storm passed a good wind came up accompanied by showers of rain; we hurried to a farm (it was that of Jacobus Vermaak, now deserted), we arrived $^1\!/_2$ past 5 at the homestead which consisted of two houses not of the best, in which we established our night quarters in a large room, where the light came from the door, yet this was no obstacle to spreading our mattresses in it and sleeping soundly. The dry clothes made us forget the wetness of the storm, but not the majesty of the thunder and lightning.

The colonist Dirk van Reenen, who travelled with them and kept his own journal, also recorded the storm: "The General, riding ahead on horseback, was undaunted and was so fascinated by the magnificent sight of the lightning flashes, so sudden-ly followed by the awful peals of thunder, that for a considerable time he stood still in the heavy rain to contemplate this spectacle, without thinking of seeking shelter in the wagon, which had a good covering."

ALL SORTS OF GRIMACES
We made a good fire in the camp, not far from it the Hottentot leaders and wagon driver had theirs, they played at cards in their manner, which con-sists of very small pieces of wood, which are held between the fingers. I shall write down here as much as I was able to know and understand about their game. As many as there are, sit on their haunches around the fire, each one holding one of the little pieces of wood mentioned above in the hand; the one half of the players at the start in the right, and the other in the left hand. The most dextrous then starts with all sorts of gesticulations and stripped half naked to talk unbelievably fast in the Hottentot language, and to switch his wood from one hand to the other, making all sorts of gri-maces, bending movements, turns and comic contortions and so on to the one sitting opposite him, who does the same; after continuing to do this for a long time with great agility, one of the two suddenly shows his hand with the wood; if the other holds it in the wrong hand he is beaten but the game is not ended. The winner must have defeated the entire row opposite him to be triumphant, this causes them all to speak at the same time, they con-tort themselves, stamp, and adopt the most laughable postures; if a man loses, one of his previous victories does not count any more, so that the game can last very long. The person who has lost to the whole row, his wood is burned with much gesturing and gurgling of the throat, this is what we could understand of it; the game animates them strongly, so that gradually they remove their clothes, to bend and somersault more flexibly.

HOLDING HIS EARS
In the Eastern Cape, Janssens tried unsuccessfully to broker a settlement between

Janssens meets the Xhosa chief Ngqika on the Kat River.

warring factions of the Rharhabe, or western Xhosa. *The chiefs in the Zuurveld (who included Cungwa of the Gqunukhwebe, the "Conga" mentioned here), were understandably suspicious of his motives, and refused to go anywhere near his encampment at Fort Frederick in Algoa Bay.*

Thursday the 19 May the emissary of Conga was presented with some trifles that were very attractive to him, and was asked if he wished to ride the following day in the company of the governor to his chief, which he accepted eagerly, after which the burger Stolts took him for a walk. The Asiatic ship the Verwachting attracted his attention somewhat, the approaching chaloupes which were debarking goods, and rapidly rising and falling in the strong surf, filled him with wonder; on the offer, that they made to him to go on board, he declined, remarking that he did not like to go over the water. When he passed the barracks, he saw the troops eating, which pleased him greatly, as did fort Frederick. The governor asked him, if he wanted to see and hear the cannons he was admiring being fired, which he wanted, but without signs of fear, at the shot he suddenly jumped up, whistled with a very long breath, holding his ears looking in the direction the cannon pointed, he asked what distance one could shoot, and how many people one could hit at the same time; at this an indication of a distance far past the ship was given to him, and a hundred people mentioned (that could be killed in one shot), at which he showed no surprise. The governor asking him if he wanted to hear another cannon shot, he declined it with much gesturing and bowing. At his return from the fort he went again into the barracks, and remarked that the Caffer chiefs also had people, who lacked nothing, but that this must be an extremely powerful chief, to have so many and such a rich people under him, that he did not understand how everyone could find their own things among so many goods. The shiny buttons of the jaegers particularly attracted his notice, and he said that if everybody gave him just one, he would have a great number and they would also have many left over. The gold epaulettes of the governor attracted his attention; he inspected them closely and touched them, he whistled just as when he saw the beautiful outfits of the jaegers in the barracks. He asked for brandy with the explanation that nothing gave him more pleasure; he said in broken Dutch: ["] it too nice for me." The name of this Kaffer who appeared to have so much judgement is Nacabanée, his rank with the chief Conga is the same as what the colonists call heemraad; he is a man of generously tall stature, middle age, well-made and with an assured presence, he has four wives and said, now he had bought them all, he did not have many cattle left.

Van Reenen said the Xhosa did not show the least fear when the cannon was fired "but simply requested that it should be discontinued because their ears could not stand the din".

HEINRICH LICHTENSTEIN

Lichtenstein, a German doctor and naturalist, came out to the Cape in 1802 as tutor to governor Janssens' son. He amassed a wealth of specimens and information during a six-month tour of the colony in 1803-04 and a journey to the Tswana in 1805. On his return to Germany he began a history of the Cape, and published a two-volume account of his travels as well as papers on subjects as diverse as the biology of the ostrich, a dysentery epidemic among troops badly quartered outside Cape Town, and African languages.

A HUNDRED EXPERIMENTS
In the Karoo, somewhere near present-day Sutherland – which can still be a very cold place.

When we arose in the morning, and went out of our tents, we found the whole surface of the ground white with hoar-frost; a thick fog was spread over the plain, and the water in our saucepans was frozen as thick as the little finger. To most of our company this was a pefectly new sight; and the astonishment of our slaves, who had never seen any thing like it, either at Mozambique or in the Cape Town, afforded us infinite entertainment. It was utterly incomprehensible to them how they could take water in their hands as a solid mass. They made a hundred experiments with it, holding it up against the light, sticking it in the fire, endeavouring to bite and to chew it: they were just like a group of children.

OUR JOVIAL YOUNG MEN
Our business, while we rested here, was confined to writing down our journals; to little excursions about the country; and to some domestic labours for the advantage of the whole party. As night closed in, the whole company assembled round a large fire near the camp, and weighed, in common, the hardships and dangers which had been surmounted, and those which the following day might bring. Not far from us several small fires had been made, and the slaves were occupied in preparing our supper. The Hottentots, more accustomed to the want of wood, were content rather to suffer somewhat from cold, than take the trouble of collecting bushes to make a fire. We found them even sleeping near our fire, and permitted our jovial young men to make a noise and frighten them, that they might recollect they ought to be upon the watch. While they were sitting half asleep, our wags went slily to a little distance, and shot a couple of arrows from a Bosjesman's bow. No sooner did the slumberers hear the twang of the spring, and perceive the shafts falling by them, than they sprang up hastily, almost tumbling over each other, to get their arms from the waggon. They were received there with a loud burst of laughter from the people about.

For this joke they afterwards took ample revenge. As the same young men were amusing themselves one dark evening with setting fire to some dried reeds, about two hundred paces from our camp, and were vastly delighted with the cracking and sparkling they made, some of the Hottentots stole directly behind the reeds, and, with the shell of an ostrichs'

egg, imitated the roaring of a lion so naturally, repeating it three times, every time as if nearer than the former, that at length the young men, recollecting that these reeds were a favourite haunt of the lions, ran away, screaming violently, and came almost breathless to the camp.

A TRIFLING PIECE OF DECEIT
Lichtenstein is here surrounded by curious Tlhaping at their capital Dithakong, near present-day Kuruman.

It was somewhat extraordinary, that notwithstanding the abundant opportunities afforded for stealing, and the impossibility of keeping all our things out of the way, or watching them, that scarcely any thing was ever missed, except now and then some pieces of meat or other articles of food. A trifling piece of deceit, which I myself experienced in the course of this day, was almost the only one of which they were guilty towards us. I had given a woman a little piece of tobacco in exchange for an ivory ring, when another, who was standing by, and who had for some time been begging for a little tobacco very earnestly, and who saw two more pieces in my hand, again urged my giving them to her as a present. I, however, represented that it would be unjust, when I had required payment from the other woman, to let her have any gratuitously; but if she would give the same price I was ready to part with my tobacco. An ivory ring was immediately produced by her, which I put in my pocket, and paid her for it; this was no sooner done than a third was offered me, for which I gave my last piece of tobacco. I now withdrew from the crowd, in possession, as I supposed, of my three rings, but when I examined my pocket I found only one: it had been twice taken thence for the purpose of being resold to me.

A SHEW OF COURTESY
In 1804, as the threat of a second English invasion loomed large, Lichtenstein joined a group of officers, including Paravicini di Capelli, on a trip to Swellendam to establish a gunpowder factory, a magazine and storehouses for provisions.

On the seventh of September we proceeded farther down the river Zonder-end, crossing it several times, and halted at length at the house of our friend Holzhaussen, the son-in-law of the Postholder Theunissen. As we could not all be accommodated here, some were obliged to go for the night to a neighbouring farm. It happened, however, as is not often the case, that this visit was not agreeable to the master of the house, who had therefore absented himself with his wife. The two gentlemen having, however, had some intimation of the disposition of these people, made no ceremony, but quietly took possession of the house in the true military style; and ordered the slaves to prepare them a good supper from the stores that it contained. This was attended with the consequence they expected, for the master of the house now came forth from his concealment, making at least a shew of courtesy and hospitality. The wife, however, who on our former journey had refused to let her house be made a lodging-place for some of our people, notwithstanding the change in her husband's behaviour, could not be brought to anything like civility, but continued, to the very moment of our departure, altogether rude and ungracious. A hint upon this subject, which she received from Captain Paravicini, gave occasion to a truly comic scene, since she chose to ascribe all her ill-humour to her husband, because she had wanted to prevent his talking against the government and the Governor. Not being disposed to interfere in this matter, we left the loving couple in a most warm matrimonial dispute.

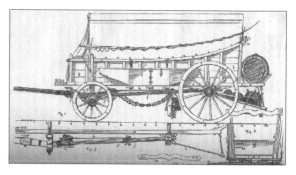

On the return journey the entire party spent the night at Holtzhaussen's, and …

His gruff uncivil neighbour, was now, as a punishment for his former want of complaisance, obliged to furnish oxen for a relay to our waggons. He found, however, a means peculiar to himself, of giving vent to his ill-humour, even under this punishment. In harnessing the oxen to a waggon, at two of them, who were called *Holland* and *Lieutenant,* he swore and cursed most furiously, while he did nothing but praise and caress a third, which had the name of *England.* Nobody, however, thought proper to indulge him with taking the slightest notice of this: so far, indeed, were we from being disposed to any thing like dudgeon upon the subject, that the humour of the thing somewhat reconciled us to him.

ANONYMOUS

The British did come back, and re-occupied the Cape – permanently this time – after a one-sided exchange of cannon balls at Blouberg on the eastern shore of Table Bay in January 1806. This unidentified English gastronome, here writing to his mother, is describing a brief stopover at the Cape on his way to India at the end of that year.

PRETTY GOOD BREAKFASTS

First thing we had to do was to find out an Inn and order dinner which we did soon, and then having heard before I left the ship that fortunately there was the "Georgiana" packet going to sail next day for England I hunted out for the Post Office which I soon found in the Castle and deposited my packet for which I thought I paid a great deal which was 5/6d as the weight was equal to eleven letters and it is 6d a letter.

The next thing I hired a horse and rode to Camp to see Captain Hulton of the 21st Light Dragoons and found him at his tent, but I should have mentioned before I set out we had a luncheon of cold mutton, new bread and some Cape wine – Memorandum Nasty stuff – and beautiful water. I rode to Camp which was four miles and a half and as soon as I got there I had another luncheion of poached eggs and cold ham and some excellent claret and was so much pressed to dine there could hardly get away, but as I had engaged to dine with my friends at Cape Town at last got away after having promised to dine there Christmas Day, if I should stay so long on shore.

Got back at 3 o'clock and walked about town until 4 o'clock and then sat down to dinner to some very fine fish, beautiful leg of mutton, potatoes, carrots, turnips, fresh beans and cucumber etc., apricot tarts and apricot jam puffs. After dinner only then on the 23rd December we had oranges, walnuts, apricots, figs, almonds, raisons, mulberrys, strawberrys, peaches in great abundance. Every apricot I ate I thought of you and the apricots I brought you from Lawrence's in my pocket and they all smashed in such a horrible mess.

After dinner walked in the Company's public gardens (something in the style of Kensington Gardens as far as being The Mall) till dark and went back and had coffee and tea, new bread and very good butter and sat chatting till 12 o'clock.

The next morning got up and breakfasted at 9 o'clock for the breakfasts are not as in England; at their hotels they are public as at Harrogate, one large table with a servant at each end to make tea and coffee etc. We had tea, coffee, hot beef steaks, cold ham, cold tongue, eggs, turnips, radishes, common radishes, hot rolls, good butter, apricots, strawberrys and cream, buttered toast, pretty good breakfasts, I think.

PETRONELLA CAMYN

Literary daughter of a Swellendam landdrost, Camyn visited the Cango caves in 1808 with a large party of companions. Her account was published 16 years later in Het Nederduitsch Zuid-Afrikaansch Tydschrift *under the sobriquet "een Kaapsch meisje". Here they have just passed the outer entrance to the caverns.*

VAULTS OF NIGHT

Having reached this point, we breathed as in a dark night of terror and doubt, where deathly quiet and silent majesty reigned. Doubt overcame me, while an anxious sweat covered my face, however much I tried to keep courage alive.

An unpleasant smell, here poisoned the air, and this stink, which would affect even a coarse female Hottentot, coupled with the close heat that one encountered here, and the cloud of dust that our company spread, obliged us to fortify ourselves with strong scent-water against fainting, which would certainly have been our lot had we had none. Every step we took on this sandy soil, resounded with a hollow noise through the rumbling earth, and each word one uttered, bounced muttering back off the rock faces, with an echo, that grew fainter and fainter, until it eventually vanished completely. After we had proceeded in this way for an estimated one hundred and fifty paces, (leaving aside a number of deep and shallower windings in the path, in which, according to the tracks we discovered, many tigers, porcupines, dassies and other wild animals had set foot,) we came unexpectedly to the opening, the size of an ordinary house door. Here the necessary apparatus, ropes as well as wooden ladders and a chair (for use of the ladies,) were put in order. The fact that the weakness of my sex dominated here, was apparent from the dismay that seized me at the sight of the preparations being made for the execution of our descent into these gloomy vaults of night. I would certainly have shrunk back, had it not been for the cowardly conduct of one man, who at that moment saying to me – "Oh, Heavens! young miss, I am becoming very afraid, one of our company has already fled, and if it could be done without danger to life, I would follow him; this cavern has not been visited for a year, who can assure us, that we will not be surprised by a tiger?" inspired me with heroic ardour, and I recovered my previous courage, to overcome my feminine weaknesses to his shame. Everything having eventually been set in readiness, as a precaution we sent some burning candles to the bottom, then fastened the chair as carefully as possible, placed the ladder in the most suitable way, and began to descend one after another. The spectacle of this so shocked my emotions, that I almost thought aloud:

> Will from this awful hole
> The cheerful meeting again come forth?
> Imagination! why then am I
> Murdered by fear?

Because truly the view downwards to the men who were walking around with the light, was so alarming that one would almost fancy that one had been transported from among humankind to a ghost world, just as an overheated imagination, assisted by many writers of spirit and ghost stories, often paints it.

Eventually my turn also came to be lowered into the depths; – being above terror and fear, I bravely placed myself on the chair, held onto what I could, and like this descended gradually, until I reached a rock, where it was less steep and somewhat uneven.

With the aid of good guides, who had positioned themselves on this protruberance, I climbed carefully off, until I eventually reached the ladder, by which I came to the bottom, and was as if transported into another existence.

Here we found ourselves, as far as could be seen, instead of being in a cave, in a spacious hall, which was at a guess more than 80 feet high and wide; as beautiful as ever my eyes had beheld, and lovelier than the wildest imagination might conceive; how less equipped then is my pen, so weak and impelled by ignorance, to properly portray its excellence. Here even the God-denying freethinker, ashamed of his senselessness, must renounce this deep-rooted false faith and with heart and voice confess: Jehova! I acknowledge your almighty power: yes, – You live and reign in Eternity!

The rapture continues with psalms amid the stalagmites as she enters chambers with formations "spattered with silver and woven with millions of pearls and jewels". She and her companions break off translucent stalactites as souvenirs before stumbling back into the sunshine "which", she declares, "I would not exchange for all the treasures of the earth".

JOHN GRAHAM

The Palmiet River, on the route from Cape Town to the eastern districts, had no bridge in 1809, and the owner of the ferry appears to have expected people of colour to get wet rather than trouble him for the boat. Colonel Graham, commander of a corps of Khoikhoi troops, confessed to his diary that he could not avoid feeling an "inward satisfaction" at the spirit his men showed here.

THEIR BARE BREACH

The owner of the boat made a bitter complaint against some of our Hottentot soldiers who were going on pass who he said had not only been extremely unruly and troublesome in his house by insisting on having wine etc but which he allowed they had paid for – but also and what indeed seemed to offend his feelings still more they had carried his boat to the opposite side of the River where having arrived in safety they were ill mannered enough to draw up in a line on the top of the bank and expose their Bare Breach for the inspection of the half caste gentleman above alluded to.

WILLIAM BURCHELL

Spurned in love by an English rose, the botanist Burchell diverted his energies to a journey through the interior of the colony. It lasted almost four years, from June 1811 to April 1815, and established his reputation as the greatest of the score or so of scientific travellers in southern Africa of that era. His friend James Alexander described him as "one of the most painstaking, industrious, and intelligent of travellers". He took more than 60,000 natural history specimens and about 500 drawings back to England.

SOME SUPERSITITIOUS NOTION
Encamped on what he called the "Ky-Gariep", but was in fact the Vaal River, he was visited by a group of San living nearby.

By the temptation of a good piece of tobacco, I induced one of them to sit quietly for a quarter of an hour, while I drew his *portrait*. The whole affair was quite unintelligible to him and his countrymen, none certainly ever having seen a portrait taken before. Observing them look very serious all the while I was drawing, I began to fear that some supersititious notion might lead them to imagine I was practising sorcery, to injure the kraal, or to cause the death of the man; for tales of this kind had often been related

to me. After it was finished, and the tobacco paid, I explained that in my own country it was esteemed a mark of great friendship and good will, to desire to possess the likeness of another person; and that this was the reason of my wishing to have his: that my having given him so much tobacco, was a proof of it, and that I should give him a little more, together with the drawing, which he was to  keep in his hut, to remind him of his friend, the white man. On saying which I left them, and retired to my waggon, as if to fetch the tobacco, when I tore the drawing out of my book, and quickly made a copy on the next leaf, and bringing it before the party, tore it out, and gave it to him. With all this they seemed perfectly satisfied, and went away persuaded that the matter was exactly as it had been explained to them. In this little affair, it was certainly I who ran the greater risk of incurring harm; for had the man died shortly afterwards, or met with any accident or sickness, my drawing would have been pronounced to be the cause, and myself devoted to the revenge of his relations, and a poisoned arrow have been my fate.

Almost suffocated
At a farmhouse north of Graaff-Reinet.

The rooms in the principal house being but three (that is, one in the middle in which the family sit and take their meals, and one bed-room at each end) a visitor could not be accommodated with a chamber to himself. A bed was therefore prepared for me, in the same apartment with the meester and his three scholars.

This tutor was in every respect, qualified for finishing their education, and for completing them for Dutch farmers; for a man who does not *smoke*, is a rare phenomenon in this colony, and is generally looked upon by the boors as an imperfect creature; a disadvantage which I myself laboured under, but which, for want of any natural talent for this accomplishment, I was never able to overcome. I might perhaps have partly retrieved my character in their estimation, could I even have shown them that I enjoyed it in taste; or even in smell, by exhibiting both nostrils blackened, and hermetically closed, with that elegant and fashionable dirt, called in England, *snuff*: but in both these arts, unfortunately, I was equally deficient.

This tutor, then, as soon as he was in bed, placed the candle by his side, as I at first thought and hoped, to extinguish it, that I might be left to close my eyes for that sleep which nature demanded after two days of fatigue with little intermediate rest. But finding that the light still remained, I turned my head towards it, and to my double mortification, beheld the *meester* lying very quietly, with a short crooked German pipe hanging from one corner of his mouth, while from the other, arose clouds of smoke rapidly following each other, till the room was filled with the fume of tobacco, and myself almost suffocated.

At length when that pipe was finished, I had some little respite, but it was only while he was occupied in filling it again. In this interval, finding that I was not asleep, a circumstance not much to be wondered at, he began to relate to me some of his *adventures* in foreign parts; and these reminiscences afforded him so much satisfaction, that he allowed himself to talk and smoke in alternate fits, so that the second pipe, unfortunately, lasted twice as long as the first. But, as it would ill become a guest so hospitably received, to interrupt his entertainers' enjoyments, I endured it all with perfect patience till the last; though, at an hour when most mortals desire to be "lulled into sweet oblivion," his candle, his pipe, and his conversation, kept three of my senses in a state of continued irritation.

By degrees the smoking became fainter; the anecdotes of Malacca, Batavia, and Moccha, were at length all exhausted; he stretched forth his arm to put out the candle; and bade me *Goodnight*. But the long-wished-for hour of sleep was not yet come; and it now fell to his turn to be annoyed. Scarcely had we begun to doze, when repeated claps of the most violent thunder, roused us again; and flashes of lightning glaring through the window, gave us opportunities of beholding each other once more.

In a few minutes after this, the sound of the rain out of doors, pouring down in torrents, made me, notwithstanding the tobacco smoke, consider myself fortunate in being at such a time under the *shelter of a roof*. Presently, I heard the meester start up, and, with furious rattling, begin dragging his bed, with the frame which supported it, from one side of the room to the other. He cried out, in a mixed tone of lamentation and surprize, that the rain was running down upon him in a stream, from the *groot gat in het dak*; and truly enough; for on looking upwards, I saw, what I had not noticed before, a "great hole in the roof," just above the place whence he had so long been issuing his fumigations, and his anecdotes of Malacca, Batavia, and Moccha. When I saw this, I began to regret that the storm had not commenced an hour or two sooner.

JAMES EWART

Lieutenant Ewart was with the 93rd Highlanders at the Cape from 1811 to 1814. He spent a month's leave travelling with two brother officers north of Cape Town as far as the Piketberg area, enjoying the hospitality of local farmers, who he uncharitably described as "amazingly fat".

GENTLY FROM HIS HEAD
The best trait in the character of the Boor is his acknowledged hospitality, a virtue which may have developed from necessity, for when traversing the almost trackless region over which they are dispers'd, they must depend entirely upon each other.

A Boor on entering the house of another methodicaly puts his left hand to the back part of his hat which he raises gently from his head, at the same time stretching

124

out his right hand to seize the proffered one of the landlord which having shook, he in the same manner salutes all the males of the family. He then (beginning with the landlady) kisses all the females, which ceremony being ended, he takes a seat and joins in the conversation, which generaly turns on the object of his journey, if to Cape Town, what he expects to get for the produce he is carrying there, or if returning, how many rixdollars he procured. When dinner, or other meal is announced, he draws to the table with the rest, an invitation to do so being thought unnecessary. When he has finished his repast and his horses or bullocks again yoked, he takes his departure with the same formality as when he enter'd.

So ignorant are the Boors of the rules of society or the ways of the world, that they naturaly judge of every other people by themselves, and consequently expect the same freedom and unreserve in strangers as they use towards each other, indeed so deep is this ignorance rooted, that should a person unacquainted with their customs, enter one of their houses with the formality he has been accustomed to in the civilized world, instead of taking a seat and asking for what he wants, his good breeding would be construed into pride, and the chance is that were he ever so fatigued or hungry, he would be allowed to depart without either rest or refreshment.

JOHN CAMPBELL

Campbell, a director of the London Missionary Society who looked rather like Dr Dolittle, visited South Africa twice and made impressive journeys to the interior in 1813 and 1819-20 to inspect the society's stations. The names he bestowed on geographical features, such as Shrubsole Fountain and the Society Hills, have faded into merciful obscurity, as has the verse that the landscape inspired. An example:

John Campbell

> *I'm far from what I call my home,*
> *In regions where no white men come;*
> *Where wilds and wilder men are found,*
> *Who never heard the gospel sound.*

Incidentally, on the first trip he kept a meticulous tally of the creatures he and his attendants killed on the way, including five buffalo and 17 scorpions.

As if we had all been dead

Thermometer at sun rise, 86. At noon in the shade 101, which was rather alarming, as noon is never the hottest part of the day. A breeze of wind rendered it more tolerable than it must otherwise have been. The common flies were numerous and troublesome; the perspiration on the face attracted them, and though driven away, they returned in an instant, walking over the whole face, especially about the eyes. They likewise rested on the inky part of my pen, so that I could not see what I wrote; to drive them away was useless, it was only making way for successors. The lowness of the ground, which was surrounded by hills, increased the heat. At half past three the thermometer stood at 102 when completely shaded from the sun. My silver snuff box in my pocket felt as if lately taken out of a fire, though I sat under covert of the tent; all the water was warm, and our butter turned into oil. Our dogs, though screened from the rays of the sun, lay breathing quick, with their mouths open, and their tongues hanging out, as if in a high fever. My ink, though mixed with water, got thick in a few minutes. All was silence around, all employed in sheltering themselves from the sun's scorching rays, in the best way they could. The crows were walking about our waggons as if we had all been dead.

TEMPORARY RELIEF
The flies are very numerous and very troublesome all the year. They [the Nama] have a strange method of obtaining temporary relief from them. They rub milk over their sheep, and placing them before the door, drive out the flies, which instantly light upon the sheep whose backs are wet with milk, when they are driven to a distance.

THINGS OF NO USE
Many of the Caffres travel into the countries which surround them, sometimes to plunder, at other times merely to gratify curiosity, and to bring back any thing they judge useful or curious. They always travel on foot, carrying no more than their cloak to sleep in during the night. On their return they entertain their friends by relating the most minute circumstance that happened – where and what they ate, where and what kind of water they drank, and every thing they saw or heard, and he who does not do so is despised. When any of them have visited Cape-town, on their return they used to describe how the people dressed, how they washed their mouths, their houses, &c. but never imitated or endeavoured to introduce any of their customs. They expressed surprise at many things which they saw, but never think the white men are more wise or skilful than themselves, for they suppose they could do all that the white men do if they chose. They consider reading and writing as insignificant things of no use.

HEART OF STONE
From his second voyage to the Cape: in July 1819 he visited the Eastern Cape missions, including Bethelsdorp at Algoa Bay, where he had a disciplinary matter to deal with. The missionary James Read had been setting a bad example to his flock by two-timing his Khoikhoi wife Sarah. Campbell did not believe white missionaries should marry women of colour, let alone commit adultery with them. "They [the Khoikhoi] view and treat him as become one of themselves, he loses his authority, and all his wife's friends drag from him as much as they can get. I am convinced such marriages are obstructions to the best interests of the heathen." Dr P. is John Philip, newly appointed superintendent of LMS missions in South Africa, who accompanied Campbell from Cape Town.

At 3 O clock PM the Church assembled – began by praise and prayer – Mr Barker, their present pastor, then read to them the parts of scripture referred to last night, with some remarks, pointing out their duty in obedience

126

to Christ, which, however painful, they were called upon to do, mentioning the sin of Mr Read which was of public notoriety. When they were formally called upon [as] a church, (after some apropriate remarks by Dr P.) Samson a member asked to be heard, but the loud crying of every Hottentot there, rendered it impossible for any mans voice to be heard – All continued for about half an hour giving vent to the most pungent sorrow. When quiet was a little restored, and some returned who ran from the meeting Samson made a most affecting speach. He said he believed it was right to cut off brother Read but they could not but feel in their hearts when they did it a man who had stood between us & bullets & assagais – a man who was a father to us, and taught us the word of God when we were beasts, heathens; who bore with our ignorance and hardness, and treated us like his children – here he burst into a flood of tears and was instantly joined by the whole Church, men and women.

When called upon to rise, to express by that action their detestation of the sin and assent to his exclusion, not one could move out of their seats. After waiting long for an end to their weeping, they were asked to remain in their seats who approved of the exclusion, and those who did not, to rise. All continued to sit, so it was told them they were unanimous for his exclusion, to which no one objected.

Sabina Pretorius, with whom Mr Read had the illicit connection; and Mr Corner missionary for the same crime were also cut off. As a whole, it was the most affecting scene I have ever witnessed – A heart of stone would have felt for the poor Hottentots. I hope it will be blessed to the excluded, I have no doubt but it will be useful to the Church. I was at one time afraid their affecting to Read would blind them as to their duty to Christ, but the truth, the will of Christ, so clearly set down in the new testament, gained a compleat victory, contrary to their feelings they performed their duty.

THE IDEA OF WASHING
An encounter north of present-day Beaufort West, on his way to the northern limits of the colony in 1820.

I advised the Bush people, who were extremely dirty, to wash themselves sometimes in the adjoining pools. They were much diverted with the idea of washing, but seemed unable to comprehend what end could be answered by it.

Dithakong

SO MUCH OF IT
On the way to Dithakong.

In the morning, though no more rain had fallen, the weather still appeared gloomy; the three holes near the waggons were filled with water to the brim, containing sufficient for man and beast. About midday the rain again descended, and continued for two or three hours. During the

rain, Morokey, the Mashow rain-maker, came and sat down in the tent, and after remaining silent for some time, he told us, with much seriousness, and in a tone of voice as if what he said was unquestionably true, that this rain was his, but he had not intended so much of it. I said he must know, in his own mind, that he had no more hand in causing the rain which had fallen than the waggons had. Instead of making a reply he asked for some snuff.

WITH A LOUD VOICE
Domestic life in Dithakong.

Should a wife not give her husband what he considers enough for supper, he takes his stand before the house and proclaims her conduct, with a loud voice, to the whole neighbourhood. The wife, on receiving chastisement from her husband, repairs to the same place, and publishes the whole story to the neighbours. When a man has lost any thing he makes it known in the same manner, by which means the article is frequently recovered.

STARS UPON IT
A Tlhaping chief, Moeketse, told the missionary of a cattle-raiding expedition his people made against the Mampuru, who lived far to the north, on the other side of the Kalahari desert. The Tlhaping had heard of the Mampuru only through their neighbours, the Kgalakgadi, who were in turn relaying information from San. The raiders captured barely 150 animals, and were forced to eat most of them on the long trek back. The "Great Water" mentioned here might have been Lake Ngami, then an expanse of fresh water in northern Botswana, but now dry more often than not. In Campbell's orthography, Dithakong becomes Lattakoo.

It occupied only two moons in going, travelling every day from sunrise to sunset; and three moons returning, being retarded by the cattle they had captured. They had taken some pack-oxen with them to carry food, but obtained so little to eat upon the road, that after their provisions were exhausted, they were obliged to kill the oxen, and all these were consumed before they reached their place of destination. The track by which they travelled was interspersed with many mimosa trees from Lattakoo to Kalliharry, and from thence to Mampoor they met with trees that were new to them, resembling the Kurree, or the willow.

Many of the Kalliharry people accompanied them as guides on the road, and to the pools of water. They likewise assisted in plundering the natives of Mampoor. At one part of the road they were ten days without finding any water, using wild water-melons in its stead. On one occasion they came to a pool in which elephants had been standing during the night; they all drank of the water, which occasioned violent sickness. They found a pool in a large cave under a cliff, into which the oxen went and drank; and on the seventeenth day afterwards they came to the Great Water, (or ocean,) of which they were all afraid; it had stars upon it, (perhaps meaning those parts that reflected the sun's rays,) and great waves that ran after them, and then ran back again; they had never seen any such sight before. The water was like a great country that had no end. They saw swarms of locusts fall into the water, which were all drowned. The country was level near the sea, but there were hills at the distance of ten miles.

PIECES OF DIRTY PAPER

The fair mentioned here would have been at Beaufort West. "Matchappee" is Campbell's spelling of baTlhaping.

On reaching Lattakoo we found all the people returned from their four months' journey to the fair at Beaufort in the colony, excepting three Matchappees who had been drowned in crossing the Great Orange River on a raft, as reported to us at Turreehey. There had been great lamentation for them at Lattakoo, and the white men were blamed for advising them to go to that place for beads, none having been obtained there. The raft on which they attempted to cross the Great River was only large enough to carry five persons, yet, contrary to advice, ten crowded upon it with their property. The consequence was that one side of the raft sunk down. Three of the Matchappees were carried away by the strength of the current. However, we were glad to find that Mateebe censured none but the people themselves who had been drowned, and these for going upon the raft contrary to advice and warning. All spoke in commendation of the King of the place, which was the title they gave to Mr. Stockenstrome, the Landdrost of Graaff Reynet. He was present and superintended the market, and had treated them with much kindness, of which they were fully sensible; but they complained of some of the farmers, who had either ridiculed or used them roughly. Their anger, however, was not great, as the Landdrost had desired to be informed if any one treated them ill. The Griquas were also greatly disappointed at not being able to obtain tools, plough-shares, tar for their waggons, or any thing that they wanted. Nothing was to be had but clothing.

It will, probably, be difficult to get the Matchappees to attend the market again, from its great distance, and the disappointment they felt at not obtaining beads, which their hearts are chiefly set upon.

They expected to find every white man in the colony a Missionary, and were surprised when they halted near a farmer's house, that they were not called in to worship. When at Beaufort they wondered to see the farmers sit with their hats on during the time of worship, and some of them throwing small stones at each other; they did not know what to make of this.

When the Matchappees at the fair received paper money for the articles they had to dispose of, they could not be made to understand its use; after farther explanations they supposed they could procure any thing they chose for it, whether the paper was for one, two, or more rix-dollars. Their money being rejected as too little for the articles they wanted, they thought they had been cheated by the persons who had given them the paper, and gave it for any thing they could obtain, despising small pieces of dirty paper.

On their return to Lattakoo, every day some of them were making mock sales, imitating the auctioneer, calling out in the Dutch language his very words, "Once, twice, thrice! Who bids more?" &c., which afforded great amusement to the natives.

WITHOUT A BULLET
South of the Molopo River Campbell's men killed a rhinoceros, the first he had seen, and they and the Tlhaping travelling with them cut it up in anticipation of the evening halt.

A little before we halted, we saw two rhinoceroses running before the waggons. We wounded also a quacha, which was afterwards found dead by Pelangye and his men. They endeavoured to conceal this circumstance from the others. The fact is, they had overheard our Hottentots tell us the evening before that they had severely wounded a quacha, and that he must have died; but daylight being nearly over, they thought it too late to pursue him. Pelangye, a tall, powerful man, who was captain of the Matchappees from Old Lattakoo, clever, and possessed of much cunning, dispatched a party in search of the quacha after midnight, it being clear moon-light. They were successful in finding the animal lying dead, and, on cutting it in pieces, quietly brought it to their temporary inclosure, near the waggons, before the others were awake. However, the others soon discovered what had taken place.

After all had eaten heartily of the rhinoceros's flesh at the fifteen fires, a man from a distant part called aloud, so as to be heard by all, owing to the stillness of the night, "I smell quacha flesh, who has it?" Pelangye hearing the question, and probably knowing that the business was discovered, immediately answered "We have got it." "Where did you get it?" asked the same man with a loud voice. "In the field." "Did you give the Makooa-Shou [the white men] the bullet that was in it?" Had Pelangye acknowledged a bullet to have been in it, this would have proved that it had been shot, and ought to be divided as public property. Perceiving the artfulness of the question, he evaded it by simply answering, "We found it dead in the field." "Ay, ay, dead in the field! Did it die without a bullet?" "There was no bullet." "So we shall now find quachas dead in the field without bullets! shall we?" Here the conversation ended without a direct accusation, as the accuser had no proof to adduce that the quacha was shot, it having been cut in pieces in the field, and perhaps that part of the skin, through which the bullet entered, thrown away. However, all heard the conversation, and considered the transaction to be a nefarious one.

HE FORGOT HIS TROUSERS
Kleinveld was one of Campbell's Khoikhoi servants.

Kleinveld in the evening when it got cold could not find his caross [or] cloak – his whole dress during the journey has been lost one way or other; the dogs eat his shoes in the Mashow country, he forgot his trousers at Griqua town, his cap is he knows not where, and now his last article of clothing, his cloak is also gone, in the Bushman country, he leaves something behind in [e]very land. He has nothing now to leave behind but his skin, yet he seems perfectly indifferent about all his losses, like other Hottentots he cannot be at the trouble to think – he now sleeps in the inside of the tent sack, and seemed fast asleep in less than 5 minutes after he crept into it.

HE GENTLY TAPPED HIS NOSE

Although Muliaily, a Tlhaping, acted as a cattle herder for Campbell on the missionary's return journey from Dithakong in 1820, he appears also to have been an emissary from the Tlhaping chief Mothibê: he and his two countrymen demanded – and got – a meeting with the governor at Cape Town before returning home laden with gifts.

When dining one evening at H.E–'s, Esq., with several officers of the army and their ladies, the dinner being removed, and the table covered with decanters, wine glasses, fruit plates, and with many wax candles, whose brilliant lights were so reflected, by long mirrors reaching from the ceiling to the floor, as almost to change the night into day, one of the company asked me what Muliaily, the man I had brought from Lattakoo, would think of all this finery, were he present. I could not say, but suggested that, as he was not far off, he might be tried.

The man-servant went, and soon brought him. The night being dark, was not a good preparation for entering such a glare of light. On the room door being opened for his admittance, he immediately placed both his hands on his eyes, taking them off several times, and putting them on again, before he moved a step in advance. At length, being able to view what was before him, he looked with astonishment. The first thing that attracted his notice, was an ornament of several rows of pearl beads, hanging round the neck and resting on the bosom of an elegantly dressed lady, to reach whom he had to go round the end of the table. On approaching her, he raised up the lower part of the beads from her bosom with his black hands, saying, with a smile to the lady, in Dutch, "These are very beautiful!" Whether he expected the lady then to give them to him was uncertain, but unquestionably he coveted them. As soon as he could take his eyes from the beads, he observed the branch candlesticks; being a tall man, he could examine them over the heads of the ladies and gentlemen. While doing so, the long mirrors diverted his attention, in which he beheld a whole-length likeness of himself, at which he desired me to look, while he gently tapped his nose with his fore-finger, and heartily laughed at the figure in the glass imitating him in all his actions. On taking a glass of wine that was given to him, he looked at me, saying, "Mynhere," (sir,) and drank it off. He only remarked that it was sweet. He then pranced with perfect ease round the table, when he appeared satisfied with what he had seen, and was allowed to go home to relate the wonders he had beheld. From the unembarrassed, independent manner in which Muliaily acted during the whole time he was in the room, Mr. E. remarked that he must have lived in a free country, or under a free government; which was certainly the case.

ANONYMOUS

The Abeona, a transport packed with Scottish settlers bound for the Eastern Cape, caught fire as she was about to cross the Equator in November 1820. The passengers and crew who were able to crowd into three small boats watched in horror as those left behind either burned alive or, like the couple here, were driven into the sea by the flames. Of the 112 who perished, all but two were emigrants. Forty-nine humans and three pigs survived.

THEY DISAPPEARED TOGETHER

Seeing all hope of escape cut off, M'Farlane, who had been married only a short time before they left Greenock, bound a rope round his wife, and attaching it to himself, they both, with undaunted resolution, jumped over the starboard bow, into the sea, in hopes of reaching the boats by his exertions. A dog, impelled by the same natural attachment to life, leaped also from the ship, into the water, and while the young couple were making the greatest exertions to preserve their lives, the dog got upon the top of them; which incumbrance, with the husband's exhausted strength, soon terminated the unequal struggle. They disappeared together and perished.

The Library of Parliament in Cape Town has a presumably contemporary broadsheet "Elegy" commemorating the disaster; eleven stanzas worthy of the great William McGonagall, though he was born only ten years later. A sample:

How shocking and sad is the thought to remember,
Of families divided, some sav'd, and some lost,
While the woes of the dire twenty-fifth of November,
Will be felt while their bones by the ocean is tost.

THOMAS STUBBS

Young Thomas was barely out of school when he and his family embarked for the Eastern Cape with one of the 1820 settler parties on the Northampton. *Smallpox broke out during the voyage, and claimed a number of lives, but the Stubbses survived.*

A PAIR OF SHOES

My mother had a small cabin to herself. She was ill nearly the whole voyage. My father and us boys, had berths just below the fore hatch, where the other part of our party, were stowed. We had a servant woman about eighteen years old. We called her, "Black Bet", as she had dark rings round her eyes. She was rather a rum one. She occupied the berth under my father, they ran in tiers (that is two deep). One night, my father heard something like a man's voice below him, and on getting out, saw a man jump out of Bet's berth and run upon deck. He found a pair of shoes and on looking at them saw the name of Becky, our first mate. My father showed him the shoes the next morning, when he said, "By Jove Mr Stubbs, where did you find them?

Settlers landing at Algoa Bay.

Some one took them out of my cabin." "I have no doubt of it," said my father, "But I would advise you, to keep yourself and your shoes from my quarters." Poor Bet was married to our butcher Dan Wood on board a man of war before we left Algoa Bay and I believe turned out an honest woman.

WE WILL BEGIN

The settlers were dumped with their boxes and bundles in the Albany bush, and effectively left to fend for themselves. The Stubbs family was mistakenly offloaded 13 kilometres from the rest of their party, and after some time managed to secure a wagon in order to carry their goods to the correct spot – at which juncture this extract begins.

Old Bobby, our wheelwright, began making yokes and skeys [and] all the ropes from the packages were collected, so it was not long before every-thing was ready. The oxen we had, had been supplied by government as rations, [and] were as wild as bucks. Every thing being now ready, all hands in the camp turned out to assist. The oxen were surrounded and were frightened almost to madness seeing so many strange looking people. I suppose they had never seen men in tail coats and knee breeches before! After much running and sweating, six of them were caught and made fast to the bushes. As it took nearly all day, it was arranged they should remain fast until the morning. It was not considered safe to put them to the wagon at first, so a large bush was fastened to the end of a stout rope which was to answer for a trek tow and yokes fastened on. The inspanning com-menced. After many knocks down and kicks and runs after oxen that had pulled away, they were got into the yokes, a man holding each ox by a rope. All was now ready for a start, but, as there was some doubt about the oxen understanding English, a long consultation took place. At last it was decid-ed that old Fancutt (one of my father's men) who had driven a cart and horse in Covent Garden Market before leaving England, was the man. He had brought his cart whip out with him, and he had noticed on the road from the Bay the Boers called out "Trek, Trek, Lope."

Old Fancutt said, "Now Master if you are ready we will begin." He had hardly got the word "Trek" out, when off the oxen started at full gallop off into the veld, leaving some who were holding them lying on the broad of their backs, the rest chasing and hallowing after them like mad. Old Fancutt standing with his whip on shoulder [said] "Well! I'm blowed if they'nt off with a vengeance, that's sartain." They were soon out of sight towards the Fish river bush. After another consultation, for I must remark they always had a meeting before anything could be done, it was arranged they should go in search, some to go one way, some another. Off they start-ed, but not knowing the country soon were lost. There were at that time a great many foot paths in all directions made by the game which was very plentiful, so that when the search for the oxen was given up and they wished to return to the camp, they took the wrong way and instead of reaching it had to remain in the veld all night. The next day they com-menced again but acted more wisely, for they took some pieces of rag, and as they proceeded fastened them on the bushes as they went along; but this also bothered them for as they went in different directions, the one party returning found the rags fastened by the others – which led them on their spoor. It was laughable to hear their different tales they told on their return.

The Stubbses eventually got their goods to the right spot – even though the wagon overturned on the way – and the oxen were trained to respond to commands in English and to English names. John Stubbs, the father, was killed by Xhosa cattle raiders three years later.

HENRY DUGMORE

In 1870 Grahamstown celebrated the golden jubilee of the arrival of the settlers. One of the highlights of the occasion was a lecture by Dugmore, a respected Wesleyan missionary who had been a settler child. His reminiscences, punctuated by choral interludes, kept a capacity crowd engrossed for four hours. This is one of them.

LIKE A GLOVE

A "ladies' shoemaker," who had worn out his own shoes, wished to take a walk from Wilson's party to Graham's Town. A neighbor suggested that it would be easy for *him* to supply himself by making a pair of the material which the hides and skins of the ration cattle provided. He did so, and remembering his own neat style of workmanship in the "ladies' line," he seems to have applied it in his own case. The shoes, put on damp and soft, fitted "like a glove," and he started on his journey. But the farther he walked the tighter the fit grew, and the harder the green hide, now becoming dry very fast from the heat of the dusty road. His plight soon became as bad as that of the poor fellow who was sent for penance to Loretto with peas in his shoes, and hadn't the wit to boil them before starting. In fact our settler's case was the worse of the two, for when he wished to relieve himself from torture by walking barefoot, he couldn't get his shoes off again. He had to endure his misery as far as Cadell's Hill, where a friend assisted him with his knife in the eel-skinning process of getting rid of his close-fitting appendages, and lent him a pair of his own for the rest of the journey. The ladies' shoemaker never forgot his walk, and perhaps never repeated it, for he took up his residence in Graham's Town.

ROBERT MOFFAT

At the age of 14 Robert Moffat was working as a gardener in Manchester. In 1816, aged 21, he sailed for Africa to plant the seeds of the Gospel in the hearts of what he called the "black, barbarous and benighted" people of the continent. Moffat laboured courageously for nearly 50 years at the Kuruman mission, weathering war, drought and the scepticism and hostility of the Tswana. When he tried to convince the Tswana of their state as sinners, "they would boldly affirm, with full belief in their innate rectitude, that there was not a sinner in the tribe", he wrote. There were also initial language problems: "The interpreter ... who understands very partially what he is translating ... will, as I have often heard, introduce a cart-

*wheel, or an ox-tail into some passage of simple sub-
limity of Holy Writ, just because some word in the
sentence had a similar sound."*

ARMS INTO BAGS
*The Tswana thought European customs clumsy and
troublesome, said Moffat.*

They could not account for our putting our legs,
feet, and arms into bags, and using buttons for
the purpose of fastening bandages round our
bodies, instead of suspending them as orna-
ments from the neck or hair of the head. Washing the body, instead of lubri-
cating it with grease and red ochre, was a disgusting custom …

Moffat preaching.

WRONG NAMES
I speak from experience when I say, that on some points travellers are very
liable to be led astray. For instance, I once, while writing, heard a traveller ask
his guide the name of the last halting place they had passed. The guide, not
understanding, replied, "Ua reng," which the traveller, with all simplicity, was
placing in his log book; when, interrupting him, I said, "What are you writing?
that is not a *name*: he merely asks you what you say." Accidents like the above
frequently give rise to wrong names being applied to places; in another
instance, "mountains" was the reply, instead of the name of the mountain.

FAST IN THE MUD
Travelling through territory where water-holes were few and far between.

About noon we came unexpectedly to the stream, into which men, oxen,
horses, and sheep rushed promiscuously, presenting a scene of the most
ludicrous description. One man is pushed down by an ox, pleased with the
refreshing coolness of the water; another, in his haste, tumbles headfore-
most over the bank, followed by a sheep or a goat. One crawls between the
legs of oxen, another tries to force himself in between their bodies. One
shouts that a horse is trampling upon him, and another that he is fast in the
mud. But while all this was going on, there was no disposition for merriment, till every one was satisfied and withdrew from the water; when wet,
muddy-looking spectacles presented themselves, which would have
caused even gravity itself to laugh.

SCENES OF DESOLATION
*Towards the end of 1829 the feared Ndebele king Mzilikazi sent two ambassadors
to Moffat's Kuruman station. The fact that the men were completely nude shocked
the Tswana, but the visitors cheerfully acquiesced to their hosts' suggestions for
"decency and propriety". Moffat reluctantly agreed to accompany them back to
meet Mzilikazi. The king, who executed prisoners by having them thrown into a
crocodile pool, developed a near-infatuation for the bearded missionary, and Moffat
returned several times. Here, on the first visit, Moffat is approaching Mzilikazi's
territory, travelling through land ravaged by Ndebele raiders.*

We now travelled along a range of mountains running near E.S.E., while the country to the north and east became more level, but beautifully studded with ranges of little hills, many isolated, of a conical form, along the bases of which lay the ruins of innumerable towns, some of which were of amazing extent. The soil of the valleys and extended plains was of the richest description. The torrents from the adjacent heights had, from year to year, carried away immense masses, in some places laying bare the substratum of granite rocks, exhibiting a mass of rich soil from ten to twenty feet deep, where it was evident native grain had formerly waved; and water-melons, pumpkins, kidney-beans, and sweet reed had once flourished. The ruins of many towns showed signs of immense labour and perseverance; stone fences, averaging from four to seven feet high, raised apparently without mortar, hammer, or line. Every thing was circular, from the inner walls which surrounded each dwelling or family residence, to those which encircled a town. In traversing these ruins, I found the remains of some houses which had escaped the flames of the marauders. These were large, and displayed a far superior style to any thing I had witnessed among the other aboriginal tribes of Southern Africa. The circular walls were generally composed of hard clay, with a small mixture of cow-dung, so well plastered and polished, a refined portion of the former mixed with a kind of ore, that the interior of the house had the appearance of being varnished. The walls and door-ways were also neatly ornamented with a kind of architraves and cornices. The pillars supporting the roof in the form of pilasters, projecting from the walls, and adorned with flutings and other designs, showed much taste in the architectresses. This taste, however, was exercised on fragile materials, for there was nothing in the building like stone, except the foundations. The houses, like all others in the interior, were round, with conical roofs, extending beyond the walls, so as to afford considerable shade, or what might be called a verandah. The raising of the stone fences must have been a work of immense labour, for the materials had all to be brought on the shoulders of men, and the quarries where these materials were probably obtained, were at a considerable distance. The neighbouring hills also gave ample demonstration of human perseverance, with instruments of the most paltry description.

In some places were found indigenous fig-trees, growing on squares of stone left by the quarriers, the height of twelve feet, and held together by the intersecting roots of the tree. On some of these we found ripe figs, but, from the stony basis, and uncultivated state, they were much inferior to those grown in the gardens of the Colony. Many an hour have I walked, pensively, among these scenes of desolation, – casting my thoughts back to the period when these now ruined habitations teemed with life and revelry, and when the hills and dales resounded to the burst of heathen joy. Nothing now remained but dilapidated walls, heaps of stones, and rubbish, mingled with human skulls, which, to a contemplative mind, told their ghastly tale.

To purchase his own children

It has been before stated that I was accompanied to Moselekatse by Mokatla, chief of the Bahurutsi. Dreading being driven with his subjects from his own native home, and picturesque wilds, and the tombs of his forefathers, and perhaps extirpated, as other tribes had been – whose bones lay withering in the blast, on the plains and vales which lay in our course, – he placed himself and attendants under my protection, though I was myself a stranger, and had not seen the object of his terror, and that of the tribes around. He hoped that as the missionary character had recommended itself to him, also a savage, he might go and return unscathed, and obtain the friendship of one who, as he sometimes expressed it, "prevented his peaceful slumbers." His attendants were respectable, all anticipating feasting and favour from one who wallowed in the spoils of war. There was one exception. This was a poor man, whose appearance, dress, and manner, informed me that he was truly the child of poverty, and perhaps of sorrow. This led me to take more notice of him than any other of the chief's attendants. I felt sympathy for the man, supposing he had been compelled to follow the train of his chief, and leave behind him a family ill-supplied, or some beloved member sick. No; his downcast looks arose from other causes. He had two sons, about the ages of eight and ten. These had been absent in a neighbouring glen, when a party of Matabele warriors seized the boys, and carried them as spoils to head-quarters. He and his partner in affliction had for more than a year mourned the loss of their children, and, by taking a few trinkets and beads, his little stock of ornaments, the father hoped to obtain their release. After a journey of deep interest and a flattering reception, and days passed in festivities and displays of kindness to the strangers, the man sent in his humble petition by one who could approach the presence of the king, offering the little he had to redeem his two boys. Some time afterwards the proprietor of his sons came and seated himself before my wagon, as I drew near to witness the transaction. The poor man spread his ragged mantle on the ground, and laid on it a few strings of beads and some native-made ornaments, valuable to him, but on which the haughty noble would scarcely deign to cast his eye. The father sighed to see his look of scorn. He then drew from his tattered skins, which he had brought with him, and on which he reposed at night, a small dirty bag, containing a few more strings of half-worn beads, and placed them beside the former: these were borrowed. The scornful look was again repeated. He then took from his arms two old copper rings, and rings of the same material from his ears. The chief answered the anxious eyes of the now desponding father with a frown, and an indignant shake of the head. He then took from his neck the only remaining link of beads which he possessed, and which it was evident he had worn many a year. This, with an old, half-worn knife, he added to the offered ransom. It was his all; and it is impossible ever to forget the expression of those eyes, which, though from national habit would not shed the tear of sorrow, were the index of the deepest anxiety as to the result. Neither the man nor his ornaments excited the smallest

Matabili Hut.

emotion in the bosom of the haughty chief, who talked with those around him about general affairs, maintaining the most perfect indifference to the object of paternal agony before his eyes. He at last arose; and being solicited by one who felt something of a father's love, to pity the old man, who had walked nearly two hundred miles and brought his little all to purchase his own children, he replied, with a sneer, that one had died of cold the preceding winter, and what the father offered for the other was not worth looking at; adding, "I want oxen." "I have not even a goat," replied the father. A sigh – it was a heavy sigh – burst from his bosom: one dead, and not permitted even to see the other with his eyes. The chief walked off, while the man sat leaning his head on the palm of his right hand, and his eyes fixed on the ground, apparently lost to every thing but his remaning son, now doubly dear from the loss of his brother, and he, alas! far beyond his power to rescue. On taking up his mantle to retire, he and his party being obliged to leave early to return to the place whence they came, he was told to be of good cheer, and an effort would be made to get his son. He startled at the sound, threw his mantle at my feet, and spreading out his hand to what he had offered, said, "Take these, my father, and pity me." "Retain them for yourself," was the reply. He kissed the hand of his pledged benefactor, and departed, saying, *Ki tla na le boroko.* "I shall have slumber," (peace of mind.)

In the course of the following day, a favourable moment was sought to bring the case before the king. He instantly ordered his brother, the individual who possessed the boy, to wait upon me, which he promptly did; and on receiving several pounds of a valuable kind of bead, he immediately despatched a messenger to bring the boy, who was at a distance, and who arrived the following day.

On my return to Mosega, and approaching the base of one of those hills amidst which the town lay embosomed, a human being was seen rushing down the steep towards the wagons, with a rapidity which led us to fear that she would fall headlong. Every eye was upon her, while some said, "It is the alarm of war." The wagon-driver, who sat by me, most emphatically exclaimed, "It is a woman, either running from a lion, or to save a child." Yes, it was the mother. She had heard from some of the party who preceded the wagons that morning, that her son was there: she had ascended the hill behind which the town lay, and gazed till the wagon emerged from a ravine. Frantic with joy, she ran breathless towards me. To prevent her coming in contact with the wagon wheels I sprang to the ground, when she seized my hands, kissed and bathed them with her tears. She spoke not one word, but wept aloud for joy. Her son drew near, when she instantly rushed forward, and clasped him in her arms.

THOMAS HODGSON

Hodgson, a Methodist, played a leading role in setting up the first Christian mission beyond the Vaal River. He arrived there in 1822, in time to witness the horror of the Mfecane. This cataclysmic social upheaval, probably caused by a combination of slaving, environmental factors and power struggles, scattered and devastated communities throughout the interior.

COOKING THE BRAINS

Inspanned at sunrise, hoping to meet with the other waggon at the place we had designed reaching last night. In this, however, we were mistaken, as Wm. had deemed it prudent to rest by some bushes a little behind us and he joined us about an hour after our arrival at the appointed place. As we approached the bushes where we had rested on the night of the 12th ult., we were surprised to behold a fire which two natives appeared to occupy in cooking at, while another was laid apparently asleep adjoining them. The two former attempted to conceal themselves under the bush, supposing, I presume, that we should pass them unobserved. After outspanning, my driver and I approached them, and to our utter astonishment found they were cooking the leg of a human being. From their persons, dress and language, [we] were satisfied they were a part of the much dreaded commando, and, from the appearance of the ground adjoining, it was evident the commando itself (or perhaps a part) had been there only two days ago at most, and possibly had only left the place the very day before, as the dung of the oxen, sheep, etc., was still moist. We were filled with horror at the sight we witnessed, and I was truly thankful that my dear wife was not exposed to such a dreadful scene, while constrained to acknowledge the kind providence of God which suffered us to wander from our path and thereby escape beholding this work of darkness in the shades of night, alive as we should have been to possibilities of being attacked by those who would rejoice in our destruction and afterwards feast upon our bodies. Horror-struck at the sight, I hastily retired from the scene to consider how to act; but after composing myself a little and making the necessary arrangements for quitting the spot as soon as possible after being joined by the other waggon, I returned to the wretched beings I had withdrawn from, and found the skeleton of one full grown person (the bones of which were well cleaned), and part of the body of another, one leg and one arm having been taken off, its head picked, and, the bowels, etc., being taken out, the internal part of its body was exposed to view. One woman was actually roasting a leg upon the ashes, and the other was engaged, with the man, [in] eating with greediness that which they had just cooked. I was sick at the sight, and it made me cringe as I approached to hear them breaking with a stone the bones of the deceased and then sucking them with apparent delight; and I was constrained to turn off from the awful scene after showing my abhorrence of such practices, which, however, appeared to make no impression, as the man took no notice of me, and the woman merely looked to the dead body before them and pronounced, as I supposed, the name of the deceased. One of the men saw them cooking the brains of one of the deceased. At first I thought the women apprehended we should kill them, but, finding that this was not the case, they appeared to view us with indifference. As we understood that the commando had gone to the Gt. river, which we were near, on their way to Sibbonel, and not having the means of preventing the people from satisfying the cravings of hunger upon the bodies of their fellows, we hastened away from the awful scene.

Another Methodist missionary, John Edwards, travelling on the upper reaches of the Caledon in the early 1830s, wrote that as his wagon went through long grass, "something was heard crushing, crushing under the wheels". He was riding over the skulls of people who died in the Mfecane.

WILLIAM OWEN

Captain Owen, in command of HMS Leven, was instructed in 1822 to carry out a hydrographic survey of the east coast of Africa, and to gather information on the "numbers and character" of natives he encountered. His commission was later extended to cover the west coast and a portion of Arabia. The voyage, which included visits to the Seychelles and Madagascar, lasted almost five years, and Owen's two-volume account tells of attacks by hostile tribes, hippo and elephant hunts, deaths from fever, and the magical sights and sounds of tropical seas. Henry Francis Fynn recorded that the crew of the Leven looked "most unsailorlike", as Owen encouraged his men to grow immense beards to ward off mosquitos. The starchy commander of a British frigate at Simon's Town invited one of Owen's lieutenants to dinner on condition he first shaved off his facial hair. The lieutenant's place that evening remained empty.

THE CUBE OF X

During this voyage a weekly newspaper was published on board the Leven by the officers, in which there were some papers written by Mr. Browne, that for elegance of expression have not often been surpassed. The editor of this weekly production was Mr. Owen Fisher, a most promising youth in every good qualification. Perhaps the fond partiality of friendship may be excused recording one of his numerous jokes, which served better than medicine to cheer the spirits of his companions.

It has long been the fashion to attribute every shipwreck to some fault in time-keepers and other instruments, but particularly to the deviation of the compass since its discovery by Captain Flinders, and on which so many useful experiments have been made during the polar voyages. The Leven was fitted with plates on Mr. Barlow's plan for measuring the quantity of this deviation, and the Leven's quarter-deck, as well as that of many others, was nailed with brass instead of iron.

Although it is manifest that, in nine cases out of ten, shipwrecks arise from unpardonable ignorance or neglect, yet good has resulted from the many assertions that "the compass was false," "the time-keepers wrong," &c. because enquiry has been directed to these instruments; their nature and uses are better understood, and the above-mentioned excuses will be ultimately taken from future carelessness or stupidity. In the course of these enquiries many minute calculations and formulae have appeared, which superficial observers suppose to contain some latent mystery, only attainable by the initiated, and that the art of critical navigation is only to be acquired by the learned few. The affectation of extreme minutiæ and of reasoning on new hypotheses to account for all possible effects, and to make the Royal Society a stepping-stone to the honours and benefits of our service, has certainly produced more injury by discouraging the unpresuming man of real professional merit, than it has done good by raising talent from obscurity. Young Fisher had sense enough in the few years he had lived in our service perfectly to understand the nature of the game of humbug, as it is generally termed, which it was his particular delight to satirize.

Whenever midshipmen or lieutenants from other ships came on board, he undertook to keep up our character for science in the cockpit. All the youngsters were seated by him at table over books of abstruse science, and as the stranger looked in he heard confused sounds of A, plus B, minus the cube of X, divided by the square of Y, is equal to the cube-root of Z, &c., by which artifice some of the younger part of his visiters were actually persuaded that the Captain never suffered the ship to be worked by any but algebraic rules.

One of his papers described these visiters going round the ship until they came to Barlow's plate; this he describes as an instrument for detecting whether men have drunk more than their allowance of water, which, being kept in tanks, must necessarily be impregnated with iron, and he most gravely states that it has been found highly dangerous to trust a man at the helm who shall have drunk more than his six pints; he then goes on to relate how this extraordinary property of tank-water was discovered, in consequence of the captain of the hold having taken advantage of his situation to rob one of the tanks of an extra gallon for his own private use, and unwittingly, by coming to the helm, the compass was found to deviate most unaccountably. The circumstance was reported to the Captain, who immediately ordered the man to be tried by Barlow's plate, when it was found that he had drunk seven pints and a half of tank-water more than his allowance; since which every man is tried by the plate before he is allowed to take the Leven's helm; and this method he recommends for general adoption in his Majesty's navy.

CONSCIOUS OF HIS SUPERIORITY
The man Owen calls Jackot here was a Xhosa, Jacob Msimbithi, who was kidnapped from chief Ndlambe's territory at an early age by a farmer seeking stolen cattle. He stayed with the farmer long enough to pick up a knowledge of Dutch that stood him in good stead on the turbulent frontier in the years that followed. Eventually arrested for stock theft himself, he had the distinction of making the journey to Robben Island along with the captive Xhosa prophet Nxele. Msimbithi was one of seven islanders promised their freedom in return for acting as interpreters for Owen's expedition. Here they are at Delagoa Bay in southern Moçambique.

A black interpreter, who spoke Portuguese, of which Lieutenant Vidal also had some knowledge, was hired from the factory, and, supposing the pretensions of sovereignty set up by the Portuguese to be valid, the captain applied to the commandant to give him some people to protect our boats against any attack from the natives. The Commandant, however, acquainted

us that he had no authority whatever over them, and that, so far from giving assistance to us, he was himself in hourly expectation of an attack from the Vatwas, when he should hope for *our* aid. As this explanation settled the affair at once, Captain Owen never considered it necessary to consult them afterwards upon any of his movements or operations.

We were not aware that our Kaffers were of the same people, (although a different tribe,) as the Hollontontes, and therefore did not send any of them with our boats, nor indeed had we yet sufficient confidence in them; two, however, Jackot and Fire, had by their conduct much gained upon the estimation of all.

Jackot had been a Chief "famed for deeds of arms." Fire had rendered himself a universal favourite with the sailors, and took his part in all their duties and amusements. He afforded much diversion by his close imitation of their gestures and manners, as well as by a natural wit and archness; both men amused us at times by their war exercises, and showed a thorough contempt for the Portuguese and all the natives of Delagoa.

Jackot, when one day on shore, persuaded a native, in the presence of a large party, to try his assagaye at a small tree, which he did from about forty yards, and missed; upon which Jackot took it up, and going about twenty yards further off, first poised, and then, giving it a tremulous motion in his hand, threw the spear with such force and dexterity that it entered the centre of the tree so deep as to be with difficulty extracted. The natives were all astonished, but Jackot walked off without altering a muscle of his features, apparently conscious of his superiority over them.

While our boats were hauled on shore to fit and equip for the exploration of the rivers, it was necessary to guard against the thievish propensity of the natives. We therefore placed sentinels over them, when not at work; but having so many men absent we occasionally employed our Kaffers on this duty. Fire was so delighted with this mark of confidence, that he could hardly be persuaded to be relieved; and he and Jackot actually slept under the boat, whilst hauled up on the beach, and would never quit their post without the intervention of absolute authority. One night a native approached with caution, no doubt intending to steal some of the iron or copper which was in use for her equipment. Fire levelled his musket and fired just over his head. The report brought our officers and people to the spot, who saw the rogue making his escape, when Fire boasted that he would not kill the fellow, considering him as too contemptible. This is a purely native trait, and sufficiently indicates the manly character of these people.

Msimbithi and Fire sailed with the expedition to Zanzibar, Madagascar and the Seychelles. After their discharge they were engaged by the ill-fated Francis Farewell for a trading voyage up the east coast. Fire was "shot accidentally some-time afterwards", Owen says. Msimbithi deserted and established himself as a favourite at the court of the Zulu king Shaka, who gave him the name Hlamba-manzi, the one who has swum the water.

142

DOWN HIS THROAT

Lieutenant Arlett was a member of a Leven *hunting party at Delagoa Bay. What he hoped was a hippo in tall reeds turned out to be an angry elephant, which initially merely ran over him, severely bruising his ankle. But worse was to follow.*

As soon as he had passed, Mr. Arlett arose, and, limping with pain, attempted once more to retreat, but the animal returned to the attack; his trunk was flourished in the air, and the next moment the unfortunate officer was struck senseless to the ground. On recovering himself his situation appeared hopeless, his huge antagonist standing over him, chaffing and screaming with rage, pounding the earth with his feet, and ploughing it with his tusks. When the party first saw them, Mr. Arlett was lying between the elephant's legs, and had it been the intention of the animal to destroy him, placing a foot upon his senseless body would in a moment have crushed him to atoms; but it is probable that his object was only to punish and alarm, not to kill – such conjecture being perfectly in accordance with the character of this noble but revengeful beast.

Mr. Arlett was with much care instantly conveyed on board the schooner, when, on examination, it was found that his body was severely bruised, yet no bones were broken, excepting the fibula of the left leg, which was supposed to be slightly fractured. It appeared that the elephant, on his last return to Mr. Arlett, had filled his trunk with mud, which, having turned him on his back, and forced open his mouth, he blew down his throat, injecting a large quantity into the stomach. It was this that produced the inflated appearance of Mr. Arlett's countenance, for he was almost in a state of suffocation, and for three days after this adventure, he occasionally vomited quantities of blue sand.

HENRY FRANCIS FYNN

Fynn has become embedded in colonial history as the first white settler in Natal, "the forerunner of that stream of intrepid men and women to whom Natal and South Africa owe so much". Born in England, he came to Cape Town at the age of about 15 to join his father, a trader. He claimed to have been drawn to Natal, where he arrived in 1824, by an ivory-trading venture inspired partly by a fanciful report that Shaka's cattle enclosures were made of tusks. However, one East Cape official in later years remembered a Fynn who had robbed the store at Bathurst, and fled east to escape justice. Fynn fought for Shaka against other tribes, and established himself as a feudal lord with a following over whom he assumed the power of life and death. In later years he was appointed to government administrative posts in the northeastern Cape and Natal.

Henry Francis Fynn

BY THE FOOT

Arrival on the beach at present-day Durban. These "wolves" would have been uncharacteristically bold hyaenas.

On landing there with provisions and bedding, I sent the boat back to the vessel and strolled about the Khangela flat on the chance of

143

Port Natal

finding some natives. We strolled both to the right and left of Khangela to select a spot for building, until sunset, but met with no trace of any inhabitants being in the country. Traces of sea-cows everywhere abounded. We selected a hollow or dip under rising ground to protect us from the winds, and then began to prepare for the night, cooking food and arranging beds.

Moderately tired after our walk, we soon went to sleep. We had, however, not been long in that condition when, about midnight, a storm broke over us. Not only we, but our bedding, became thoroughly drenched, and a stream of water which rushed through the hollow forced us to move to higher ground. Fortunately, we had collected a large quantity of fuel, and having some large logs on fire we removed them and the fuel to higher ground. Sleep was impossible. We employed ourselves in making a blazing fire and wrapping ourselves in our wet blankets. While thus occupied we were surprised by the howling of troops of wolves, which were coming from different directions, to where we had located ourselves. We increased our fire as far as the rain would permit us, in the hope that the wolves would be kept at a distance, but, in defiance of the fire and our yells, they approached and stood before us. To see them was impossible. We had not brought firearms with us, and as the wolves approached nearer and nearer, we had no better mode of defence than by standing back-to-back with firebrands in our hands. Several came so close as to snap at us, and we were able to strike them with firebrands.

In rushing to our standing position, we had separated from our bedding. One of the wolves seized therefrom the leather trousers belonging to Ogle, in which he had a Dutch 60-dollar note. This he was determined to defend. He rushed forward, caught hold of the band of the trousers as the wolf was dragging them, and succeeded in recovering them with the loss of only one of the legs. Although all of us had rushed to his assistance in the dark we succeeded only in beating the wind with our firebrands, though that had the effect of scaring the wolves away.

The Prussian, anxious to secure his bedding, was on all fours rolling it up when a wolf came and caught him by the foot. He screamed out most vociferously: "My toag! my toag!" meaning his toe. This caused a roar of laughter, as we were now less fearful, finding we were not likely to be rushed upon en masse. A firebrand thrown at the wolves released him from his predicament. The troops of wolves had regularly besieged our position, and we momentarily expected to be torn to pieces. We then all stooped down together to extend the fire round our position. In this we only partially succeeded, owing to the scarcity of the fuel, while the smoke almost blinded us. To obviate this, still back-to-back, we took up a sitting posture; we talked to one another and Ogle sang songs at intervals. We continued in this way, momentarily expecting the wolves would rush upon us, until day had fully dawned, when we put up a signal for the boat. On its arrival we returned to the vessel.

THIS DENSE MASS OF NATIVES
The next morning Fynn and three of his servants set off to find Shaka. Fynn grossly exaggerates his numbers, something worth remembering in the face of this seemingly endless stream of warriors. Frederick was the interpreter.

After travelling about three miles we crossed the Umngeni River. Mahamba showed great fear of the crocodiles and sea-cows which were in great numbers. We, however, passed by without harm. As there were no footpaths or human footprints, only elephant and sea-cow tracks being observable, I decided on keeping to the beach. When about 12 miles from the port I found myself so completely tired out that I sat down and ordered coffee. Mahamba produced fire from the friction of two sticks. While the kettle was being brought to the boil, I sat on the beach and as I was looking across the sea, then at low tide, I saw on my right a dense mass of people coming fast from the direction I had come. My view extended over several miles of the beach, but I could not see the rear of this immense black and continuous mass of natives, all armed and in their war-dresses. Our surprise was great and had I known the character of these people and the danger I was in, as I now know it, it is a question if I would have stood my ground, though an attempt to run away would not have saved me.

I immediately concluded they had come in pursuit of me after having already destroyed the party I had left building. The bush along the beach was dense and, as I was sure they had seen me, flight appeared inadvisable, though strongly urged by Jantyi and Frederick. Mahamba at once disappeared. On the approach of the head of the column I was struck with astonishment at their appearance, for it was sufficient to terrify. Evidently they were equally surprised at mine, and looked at me with a kind of horror. I stood up on their coming close towards me in the hope of communicating with their commanders through my interpreter and telling the object of my being in the country. When I was telling the interpreter what to say, viz: that I had come across the sea and was desirous of seeing Shaka, one of the foremost men made a sign by spanning his hand round the front of his neck and pointing to some beads round the neck of another native, evidently asking for beads. This sign was no sooner observed than Jantyi fled precipitately into the bush, and Frederick immediately followed his example, leaving me alone to my dumb show efforts at communication, and, no doubt, with misunderstanding on both sides. The signs consisted in pointing in the direction from whence I had come, and in that in which I wished to go; moreover I frequently repeated the name of Shaka. The leaders talked much among themselves, but at length passed on along the beach.

This dense mass of natives continued to pass by me until sunset, all staring at me with amazement, none interfering with me.

I have since been of the opinion that my coolness, for I certainly felt no fear, saved me from instant destruction. In the passing of this force I could not but remark that they moved in divisions, the leader of each showing me the immense control they had over their followers; they frequently struck at them at the slightest appearance of disorder.

My bodyguard, Frederick and Jantyi now appeared with Mahamba. They were surprised to find me not dead. Jantyi exculpated himself by declaring that the signs the man made by spanning round his neck signified nothing less than an intention to hang us, whereas all the man meant to convey was a request for beads to put round his own neck. That this view is correct was shown by what we afterwards heard had occurred at the port, namely, that one of the native fishermen had beads, which he had procured from us, taken from him by one of these men.

SIX IN ALL

In fact it was only some weeks later that Fynn, now joined by the backer of the venture Francis Farewell, and travelling on horseback, made the journey to Shaka's residence Bulawayo, near present-day Eshowe. They handed over gifts that included lacquered brass bars, a full-dress military coat, and a pig. Shaka demanded medical treatment, and threatened to send Fynn back to King George to be executed if he did not comply.

During my absence Mbikwana informed Shaka that Mr. Petersen also had medicine. Mr. Petersen was requested to produce it and state its virtues. He produced a box of pills which he said were good for all diseases and strongly advised Shaka to take two. The King took four and giving one each to four chiefs, made them swallow them. Mr. Petersen was also desired to take four. Mr. Petersen after vainly endeavouring to convince the King that four were too much for one person was reluctantly compelled to swallow the four. Shaka asked the chiefs how they tasted; they replied: "Not at all," they having swallowed them as directed. The King now swallowed two and ordered Mr. Petersen to keep him company. This Mr. Petersen peremptorily refused to do, but the King insisting, and the chiefs adding the pressure of the argument that one who recommended medicines should not refuse to take them himself, Mr. Petersen was compelled to swallow two more, that is, six in all. The consequences of this to a person of 63 does not require to be explained in detail.

A MERE CHANCE SHOT

On hearing of the wreck of the *Mary*, Shaka requested the whole European party to pay him a visit, Farewell, King, Isaacs, King's friend, and I, together with the ten remaining men of the crew. We accordingly proceeded to Shaka's kraal, some 140 miles from Port Natal. Shaka sent a four-horned bullock to meet us. He received us in a most affable manner and gave us two oxen to slaughter. We managed to pitch our marquee and tents by sunset. Shaka then sent for me. I was taken into his seraglio. This was now his regular practice whenever I visited him, and he rarely ever allowed me to leave before twelve or one o'clock, owing to the intense interest he took in the different subjects he questioned me about. On the evening in question he amused himself by treating with ridicule the power of European firearms, urging that native assegais were far superior. I contended that, with our guns, we could kill elephant, sea-cow, buffalo and all other kinds of game, as well as the birds of the air, and do so at a distance their assegais could not reach. He, however, persisted in his argument until I retired to rest. Dancing and feasting occupied the morning of the following day; at midday we retired to our marquee. About an hour later a messenger appeared to say that Shaka required our immediate presence with our guns, as a troop of elephants was close at hand. I immediately went to the King and begged him not to require us to shoot the animals as the guns we had were fit only for killing birds and small game. I told him that the one used for shooting elephants was of a larger kind. I merely got laughed at for my pains and on being reminded of the conversation of the previous evening, found there was no alternative but to comply. He insisted on our going, so off we went. Our army was eight to ten strong. We had among us only three fowling pieces, two blunderbusses and four muskets. I must say it was fully in expectation of being afterwards laughed at by everyone that we reluctantly set forth on this venture. We arranged among ourselves to approach to within 40 yards of the animals, then to fire a volley with no other hopes than that the elephants would turn and make off. It was evident, as we proceeded in the direction of the elephants, that the several Zulu regiments that accompanied us depended solely on our efforts, or, at least, were determined not to use their own weapons until we had failed. We had travelled about half an hour when we suddenly came upon a troop of 16 elephants. We marched slowly and cautiously towards them, but as we were manoeuvring to get within the distance we had decided upon one of the sailors suddenly fired at the nearest bull. To the astonishment of the Zulus and our own far greater astonishment, the elephant dropped dead. It was some time before we could satisfy ourselves of the fact as to how such a thing could have occurred, for in those days it was considered almost impossible to kill with leaden balls. Shaka's consternation was great, and he admitted that our weapons were superior to his own.

On examining the elephant, we found the bullet had penetrated the ear. It was a mere chance shot. The sailor was certainly not accustomed to using a gun, he had no more knowledge of shooting than sailors usually possess, nor had he ever seen an elephant before.

DINYA KA ZOKOZWAYO

Dinya told James Stuart that he had been conceived during the mourning for Nandi, Shaka's mother, which Stuart says would fix his birth about November 1827. In the 1830s he served as a youthful interpreter between claimant to the Zulu throne Mpande and his allies the Voortrekkers, who he recalled would think nothing of halting their wagons besides people's mealie gardens and helping themselves to the crop. "Any man interfering would be lashed and skinned with the whip," he said.

AS WHITE AS MILK

The first white man arrived with Nhlamba at the kraal of Sinqila ka Mpipi, chief of the Amangati tribe (offshoot of Cele tribe). Sinqila went out to look for his beast which had calved in the veld. He found all his women and children running away from the wild beast, viz. a white man who was mounted on a horse. This man had, in Sinqila's absence, arrived at the kraal, causing women etc. all to run away. They said his hair was like cattle tails, and the horse some strange bogey. (Hasazi comes after Sinqila in order of birth. Hasazi's other name is Koviswayo.) This European, Dinya says, must have been Fynn.

The extraordinary thing to the natives was this strange being on top of another strange animal. The white man was accompanied by Nhlamba, who acted as interpreter. Sinqila sent at once to report the incident to his chief Magaye. Magaye was then living at Mhlali in his Mdhlazi kraal. Sinqila gave a full account of the white man, saying how he was dressed, that he had an *imbenge* on his head, that something (a bottle in which he carried milk asked for at the kraals visited) was very peculiar, inasmuch as it shone, and the gun he carried. All these features were surprizing, and all this Sinqila, having brought a gift of food for the small children, reported to his chief (also of the Amangati tribe) as he (Sinqila) stood outside his hut.

After hearing this, Magaye sent for the principal members of his tribe. He called his *induna* Nhlasiyana ka Nomunga ka Mkokeleli, the *induna* Cunge ka Nodinga, Mvivinyeki of the Emanhlokweni tribe, and Mpangu of the Gumbi, a section of the Qwabe tribe which *konza'd* to the Cele. Others came in addition to these. Sinqila once more stated exactly what he had seen, causing a great impression on those who listened. Magaye proposed the man should be brought to him to see. Sinqila said he must not run away on seeing the monster. Magaye, after Sinqila went off to conduct the stranger to him, called up his regiments and set them on both sides of him as he sat in the open space in front of the cattle kraal. His children and relatives stood behind.

Presently the stranger arrived, mounted on a horse, with hat on head, gun in hand, hair like cattle tails, and so forth. All present were moved with wonder and awe, so much so that the regiments shuffled back as far as the fence, whilst Magaye himself moved backwards with such vigour as to sprain one of the children (girls) behind him. When the white man halted and got off and stood, the onlookers were reassured, the more so when he did as asked by Magaye through his interpreter, namely to remove his hat, to turn round and so forth in order that full opportunity should be given of surveying him well at a distance.

Magaye now ordered that an ox should be presented as food to the stranger. A dark-brown one was got and given him, and he was told to go and pass the night at Mziboneli's kraal, this man being a brother of Magaye and son of Dibandhlela. Mziboneli was much concerned at having to receive the monster into his own homestead, but did in accordance with orders, namely at his kraal known as kwa Mabola. Here the dark-brown beast (ox) was slaughtered. It was not stabbed, it was shot, and as the shot was fired all lay down on the ground. The white man proposed this, and after warning all to be on the lookout for a report like a thunderclap, fired at and killed the beast without touching it. He then cut its throat to let it bleed freely. He asked what part should be presented to the chief. They told him the meat covering the ribs, (as well as) the ear. So the white man, after having these parts carefully cut out, himself took and presented them to the chief. Magaye was much impressed with this stranger, and in view of what had occurred decided at once to report to Tshaka.

Magaye observed that he had previously heard of a stranger like this riding on a peculiar animal, when on a visit to the Qwabe tribe in Zululand, for his mother Siwetu was a sister of Nqeto. He had heard the white man had come from the Cape and was bound for the coast, and that he had been put to death by the Mtetwa people over whom Dingiswayo was chief. This is the white man of whom people sang, "Ngqwabangqwaba, go away!" to keep him from approaching their kraals.

Magaye was advised to go and report to Tshaka in person. He did so. He directed Nhlasiyana to take a detachment of 30 to 40 men with him and conduct the white man to Bulawayo kraal at which Tshaka was then staying, whither he would himself go on ahead and be present when the party arrived. When the party got to Bulawayo they found Magaye there, seated with Tshaka. They had been directed by Magaye to enter the kraal by both gates and then to advance up the meeting place of the council towards the *isigodhlo*. They were to halt with their charge as soon as they got a short distance off it, and then one and all to raise their right arms into the air and together exclaim, dwelling a long while on each syllable, as if singing, "Magaye says that the cockroaches are crossing the council place!" This expression was to be sung out three times, each time as before. (This is an expression meaning that good luck has befallen one.)

They did as ordered. No sooner did Tshaka hear them exclaim thus than he ran out of his hut, dragging his skin cloak with him, to see what it meant. He said, "Hear, my people! Magaye says the white men have arrived in his country." He presently noticed the white object among them. He gave the bystanders various orders as regards making the white man do this and that. He took it into his head to cause the white man to undress and put on his, Tshaka's, loin-cover, which was fetched from his hut. Having a sense of decency, Tshaka ordered 30 or 40 men to stand round about the white man so as to hide him whilst he undressed. This was done, and Fynn presently appeared in the garb of a Zulu, his flesh as white as milk, only to be called "Mbuyazi (Mbulazi) of the Bay, the long-tailed finch that came from Pondoland", this being the praise-name made up by Tshaka.

Fynn's account of his first meeting with Shaka does not include the undressing described by Dinya.

NATHANIEL ISAACS

Like Fynn, Isaacs made the transition from England to Africa when he was still a teenager, arriving in Natal as a member of what was ostensibly an ivory-trading venture in 1825. Like Fynn, Isaacs was devious, violent and unscrupulous: circumstantial evidence suggests he and his companions, including Fynn, may have been trafficking in slaves. The Shaka that emerges from his ghostwritten Travels

A supposed portrait of Shaka: from Isaacs' book.

and Adventures *is a monstrous tyrant, "unrestrained in his bloody designs" – all the more reason why the British government should heed Isaacs' appeals to annex Natal and grant him land there. Thwarted, he moved on to West Africa, where he made his fortune as a trader and narrowly escaped prosecution for slaving.*

BY A SUDDEN WRENCH
From Isaacs' account of his initial encounter with Shaka.

Three boys came with water, carrying it over their heads with their arms extended, which I perceived was the usual way they bore everything to the king. One held a broad black dish before him, while another poured in water for his majesty to wash, and a third stood ready with a further supply in case of need, holding it in the position before described, without daring to put it down.

Chaka, while bathing from head to foot, conversed with his people near him. After this was concluded, another attendant came, bearing a basket, which he presented to the king at arm's length. His Majesty took from it a sort of red coloured paste, with which he ornamented, or rather besmeared his body, but kept rubbing until the whole had disappeared. After this another attendant came with some greasy substance, which the king likewise applied to his body, over which he rubbed it, and this gave him a fine glossy appearance.

At this period, a body of natives arrived, about three hundred in number, every one saluting as he went on, "Biet tu Barber;" whilst some would say also, "Whenua cong Caswa," or "you who are as large as the world." On a sudden a profound silence ensued, when his majesty uttered one or two words, at which some of the warriors immediately rose and seized three of the people, one of whom sat near me. The poor fellows made no resistance, but were calm and resigned, waiting their fate with apparently stoical indifference. The sanguinary chief was silent; but from some sign he gave the executioners, they took the criminals, laying one hand on the crown and the other on the chin, and by a sudden wrench appeared to dislocate the head. The victims were then dragged away and beaten as they proceeded to the bush, about a mile from the kraal, where a stick was inhumanly forced up the fundament of each, and they were left as food for the wild beasts of the forest, and those carnivorous birds that hover near the habitations of the natives.

After this savage execution of the criminals, the cause of which I could not discover, Chaka having given orders that his warriors should disperse, retired to his palace, and I retired to my hut with feelings not a little excited by a scene which sinks man to a level with the brute.

Isaacs claimed to have witnessed several massacres ordered by Shaka, including a fortnight-long slaughter following the death of the king's mother Nandi. He urged Fynn in his own writing to make Shaka out to be "as bloodthirsty as you can".

WITH AN EXPRESSION OF FEAR

The looking glass greatly attracted him [Shaka], exciting his curiosity and admiration; he directed me to hand it to his people. For a time it afforded me a fund of amusement, and notwithstanding my troubles, I could not refrain from laughing at their attitudes and gestures. They all looked at it with astonishment; at the same time they held their mouths, and sought as if they thought to catch the figure by placing their hands behind it. Some put their hands before their eyes, occasionally glancing from the corner, to take a peep to see if it were imitating them. Chaka now perceiving that his warriors were in a consternation, wanted to assume the appearance of being bolder than his subjects; he, therefore, ordered me to place the glass at a little distance in front of him, when he looked with one eye on the object, while he nearly stared me out of countenance with the other; and with an expression of fear, he led me to understand, that he expected me not to play any tricks with him. I advanced it nearer to him gradually; and at last impressed him with the knowledge that it merely reflected his own figure, that there was nothing in it alarming – nothing the work of enchantment, but that it was simply a production of art, and used in the white man's country for the purposes of his dressing-room.

I HAD TENDER FEET
Returning to the coast, Isaacs' horse collapsed.

I was at this time about sixty miles from my residence, and had only an old pair of shoes to walk in, which was as painful as walking without any. As necessity on this occasion made me a pedestrian, so it also drove me to every shift to get on as easily as possible. It was a hot day, I had tender feet, and the road was at times strewed with thorns, when we approached near the thorn-bush jungles. I, however, discarded my shoes, for I could not

From Isaacs: "A Zoolu warrior & his daughter."

walk in them with greater ease than the poor pilgrim who was doomed to do penance by walking with peas in his. Every now and then, therefore, I was obliged to submit to the operation of extracting thorns from my feet, by operators not the most skilful in the world, though occasionally expert. After having extracted them, they tried to induce me to put the offending thorns into my mouth, and chew them, as a charm against future inflictions, which they averred would prove effectual. Their superstitious customs, however, I heeded not on this occasion, and in a few minutes I had another cause of conviction of their inefficacy, when my attendants, with astonishment and the most imperturbable gravity, attributed a second misfortune to my inexperience in travelling.

SCANNING OUR PERSONS
When they had to cross a river in which there were crocodiles, Isaacs' Zulu companions "performed their usual ceremony of first chewing the excrements of the alligator, and then spread-

151

ing it over the body as a charm to keep off those voracious animals". The inyangas *were apparently professionals at helping people ford difficult crossings.*

About 10 A.M., just as the sun was shedding its influence on the dew-covered foliage below, the "inyangers," or water doctors, arrived to take us across the river, which in parts was five feet deep, with a rapid current. It had an appalling appearance. Above us it was somewhat extended, but at the place of our crossing it became contracted, so that the force of the stream had increased to a fearful velocity. Several large rocks whose tops were visible on its surface, invited us to effect a passage by them, but we found that they increased the difficulty, as the current near them rushed by with much greater impetuosity. The bed of the river also had a most uneven surface; large stones, slippery, and dangerous to tread upon, were strewed in every direction, making it dangerous to step. With all these formidable obstructions, however, the river doctors selected this place for our passing, because they said the unevenness of the course made it a likely place not for alligators to be found in. It gave us also awful apprehensions that it was never designed for Europeans, or any human beings to attempt to buoy themselves through its fearful and impetuous current.

The natives had congregated on its banks in great numbers, and with eager curiosity to see a white man without his habiliments, that made us smile. The women and girls in particular, were more than ordinarily diligent in scanning our persons on the moment of our stepping into the water. They contended, with some strife, to obtain the best situations for a full and unobstructed view, and in these efforts to maintain the nearest margin of the river contiguous to us, one of the females fell into the stream, and with great difficulty escaped being drowned. During this moment of confusion in securing the female, we entered into the water, having two stout able natives on each side of us, by whom we were supported, and after indescribable difficulty, and being driven against rocks and stones with no little pain and fear, we got safe over. The inyangers from their great muscular power, and experience in their occupation, kept us above the water, which no skill or exertion of our own could have effected. Our supporters got severe bruises, but they disregarded them, and only asked us for a string of beads to buy medicines.

MAKUZA KA MKOMOYI

Makuza, another of James Stuart's informants, was born some 20 years after the events he describes here. The embassy got only as far as Port Elizabeth.

SMELT OUT BY THE WATER

When Tshaka, through being profoundly impressed with the power of a gun, wished to establish communication with the English people as makers of such a weapon, his first impulse was to go across the seas himself. But gratification of the impulse depended on what the sea itself wished in respect of the one desiring to cross it. Hence arose the idea that sticks should be thrown into the sea in order to see what became of them. If they were carried away altogether, it would be clear that the owner of such stick would himself be carried away and not suffered to return to the country. If, however, the sea brought it back, it would indicate that the owner would be permitted to return in safety to Zululand. When at the Isibubulungu with his regiments, Tshaka directed all the men to come to the seashore, and one and all, including himself, were to fling their sticks into the sea and watch the result. The sticks were accordingly thrown, the men standing along quite a considerable stretch of coast. The waves brought back the vast majority, but not that of the king. Search for it was continued until nightfall, without success. There were other sticks that did not return, namely those of men who were known to have killed others, especially the sticks of the great men of the nation, and of those whose children or wives had been in the habit of dying rather freely, as well as of those whose blood was bad.

As the king had thus been "smelt out" by the water, it was out of the question for him to undertake the voyage. He accordingly asked for volunteers from his people as a whole, but no-one would come forward, as they would not dare to cross the sea, as it and the sky seemed to be one and the same, i.e. the sea seemed to merge into the sky, especially in regard to the deepest and most awe-inspiring waters remotest from the land. Tshaka discussed the matter with his men. They said, "Let men of good blood go, not men of bad blood." He said, "If I were to go, people in England would put faith in me, being the king, but as I can't go, having been smelt out by the water, someone else must do so." He then thought of Sotobe ka Mpangalala. Now Sotobe's stick was among those which had been cast back onto the shore, so there was no objection on that score to his undertaking the voyage. Sotobe and Mbozamboza accordingly were deputed to go under the charge of Hlazakazi (Lieutenant King). They went, and later returned, upon which cattle were killed as a thanks offering to the spirits for the ambassadors' safe return, whilst he, Sotobe, himself was made a present of cattle that filled the enclosure.

THOMAS PHILIPPS

Not the settler of the same name; spent just over two months exploring the Eastern Cape in 1825. Here he visits a Thembu village at Tyumie.

IT WAS VERY WICKED
Whilst they were conversing with our interpreter, we amused ourselves in noticing the children. One little babe, about a twelve-month old, very readily allowed me to take it in my arms, and it was soon observable how gratifying this attention was to the fathers equally as to the mothers. An interesting little girl, about four years old attached herself to us, and played a thousand little tricks to engage our attention: one of the party gave her a sixpence, – she looked at it attentively for some time, and then returned it to him, speaking quick, and putting her little hand across her throat. The interpreter explained to us that she meant to say it was very wicked to cut off the man's head, – alluding to

the impression of the king's head only being on the coin. Attention to the children is the readiest way to ingratiate yourself with the savage.

COWPER ROSE

Rose was an officer of the Royal Engineers who appears to have been stationed in the Eastern Cape for several years in the 1820s. Despite his rectitude here, Rose had a keen eye for the ladies, and flirted his way through Xhosaland. He was most taken by an Ndlambe girl named Namarké, whose "small and beautiful ankles were defined and encircled by a single string of small blue beads". Hintza, king of all the Xhosa, had the top of his head blown off in 1835 by a colonial scout.

THE ROYAL SUFFERER

An ox was killed for us, of which the Chief and principal captains, or influential men, (to use the missionary phrase,) partook largely; and in the evening, while sitting round the fire, Hinza requested that we would send the Kaffers away, as he had something to impart; nor were we a little surprised to find him commence on the subject of his queens. He said, "that it was a fine thing to have nine wives, as they were of use in working in the fields; but then it was a difficult thing to keep them in any kind of order, and that he feared strange improprieties happened; that he had taken the cattle of the offenders, and banished them; but much that was incorrect, he believed, still went on." We tried to comfort the *royal sufferer*, by telling him that his case was by no means singular; that it was the same every where, even with those who had but one; while we could not understand why he should impart his griefs to us; but this was in some measure explained, when, on retiring to our sleeping hut, two of his wives and two of his daughters crept into it: Hinza probably reasoning, that what he could not keep from his subjects, he might as well give to his friends. The ladies crouched near the door of the hut, feeling all the awkwardness of their situation; and appeared glad to escape, when through our interpreter we dismissed them.

One of them [Rose's Xhosa travelling companions], Ikey, had a jest, on which he much valued himself, exhibiting, in an amusing manner with his hands, the superiority of their mode of travelling over ours. At first, the race seemed in favour of the horse, the hand that represented him starting off at an easy canter, but quickly halted, and began to kick and snort, then went on for a time, again stopped, and again proceeded; and the Kaffer imitated the horse's panting, and finished by making him knock up; while the other hand, denoting the walker, continued the same even pace to the journey's end.

STEPHEN KAY

Kay was a Methodist missionary who devoted considerable energy in the 1820s and '30s to combating what he considered the heathen customs of the Xhosa and the activities of their diviners and rainmakers – "the very pillars of Satan's kingdom". Ironically, in detailing these unchristian practices, he left a valuable record of Xhosa beliefs.

ADD ANOTHER STONE

In various parts of Caffraria, and, according to the accounts given by the Amafengu, in the still more distant regions likewise, are found large stone heaps; to which the natives attach a kind of sacred character, and which by the Kaffers are called the *isivivani*. They consist simply of round piles of small stones, thrown loosely together, and are generally met with on the sides or upon the summits of mountains. Their size, of course, varies according to circumstances; but their form is always the same, obviously unstudied and devoid of all art. They are invariably erected within a few paces of the path. Every passenger regards it as a duty incumbent upon him to add another stone to the number, or otherwise a green branch taken from one of the neighboring trees for the purpose. While engaged in this act, he prays that his journey may be prosperous; that he may have strength to accomplish it; and that he may obtain an abundant supply of food on the way. This constitutes the great object of his petition; in concluding which he spits upon the article held in his hand, casts it upon the heap, and then proceeds. Should he on any occasion pass one of these rustic piles without attending to every punctilio of this pagan ceremony, and subsequently fail in his pursuit, or become weak and sickly on the path, such ills are immediately ascribed to his negligence at the *isivivane*, over which he mourns and bitterly grieves. With regard to the origin of this custom, the oldest men among them are unable to give us any satisfactory information. Heaps of a somewhat similar construction were formerly raised by the Hottentots, over the graves of their deceased relations; but this is not the occasion in the case before us. Whether therefore it may not be a relic of some system of idolatry that existed amongst their forefathers, or the remains only of a kind of patriarchal mode of making vows, are questions which may perhaps afford subject matter for speculation.

MARTEN DOUWE TEENSTRA

Teenstra, forced out of farming by money problems, left Holland for Java in 1825 to seek a civil appointment. He was forced to make a four-month stopover at the Cape to recover from an illness – probably rheumatic fever – contracted on board ship. He used the time to compile a detailed and accurate account of life at the Cape, with a heavy emphasis on agriculture. For students of the evolution of Afrikaans, the gem in it is Teenstra's rendition of a conversation in "verbasterd" Dutch between an Overberg farmer, his wife and a slave. "Sies!" says the wife as the family's pet baboon escapes his chain. "Ik ben bang, dat hij hier komt."

DEN OF GHOSTS
On his doctor's advice Teenstra followed Govert Cnoll's pilgrimage to the hot springs at Caledon, and lodged in the bath-house there, which he found thoroughly depressing. His gloom was heightened by the death, within a few hours of his arrival, of the only other patient in residence; Teenstra's window looked out on two gravestones.

Now everything was deathly silent in the bath house. Arend, my servant, provided me, without speaking, with food and drink; meanwhile my soul hungered, and languished from thirst: I lacked that necessary nourishment, for in this Mohammedan I had much less companionship there than I would have received from the dog I left behind me. O! what would I not have given, what would I not have whistled, if by doing so I could get my so handsome and fleet, so faithful and friendly *Carroo*! what balm would this not have brought to my smarts and homesickness! In addition, Arend had haunting on the brain, so he, for fear of evil spirits, which he had seen in fearsome form, and had heard now and then with a disturbing hissing and strange noises, abandoned me without telling me of his intention.

The bath-house at Caledon.

There I lay now completely devoid of human company, left to myself in that awful den of ghosts – yes, a den of terrors! and although I was afeared of no haunts, my anxiety nevertheless now began to increase markedly. The whole night I spent in this solitude, hearing now and then a bat flitting in the passage.

The next day no person came to care for me, and being too weak to risk entering the bath alone, I remained in bed, without hearing any life or noise; then at dusk I heard movement in the kitchen; and since there was no further development, I stood up and hobbling on two crutches went through the dark passage to see what it was – and behold, it was one of my chickens, that wanted to take her night's rest. At once I shut fast the kitchen door, and bolted it, so that the house was now completely closed up; now I was determined to catch that fowl, and cook it. Deed followed decision: with one of my crutches I dealt the chicken a blow that nearly killed it, and knocked it off the brushwood, that lay here for firewood, so that we both fell to the ground. Then there began in the ghosts' den a hunting and shrieking; but eventually I was fortunate to overcome the hen in a corner of the room, and having now killed her, I tried to get the fire going again; but it was as dead as the hen lying before me. Then I went back to my room with my dead fowl, and began to remove its feathers; then the fatigue and increasing pain drove me back to bed, to which I also took my chicken, to continue my labour, but the darkness hindered it anew. I then laid down my head, in the hope of being able to obtain a result in the morning. The night, which was a week long, eventually came to an end, and now my first job was to seek the tinderpot, and make a fire, which I happily managed swiftly, after which I set the still-filthy pot with water on the cooking-range, and after having plucked the remaining feathers of my chicken, thrust it in the pot, and afterwards fished it out of the ocean of soup with a stick, and holding it in my hands, started gnawing at the meat. – Then, what joy! the good Kleijn came to visit me, and saw with wonder my condition, saying, that Coetzée, my host, was out riding to *Genadendal*, and would not return before Thursday. Kleijn therefore went off in all haste, to send me someone to help me as swiftly as possible.

THE ART OF CHANGING HIMSELF
In the Riviersonderend valley, on his return journey from the hot baths. Hendrik Wessels was a Caledon tanner whom Teenstra had hired to accompany him on excursions.

From here we now rode past the place of du Toit, which was prettily situated against the slope of unusually high ridges. In the deep kloofs one saw here many small trees and thickets. Wessels related to me, (which I record here as an instance of superstition,) that on one occasion he had to take a Hottentot, who was in chains, to the veld-cornet; but that this man, like many Hottentots, understood the art of changing himself into a jackal. Here at this spot it happened to him, and the Hottentot abruptly changed himself into that particular animal, and thereafter plunged into the depths of the kloof, after which he never saw him again. Another Hottentot, named Klaas, for a joke changed himself into a lion at *Caledon*, in front of many onlookers, and in that shape caused a tremendous fright: known afterwards as Klaas Leeuw, he is still alive, coming now and then to *Caledon*.

DESERVING OF PUNISHMENT
Back in Cape Town. As is apparent from this piece, Teenstra was a philanthropist; he went on to write books on slavery and Christianity. The Mosaic law he talks of here maintains a beating should be no more than 40 strokes. Thus the 39, so you don't incur the wrath of God if you've miscounted one.

157

I now walked to the *tronk*, or the place of imprisonment and punishment of the slaves, situated on the lower or north side of the Strand street; but we shall not stop here long: because I am convinced, that it will quickly bore you there, as well as me. Imagine that one first passes through some cages, where these unfortunate beings, some chained and nearly mother naked, are shut up, and, since one finds many of them in one cage, where the filthy slaves and Hottentots who, smearing a certain mixture of fat, oil etc. in the hair on their heads, make an unbearable stench, while they lie on the grounds like creatures void of reason. Worse, yes much worse, than we do the animals at home, they treat the poor natives of this land. – Christians! no, you only bear the name, – white Europeans! who wish to have the reputation of enlightened; Africans, descendants of the Europeans! search your own heart and look on your slaves with more compassion! Are they not our fellow-beings? are they not also our brothers? are they not with us children of one and the same God and Father? – Consider, that they after a few days are equal to their master and to the most powerful king; – know, that they, though you bury them in a separate place, set apart from your churchyard, know, I say, that they will appear with you before one and the same Judge, standing there equal to you in everything. – Then taking a closer look, going further into the prison, and further among these cages, my heart became anxious on hearing the screaming of a maid, whom they had bound fast to a whipping post which stood on the inner square, and there, at the request of her owner, were administering a beating; a beating consisted of 39 blows with a bundle of 5 or 6 thin canes or also with a rope-end. See, this is punishment according to Jewish law. It happens on request of the owner, without any judicial investigation. Whatever the request of sir or madam might be based on, the maid or the boy receive a beating; and if they can no longer get along with the slaves, then they send them to the treadmill, or put them up on an auction for sale, just like we would bring a horse for one or other reason to a market or auction, to be sold there or disposed of to a bidder.

From here one comes then eventually to the so-called treadmill, the nearness of which is made known by an unpleasant sweaty smell. Here 10 or 12 slaves are treading the wheel, with nothing more than breeches on their bodies, for their punishment. The wheel is an oblong cylinder, of about 6 or 7 Dutch ells in length and 2 Dutch ells in diameter. Around it there are 24 or 25 small strips of wood, of 10 or 12 Dutch inches wide, with the inner edge pointing towards the centre of the wheel, like the ribs on a threshing machine, onto which 10 to 14 slaves climb up at the same time, holding onto a pole placed above the wheel. A police servant, here called Kaffer, generally extremely slovenly dressed, being great drinkers and unfeeling creatures, keeps an eye and a cane on things there. The treading lasts from 7 in the morning, or when the day-gun sounds. (The rising and setting of the sun is announced every evening and morning to the inhabitants of this city, by the firing of a cannon from the old castle.) In the morning at 7 o'clock then the slaves begin to tread the mill, and this continues, with small pauses for rest, to 12 noon, and then from 1 o'clock in the afternoon to sundown or the evening gun. I have seen them come off, unable to speak one word, with their naked chest and abdomen rising and falling like a smith's bellows. Some owners of slaves send obstinate ones there 6 or 8 days in a row; and what is worst about this, is the *absolute necessity* to have slaves to drive this flour machine; because this treadmill belongs to the government, and is assigned or hired out by contract, for a period of a year, to someone or other, and this by the fiscal or prosecutor of the accused slaves or Hottentots. Here there must therefore be people treading the treadmill in the same way as there must be wind to turn the windmills in our fatherland; without wind ours stand still and without criminals this mill does not turn: therefore slaves and Hottentots deserving of punishment often have to be sought out. When this need arises, the aforesaid servants of justice often, and particularly on Saturday and Sunday evenings, seize any drunken, rowdy or fighting slaves or Hottentots in the streets; because without wrongdoers the miller would be not be able to grind any flour and he would not be able to pay government the hire, and there must also of course be flour. This rabble must therefore be sought out, whether or not there is adequate reason to accuse them or not; because otherwise this machinery would have to stand still and this could not be – no, if you have not deserved it, then your father or grandfather must have, off you go!

ANDREW GEDDES BAIN

Bain was a trader, explorer, road builder and geologist, whose dinosaur discoveries earned him the title of father of South African palaeontology. He visited Sebego, a Ngwaketsie chief living north of the Molopo River, in 1826. Bain was searching for the "Mines of Mileta", which he believed would be rich in a variety of metals.

To pull our noses
This morning we had an invitation from Sibigho to visit him, which of course we immediately complied with & found him seated under a tree surrounded by a great number of petty Chiefs & others. He asked permission to pull our noses in token of friendship & held his own out that we might return the compliment. This ceremony was also performed by his two brothers, one of whom was seated on each side of him, & we gave each a good pull to the no small danger of soiling our fingers which was, however, received as the warmest expression of friendship. This was the first time we had seen this mode of salutation & it was no small fund of amusement to us.

Partners for the night
On the Mngazi River, south of present-day Port St Johns, in 1829.

On coming up to the craal where we had spent the night preceding I found a very great show of Amapondan virgins seated in regular order on the ground when, after some refreshments had been offered us, the ladies were desired to choose themselves partners for the night from the men then present. To my astonishment the first fixed upon me before I understood the meaning of the entertainment. The second fixed on a Caffre (one of my train) who, more gallant than his master went up & kissed the damsel's hand as a sign of his approval. The next also chose the Malunga, or white man, & of course I took the hint to kiss the hand of my fair one. This fun went on till all the ladies were disposed of & four of them fell to my share, so that if I had been disposed to stop another evening at the Kraal I should have been well supplied, but as I was anxious to return to the waggons the disappointed ladies were obliged to take the will for the deed; but as a small consolation (which by the bye was I believe all they wanted of me) I gave each a present of some beads for her good intentions towards me.

I was afterwards given to understand that it was but a common rite of hospitality that was here practised upon us, & that all the Amapondan virgins are *broken in* by strangers. I considered those people the most friendly I had yet found among the Caffre tribes & left them with regret ...

James Holman

JAMES HOLMAN

Holman joined the British navy, but lost his sight at the age of 25. Undeterred by his blindness, he decided to travel the world. After an initial excursion to Siberia, he set out in 1827 on a three-and-a-half-year voyage that took him to Brazil, the west and east coasts of Africa, India, China and Australia. At the Cape he made his way, largely on horseback, to the eastern frontier and back. Holman appears to have dictated diary notes to helpers as he travelled, but he also had use of an apparatus called the "Nocto via Polygraph", invented by a Mr Wedgewood, which enabled blind people to write "very clearly and legibly".

SECURE UPON A PRECIPICE
At Cape Point.

We re-ascended the cliff, and made our way to the top of a rock over the cave, 276 feet above it, in a perpendicular line; and where it was, with great difficulty, that I persuaded my friends to allow me to sit on the extreme point; and I was obliged repeatedly to assure them, that my confidence was founded on experience, before I could gain their consent. I must admit, that the seat was very dangerous; especially as the occupier must allow his legs to hang over the rock: but to me, it was less so than to those who enjoy the blessing of sight: for, strange as it may appear, it is no less true than singular, that since my loss of vision, I have ever felt myself more secure upon a

160

precipice, than while I had the power of looking down upon the dizzy scene below. This does not proceed from bravado, or insensibility to the danger, because I always wish *that* to be clearly explained to me, and the better I understand it, the more confidence I feel in my own power of self-possession: it enables me to turn my whole attention to the sense of *touch*, which having ceased to be acted on by the nervousness communicated from the visual organ, is firm and secure.

To celebrate finding himself on "the highest pinnacle of Southern Africa", he drank a toast to King George out of a limpet shell.

AT FULL GALLOP
Leaving Plettenberg Bay.

When I was mounted ready for my journey, my Hottentot guide, who was engaged arranging the reins, gave me, by some mistake, the leading rein instead of the bridle, upon which the horse, being a noble, fine spirited animal, feeling himself free, set off with me at full gallop. The Field Cornet had previously expressed his fears that I should find him difficult to mount on account of his spirit, but had assured me that, after a breathing of a few miles, I should find him a gentle and a pleasant creature, and the only one in his stable equal to the difficult journey I had to perform over the mountains. My reply had been a jocular one, that I believed myself able to mount a capering horse, having already had some experience in that way (alluding to my recent tumble), and that if I was once fairly in the saddle, I fancied I could contrive to keep there; and thus was I put to the test, for the animal made a rapid sweep of at least half-a-mile to return to his stable, into which he would have dashed headlong, and sent me the Lord knows where, if the Field Cornet and Mr. John Rex had not anticipated his movements by running to shut the stable-door, where they caught hold of his bridle the moment he approached.

The Cape of Good Hope

After reassuring his friends, he set off again on the same horse "and found him precisely what his master had described him to be, good-tempered, and powerful, completing his work admirably".

CHAPTER FOUR

1830 to 1850

In which a young lady inadvertently exposes her
knees, a missionary goes lion hunting with an
umbrella, frogs get into the soup, a Voortrekker is
overcome by grief, a troopship is driven onshore
in a gale, a fish makes a noise during prayers,
and a thief is condemned to death.

JOHN HERSCHEL

*Astronomer, natural scientist, pioneer photographer and social reformer, Herschel
dominated British science for 50 years. He travelled to the Cape in 1834 specifically to survey the southern skies, and installed a 20-foot reflecting telescope at his
home in what is now the suburb of Claremont. Over the next four years Herschel
recorded an astonishing 1,200 pairs of double stars, and 1,700 nebulae and clusters. On his death in 1871 he was buried in Westminster Abbey near Isaac
Newton. This is a letter written to a friend soon after his arrival at the Cape.*

FIELDS FULL OF LIGHT
The 20 feet has been erected and at work since the latter end of February
and I have already examined by sweeping a considerable portion of the
sky. The Southern heavens are very rich and full of extraordinary objects. I
cannot help believing that we are *nearer the stars* here. I mean that the Milky
Way is not equidistant from the earth all round – but that we are situated
excentrically in it, & nearer to it in that quarter which intervenes between
Canopus & α Centauri. I have not room here
to state the grounds of this opinion. Meanwhile, whether owing to proximity or to
intrinsic constitution, some of the globular
clusters such as ω Centauri & others are
objects of such magnificence as of themselves
to repay the trouble of bringing a large telescope to view them.

The Magellanic clouds however are the
most wonderful and mysterious objects
which these heavens present. They consist
partly of stars, partly of globular clusters of
clustering groupes of irregular form – (and
some very strange ones) and of great regions

The 20-foot tele-
scope in place.

162

of *irresolvable nebula* especially the Nebecula Minor, the greater portion of whose extent is beyond the reach of the space-penetrating power of the 20-feet and offers the appearance of fields full of light, with few discernible stars, & occasional knots & starry & nebulous patches.

HARRIET LOW

Low, daughter of an upper-class family from Salem, Massachusetts, was awed by the massive breakfasts she was confronted with at her lodgings in Cape Town. She confided to her diary that she expected before long to be what the Dutch called "a dicker fatty". She was travelling from the Far East with her aunt and sick uncle, a Macao trader who had been told to seek a healthier climate. Though they moved on doctor's orders to a cottage at Kirstenbosch, and the uncle took a medicine "made of herbs from the Caffre country", he died at the Cape. Low is here amusing herself soon after their arrival in January 1834. Mr Jones was tutor to a local family.

MY POOR BONES

About half-past three we mounted our steeds, and commenced our ride to "Bergvlyt", the residence of Mr. John Eksteen. We arrived about five, and I must say it was anything but pleasure to me. In the first place, my horse was lazy, and if perchance by whipping him I urged him into a canter, it was almost at the expense of my poor bones, for I had not yet recovered from yesterday's frolic. To add to my miseries, the breeze was strong, and the pins came out of my dress, and I had great difficulty in keeping it in decent order. Then my bonnet kept blowing off, and what with my lazy horse, my sore bones, my whip, the reins, my bonnet, and my dress, I had more than I could manage. I could have cried almost, with vexation. Whether Mr. Jones saw my knees or not, I do not know, but he was kind enough to keep in front a little. Before we got to our destination, my comb had contrived to make its escape, and my hair was hanging over my back, so you may judge how I looked, but I cannot tell you the agony I was suffering. Miss E. had an easier horse and an easier saddle, and was enjoying herself comparatively, though her hair plagued her some. We arrived at last, and, having arranged our hair and our dresses a little, took a walk in the garden with the young ladies. It was as romantic a spot as I ever saw. We sat there some time, and then prepared for our return, which I dreaded, my bones were so stiff. I gave my horse to Mr. Jones, and took his, hoping it might be easier. It was not quite so lazy, but cantered harder. There was not so much wind going home, and, saving the pain I endured, it was pleasant. I certainly never was so tired before.

HENRY BUTLER

Butler, an officer in the Royal Inniskilling Fusiliers, was given command of a post on the Fish River during the 1834-5 war against the Xhosa. His first challenge was when an Mfengu chief came to share an offering of milk in a "large white vessel of English earthenware, with one handle". "The chief was at last made sensible that there was something in our religion which forbade its use as a drinking cup, and a calabash was substituted," Butler said.

SOME STRANGE NOISE

The Great Fish River, in dry weather an insignificant stream, though running deep in a rugged bed, has its sources remote among the high mountains of the interior; it is subject to sudden and violent floods from the bursting of the thunder-storms which hang about the summits of the latter – a crash is heard through the forest louder and more articulate as it approaches, and down comes the torrent in three rolling billows of water like red liquid mud, toppling one over the other to the height of forty feet, and bearing with them uptorn trees and fragments of waggon tops and oxen that have been overtaken at the drifts, and not unfrequently a luckless Hottentot, or other ill-fated traveller.

On the banks of this river was our encampment, and that night afforded us a further initiation into a frontier life not a little startling, to those so recently cast among the grim scenery and circumstance of an African bivouac.

I had fallen asleep, with my head against the wall of my tent, and was roused by some strange noise beside me, as if a dog were sniffing at my ear; a low moan, immediately afterwards, which I recognised as the cry of the hyæna, caused me to spring to my feet with my double-barrelled gun, which lay beside me, ready for action. As soon as I had sufficiently awakened my faculties, and ascertained that the noise had been from the outside, I passed through the opening of my tent, and immediately before me, between me and the moonlight, stalked a monster as big as a calf, in whose shambling gait and drooping quarters I recognised the beast that the beef-eater loves to characterise as the "untameable" – the "laughing." The first impulse was

to fire into his head – a moment's thought, and I saw the ground beyond strewed with blankets, under each of which lay buried in sleep a Hottentot militiaman. While I was moving about to procure a fair shot, without the risk of bagging one of the sleepers, or of my own men, whose tents were pitched around, the monster strode off slowly into the darkness, his head turned bashfully over his shoulders, watching my movements with a phosphoric wink in his eyes. A few paces from me was a sheep kraal, in the shady side of whose fence, my eyes having become now accustomed to the darkness, I distinguished no less than eight of these grizzly monsters pacing up and down, impatiently sniffing the mutton within, and picking their steps among the blankets where the Hottentots snored supine. To fire among such a crowd was out of the question, though the brutes seemed very little disposed to hurry out of my way; the risk now also occurred to me of raising an alarm in the camp; a shot fired by accident some time previously, had set two companies of Highlanders firing into each other, nor was the panic allayed before several had been killed and wounded. After gazing for a while upon the strange scene, and observing how completely the aboriginals, who must be best acquainted with the natural history and habits of the beasts of the desert, trusted to their honour, I resolved to trust to their honour too, and muttering to myself that fragment of the wisdom of our foremothers, that the devil is never so bad as he is painted, flung myself down in my cloak within my tent again and in five minutes was asleep.

THOMAS ARBOUSSET

Arbousset and two other French Protestant missionaries established the first mission among the Sotho in 1833. For decades Arbousset acted as an adviser to King Moshoeshoe: in 1858 during the first war between the Sotho and the Orange Free State, his house at Morija and books were burned by Boers who suspected him of supplying arms to their foes.

OH! MY WHITE MEN
Here Arbousset and fellow missionary Francois Daumas are on an 1836 trip to the north of Moshoeshoe's kingdom. During this journey they named Mont-aux-Sources, which for more than a century afterwards was considered the highest peak in southern Africa.

From Kokuatsi we came to Sisiyue, passing through Tsikaniane, where we preached the gospel to the inhabitants. They pointed out to us at a little distance from the road Moghotli, Monchunyane, and Chupane, three villages of Lighoyas, who but a short time ago were cannibals, as were also the inhabitants of Sisyue. The extreme wretchedness and frightful manners of the inhabitants of the place, forced themselves on our attention, but notwithstanding their ferocity, they fled at our approach. Almost all left their cabins, though it was nightfall and the weather very bad. It was not till the next day that they permitted us to get near them to give them some tokens of our good will, and to tell them what we had to say to them about the Saviour.

Moshoeshoe

A man, with numerous gashes in his face, sang, danced, and pirouetted near the wagon, assuming a thousand low comic attitudes. "Wonders!" cried he, "Wonders! what have we here? Yesterday, on perceiving this *house* in the plain (the wagon covered with a large linen sail) I swore that it must be a *walking rock*. To-day I see heads with crops of *horse hair* (our locks, every where wondered at, sometimes envied, sometimes ridiculed, happening not to be crisp,) I see white faces, white hands, oh! oh! my white men, oh! oh!" This old cannibal ridiculed many other things about us; but when we put a mirror before his eyes, in order to procure for him once in his life the pleasure of beholding his hideous figure, he made some amusing somersets, and fell on his back, on which he lay for several minutes laughing at himself like a great fool.

Thaba Bosiu

Tree of the Skirts

In 1840 Arbousset made another journey through the kingdom, this time in the company of Moshoeshoe himself. On the earlier trip, the missionary had heard first-hand accounts of the cannibalism rife during the Mfecane, and now he again encountered evidence of anthropophagy.

But, while in the midst of this delightful nature, what sorrow to find there, along one of the paths, a lonely tree, such as we saw at four o'clock, withered from the roots up to the branches. It must have been, I imagine, like the fig tree of the Gospel which was cursed by the Lord! I am speaking about the sad Lithethana, or Tree of the Skirts. This name originated from the horrors perpetrated by the Bechuana cannibals about twelve years ago. When those ferocious animals stopped travellers on the road, in order to eat their flesh, they would hide in the forest of Lithethana, through which I have not passed without shuddering. If it was at night, they would spread on the valley floor a strong rush cord designed to make the travellers stumble, and they would immediately charge upon them to cut their throats. During the day they would dart forth from their horrible shelters, like infernal demons, and swoop down on their victims. Then they would seize them, tie both their hands behind their backs, and lead them like that to the kraal, while beating them with sticks and even assegais. Added to their misfortune, the women had to strip off their skirt-like garments or leather aprons, which were hung by their executioners like a spectacle on the branches of the Lithethana. Then the women were driven or dragged to the den of these bandits.

Pleasant memories

Still with Moshoeshoe, this time in his youthful haunts.

All of the places which Moshoeshoe saw were filled with childhood memories, those kinds of pleasant memories of such exquisite delight that everyone preserves them enshrined in his heart as the best and most enduring of all. Over there, on a beautiful plateau, he had often raced with his friends, sometimes naked and as free as the desert gazelles, sometimes mounted on three year old calves, which they themselves had broken in to carry them across the plains.

Further away in the beautiful midst of the valley, his initiation lodge had been built. It was what he nowadays jocularly calls his prison. It was there in a simple hut, isolated, as these people live, that for six full moons he had undergone his harsh education for manhood and military service. Only afterwards could he come out of the circumcision school and return to see his mother.

The mountain of Makosa offers an imposing appearance. It is large, high, covered by forests in its kloofs, and very steep.

"Follow me", Moshoeshoe cried out to me, as he climbed up. "I know this rugged and winding path well." He made me sit down at the spring of cold water called Maruru. "I used to quench my thirst every day here", the Basotho king told me, "when my father lived on the plateau which crowns this mountain."

Thereupon I asked him: "How does the heart respond to a man who sees again the place of his birth?"

To this question, he replied: "I have joy in my heart such as and even more than if I were returning home to Thaba-Bosiu and into the midst of my family."

Then he cast his eyes in all directions. "Over there", he said, "rises the mountain where Mokhachane was circumcised. To the right of that, you see the place where he lost a famous battle. Look at these remains of ancient kraals opposite us: they belonged to the wise Matete. What you are seeing in the same direction, a little farther off, are the ruins of the village of Mahao. Oh, how many human skulls lie in the depths of these valleys! How sad they seem! In olden days these mountains were alive with people; the cattle delighted in going out to pasture on those heights over there; all those hills facing us were cultivated … nowadays I see nothing but death, I hear nothing but silence."

"Bana beso!", exclaimed the Mosotho prince turning towards his subjects. "Brothers! How old this country has grown!", and he put his hand on his mouth as a sign of astonishment. After a long silent pause, when everyone was thinking about continuing on the way, the chief ordered them to wait, and he asked to be served a cup of tea. At the same time he again spoke extensively and almost entirely about the land of Makosa, which, incidentally, he wrongly considered to be more beautiful than the country where he now resides; but since his illusion was pardonable, no-one thought of disagreeing with him.

AND AN UMBRELLA
Sleeping in a cave at Ha 'Meea, the travellers were woken before dawn one morning by a cry of alarm: a pair of lions had killed and partly eaten two horses, one of which was Moshoeshoe's favourite steed Valiant Black.

We were going on a lion hunt, nobody could fail to be aware of that, and that was all that mattered as far as our young men were concerned. No wonder then, if in their extreme haste, some of them only picked up their trousers, while others wore less still, since they went wearing just an upper garment, even though it was more than a little cold.

Moshoeshoe, in particular, left in his drawers, a kerchief around his neck, coming in two bands crossing his chest, continuing to where they were tied beneath his shoulders. His Majesty was wearing buskins, but was bareheaded; and like the rest of the party he was on

foot. I was the only one walking beside him, because all of the hunters had gone ahead of us, with the exception of two young men who carried our guns, and therefore could not leave us. Besides my musket, I had armed myself with an assegai, a bamboo lance, and an umbrella, because I had heard it said that the lion stops short with fright when he sees an umbrella opened in front of him. So this means of minor protection could be useful to me in our undertaking.

The hunters cornered the beasts in a patch of forest and wounded one, but were unable to flush them out. So everyone went back to the cave for lunch, and Arbousset was unable to test the umbrella theory.

EUGENE CASALIS

Casalis was the third of the French missionaries in Basutoland. Known among the Sotho as mahloana-matsoana, *the man with the small dark eyes, he broke his glasses on the trip up. Here the short-sighted missionary and his one-eyed horse are trying to rejoin the party after returning to Graaff-Reinet in an unsuccessful search for replacements for the spectacles.*

SIX MORE LIONS

We were approaching one of the ill-looking defiles of which I have just spoken, when I saw something coming towards us, apparently in a rational manner, with none of those suspicious movements which indicate the presence of evil passions. Oh, joy! it was a dog! Yes, a dog, in real flesh and blood. I seem still to see him. He was of russet colour, of good size, and with a well-fed appearance. He was travelling with an air of quiet assurance, as of an animal that perfectly knew its way. No capricious stoppings on the road, no distractions, no more speed than was necessary. Unfortunately, he was going in a contrary direction from that which a confused remembrance counselled me to take. He hardly paid any attention to us. What would you have? He knew where he was going. Could he suspect we were less competent travellers than himself? How I should have liked to interview him, if only to get from his glance some sign of helpful sympathy! Hastily repeating the proper names most in use at the Cape amongst the canine tribe, I tried to stop this most respectable animal. It was lost labour. However, the meeting with him was not without use. My nerves, before somewhat over-excited, had need of this respite.

Some instants afterwards, what should I see but a monstrous head, which appeared in the midst of a thicket of mimosas, and an entire animal disengaged itself from the brushwood. It was as to size something like a small pony. My spectacles did not allow of my distinguishing the outlines in detail, but the whole appearance awakened in me certain recollections of the menagerie which were anything but agreeable – to wit, a mane, a bearing assured and menacing, and a tail ceaselessly lashing the hollow flanks. Without doubt it was a lion, and of a large size! One thing astonished me – that my nag in no degree shared my emotion. I observed, however, that the wind was not coming from the direction of the dreaded beast, and I had heard say that it was the smell which usually revealed to the domestic animals the presence in their vicinity of the king of the forest.

What was I to do? Go back? I should only draw on the enemy, in the hope of an easy triumph. Send my horse along at full speed! But that would make him desirous of showing me how far one of his great bounds could carry him. Having no weapons, any idea of resistance was out of the question. It remained then only to resign myself: to wait upon God, and to let the pony continue his steady trot.

It was not without a certain shrinking within myself, nor without a little mist in the eyes, that I reached the point where the lion would probably fall upon me if he wished to profit by his opportunity. Once there, I felt no more fear. It is an experience which I have gone through since in more than one encounter. I looked fixedly at the monster, but still without seeing him distinctly. There was nevertheless in his attitude something that seemed to me to betray uneasiness; a brusque movement forward, followed by a recoil, and stampings, apparently of inquietude rather than of anger. I do not recollect now of which eye my horse was blind, but he went on as if he saw nothing.

Thanks to the steadiness of his trot, I soon found myself at a reassuring distance from the object of my terrors. "That's enough for one day in the way of a fright," said I to myself, wiping my brow; "I have had the honour of exchanging looks with a lion in full daylight, and in his own domains!"

But my adventures were not yet over. I was in vein for heroic encounters. Soon after, behold six more lions, all as large as the first, and placed as if an evil genius had assigned to each one his post! I passed them, and yet lived!

The evening of this adventurous day, thanks to the perseverance of my little nag, and to the directions given me by a traveller whom Providence threw in our way, I found myself at the bivouac of my friends, seated with them before a great fire. Without asking me the date of my last repast, they treated me as a man dying of hunger. When at length the time for talking arrived the lions were not forgotten. "Seven!" murmured M. Lemue; "seven, and here am I without having yet seen a single one at close quarters!"

The next day our wagons were pleasantly rolling along. I had taken my place by the side of my incredulous friend, and was repeating to him how happy I was to have escaped. Suddenly, seizing him by the arm, I cried, "There are the lions! You will believe now how this country is infested with them!" Without moving, he said to the Hottentot who was driving, "Go quick with your whip, and chase my friend's lions over there!" – "No, no!" replied the other, roaring with laughter, "better give me your gun, I will make him eat some steaks off them!" They were gnus! a very inoffensive kind of antelope!

I have had since the consolation of knowing that others have been deceived by them in the same way. In order that the mistake may be possible, it is necessary to be shortsighted, or not to have good glasses, and also that the animal be facing you, with his head down, which renders the horns less visible. He is not the only one who, in this world, in order to conceal his own terrors gives himself ferocious airs.

ANDREW SMITH

Smith, a close friend of Charles Darwin, was appointed first superintendent of the South African Museum when it was established in 1825. He undertook three journeys to the interior, exploring the politics of the region on behalf of the Cape government and amassing a wealth of scientific information. These extracts are from his accounts of the final and most important of his journeys, a one-and-a-half-year expedition that began in late 1834 and took him and about 40 companions, including the artist Charles Davidson Bell, beyond the Limpopo to the Tropic of Capricorn. They brought back a mass of natural specimens and ethnological items, including 180 skins of "new or rare quadrupeds" and 3,379 of birds; three barrels of snakes and lizards; and hundreds of weapons, household items and personal ornaments from tribes they visited. Smith returned to England in 1837, where he rose to director-general of the army medical department just in time for the Crimean debacle – which he survived with reputation intact. He compiled a five-volume work on the zoology of South Africa, and had embarked on a massive ethnographic survey of the entire African continent when he died.

A GREAT QUANTITY OF WIND

Some days ago Mr. Bell's horse appeared sick, and to-day one of Kruger's was affected in the same way. K. considered the disease as constipation occasioned by eating locusts. Had his horse exercised sharply which caused him to evacuate both faeces and a great quantity of wind. Says when grass is scarce horses devour immense quantities of locusts and that they have the effect mentioned.

THE MAN JACKAL

The goal being reached and the cattle very tired, preparations for cooking the evening meal were immediately commenced, and while that was preparing a warm discussion ensued relative to the merits and demerits of the different oxen. But as that apparently had reached its highest interest

and as the tongues of all concerned were most loud, a sudden yelp from a jackal put a stop to the altercation. All immediately appeared to forget the subject and one feeling instead of the many which had previously existed seemed to pervade the members of the fireside group. No one denied but that [the] animal which had intimated his near approach was the "Man Jackal," and all were unanimous in regarding the visit as extremely unfavourable. The individuals best acquainted with the opinions entertained relative to such occurrences commenced immediately the ceremony recommend[ed] on such occasions which consisted in certain gestures and a fervent supplication for mercy. The latter is uttered in a tone so as to be audible to the animal, and it is believed if with that it ceases to call, the intercession has been successful, but if its cries are repeated, misfortunes will certainly occur. To the supplications of this evening it was, however, indifferent, and in its progress, uttered from time to time what led to the most awful forebodings. Some women who were present began to cry and there was scarcely one of the party who did not auger bad luck either to himself or his friend, and several predicted that some serious mishap would certainly happen before we should return to the colony. Among the most ready in drawing unfavourable conclusions was the man who it will afterwards be seen was killed by a lion.

NOW YOU ARE A MAN
Dingane was Shaka's brother and successor as king of the Zulus.

Whatever superiority he or others, however, may concede to the system of the white man is generally to be viewed simply as an indication of deceit, for the barbarian is not to be found who does not consider his own system the best and does not immediately advocate and practice it the moment after he may from policy have been professing an opposite opinion. In proof of this I may merely mention the following fact: while travelling from Port Natal to the residence of Dingan I had occasion to pass over a portion of road very hard and thickly covered with gravel. As may easily be supposed, shoes proved a great convenience, with which I endeavoured to impress the Zoolas who escorted me. They readily admitted the truth of what I stated. In a short time, however, the shoes I wore gave way so as to render it impossible to keep them on my feet, and not being supplied with others, I removed them and gave them to one of my attendants for the purpose of getting them repaired when we should halt and advanced in the best possible manner I could barefooted. The moment my condition was discovered a universal shout of joy proceeded from the escort and the chief in command approached me, slapped me upon the shoulder, "Now you are a man; before you were a woman. A man is disgraced by covering his feet!" And so much effect had this circumstance upon them that this was one of the things they communicated to their king and applauded me for having walked part of the way without shoes.

AND ALSO A LARGE DOG
The "tracto" is the braided leather trek-touw *used to pull an ox-wagon.*

We had now reached a country where it was necessary to be supplied with water before the darkness set in as crocodiles were to be found from hence in all the rivers, which were in the habit of seizing persons who might approach their haunts at night or even wander in their vicinity. David Scoon, a trader and a man of veracity who formed one of our party, when halting upon the banks of the Mariqua on a former occasion lost his *tracto*. Every search was made to recover it, but without success, and it was not till the following day when a crocodile made his appearance at the ford where Scoon's people were in the habit of scooping their water and for his boldness received a musket ball through his head that the fate of the tracto was discovered. The distended state of the reptile led the man who had shot it to suspect it had just made a hearty meal and, with the view of ascertaining upon what it had feasted the belly was slit open, when to the men's surprise they found the tracto unaltered, and also a large dog. The former, it was found, had been swallowed whole and no care had been taken to detach the four massive iron rings by which it is attached to the yokes.

SUCKING AT THEIR CLOTHES
24th June 1835

Towards evening of the day after we left this place, some of our hunters encountered a black rhinoceros with her young one, and on firing several shots at her she fled with great rapidity and in the flight which took place among dense brushwood the calf lost her. As soon as that took place the little beast, which was closely pursued by one of the assailants, turned upon him with the appearance of being highly infuriated and as if determined to revenge the injury he himself had sustained and likewise that of his mother. The man fled with precipitation to the highest tree he observed and he had not ascended that sufficiently high before he received a violent blow on one of his limbs from the head of the little combatant who was not larger than a moderate sized pig. He soon, however, reached a place of safety, and though beyond the reach of immediate danger he did not feel secure from consequences, as the little beast continued butting the trunk of the tree with the utmost violence and each time causing it to yield, so that fears were entertained it might in time give way. In a few minutes the entire of the bark of one side was displaced and marks were even left in the solid wood portions of which some began to peel off. In this position was the prisoner when several of his companions attracted by his call reached the spot, and the instant they approached the enemy abandoned the tree and made towards them. On their flying he did not follow but returned to the tree and pursued his employment as if he had actually settled within himself that by perseverance he was to succeed in getting the individual who had been a prominent actor in depriving him of his mother into his power.

By this time the waggons had reached close to the spot and cords were immediately supplied to secure the beast, and dogs were also taken to confuse him while he should be entangled in the [cords] which were prepared for him. The plan was successful, but the instant he discovered himself in the power of his enemies he got doubly infuriated, and it was impossible to manage him until two ropes were fixed so as to pull in opposite directions by which he was prevented from approaching those who held either. The result of the last measure served to excite him violently. Instead of running furiously onwards as he had done hitherto, he now held back and it was feared he would be strangled in the endeavour to get him to the spot where we had established our camp for the night about a quarter of a mile distant. With patience, however, he was carried safely to the spot, but not till after the holders of the cords relaxed them alternately so as to give him hope that by a violent rush he might reach some one of his [assailants], all

172

of which keeping constantly in advance of him. Though panting to a degree inconceivable from the exertion he had made, and apparently almost unable to stand, nevertheless, on reaching the waggons, renewed his efforts against whatever attracted his attention, and on finding himself unable to reach living objects he set to butting with determination every substance that was within his reach.

Pity for his suffering and a conviction that perseverance in such proceedings must soon terminate his existence, his feet were tied with a hope of putting a stop to his efforts. In this, however, we were not successful, for though he was reduced to a condition in which he could not stand, he, nevertheless, persevered in dashing his head so violently against the ground that in a short time he effected the destruction of the thick skin by which it was covered in several places besides breaking up the hard soil upon which he was lying. A few hours of continued exertion, however, completely exhausted him, and at last he lay as if dead and did not notice any persons who approached.

25th June 1835
Next morning he was to appearance disposed very differently to what he had been previously. When approached he raised his head from the ground, looked good natured, and almost courted caresses. These were bestowed without any effort on his part towards resentment, which led us to untie him. The moment he was let loose he ran towards the nearest person, but with no symptoms of rage or an appearance of offering violence, commenced sucking at their clothes and manifested every evidence of suffering under extreme hunger and in hope of acquiring food. Now he was

docile, affectionate, and imploring, there was the most perfect safety in his company and his condition called forth general sympathy, so that his life was taken but not without reluctance.

A LITTLE CLAY
The Baquans when they have not seen each other for a long time take a little clay, place it on the fingers near the points, and then apply it to the forearm of the other a little above the wrist, he doing the same to the other; each then pulls his fingers down towards his acquaintance's hand and thus smears the wrist with it. They do this before speaking in order that when they converse they may not get headaches. At our encampment three did it with dung.

JAMES ALEXANDER

Before he undertook a commission from the Royal Geographical Society in 1836 to visit Namaqualand and Damaraland, Alexander had seen military service in Burma, the Balkans, and an 1826 war between Persia and Russia. This helps explain why he included in his equipment for the African expedition various articles for "offence and defence", including double-barrelled guns, fusees, rifles with bayonets, swords, pistols, boarding pikes, seven rockets, 100 pounds of gunpowder, plus lead, flints, bullet moulds and 600 rounds of ball cartridge "for a stand, in case of being attacked".

BLACK BLOOD
Though the farmers affect to have a great abhorrence for any admixture of black blood, yet, strange to say, I saw, at a farm house, several dark children running about, who, I was told, were the offspring of one of the daughters of the family by a Hottentot youth. Another of the daughters of the same family married a Boor, and, seven months after marriage, produced a black child, which a trader seeing, asked "Hoe kom dat?" (How did that happen?) When the husband coolly replied, "that one day his wife was going out and was frightened by a black man, whom she suddenly saw behind the door, and that the child became black in consequence." The wife was by, and on hearing this she merely laughed. So both parties "thought no harm."

A MASS OF FAT
The sun, by some of the people of this benighted land [Namaqualand], is considered to be a mass of fat, which descends nightly to the sea, where it is laid hold of by the chief of a white man's ship, who cuts a portion of tallow off it, and giving it a kick, it bounds away, sinks under the wave, goes round below, and then comes up again in the east next morning, its fat having again grown.

LIKE BADLY COOKED LIVER
In the evening we were rewarded for our dull day's journey by finding ourselves in the midst of scattered trees like those in an English park, with broad pastures and plenty of water: this was at the Huntop or Springing river, one of the finest in this part of Boschman land.

My four European followers cooked for me and for themselves day about, and the cook here incautiously filling his pot in the dark, we got in the soup substances which, between the teeth, felt like badly cooked liver, but which, on being held up to the light of the fire, turned out to be frogs!

THEY RAN AWAY FROM IT

The Boschmans here saw three new things, white men, horses, and a waggon. Of white men, they thought that they were not particularly handsome, but, I fear, "rather the contrary;" that is, we were thought to have been flayed! My horses, they imagined were a sort of ox without horns, and said they supposed they would eat very well; the waggon they believed at first was alive, and afterwards, that it was one of the strange white things (ships) which had come out of the sea, and was now travelling over the land.

The Boschmans in the neighbourhood of the Great River even, used lately to be very much afraid of waggons: thus, Mr. Schmelen's people once caught a Boschman, and he told them that the first time he and his people saw the missionary's wagon they ran away from it for a whole night, thinking it was some terrible monster, and that they always jumped over its spoor, and would not touch the wheel tracks on any account.

On another occasion, Mr. Schmelen sent out an old waggon with a hunting party, when one of the fore wheels was broken, and the waggon remained standing in the field for two months, at the end of which time a Boschman came to Mr. Schmelen's place, and said that he had seen the missionary's *pack ox* standing in the field for a long time, with a broken leg; and that as he did not observe that it ate any grass, he was afraid that it would soon die of hunger if it was not taken away!

I COULD HAVE EATEN MY SADDLE

We had not got any game for some days; the sheep were almost all eaten, and the broken-backed and lame bullocks devoured by my forty followers. Not knowing that we should obtain any supplies at the sea, (and we were almost certain we should find no game there), we were now reduced to very short commons. A sheep was made to go a long way, and none of us had ever sufficient to appease our hunger. The Namaquas asked for a bullock's hide, which we had kept to make shoes of,

Nama hunters

and roasting it at the fire, they pounded it between stones, and devoured the whole of it. I partook of it also, and found it very tough, but not disagreeable to the taste: to be sure, at the time, I could have eaten my saddle for hunger; and I certainly thought that our leather trousers must soon furnish a meal. Old Choubib was a great talker and a great eater; and when he got a mess of meat before him, he made always a large hole in it. An ingenious device was fallen upon to cheat him of his usual portion. When he sat down to eat, one of the white men asked him a question on some subject, he answered it at length; then another would ask his opinion on something else,

175

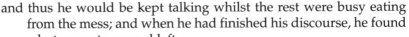

and thus he would be kept talking whilst the rest were busy eating from the mess; and when he had finished his discourse, he found but a scanty morsel left.

SNAKE OF THE FOUNTAIN

After a day's halt to refresh the cattle, we continued our journey along the cold and flat summits of the Bulb Mountains, and turned aside to get water at the fountain 'Ahuas, or blood. In this was said to dwell a snake which guarded it, but strange to say, when the fountain was reached, it was found to be dried up, and a water snake, about six feet long, brown above and yellow below, lay dead beside it. The Namaquas immediately cried out, "Some one has killed the snake of the Fountain, and it is therefore dried up."

Not far from the Fountain of Blood, a young Boschman and his wife were met, and the woman accused her husband of having committed a great crime; she said, that the day before, they had drank at 'Ahuas, and the Boschman seeing the snake there had killed it. He excused himself by saying that he was a stranger in that part of the country, and did not know that the snake he had killed at the edge of the water, was the snake of the Fountain.

LOUIS TRIGARDT

After several decades farming stock on both sides of the Eastern Cape frontier, Trigardt trekked north, complaining that the area had been "ruined" by the blacks. He left probably in early 1835, with his sights on the Moçambique coast, which he hoped would be suitable for settlement. Trigardt and a handful of followers marked time for just over a year in the Soutpansberg area before making an arduous crossing of the Drakensberg some 64 miles north of modern Lydenburg. When the wagons had completed the descent, three of the boys in the party – Isaak Albagh, Kootje Scheepers and Frederick Botha – ran away one night, taking three guns, including the one Trigardt's adult son Karel (whom he calls Carolus in the journal) had been using. The grown-ups made half-hearted efforts to find them, Karel swearing to cut off the ears of the youngster who took his gun. Five days passed before the errant juveniles returned.

CRY THE WHOLE NIGHT

When they arrived at the wagon, we asked them for their reasons for doing what they did. They said that they wanted to go out to our former land, but when they had been away for three days, Frederick began to repent. The fourth morning he said that he wanted to return to his parents and had done nothing but cry the whole night. Albagh then began to take pity on him and also started crying. They turned back to the wagons but Koot did not want to, but seeing that they started off, he followed. They had shot one red buck and one wild fowl.

We found everything they had taken away or stolen except 36 bullets of Anthonie's, and some powder of his was also missing; one bridle of old Albagh; two ox-riems of Carolus.

Albagh asked me what I wanted to do with his child. I replied that as they had returned on their own and had brought back nearly all the goods, I for my part would forgive them this time. Mrs. Schepers said that she would not be satisfied until her son had received a thrashing. She called Carolus and a few others; had them hold him fast; gave him a thrashing with two straps, and Albagh did the same to his son; and then Botha also to his.

Carolus gave Albagh's son a blow with the fist above his eye, so that he had a wound. I asked him why he did it. He replied that the Bastard was too arrogant in his appearance. I said that he should leave it to the parents; that each parent should punish his child according to his feelings. After they had had their whipping, we forgave them all for this time.

GRIEF OVERCAME ME

The party reached Lourenço Marques, present-day Maputo, in March 1838, at the height of the malaria season. Surrounded by swamps, with inadequate grazing and water unfit even for cattle, it was far from a promised land. Soon after their arrival, the trekkers began to go down with fever, among them Trigardt's wife, Martha, and their young son Gustavus. Martha was taken into the residence of the Portuguese governor to be cared for by his lady "die veel kennis van de siekte heb".

About 3 o'clock I went to my dear wife. The lady said that I might again lead her gently through the room by her arm, so that she moved her body a little. When I was in the front room with her, I let her sit a little; the lady opened her mouth. She said she would have to clean her tongue; that she saw great danger if this was not done. I took her back to her room and with much persuasion from me, she let the lady do it.

I stayed with her until sundown, to see whether she would again get the cold fever at the time that the sun went under. But she was free of it. And the time that she got it every evening, was past. The lady said she also had to clean Goestaf. He had, as was usual, the cold and after it the hot fever. The lady cleaned his mouth. She went to fetch a piece of bread for Goestaf to give him to eat.

As she left, Mrs. Schepers came calling me; that my wife had suddenly become so ill. I ran in all haste to her room; found her speechless! I lifted her upright. She came back to her senses a little. The lady brought medicines which restored her awareness.

The lady said that I and the children could safely sleep; that her thought was that she would be stronger in the morning than now. And did not wish, if she was to

Left: Tsetse fly

177

express her preference, that we should watch her during the night; that she herself would watch in the night.

Such grief overwhelms me that I cannot think of living another day.

Thursday the 1st. In the morning when the cock crowed, I stood up to see if I could not hear how my dear wife was faring. But all was still in the house. I again lay down but could not sleep. Rose again with the second cock-crow: was still not day. Waited impatiently for the time that the lady might open her door.

I sent Carolus to knock and to get news of his mother's condition. He returned and said that his mother was reasonable, but very weak.

I went to her for the first time and bade her good morning. She spoke so softly that I could hardly understand what she said.

I asked her if my dear wife knew me. She answered, how could she not know me, but with such difficulty that I could hardly understand her words. Then I saw that my feeling was only too well founded; that I would never see her in health!

From that moment grief overcame me to such an extent that I did not know what I said or did. The Children grieved with me, which saddened my more and more burdened heart. I took leave of her for this life, and bethought to see her again in the Heavenly Father's house, and did not complain to Him but prayed that He should come to my aid. The will of the Lord must happen and all our efforts and care were in vain.

About eleven o' clock the Almighty God took her away! with firm faith in … I am! that my treasured and dearly loved Darling had undergone a blessed transformation. However I could not console myself. Grief over-whelmed me … so greatly that I was almost out of my mind. The gentle-man and lady consoled me, but for me there is no consolation on earth!

I had Carolus make a coffin for her death, when I saw there was little hope for her. It was finished that evening. Jan Pretorius asked the people to help him.

My beloved and Precious Treasure has been taken from me forever!

Martha's death, in May 1838, was followed by that of Karel's wife and little daugh-ter. Trigardt made only one journal entry after his record of Martha's passing: on August 10 the same year, when he turned 55. "I had a quiet birthday but still thought about it," he wrote. Ten weeks later he too was dead. The following year 25 survivors of the Trigardt trek were evacuated by boat to Port Natal, leaving 20 of their number buried at Lourenço Marques.

ALLEN GARDINER

Captain Gardiner was a naval officer who after more than two decades in the serv-ice joined the London Missionary Society and did pioneering work in Natal. After the massacre of the trekker Piet Retief and his followers, Gardiner moved on to South America, where he starved to death during a famine in Tierra del Fuego. His account of his 1835 journey to Zululand is raddled with his own poetry. From Sunset at Berea:

How glorious is that golden hue,
What gorgeous streams of light!
What varied tints from azure blue
To deepest crimson meet my sight …

DEARLY FOND OF A JOKE

Dingarn, with all his barbarity, is dearly fond of a joke, and one morning sent for me and my interpreter, for the sole purpose of affording some amusement. The open court which surrounds his house, into which we were admitted, was lined with seventy or eighty women, seated on mats, while he himself was standing on an earth mound, about the size of an ant-hill … from which he is enabled not only to overlook the fence, but to take a general view of the whole town; and it is from this rude pedestal that his orders are frequently given to the people without.

Dingane receiving homage from his men.

"There has been a contest," was his first observation. "My women will not believe that you can do the things that are written down, unless you were present when the directions were noted – but I tell them you can."

In order to place this knotty question beyond all further dispute, I was requested to remain at a sufficient distance outside the fence, while my interpreter, at their dictation, wrote in pencil the names of twelve or fourteen of the women, describing their relative situations, when I was again admitted. The accuracy with which I was enabled at once to point to each individual named on the paper was a source of great merriment and surprise, but still they were not satisfied, and devised another plan, which they thought would certainly puzzle. On my return, after a considerable interval, it appeared that several articles had been hid, and for which I was required to search, according to the directions given. My first essay was to produce a broom, which had been rolled up in the end of a mat; then a bead, in the closed hand of one of the ladies; afterwards, an ear ornament, concealed in the skirt of Dingarn's cloak, but here I was at default – pointing to the cloak, he shook it loose, to show that nothing was there; still I pointed at the same spot near his feet; at last, with a laugh of triumph, he lifted up one of his feet, which had been purposely placed upon the article in question. This, of course, all acknowledged was an unfair advantage; and I then proceeded to pronounce the name of his favourite dog, Marquillána, and to watch the first lizard which happened to run over the thatch of the King's house; on noticing which, my task was ended, and I doubt not my reputation for literary acquirements wonderfully enhanced.

HE GRASPED THE HEARTSTRING

Before it was slaughtered I went to the cattle-fold, where the people were assembled for the purpose, in order to prevent the poor animal from being unnecessarily tortured. Although their method of killing cattle is in general use among the Amakōsa and neighbouring tribes, I had never before witnessed it; and on being assured that it was as expeditious as any other

179

mode of taking life, I allowed them to proceed. The unfortunate animal, seized by its horns and legs, was then thrown on its back, and held down by several men until an opening was made by an assegai a little below the chest. Into this opening the man thrust his arm above the elbow, feeling his way until he grasped the heartstring, which by main force he broke, and then left the poor beast, writhing with pain, to linger several minutes before it expired, breathing partly through the gaping wound. The horror of that sight, and the feelings I endured during the barbarous act, will long be remembered; and most strenuously would I recommend all Missionaries and well-wishers to humanity to exert their influence, if possible, to abolish a practice at once so cruel and revolting.

FRANCIS OWEN

Owen, a former Yorkshire curate, tried to convert Dingane and his followers to Christianity, but the Zulu king refused to take seriously the idea that his soul was filthy and had to be washed in the blood of a man who had gone to heaven. Owen abandoned his mission a few days after witnessing Retief's death, and ended his days as a parish priest in England. Here he is among the Bhaca, on his way to Dingane.

CRAMPED BY SIN

We had now entered the country inhabited by the tribe of another chief called Napai. This is usually called, by the frontier Kafirs, the Ficani, or robber tribe; from their numerous depredations on their neighbours. The horses having strayed, we were detained all day and whilst the men were gone to look for them, a large party of natives, amounting to about 50 or 60, seated themselves by the side of my waggon. As I went towards them, they were as mute and fixed their eyes on me, as steadily, as if they had never seen a white man before. As soon as my Interpreter came, I told them I would read a portion of the word of God to [t]hem; and opening my Bible read the parable of the lost Sheep in Luke XV. When I had finished, I asked if they understood? Having no idea of the nature of a parable, they asked, if I was speaking of my own sheep, or of some others man's. Upon this I endeavoured to explain to them, how *we* were the lost sheep as we had all strayed away from God and how Jesus Christ was the good Shepherd, who had come to bring us back to God, one man, who was the chief organ of the party, denied that they were sinners, asking when had they ever ill-treated a white man, passing thro' their country. I endeavoured to explain to them the nature of God's law; and how it required duties to him, which they had not preformed, as well as to their neighbours. They seemed however to have no notion of any thing as sin, but what was an injury to their neighbours; and pressed for information respecting those points of duty, which regarded their fellow creatures; asking "Suppose for example, one man was to meet another and fight with him, would that be sin?["] I told them that unless their hearts were changed, even tho' I should acquaint them with their duty, they could not do it, as the heart was cramped by sin, and nothing good could proceed from [it]; and that this was the character of all men by nature, both white people and black. They said, that our hearts might be proud and wicked; but that they had not wicked hearts. At length after a great deal of conversation, they began to talk among themselves on what they had heard, particularly on the parable; when the master of the kraal said, they thanked me for the word of God and that when they went home, they would talk over it with their children. I asked if a Teacher were to come and live among them, would they be glad? They said, if their chief allowed him to reside in the country, they would hear him. The conversation was then renewed, when they asked me, what ought to be done to a person who bewitched another? I said it was not my business to say, what *man* should do to him; but God would punish *every* sin with everlasting fire. They said they were glad that God would punish him, as well as the man; for there were many persons in the country who went about bewitching their neighbours. I waived entering into a discussion on this subject. The whole conversation lasted about 2 hours; when the chief speaker said, the state of the grass shewed how many had been listening to me and for how long a time; and now, he hoped, I would give them a present and they would tell their friends that they had seen not a *common* white man only, but a teacher. I begged them to think of what they had heard and went away. I felt deeply interested during the conversation; and secretly prayed for wisdom, whilst my Interpreter was delivering my words. I trust I shall better know, after every succeeding conversation, the proper way of bringing forward the truth.

ADULPHE DELEGORGUE

Delegorgue was destined for the French Bar but, in the words of bibliophile Sidney Mendelssohn, became "siezed with an uncontrollable desire to visit Africa and a distaste for the legal profession". During his visit to Dingane's successor Mpande in 1842, his tent was ransacked. The culprit, a man named Fetikani, was identified at a public hearing, and condemned to death.

TO PREVENT THE CONTAGION

The 27th was rainy. On rainy days nothing is done among the Zulus. Even an execution is postponed. But on the 28th, the sun shining brightly, ten warriors of Umlandeli seized Fetikani, whom they led into a narrow valley, in the neighbourhood of their kraal. After their arrival, their business did not long occupy them. Fetikani had already confessed that he alone was answerable for the robbery. He repeated his confession while they were fastening him to a tree, and without any emotion he saw the warriors retire to a distance of fifteen paces, forming before him a terrible arc of a circle. Then the assagais with their quivering shafts were three times drawn back, and discharged together at the body of Fetikani, which they pierced through and through. Fetikani had been killed – killed for the crime of theft by housebreaking: a dreadful punishment, no doubt, for so small an offence; but under Panda there is no prison, no bastinado,

nothing but death, whatever be the degree of crime. And I venture to affirm that there is no country in the world in which thefts are so rare.

Had not Panda said at the very outset that he did not believe the truth of my charge, because he did not consider it possible that a single thief could be existing in his kingdom; and that I ought, besides, to adduce proofs and witnesses? I had endeavoured, while claiming satisfaction, to induce Panda to adopt some other form of justice, objecting that his system of inflicting death exceeded all reasonable measure of punishment, and that every execution deprived him of a man – a warrior – capable of serving him in case of need. "As to that," said he, "the whites have often repeated the same thing to me, pretending to change the usage of the black man, without ever giving me an equivalent expedient. A man is bad. I destroy him, not only on his own account, but to prevent the contagion of evil. Would you have me make a large hole in the earth and put him into it? Then he would have to be fed there at the expense of others. The painful life he would drag out there would embitter him still more against men, and, if he happened to escape, render him ten times more wicked. When a criminal is killed, everyone is quiet. As to that which relates to the loss of a warrior, as you say" – and here Panda put on a smile of pity – "my men, my warriors, everybody knows, are more numerous than grasshoppers; and when a grasshopper falls to the ground, do you miss one from the swarm?" I admit that I found no answer ready in reply to Panda's short explanation, because to change customs of this kind one would first have to remodel everything, and establish everything anew; and, as a consequence, to impose on such a people the burdens borne by civilized communities.

HARRIET WARD

Ward was the daughter of a veteran of the Peninsula campaign, and wife of a captain in the 91st Regiment. Not surprisingly, when her husband sailed to the Cape in 1842 for duty on the troubled eastern frontier, she insisted on accompanying him. Her Five Years in Kaffirland *contains vivid reportage on the War of the Axe, which erupted in 1846 and ended with the humiliation of the Xhosa chiefs at a "peace" ceremony stage-managed by the bombastic governor Harry Smith. Not that this treatment would have worried Ward. "The Kaffir has no genuine pride, for he will submit to any personal degradation to obtain his ends," she says. "In short, he is an ignoble foe, and we gain no more credit, or profit, in fighting such an enemy than if we were endeavouring to circumvent an army of baboons." Notes the introduction to her book: "The presence of an English lady in the wilds of Africa … exhibiting in her own person an example of courage and fortitude under privation – must certainly have been attended with its good effects on the minds of the gallant fellows who served during the campaign." The first call on her fortitude was on arrival in Table Bay, when their troopship, the* Abercrombie Robinson, *found itself in the grip of a northwest gale.*

YES, I DO
The wind and sea rising caused at first but little alarm; at twelve o'clock, however, the ship shivered; apparently from being struck by a heavy sea.

She trembled in every joint, and the same sensation being almost immediately after felt again, it was evident the vessel touched the bottom and with some violence. I rose from my bed, and, dressing my child and myself, we proceeded with my husband to the cuddy, where some of the officers were assembled round the stove, the night being bitterly cold. The Captain, still depending on the strength of his anchor-chains, saw no great cause of alarm, and having put my child to sleep on a chair which Captain Gordon kindly prepared for her, I retired again to my berth, and, being quite worn out, soon fell fast asleep. I was awoke by my husband bidding me rise, and come on deck immediately, the anchor chains having both snapped one after the other. My little Isabel stood beside her father partly dressed, and pale and silent. I have no distinct recollection of all that happened for the first half hour after this awful intelligence. I remember hearing the water splashing about my cabin, and our little lamp swinging violently backwards and forwards. I remember being dragged in unshod feet along the wet deck, up the steerage hatchway, while my husband carried my child. I can remember, too, her little voice issuing from my bed, into which she had crept to fasten on her warm boots, and begging me not to be frightened.

"How calm she is!" said I, to my husband.

"Poor thing!" he whispered, "she does not know her danger."

"Yes, I do," she answered, overhearing us; "but mamma has often told me that God Almighty can take care of us if he pleases; and I keep saying that to myself, and then I am not half so frightened."

I remember, at the height of the storm, when the noise of the thunder could scarcely be distinguished from the roar of the waters, and the torrents of rain, – when the elements in fact howled wildly and angrily at one another, – when the lightning pouring, as one may call it, on our decks, blazed in at the fore-windows of the cuddy, being horror-stricken at the ghastly faces assembled under the uncertain and flickering light of a broken lamp! I can remember when the water rose up to my knees, being carried between decks with my child, through rows of shrieking women and silent soldiers. The conduct of our men was beyond all praise.

For some time, I sat on a chest with my child, near the fore-hatch, the ship continuing to drive, every moment striking against the sand, and our only hopes resting on the coming of the dawn, which would show us *where we were*, the floods of rain preventing the lightning – vivid as it was – from doing this distinctly. About six in the morning, the Captain came down among us with some comfort, saying he hoped the ship was making a bed for herself in the sand. In truth, she had been all night like some great creature scratching her way through it with restless impatience. The rudder had been carried away from the first, the stern cabins knocked into one, and the sea bubbling up like a fountain in the after part of the ship. We were yet uncertain of our safety, for there were rocks not many hun-

dred yards from us, on which the Waterloo convict ship had already struck: but of her anon. Meanwhile, our people attaching a rope to a shot, fired it on shore, but in vain. All night the guns from the fort and other vessels had been giving awful warnings to the town, while the constant roll of musketry on board the convict ship, led us to imagine that the convicts were mutinous. This was, however, discovered afterwards not to be the case: they had been loosened from their bonds on the first alarm, and desired to make use of the first possible means of escape.

At length, as we neared the coast, which for some time had been crowded with spectators, we were enabled, through God's mercy, to get a boat on shore with a rope attached to the ship, and afterwards fastened to an anchor driven in the sand. As the surf-boats put off, the first of which brought Lieutenant Black, the Agent, on board, our men gave nine hearty cheers, and in a few minutes we commenced our disembarkation; the women and children being lowered into the boats first: I waited for the third boat. Such a noble example had been shown by the officers to their men, and its effects on the latter had been so important, that in spite of my anxiety to land, I felt unwilling to exhibit it by hurrying from the ship to the shore, and thus creating unnecessary fears among the poor uneducated women, whose terrors I had witnessed during the awful hours of the night. As I was carried between decks, I had been struck, in spite of my fears, with the scene that met my view there. Pale women, with dishevelled hair, stretched themselves from their beds, wringing their hands, and imploring me to comfort them. Some prayed aloud; others, Roman Catholics, called on the Virgin and their favourite saints to help them in their peril; and many bent in silent but eloquent agony over their unconscious infants. One woman who had, during the whole voyage, been considered as dying of deep decline, sat up in the hammock which had been carefully slung for her, and with a calm voice, which was yet distinguishable from the noise around her, imparted a certain confidence in the power of the Almighty to all who were willing to listen to her, or at least prepared them to view their possibly approaching fate with more resignation. That calm, steady voice

Grahamstown

184

sounded strangely amid the cries of fearful women, the hoarse voices of reckless sailors, and the crashing of timbers; while, above all, still rolled on the sound of musketry from the convict ship, Waterloo, now beating violently against the rocks, and beyond immediate help; while the appearance of hundreds on the beach striving, some to get their boats off, and others with daring spirit urging their horses through the surf, formed a scene difficult to describe, even by the pen of a mere looker-on.

Our ship was a stout vessel, and held well together. I embarked at last in a surf-boat with my child, (my husband of course waited for his company,) and with a heart full of earnest gratitude to the Almighty, I approached the land. Had I dreamt of the awful calamity which afterwards befell our unfortunate neighbour, the Waterloo, I should not have felt the exhilaration of spirit I did as the Lascars bore me from the boat to the shore through the surf ...

The Waterloo *was driven aground near the mouth of the Salt River, and her rotten timbers broke up rapidly under the pounding waves. Of the 265 people on board, 175 lost their lives. The bulk of the dead were convicts.*

NOT WORTH DESCRIBING
Graham's Town is not worth describing.

Although in truth she does devote a few sentences to it – "a great straggling place, irregularly built, and in a dirty and disorderly state".

SOME POWERFUL ANIMAL
A Kaffir will not raise his hand to remove a fly from his face; and, as he rubs his skin with clay and grease to protect it from the effects of the sun, these attract the flies, and I have known a savage sit for hours in the sun with his cheeks and brow covered by these tormenting and fidgetty insects, without attempting to remove them. It must be allowed, though, that a Kaffir's skin more resembles the hide of some powerful animal than the skin of a human being. In the early part of this war, some person procured the entire skin of a Kaffir, and had it braded in the same way that leather is first prepared for tanning. I am told that that the texture is at least three times the thickness of a white man's, and I see no reason for doubting the assertion.

PASCOE HILL

Reverend Hill was chaplain of HMS Cleopatra, *a British cruiser patrolling the Moçambique coast to enforce the ban on the slave trade. In April 1843 she stopped a Brazilian brig, the* Progresso, *and discovered that the 447 slaves packed on board had just seized control of the vessel and were busy ransacking the stores and knocking off their chains. The slaves, some already branded, had been destined for Rio de Janeiro. Fifty of them were transferred to the* Cleopatra, *and Hill joined the rest on the* Progresso, *now manned by British seamen, on a nightmarish 50-day voyage to the Cape. By the time they reached Simon's Town up to eight negroes a day were dying of disease; one, too weak to extricate himself, suffocated in the shitbucket; another was strangled by his fellows; the decomposed body of a boy was*

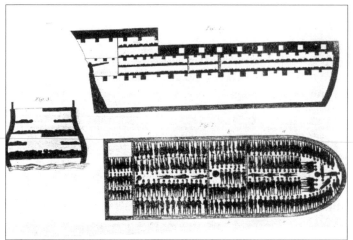

found under the ship's planks, with part of a hand devoured and one eye "completely scooped out" by rats. Some had bizarre wounds, such as an ankle joint nearly chewed through, inflicted by companions driven to the brink of insanity. In all, 175 died on the Progresso, and at least another 14 soon after landing. The fate of the survivors is not recorded, but it was official policy at the Cape to "apprentice" prize negroes such as these to colonists for a year, to work as servants or farm labourers.

We join Hill here on his first night aboard the Progresso. Concerning the size of her slave-hold: 12 yards is the exact width of a tennis court. From the baseline, seven yards takes you just over halfway to the net.

Storage of slaves on a ship.

THE SMOKE OF THEIR TORMENT

During the first watch, our breeze was light and variable, the water smooth, the recently liberated negroes sleeping, or lying in quietness about the deck. Their slender supple limbs entwine in a surprisingly small compass; and they resembled, in the moonlight, confused piles of arms and legs, rather than distinct human forms. They were, however, apparently at ease, and all seemed going on as fairly as could be desired. But the scene was soon to undergo a great and terrible change. About one hour after midnight, the sky began to gather clouds, and a haze overspread the horizon to windward. A squall approached, of which I and others, who had lain down on the deck, received warning by a few heavy drops of rain. Then ensued a scene, the horrors of which it is impossible to depict. The hands having to shorten sail suddenly, uncertain as to the force of the squall, found the poor helpless creatures lying about the deck, an obstruction to getting at the ropes and doing what was required. This caused the order to send them all below, which was immediately obeyed. The night, however, being intensely hot and close, 400 wretched beings thus crammed into a hold 12 yards in length, 7 in breadth, and only $3^1/_2$ feet in height, speedily began to make an effort to reissue to the open air. Being thrust back, and striving the more to get out, the after-hatch was forced down on them. Over the other hatchway, in the fore-part of the vessel, a wooden grating was fastened. To this, the sole inlet for the air, the suffocating heat of the hold, and, perhaps, panic from the strangeness of their situation, made them press; and thus great part of the space below was rendered useless. They crowded to the grating, and clinging to it for air, completely barred its entrance. They strove to force their way through apertures, in length 14 inches, and barely 6 inches in breadth, and, in some instances, succeeded. The cries, the heat, – I may say, without exaggeration, "the smoke of their torment," – which ascended, can be compared to nothing earthly. One of the Spaniards [from the slaver's original crew] gave warning that the consequence would be "many deaths." – "Mañana habrà muchos muertos."

186

Thursday, April 13th. (Passion Week). – The Spaniard's prediction of last night, this morning was fearfully verified. Fifty-four crushed and mangled corpses lifted up from the slave-deck have been brought to the gang-way and thrown overboard. Some were emaciated from disease; many, bruised and bloody. Antonio tells me that some were found strangled, their hands still grasping each other's throats, and tongues protruding from their mouths. The bowels of one were crushed out. They had been trampled to death for the most part, the weaker under the feet of the stronger in the madness and torment of suffocation from crowd and heat. It was a horrid sight, as they passed one by one, – the stiff distorted limbs smeared with blood and filth, – to be cast into the sea. Some, still quivering, were laid on the deck to die; salt water thrown on them to revive them, and a little fresh water poured into their mouths. Antonio reminded me of his last night's warning, "Ya se lo dixè anoche." He actively employed himself, with his comrade Sebastian, in attendance on the wretched living beings now released from their confinement below; distributing to them their morning meal of "farinha," and their allowance of water, rather more than half a pint to each, which they grasped with inconceivable eagerness, some bending their knees to the deck, to avoid the risk of losing any of the liquid by unsteady footing, their throats, doubtless, parched to the utmost with crying and yelling through the night.

A heavy shower having freshened the air, in the evening most of the negroes went below of their own accord, the hatchways being left open to allow them air. But a short time, however, had elapsed when they began tumultuously to re-ascend, while persons above, afraid of their crowding the deck too much, repelled them, and they were trampled back, screaming and writhing, in a confused mass. The hatch was about to be forced down on them, and, had not the lieutenant in charge left positive orders to the contrary, the catastrophe of last night would have been re-enacted. Antonio, whom I called at this juncture, turned away with a gesture of horror, saying, "No soy capaz de matarlos como anoche." On explaining to him, however, that it was desired he would dispose in proper places those who came on deck, he set himself to the task with great alacrity. As they climbed nimbly up, he made me feel their skins, which had been wetted by the rain: "Estan frescos," – "they are cool." – "No tienen calor, tienen miedo." It was not heat, but fear, which now made them rush to escape from the hold; and he showed me, with much satisfaction, how soon and quietly they were arranged out of the way of the ropes, covered with long rugs provided for the purpose. "Mañana no ha de morir ninguno : – acaso algunos de los que estan ahora enfermos." – "To-morrow there will not be one dead: – perhaps some of those who are now sick."

FANNY PARKES

Parkes, described by a contemporary as "abundantly fat and lively", accompanied her civil servant husband to Bengal in 1822 in the knowledge that they would have to stay there more than 20 years if he was to qualify for a pension. She fell in love with the country, learning Hindustani, recording mythology, customs and lan-

guage, and undertaking a series of expeditions, often without European companions. "How much there is to delight the eye in this bright, this beautiful world!" she writes. "Roaming about with a good tent and a good Arab [she means her horse], one might be happy for ever in India." In 1843 she and her husband spent nine months at the Cape so he could recuperate from an undisclosed illness. They lodged in Roeland Street, and Parkes spent her time sketching, walking, and gathering flowers and bulbs.

DRUNKARDS, THIEVES AND LIARS

Never did I meet with such servants as those at the Cape, – drunkards, thieves, and liars, – the petty annoyances these people give are enough to destroy the pleasure of living in this fine climate and beautiful country; had it not been for the plague of the servants I should have felt sorrow in quitting Africa. A Malay man-servant of ours, speaking of his family, said, "My father was only a lieutenant, but the father of my wife's eldest son, he was a very great man! – he was a colonel! he gave her the cottage. Though the son is but a boy he has so much English spirit in him, that I am afraid of beating him; don't you think the other children are very like me? The friends of many women are only captains or lieutenants; my wife's friend was a colonel! – we are all like this!"

Parkes knew all about servants: when she first arrived in India, she was running a modest establishment of 57 of them.

SO BEAUTIFULLY GRAND

This is later, in 1845, when her husband had received permission to return to England from India on furlough. Parkes secured a stern cabin on the poop of the Essex, *along with her ayah, or female servant, and a collection of "curiosities". The ship ran into a gale off the East Cape coast.*

My ayha, who usually got up before daybreak, to smoke her hooqŭ in the galley, made an effort to quit the cabin; I desired her not to attempt to move, or she would be thrown down from the pitching and rolling of the vessel; but the moment my eye was off her away she went: she met another ayha in the passage, who said, "Are you mad, that you want to go and smoke in such a gale as this?" My ayha, who would sell her soul for half a dozen whiffs of tobacco, persisted in going; she had not got half way through the cuddy when she fell, and I heard a violent scream. The cuddy servants ran to her assistance, and found she had broken her leg just above the ankle; the bone was through the flesh, and the wound bled very much. The medical man set her leg, and with great difficulty we had her removed into the stern cabin, where we secured her as well as we were able, but not until some time had passed, as the large heavy toonwood couch in the stern cabin had started from its moorings, and, turning over topsy-turvy, had dashed across the cabin, breaking and throwing down the table, and carrying away the trunks. Never was there such confusion as the furniture made in the cabin, pitching from side to side with the roll of the vessel. At length the carpenter secured the frisky couch, bound up the wounds of the table, and relashed them all. By this time the sea was breaking over the stern windows, and dashing into the cabin, in spite of the dead-lights, and into the quarter-gallery; much damage was done on the poop. The medical man, knowing that leeches sold at the Cape for half-

a-crown a-piece, on account of there being none but those that are import-ed, on which a heavy duty is paid, took 10,000 of them from Calcutta, secured in large earthen pots (*gharās*) full of soft mud, which were all placed on the poop, in a small boat called "Little Poppet." The water cis-tern gave way, and dashing against "Little Poppet," upset her, broke all the gharās, and the sea-water killed the leeches. The cutter that hung over the quarter was turned up on one side by the force of the wind, dashed against the side of the "Essex," was greatly injured, and rendered utterly useless; three of her oars fell into the sea, and were borne away, but the sailors secured the boat.

By noon on the 24th (Lat. S. 33° 45′, Long. E. 28°), the current had car-ried the vessel one hundred and twenty miles nearer the land, which was now only eighty miles distant; we were driving almost under bare poles, the violence of the wind not allowing any sail but one small one; another, which they wished to set, was twice blown to pieces, and could not be car-ried. The waves were striking the vessel in the most frightful manner, roar-ing in concert with the gale, and jostling and rolling against the ship as if they were ready to engulf her. Nevertheless the "Essex" bore bravely on; her captain put her about, and we ran down the side of the land for some distance. To sleep – to rest, with so furious a gale blowing, was impossible; and how the time passed I hardly remember, for day and night it was the same – pitch, pitch, roll, roll, – and the same roar: all night long two seamen were baling out the water from our cabins, – the waves poured constantly into the cuddy ports on one side, and rolled out on the other. We sat down to dinner, a plate of food was brought to each person, and we held on and ate as we could; every now and then an officer came down for ten minutes, took his food as hastily as possible, and returned instantly to the poop, – it was an anxious time.

"But where of ye, O tempests, is the goal?
Are ye like those within the human breast?
Or do ye find, at length, like eagles, some high nest?"

About 4 P.M. on the second day, the thunder rolled heavily, the lightning was very vivid, and hail fell in heavy showers. The chief officer, having caught up a handful of the large hail, gave it to me in a plate at the cuddy door, where I amused myself with eating it, and watching the scene. About this time the situation of the vessel became critical: the first officer desired the captain to observe what was coming down on the weather side; he could not tell what it was, never having seen any thing of the kind before. The foam of the sea was caught up by the wind, and whirled round and round in thick masses like smoke; it blew heavily, and the spray beat with such violence into the faces of the officers, that at times they could not see. Not a minute elapsed ere the whirlwind struck the vessel on her weather side, and the blast was perfectly *hot!* The captain called to the men to hold on; they were prepared, – and well for them they were so: with a tremendous roll the vessel was pitched over almost on her beam-ends; the thing was so sudden, and the officers were so blinded by the spray and wind, that they could not tell whether the whirlwind passed by the stern or the head of the vessel. Almost as quickly as the wind struck her on the weather side it was round to the other, and the ship was taken aback, or brought by the lee.

The mountainous waves were foaming, breaking, and dashing against her; one great sea broke off the knees of the vessel, drew out two or three of the long iron bolts, and loosened the cutwater. The thunder rolled, the lightning flashed, and every five minutes the hail beat on the decks like the pitching down of myriads of marbles. At length the horizon cleared, and the gallant ship, rising over the surge, went on her way rejoicing.

JOHN STEYTLER

Steytler, born at the Cape in 1832, wrote a wonderfully vivid set of reminiscences for his children when he was nearing his eighties. Although he spent his early years at sea, he subsequently became a shorthand writer for the Cape government, then carved a distinguished career for himself as a merchant.

MY OWN MASTER
As a boy in Cape Town.

When I was 12 years old my Father said I could go to the Country during my holidays. He lent me his famous horse "Charles", his saddle-bags & Macintosh & I set off one day with a shilling in my pocket for the whole trip, for tolls etc. Out of this shilling I bought 4d cigars, 3 for a penny, imitation Manillas. (I bought the same kind in Calcutta for 6d a hundred). Before leaving my Father gave me instructions. I was first to go to friends at the Paarl, then on to an Uncle at Porcelain Berg, next to Oom Piet at Dassenheuvel, Malmesbury district, & last to Uncle Freislich at Malmesbury. When I asked my Father how I was to find my way he said "Find out & take your chance". I was nothing loath so behold a young man of twelve, rather short for his age, outside a big horse with saddle-bags containing his clothes & a little provision, setting out to ride thirty six miles the first day. Oh! what delight to find myself my own master for a whole fortnight! Splendidly mounted, & after Salt River when I lighted my first cigar, I felt quite a MAN. I was already an experienced smoker having learnt the trick during our boating trips. After riding three hours I off-saddled in the veld. The halter being under the bridle, the horse was knee-haltered & allowed to graze while I ate my sandwiches & smoked another cigar. I off-saddled again at Mulders Vley & then went on to the Paarl after a ride of six hours with two hours' rest in between, arriving as fresh as a daisy & feeling very much a man. My friends made much of me & chaffed me about saddling & managing the horse, being such a little chap, but I took it as a matter of course having been thoroughly trained by my Father.

He made it safely to Malmesbury, from where Charles was sent home, and he eventually returned to Cape Town in a four-horse cart – which to his joy he was allowed to drive.

IN A PROPER ATTITUDE
Though Steytler's father wanted him to study law, his own dream was to become a sailor. He and a like-minded schoolmate who had been earmarked for the church decided at one point that if their parents would not agree, they would run away to sea. When he was about 15, Steytler senior arranged for the boy to crew on a schooner on a trip to Durban and back, in the hope that the experience would put him off. Unfortunately he enjoyed every minute.

A small square in the hold was arranged on the coffee bags, for us to sleep in; in that little craft we had sixteen passengers, among these were three American missionaries, with their wives, & they had Service on Deck every evening when fine.

We were becalmed off Danger Point & had some splendid fishing. Bye-and-bye the word was given for prayers, I kept my line out of sight & during the first prayer I hooked a fine fish & hauled him up carefully, but I had not reckoned on the row he would make, when he got out of the water, as soon as I heard the splashing I let go, & put myself in a proper attitude, which showed I had nothing to do with the matter. The mate nearly split with laughter.

ALFRED COLE

Bored with life as a London clerk, Cole decided to emigrate to New Zealand in 1841. His ship sank in Table Bay with all his possessions; Cole stayed on to travel and produce a book on the colony. He later became a member of the legislative assembly and a respected judge, and wrote more books, among them Lorimer Littlegood, esq., a gentleman who wished to see society and saw it accordingly. *He found these locusts north of Fort Beaufort.*

SPECKLED WITH LOCUSTS
Next day was warm enough, but the wind was desperately high, and, much to my disgust, right in my face as I rode away on my journey. After travelling

some ten miles, having swallowed several ounces of sand meanwhile, and been compelled occasionally to remove the sand-hills that were collecting in my eyes, I began to fall in with some locusts. At first they came on gradually and in small quantities, speckling the earth here and there, and voraciously devouring the herbage. They were not altogether pleasant, as they are weak on the wing, and quite at the mercy of the wind, which uncivilly dashed many a one into my face with a force that made my cheeks tingle. By degrees they grew thicker and more frequent. My progress was now most unpleasant, for they flew into my face every instant. Flung against me and my horse by the breeze, they clung to us with the tightness of desperation, till we were literally speckled with locusts. Each moment the clouds of them became denser, till at length – I am guilty of no exaggeration in saying – they were as thick in the air as the flakes of snow during a heavy fall of it; they covered the grass and the road, so that at every step my horse crushed dozens; they were whirled into my eyes and those of my poor nag, till at last the latter refused to face them, and turned tail in spite of whip and spur. They crawled about my face and neck, got down my shirt-collar and up my sleeves – in a word, they drove me to despair as completely as they drove my horse to stubbornness, and I was obliged to ride back a mile or two and claim shelter from them at a house I had passed on my route; fully convinced that a shower of locusts is more unbearable than hail, rain, snow, and sleet combined.

I found the poor farmer in despair at the dreadful visitation which had come upon him – and well he might be so. To-day he had standing crops, a garden, and wide pasture lands in full verdure; the next day the earth was as bare all round as a macadamized road.

I afterwards saw millions of these insects driven by the wind into the sea at Algoa Bay, and washed on shore again in such heaps, that the prisoners and the coolies in the town were busily employed for a day or two in burying the bodies, to prevent the evil consequence that would arise from the putrifying of them close to the town.

Roualeyn Gordon Cumming

ROUALEYN GORDON CUMMING

Striding across the veld in a kilt and introducing himself to Boers as a "Berg Scott" or mountain Scotchman, Cumming spent five years killing animals in South Africa for pleasure and profit. He returned to Britain in 1849 to write a two-volume bestselling account of his experiences. The former army officer recorded kills of up to eight elephants a day. One of the reasons he stopped hunting was that it was becoming increasingly difficult to reach the dwindling herds. Cumming, who according to the missionary David Livingstone took a Khoisan concubine with him on his travels, died of drink at the age of 46. His diary, in which he detailed not only his hunting exploits but his private life, was apparently burnt after shocked relatives had looked at a few pages.

TWO DARK OBJECTS

Night was now fast setting in, so we descended, and made for home; cantering along, we observed what we took to be a herd of quaggas and a bull wildebeest standing in front of us, upon which we jumped off our horses, and, bending our bodies, approached them to fire.

It being now quite dark, it was hard to tell what sort of game we were going to fire at; Strydom, however, whispered to me they were quaggas, and they certainly appeared to be such. His gun snapped three times at the wildebeest, upon which they all set off at a gallop; he was riding my stallion, and let go his bridle when he ran in to fire, taking advantage of which the horse set off after them. I then mounted "The Cow," and after riding hard for about a mile came up to them. They were now standing still, and the stallion in the middle of them. I made him out by his saddle, and, jumping off my horse in a state of intense excitement, ran forward, fired both barrels of my two-grooved rifle into the quaggas, and heard the bullets tell loudly. They then started off, but the stallion was soon once more fighting in the middle of them; I was astonished and delighted to remark how my horse was able to take up their attention, so that they appeared heedless of the reports of my rifle.

In haste I commenced loading, but to my dismay found that I had left my loading-rod with Hendrick. Mounting "The Cow," I rode nearer to the quaggas, and was delighted to find that they allowed my horse to come within easy shot. It was now very dark, but I set off in the hope to fall in with Hendrick on the wide plain, and galloped along shouting with all my might, but in vain. I then rode across the plain for the hill, to try to find some bush large enough to make a ramrod; in this, by the greatest chance, I succeeded, and, being provided with a knife, I cut a good ramrod, loaded my rifle, and rode off to seek the quaggas once more. I soon fell in with them, and, coming within shot, fired at them right and left, and heard both bullets tell, upon which they galloped across the plain with the stallion still after them. One of them, however, was very hard hit, and soon dropped astern – the stallion remained to keep him company.

About this time the moon shone forth faintly. I galloped on after the troop, and, soon coming up with them, rode on one side, when, dismounting and dropping on my knee, I sent a bullet through the shoulder of the last quagga; he staggered forward, fell to the ground with a heavy crash, and expired. The rest of the troop charged wildly around him, snorting and prancing like the wild horses in Mazeppa, and then set off at full speed across the plain; I did not wait to bleed the quagga, but, mounting my horse, galloped on after the troop, nevertheless I could not overtake them. Returning, I endeavoured to find the quagga that I had last shot, but owing to the darkness, and my having no mark to guide me on the plain, I failed to find him. I then set off to try for the quagga which had dropped astern with the stallion; having searched some time in vain, I dismounted, and, laying my head on the ground, made out two dark objects which turned out to be what I sought. On my approaching, the quagga tried to make off,

Cumming "drawing a snake".

when I sent a ball through his shoulder, which laid him low. Going up to him in the full expectation of inspecting for the first time one of these animals, what was my disappointment and vexation to find a fine brown gelding, with two white stars on his forehead! The truth now flashed upon me; Strydom and I had both been mistaken; instead of quaggas, the waggon-team of a neighboring Dutchman had afforded me my evening's shooting!

I caught my stallion and rode home, intending to pay for the horses which I had killed and wounded; but on telling my story to Hendrick, with which he seemed extremely amused, he told me not to say a word about it, as the owners of the horses were very avaricious, and would make me pay treble their value, and that if I kept quiet it would be supposed they had been killed either by lions or wild Bushmen.

A DENSE LIVING MASS

On the 28th I had the satisfaction of beholding, for the first time, what I had often heard the Boers speak of, viz. a "trek-bokken," or grand migration of springboks. This was, I think, the most extraordinary and striking scene, as connected with beasts of the chace, I ever beheld. For about two hours before dawn I had been lying awake in my waggon, listening to the grunting of the bucks within two hundred yards of me, imagining that some large herd of springboks was feeding beside my camp; but rising when it was light, and looking about me, I beheld the ground to the northward of my camp actually covered with a dense living mass of springboks, marching slowly and steadily along; they extended from an opening in a long range of hills on the west, through which they continued pouring, like the flood of some great river, to a ridge about a mile to the north-east, over which they disappeared – the breadth of ground they covered might have been somewhere about half a mile. I stood upon the fore-chest of my waggon for nearly two hours, lost in astonishment at the novel and wonderful scene before me, and had some difficulty in convincing myself that it was a reality which I beheld, and not the wild and exaggerated picture of a hunter's dream. During this time these vast legions continued streaming through the neck in the hills in one unbroken compact phalanx. At length I saddled up, and, riding into the middle of them with my rifle and after-riders, fired into their ranks until fourteen had fallen, when I cried "Enough." We then retraced our steps to secure from the ever-voracious vultures the venison which lay strewed along my track; having collected the springboks

at different bushes, and concealed them with brushwood, we returned to camp.

A person anxious to kill many springboks might have bagged thirty or forty that morning. I never, in all my subsequent career, fell in with so dense a herd as I did this day, nor found them allow me to ride so near them. Having inspanned, we proceeded with the waggons to take up the fallen game, and held for the small periodical stream beside which the wandering Boers were encamped, that point being in my line of march for Beer Vley. Vast and surprising as was the herd of springboks which I had that morning witnessed, it was infinitely surpassed by what I saw on the march from my vley to old Sweirs's camp; for, on our clearing the low range of hills through which the springboks had been pouring, I beheld the plains, and even the hill-sides which stretched away on every side of me, thickly covered, not with herds, but with one vast mass of springboks; as far as the eye could strain the landscape was alive with them, until they softened down into a dim red mass of living creatures.

"You this morning," an old farmer told him, "behold only one flat covered with springboks, but I give you my word that I have ridden a day's journey over a succession of flats covered with them as far as I could see, and as thick as sheep in a fold."

BY THE TAIL

Before leaving I heard that the party who had been lion-hunting had bagged two fine lions, a male and female; and as their farm lay in my line of march, I mounted Colesberg, and, desiring my servants to follow with the waggons, rode forward to inspect the noble game. I found the lion and lioness laid out on the grass in front of the house, and the Boers' Hottentots busy skinning them. Both lions were riddled with balls, and their heads shot all to pieces. This is generally the way in which the Boers serve a lion after they have killed him, fearing to approach, until they have expended a further supply of ammunition. A Hottentot is then ordered to throw a stone at him, after which the Boers ask if he is dead, and on the Hottentot replying, "Like so, baas," he is ordered to pull him by the tail before the hunters will venture to go up to him.

BLACK AND CLOTTED GORE

There are few things which a Bechuana prizes so highly as fat of any description; he will go an amazing distance for a small portion of it, using it in cooking his sun-dried biltongue, and eating it with his corn. It lies in extensive layers and sheets in the elephant's inside, and the quantity obtained from a full-grown bull, in high condition, is very great. Before it can be got at, the greater part of the intestines must be removed, and to accomplish this several men eventually enter the immense cavity of his inside, where they continue excavating with their assagais, and handing the fat to their comrades outside until all is bare; while this is going on, other parties are equally active in removing the skin and flesh from the remaining parts of the carcase. The natives have a horrid practice on these occasions of smearing their bodies, from the crown of the head to the sole of the foot, with the black and clotted gore; and in this anointing they assist one another, each man taking up the fill of both his hands, and spreading it over the back and shoulders of his friend. Throughout the entire proceeding there is an incessant and deafening clamour of voices and confused sounds, the crowd jostling, wrestling, and elbowing each other, in their endeavors to force their way to the venison, while the sharp and ready assagai gleams in every hand. The angry voices and gory appearance of these naked savages, combined with their excited and frantic gestures and glistening arms, presented an effect so wild and striking, that when I first

beheld the scene I contemplated it in the momentary expectation of beholding one half of the gathering turn their weapons against the other.

The trunk and feet are considered delicacies, and a detachment of men are employed on these; the latter are amputated at the fetlock joint, and the trunk, which at the base is about two feet in thickness, is cut into convenient lengths. Trunk and feet are then baked, preparatory to their removal to headquarters. This is done as follows: – A party, provided with sharp pointed sticks, dig a hole in the ground for each foot and a portion of the trunk; the hole is about two feet deep, and a yard in width, and the excavated earth is embanked around the margin. This being completed, they collect an immense quantity of dry branches and trunks of trees, of which there is always a profusion scattered around, having been broken by elephants in former years; these they pile above the holes to the height of eight or nine feet, and then set fire to the heap. When these strong fires have burnt down, and the whole of the wood is reduced to ashes, the holes and the surrounding earth are heated in a high degree. Ten or twelve men then stand round the pit, and rake out the ashes with a pole about sixteen feet in length, having a hook at the end; they relieve one another in quick succession, each man running in for a few seconds, pitching the pole to his comrade and retreating, the heat being so intense that it is scarcely to be endured. When all the ashes are thus cleared out over the bank of earth, a foot and a portion of the trunk are lifted by two athletic men, and placed in the hole. The pole is then used, and with it they shove in the heated bank of earth upon the foot, shoving and raking until it is completely buried; the hot embers are then raked into a heap above the foot, another bonfire is kindled over each, and by the time this has burnt down, the enormous foot or trunk will be found to be equally baked throughout its inmost parts.

The traveller James Chapman said roasted elephant's foot was "exceedingly good". He noted that after the scorched hide was removed it looked "something like the udder of a cow, only more gristly".

POOR OLD FELLOW

On the 27th we came upon a large extent of burning grass, which the Bakalahari kindle to make the young herbage spring up with greater facility, and during the day discovered a herd of bull elephants quietly browsing on the side of a hill, two hundred yards to windward of us.

I started them with an unearthly yell, and, selecting the finest, fired both barrels behind his shoulder, when he instantly turned upon me, and in his impetuous career charged head foremost against a large bushy tree, which he sent flying before him high in the air, coming down at the same moment violently on his knees. He thus met the raging fire, and wheeled to the right-about.

I followed, loading and firing as fast as could be, sometimes at the head, sometimes behind the shoulder, until the elephant's fore-quarters were severely punished, notwithstanding which he continued to hold stoutly on, leaving the grass and branches of the forest scarlet in his wake.

On one occasion he endeavoured to escape by charging desperately amid the thickest of the flames; but this did not avail him, for I was soon alongside, and blazed away at him until I began to think he was ball-proof. Having fired thirty-five rounds with my two-grooved rifle, I opened upon him with the Dutch six-pounder; and when forty bullets had perforated his hide, he began for the first time to show symptoms of exhaustion. Poor old fellow! it was now all over with him; so I resolved to expend no further ammunition. Throughout the chace he repeatedly cooled his body with large quantities of water, which he ejected from his trunk over his back and sides; and just as the pangs of death came over him, he stood trembling violently beside a thorny tree, and kept pouring water into his mouth until he died, when he pitched heavily forward, with the whole weight of his fore-quarters resting on the points of his tusks. He lay in this posture for several seconds, but the amazing pressure of the carcase was more than the head was able to support; he had fallen with his head so short under him that the tusks received little assistance from his legs. Something must give way. The strain on the mighty tusks was fair; they did not, therefore, yield; but the portion of his head in which the tusk was imbedded, extending a long way above the eye, yielded and burst with a muffled crash. The tusk was thus free, and turned right round in his head, so that a man could draw it out, and the carcase fell over and rested on its side. This was a very first-rate elephant, and the tusks he carried were long and perfect.

ALL STAINED WITH BLOOD

About three hours after sundown I called my men to come and take their coffee; and after supper, three of them – John Stofolus, Hendrick, and Ruyter – returned before their comrades to their own fireside, and lay down. Hendrick and Ruyter lay on one side of the fire under one blanket, and John Stofolus on the other. At this moment I was eating some barley-broth at my fire, which was small, for, owing to our proximity to the village, wood was very scarce. The night was pitch dark and windy.

Suddenly the appalling and savage roar of an angry lion burst upon my ear within a few yards of us, followed by the shrieking of the Hottentots; again and again the murderous roar of attack was repeated. We heard John and Ruyter shriek; still, for a few moments, we

The death of Hendrick.

thought the lion was only chasing one of the dogs round the kraal; but, next instant, Stofolus rushed into the midst of us almost speechless with fear and terror, his eyes bursting from their sockets, and shrieked out, "The lion! the lion! He has got Hendrick; he dragged him away from the fire beside me; I struck him with the burning brands upon his head, but he would not let go his hold. Hendrick is dead! Oh, God! Hendrick is dead! Let us take fire and seek him." On hearing this the rest of my people rushed about, shrieking and

yelling as if they were mad, which made me angry with them for their folly, and I told them that if they did not keep quiet, the lion would in all probability have another of us, and that very likely there was a troop of them. I then ordered the dogs to be let loose, and the fire increased as far as it could be. I likewise shouted Hendrick's name, but all was still, and, hunting my dogs forward, had everything brought within the cattle-kraal, and closed the entrance as well as we could. To help the dead man was impossible.

My terrified people sat round the fire with guns in their hands all night, fancying every moment that the lion would return and spring again into the midst of us. When the dogs were first let go, the stupid brutes, as dogs often prove when most required, instead of going at the lion, rushed fiercely on one another, and fought desperately for some minutes; after this they got his wind, and, going at him, showed us his position, and here they kept up a continued barking until day dawned, the lion occasionally springing after them and driving them in upon the kraal. The horrible monster had dragged the unfortunate man into a little hollow at the back of the thick bush, beside which the fire was kindled, and here within forty yards of us he devoured him, careless of our proximity.

It appeared that when the wretched Hendrick had risen to drive in an ox, the lion had watched him to his fireside, and he had scarcely lain down when the brute sprang upon him and Ruyter, and, roaring, grappled him with his fearful claws, biting him on the breast and shoulder, all the while feeling for his neck; having got hold of which, he at once dragged him away backwards round the bush into the dense shade.

As the animal lay upon the unfortunate man, he faintly cried "Help me, help me! Oh, God! men, help me!" after which all was still, except that his comrades heard the bones of his neck cracking between the teeth of the lion. John Stofolus was lying with his back to the fire on the opposite side, and hearing the lion, sprang up, and, seizing a large flaming brand, belaboured him on the head with the burning wood, but the brute did not take any notice of him. The Bushman had a narrow escape, and did not get off altogether scatheless, the lion having inflicted two gashes on him with his claws.

As the day broke, we heard the lion dragging something up the riverside under cover of the bank, and, having driven the cattle out of the kraal, proceeded to inspect the scene of the night's awful tragedy. In the hollow, where the beast had consumed his prey, we found one leg of the unfortunate Hendrick, bitten off below the knee, the shoe still on his foot; the grass and bushes were all stained with blood, and fragments of his pea-coat lay around. Poor Hendrick! I knew that old coat, and had often seen some of its shreds in the dense covers where the elephants had charged after my unfortunate after-rider. Hendrick was by far the best man I had. He was of a most cheerful disposition, a first-rate waggon-driver, fearless in the field, very active, willing, and obliging, and his loss to us all was very serious. I felt sick at heart, and could not remain at the waggons, so I resolved to go after elephants to divert my mind.

HENRY METHUEN

Methuen undertook an eight-month hunting trip in 1844 as far north as Tswana territory where he bagged trophies including elephant, rhino, leopard, and a string of giraffe. The flesh of young or female giraffe, he says, is "savoury and wholesome, somewhat like beef".

LIKE A BUCKET FULL OF EELS

We had ridden within a mile of the mountains, which, clad in wood at their bases, and intersected by dark ravine, formed with their rugged summits a most striking object, when we encountered some Bakatlas, armed with shields and assegais. They talked very fast, and made many signs, from which we concluded that they knew where game was, and were desirous to lead us to it. Parties of men, however, shouting with stentorian lungs, issued from the bushes on all sides; a giraffe was seen striding rapidly away; presently a herd of quaggas, pallahs, gnoos, and ostriches, showed themselves. I shot a pallah and a quagga, right and left, but only obtained the horns of the former, the natives having skinned the head. Fresh bodies of men, running and hallooing, burst in view, till we were completely mystified on the subject. The quaggas turned back, and I rode after them, and then, by the hedges on each side of me, first discovered the object of the natives, and that I had entered within the limit of their game-traps. Two wattle hedges, of perhaps a mile in width at the entrance, contracted to a long narrow lane, about six feet in breadth, at their termination, where were two covered pit-falls, with a number of loose poles placed in parallel lines above each other, at either extremity of the pits, to prevent any creature escaping, or pawing down the soil. Noises thickened around me, and men rushed past, their skin-cloaks streaming in the wind; till, from their black naked figures and wild gestures, it needed no Martin to imagine a pandemonium. I pressed hard upon the flying animals, and, galloping down the lane, saw the pits choke-full; while several of the quaggas noticing their danger turned upon me, ears back and teeth showing, compelling me to retreat with equal celerity from them. Some natives standing in the lane made the fugitives run the gauntlet with their assegais: as each quagga made a dash at them, they pressed their backs into the hedge, and held their broad ox-hide shields in his face, hurling their spears into his sides as he passed onward. One managed to burst through the hedge and escape, the rest fell pierced with assegais,

like so many porcupines. Men are often killed on these hunts when buffalos turn back in a similar way. It was some little time before Bain and I could find a gap in the hedge, and get round to the pits, but we at length found one, and then a scene exhibited itself which baffles description. So full were the pits, that many animals had run over the bodies of their comrades, and got free. Never can I forget that bloody, murderous spectacle; – a moving, wriggling mass of quaggas, huddled and jammed together in the most inextricable confusion; – some were on their backs, with their heels up and others lying across them; some had taken a dive and only displayed their tails; all lay interlocked like a bucket full of eels. The savages, frantic with excitement, yelled round them, thrusting their assegais with smiles of satisfaction into the upper ones, and leaving them to suffocate those beneath; evidently rejoicing in the agony of their victims. Moseleli, their chief, was there in person, and after the lapse of half an hour, the poles at the entrance of the pits being removed, the dead bodies, in all the contortions and stiffness of death, were drawn out by hooked stakes secured through the main sinew of the neck; – a rude song, with extemporary words, being chanted the while.

Vultures hovered over-head in anxious expectation of a feast, and Moseleli, who received us civilly, and shook hands with us, sat in his leopard-skin caross upon a dead quagga, receiving the congratulations of his courtiers, for this flesh is a very favourite food with them. His appearance was mild but undignified. We were in great luck to witness this sight, since it had been a royal hunt, such as the Highlanders practised of yore for the amusement of their chieftains. A large extent of country is encircled by men on these occasions, who, narrowing to a centre, drive all the game enclosed within their ranks to the desired point. I counted twenty quaggas as they were being extracted from one pit, not more than ten feet square and six feet deep.

JOHAN WAHLBERG

The impressive collection of southern African birds, insects and other creatures that the naturalist Wahlberg lodged with the Stockholm Natural History Museum had a hidden price: a trail of rotting pachyderms. The Swede began hunting ivory merely to supplement the shaky finances of his scientific expeditions, but the killing grew almost to a frenzied end in itself. A wounded elephant with a poetic sense of justice eventually terminated Wahlberg's career in central Botswana in 1856. This section of his journal finds him on the upper reaches of the Crocodile River in the northern Transvaal in 1844. "W" and "K" are his assistants Willem and Koos; Samok is presumably a local chief, and Maloko one of his followers; Rhinoceros simus is the white rhino and Keitloa a supposed species of the black; this Plectropterus is the spur-wing goose. The rhino were killed primarily for their meat.

CUT OFF THE HEAD
25 Wednesday. Continue on our way. K, 2 *Rhinoceros simus.* At a water-hole we discover a young dead elephant; probably its mother had been killed by other hunters, and the calf had died of hunger. Since it was still fresh, only

damaged by a cut on one of its flanks inflicted by my Basuto, I decided to prepare the hide, and we stay over here. Towards evening K once again killed a *Rhinoceros simus*.

26 Thursday. Move on a little. Here an appalling thunderstorm came on, with hail the size of hens' eggs, which ravaged the bush and the veld.

27 Friday. Resumed our return journey.

28 Saturday. Reach our other waggon at the Masubā lake. W returns in the evening with an ostrich skin. News that 4 of Samok's people were murdered on the night of the 25th on a rocky hill quite close to my waggon: the corpses hidden.

29. Prepared the ostrich. Maloko's brother killed, etc.

30. W and K go hunting elands, for food for the return journey: no success. K, 1 redbuck and 1 young white Rhinoceros. Cut off the head of one of the corpses and wash it, only to find that the cranium has been completely shattered.

1 October Tuesday. Cut off the head of another corpse, probably Maloko's brother. It was now easy to get at, having been exposed by the hyaenas. W and K hunting: in vain.

2 Wednesday. W and K shoot rhinoceros. The younger Wolverantz passes by my waggons.

3 Thursday. Move to the Moritili. W kills 1 *Keithloa*, and I cut off its head. See *Plectropterus*, and try in vain to get it.

CHAPTER FIVE

1850 to 1870

The governor throws a ball,
David Livingstone warns against constipation,
a eugenist produces the ultimate doggy bag,
a Russian priest comes close to burning down a hotel,
a hyaena gives the coup de grâce to a teapot,
and we visit a cannibal cave.

ROBERT GODLONTON

*"Moral Bob", Grahamstown newspaper owner, warmonger, settler propagandist
and advocate of separate government for the Eastern Cape, was chosen by governor Harry Smith to sit on the legislative council which preceded the first elected
Cape parliament. This is from a journal recording his journey to and stay in Cape
Town in September 1850 for his first sitting of the council. William Cock was
another Eastern Cape representative on the body.*

A FAIRY LANDSCAPE
Dressed and proceeded to Government House – where I found a most brilliant party. Sir Harry received me most graciously and at once presented
me in due form to Lady Smith, who is a charming woman, goodness beaming from her very countenance. She was most superbly dressed, in crimson
figured velvet, her head in a blaze of diamonds, and her fingers covered
almost with costly rings. The ladies in her circle were all most beautifully
attired. Sir Harry selected for my charge to the banquetting hall Mrs.
Macleay – the most lovely woman of the whole; while Cock had the distinguished honour of conducting Lady Smith herself. Cock sat on the right
of her Ladyship, I next but one to Sir Harry, my fair partner being of course
seated between us on my right hand. The saloon is a most elegant apartment and the spread for dinner was most gorgeous. There were the cande-
labra presented to Sir Harry Smith in India – an exquisite massy piece of
workmanship in dull silver. On the basement of this costly article, are the
Elephant and the Camel, much larger than those in the carved wood of the
Adderley Chair. – there is the native of Hindostan – beneath the graceful
palm branches – and a great deal more which I cannot describe all mod-
deled with exquisite skill in solid silver. There was another ornament of the
same character and of the same material, but rather smaller, presented to
Sir Harry when at home by his native town. There were several other costly things also upon the table, most of which were presented to Sir Harry by

public bodies. The dinner consisted of all the delicacies obtainable in this part of the globe, and it passed off very pleasantly. Though my position was a novel one, I found myself quite at home. Every one was agreeable and the attention paid to me was marked and flattering. There was a good sprinkling of uniforms, both naval and military, French and English – together with many of the most distinguished men of the Cape in plain clothes – both merchants and officials. After dinner we rejoined the ladies in the drawing room – and found that the company had been augmented by a large evening party – among whom I found Commissary De Smidt, Dr. Hadaway, E. Norton, Mr. Van der Byl, whose acquaintance I made a few years back, at Robeys on Manleys flat. I found he had since visited Europe. Every lady was kind and agreeable. The folding doors had been thrown open and the Ball room was seen like a fairy landscape – brilliantly lit up with gas by means of massy gilt chandeliers suspended from the ceiling – the room is richly gilt – with a looking glass on one side about 12 feet square – and costly adornments around it – the band of music was in the orchestra, and the ladies were soon whirling round in the giddy dance. The gas lights were most brilliant, shedding upon the scene a light far more intense than sunshine. Sir John Wylde was among the dancers, quite as gay as the most juvenile person, and there were many other "grave and vener-able seigniors" employed the same way, that I could not help thinking might have been much better occupied. At ten the supper room was thrown open, the table groaning beneath its load of viands of every description – fruits – sandwiches, hot and cold fowl, hams and tongues, pastry, custards, jellies – wines of all kinds etc. etc. Everybody acted ad libi-tum – that is, as they pleased – came and went as they were inclined, stood or sat, ate little or much – and were in fact quite at home. At half past 11 Cock and I took our departure, much pleased with our entertainment …

Juana Smith, incidentally, was of noble Spanish blood. Little more than a girl when she first caught Harry Smith's eye during the Peninsular campaign, by the time Godlonton met her she was overweight and dropsical. She confessed to him later that even when her feet were killing her, she was compelled by her position to "receive company with a smiling face".

203

GOULD LUCAS

Lucas, an ensign in the 73rd Regiment, shipped out from England on the Birkenhead *with reinforcements for the troops engaged in the Eastern Cape in the Eighth Frontier War. The vessel touched at Simon's Town, and on the evening of February 25 1852 steamed out of False Bay for Port Elizabeth. Lucas says in this letter to his father that he was sleeping heavily when he was awakened in the small hours of the 26th by "three distinct shocks". The* Birkenhead *had impaled itself on an uncharted rock off Danger Point; a bid to go astern gashed the iron hull even further. The bulk of the troops stood fast on the deck as the 56 women and children on board were transferred to lifeboats, and maintained this discipline until the ship made her final plunge. There has been a suggestion this was simply because they had no idea how grave the situation was. Of the 638 people on board, 445 lost their lives, and with the British penchant for turning disasters into celebrations of national virtue, a legend was born. Lucas went on to serve in India and Natal, where he co-founded Hilton College.*

HE COULD NOT SWIM

The order was given by Capt. Salmon to jump into the sea and save ourselves if we could. Almost all the officers were congregated on the poop at that time.

We were now sinking very fast. I was afraid the ship would go down with a rush by the head, for her stern was so much raised that one of the men swimming saw the heel of the rudder. Indeed it was very difficult to prevent oneself slipping on the deck. I had just taken off my clothes and got over the bulwarks ready for a jump, and was making up my mind to dive head first when I thought that, should I ever get ashore, I should be roasted by the sun in the day. I once more got over the bulwarks and groped for my shirt on the deck and put it on. I again took up my old station; Major Seaton was still on the other side of the bulwarks. We talked for a little – a few seconds, then another crash was heard. The ship forward of the

The *Birkenhead* goes down.

mainmast broke off and went down. The remaining part – that aft of the mainmast – still stood, but was sinking fast. Poor Major Seaton said to me "Now, Lucas, you had better go; there is no use in waiting." We shook hands. I said I hoped we should meet ashore; he told me he could not swim. I still remained standing; I was afraid to jump, as the water was full of men below me – many drowning as fast as possible, a sad sight. I should most likely have been pulled down and drowned. While hesitating to make the plunge, I heard my servant Collins call me. He asked if he was to follow. I knew he could not swim, so I advised his getting as high up as he could in the rigging. He said "All right, Sir! but I have brought your purse up from your cabin; you will want it when you get ashore." I never saw the faithful fellow again. I waited till the poop deck was about two feet from the water, then jumped off, and struck out as quickly as possible to get out of the suction of the ship. When I turned my head to look, I saw nothing but the mainmast and yard, the rigging was crowded with men. When I left the ship, many poor fellows in the mizzen rigging must have been drowned at once.

When I was making up my mind to leave the remains of the ship, I think what caused me to hesitate so long was that the men in the water (some swimming strong) were pulled down by exhausted men. Others, swimming strong, went down with a yell: I learned afterwards that the ship was surrounded by sharks.

I swam about 100 yards and then caught hold of a piece of wreck, rested and then struck out for a large white object, 50 yards, perhaps. It turned out to be one of the paddle box boats turned keel uppermost. I found on it five soldiers and one sailor. We were now in comparative safety, but we were much afraid of being carried out to sea instead of to land which we could see; it looked about 9 or 10 miles off. Well, I felt more regret and more uncomfortable during the first half hour I was on the boat than I did during the whole of the business – that long struggle for life. We drifted some time out to sea, and then happily a current took us towards the land. When we were about a mile from the wreck an oar passed us, and when about 50 yards off the sailor said it was gone and that it would have been of use to us. I asked the men if they would go for it, they all said no. I was the best swimmer; although very tired, as they thought it would be of use to us, I jumped into the water, got hold of the oar, and turned towards the boat. It then struck me that perhaps I should not be able to catch the boat up again. I assure you that my feelings were not of a pleasant kind. The men cheered me; I struck out and reached the boat. After about 12 hours, we drifted to about 300 yards from the shore, then got among breakers. It was a most odious coast, nearly all what is called "ironbound." A seaweed grows along the coast called "sea bamboo." These weeds grow about 15 or 16 feet long, so that for several hundred yards from the shore where these weeds were, it is nearly impossible to swim along them, for being all matted together, they catch the legs. We were now surrounded with these sea bamboes which held the boat, preventing her getting nearer the shore. The breakers were washing us off.

I forgot to mention that when I first reached the boat, I did not dare to speak lest I should be driven off by those already in her bottom. I hung on for some time up to my middle in the water. When I could hold on no longer I called out and was pulled on to the boat. I need not have feared, for the men asked me to take charge and said they would do anything I told them. The sailor was Quarter-Master Maxwell. Three of the soldiers were stark naked. I could not help them, having only half a shirt myself; but Maxwell said "I can." He had on two pairs of trowsers and three shirts, so was able to help the three naked men. He told me that he could not swim a stroke and did not know how he got on to the boat. Before we got to the shore, we drifted through quantities of wreckage to which many poor fellows were clinging, and as they passed they asked for help. Oh that I could forget what I saw that night, I would not pass such another. It is an awful sight to see despairing men fighting for anything to support them in the water.

WILLIAM FLEMING

As a junior officer with the 45th Foot, Fleming fought against the Xhosa in the War of the Axe, and against the Boers in the skirmish at Boomplaats. On leave in 1852 from peacetime duty at Pietermaritzburg's Fort Napier, he and two companions embarked on a hunting trip to the Pongola area of northern Natal.

A FEW INCHES TOO SHORT

We did not again meet with them [elephants] during our 14 days wanderings but saw plenty of all sorts of other game. The rhinoceros were very plentiful generally running in pairs but at times I used to come across them in small troops of 4 and 5. I think James would have laughed to have seen me galloping along side of them (for your horse has the speed of them) to examine their horns and try if one was long enough to make a stick for him which I thought he might value more from being my shooting but I am sorry to say that I did not succeed for the Dutch Boers have shot off all the long horned ones for the trade of sticks and to make ramrods for their guns. After I had shot one, I used to let them pass unmolested whenever, on examination, I found the horn to be short. One day when an elephant spoor (id est – foot print) I was following along I came on one apparently with a longer horn than usual. I gave chase and, after a hard gallop of about 13 miles, I succeeded in killing him with the 4th shot. To my mortification, on cutting off the horn, I found it just a few inches too short for a stick but it will make little dandy canes.

EDWARD ENSOR

Ensor, in his early twenties, was heading for Australia in a vain bid to escape the family gloving business at Milborne Port on England's south coast. His vessel stopped in January 1853 at the Cape, where he and five companions climbed Table Mountain. Here he describes distractions in the early stages of the ascent. Although Ensor was eventually reclaimed by the glove factory, he gained international repute in later life as a scholar by constructing a chronological chart covering 6,000 years of history. It was 15 metres long and 1½ wide, took 17 years to complete, and was exhibited on both sides of the Atlantic.

On enquiring our way at some cross roads we were directed to follow some Malay girls who were carrying bundles of clothes to
wash in the stream that flows through the ravine. As we ascended by the water side our mountain lassies took their bundles from
their heads and settled themselves on the blankets to wash. Here
and there we observed an old Mosambique man washing alone
but generally the black fair sex occupied the stream. Perhaps the
manner in which these nymphs performed their ablutions and
washing operations may interest and instruct some of the maid-
ens on board who hope to soon have similar work to perform in
the Bush for husbands and children. Well as the work was arduous and the sun nearly vertical, they divested themselves of their
upper and lower clothing, reserving just so much that it would
not interfere with the free use of their arms and shoulders above
and be hanging in the water below as they were standing knee
deep in the middle of the stream. In fact one slight garment fastened round the waist answered the purpose. After they had
arranged their toilet they took their work and soaked and soaped
it, rubbing it well and cleansing it in the current. They then
exposed it to dry on the rocks and bushes around them. I suppose
there must have been two hundred thus employed.

DAVID LIVINGSTONE

*After a youth of drudgery in the cotton mills of industrial Scotland, Livingstone
completed a medical degree and was accepted by the London Missionary Society for
a posting to the Cape. He survived mauling by a lion to make the first authenti-
cated European crossing of the continent (it had been done before by half-caste
traders and Arab explorers), name the Victoria Falls, rekindle English outrage
against slavery and lay down the moral imperative for British expansion in Africa.
He displayed determination verging on obsession, and undisputed courage, qualities that earned him iconic status in Victorian England. "I ... always believed that,
if we serve God at all, it ought to be done in a manly way," he wrote. But at the
same time he was plagued by self-doubt and harshly intolerant of weakness in others. He deliberately played down the dangers he had been through, with fatal consequences for those who tried to follow, and died a lonely death trying doggedly to
persuade himself that he had found the source of the Nile. Livingstone left detailed
letters and journals, as well as published accounts of his journeys that became bestsellers. However, he claimed to find writing for public consumption irksome and
laborious. "I think I would rather cross the African continent again than undertake to write another book," he wrote. The first extracts here cover pioneering journeys through the eastern Kalahari to the Zambezi, from 1849.*

YOU SPEAK LIKE A CHIEF

All around Serotli the country is perfectly flat, and composed of soft white
sand. There is a peculiar glare of bright sunlight from a cloudless sky over
the whole scene; and one clump of trees and bushes, with open spaces

David Livingstone

between, looks so exactly like another, that if you leave the wells, and walk a quarter of a mile in any direction, it is difficult to return. Oswell and Murray went out on one occasion to get an eland, and were accompanied by one of the Bakalahari. The perfect sameness of the country caused even this son of the Desert to lose his way; a most puzzling conversation forthwith ensued between them and their guide. One of the most common phrases of the people is "Kia ituméla," I thank you, or I am pleased; and the gentlemen were both quite familiar with it, and with the word "metse," water. But there is a word very similar in sound, "Kia timéla," I am wandering; its perfect is "Ki temétse," I have wandered. The party had been roaming about, perfectly lost, till the sun went down; and, through their mistaking the verb "wander," for "to be pleased," and "water," the colloquy went on at intervals during the whole bitterly cold night in somewhat the following style: –

"Where are the waggons?"

Real answer. – "I don't know. I have wandered. I never wandered before. I am quite lost."

Supposed answer. – "I don't know. I want water. I am glad, I am quite pleased. I am thankful to you."

"Take us to the waggons, and you will get plenty of water."

Real answer (looking vacantly around). – "How did I wander? Perhaps the well is there, perhaps not. I don't know. I have wandered."

Supposed answer. – "Something about thanks; he says he is pleased, and mentions water again." The guide's vacant stare, while trying to remember, is thought to indicate mental imbecility, and the repeated thanks were supposed to indicate a wish to deprecate their wrath.

"Well, Livingstone *has* played us a pretty trick, giving us in charge of an idiot. Catch us trusting him again. What can this fellow mean by his thanks and talk about water? O, you born fool! take us to the waggons, and you will get both meat and water. Wouldn't a thrashing bring him to his senses again?" "No, no, for then he will run away, and we shall be worse off than we are now."

The hunters regained the waggons next day by their own sagacity, which becomes wonderfully quickened by a sojourn in the Desert; and we enjoyed a hearty laugh on the explanation of their midnight colloquies. Frequent mistakes of this kind occur. A man may tell his interpreter to say that he is a member of the family of the chief of the white men; *"Yes, you speak like a chief,"* is the reply; meaning, as they explain it, that a chief may talk nonsense without any one daring to contradict him. They probably have ascertained, from that same interpreter, that this relative of the white chief is very poor, having scarcely anything in his waggon.

NO CHIN AT ALL

All the black tribes have the idea that beauty and fairness are associated. The Basutu are much fairer than the river tribes & prize themselves accordingly. They seldom carry burdens. But in other respects all have the same ideas of comeliness with ourselves. Their remarks on first seeing themselves in a looking glass are amusingly ludicrous. "Is that me?", "What ears I've got", "What a big mouth", "I have no chin at all", "I would have been beautiful but for these high cheek bones", "I am destroyed by these cheek bones", "See how my head shoots up in the middle", "My ears are like pumpkin leaves" – and laughing heartily all the while because the disparaging remarks are made by themselves. One man asked [for] the looking glass in the evening, and when I was lying as if asleep I observed him taking a long scrutinizing look and, after twisting his mouth in different directions, [he] remarked to himself, Kana ki mashue yan! How very ugly I am!

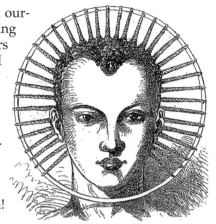

THE GREAT SOW
Sekeletu was the young chief of the Kololo.

Katongo was the best place we had seen; but in order to accomplish a complete examination, I left Sekeletu at Naliele, and ascended the river. He furnished me with men, besides my rowers, and among the rest a herald, that I might enter his villages in what is considered a dignified manner. This it was supposed would be effected by the herald shouting out at the top of his voice, "Here comes the lord; the great lion;" the latter phrase being "tau e tŏna," which in his imperfect way of pronunciation became "sau e tŏna," and so like "the great sow," that I could not receive the honour with becoming gravity, and had to entreat him, much to the annoyance of my party, to be silent.

HIS COLD WET NOSE
In November 1853 Livingstone and a party of Kololo companions set off from Linyanti, on the Zambezi, for Luanda, more than 1,600 kilometers to the northwest. Livingstone, who believed exposure to English commerce would help civilise the interior, hoped to open a trade route to the coast. Overcoming fever that at times totally incapacitated him, and other disease that left him vomiting blood, as well as hostile tribes and hellishly daunting geographical obstacles, they took two years to get to Luanda and back. Livingstone had to admit to himself that the route was impractical. These next pieces are from that journey. The Manenko here was the energetic and strong-willed daughter of a chieftainess of the southern Lunda in what is today eastern Angola. She led Livingstone on an enforced five-day detour to the town of her uncle Shinte, paramount of the tribe.

Livingstone at Lake Ngami.

During the night we were all awakened by a terrific shriek from one of Manenko's ladies. She piped out so loud and long that we all imagined she had been seized by a lion, and my men snatched up their arms, which they always place so as to be ready at a moment's notice, and ran to the rescue; but we found the alarm had been caused by one of

the oxen thrusting his head into her hut, and smelling her: she had put her hand on his cold wet nose, and thought it was all over with her.

AS LARGE AS LIFE

Shinte was most anxious to see the pictures of the magic lantern, but fever had so weakening an effect, and I had such violent action of the heart, with buzzing in the ears, that I could not go for several days; when I did go for the purpose, he had his principal men and the same crowd of court beauties near him as at the reception. The first picture exhibited was Abraham about to slaughter his son Isaac; it was shown as large as life, and the uplifted knife was in the act of striking the lad; the Balonda men remarked that the picture was much more like a god than the things of wood or clay they worshipped. I explained that this man was the first of a race to whom God had given the Bible we now held, and that among his children our Saviour appeared. The ladies listened with silent awe; but, when I moved the slide, the uplifted dagger moving towards them, they thought it was to be sheathed in their bodies instead of Isaac's. "Mother! mother!" all shouted at once, and off they rushed helter-skelter, tumbling pell-mell over each other, and over the little idol-huts and tobacco-bushes: we could not get one of them back again. Shinte, however, sat bravely through the whole, and afterwards examined the instrument with interest.

SLAP HIS NOSE
The trials of riding an ox.

The forests through which we pass are becoming more dense, and the numbers of parasitical and climbing plants so numerous it is very difficult to pass through them. Many of the latter are from an inch to three or four in diameter, and hanging loosely accross the path require to be quickly lifted over the head or ducked under with dexterity, for the ox invariably rushes on more quickly if there is any difficulty. He sometimes leaves the path without any apparent cause except for the purpose of hanging his rider like Absalom among these tough and strong climbers. The bridle or string attached to a piece of wood through his nose is of very little use, for he persists in his course though his head is turned quite round. The only effectual means of turning the wayward animal is to slap his nose with a switch towards the proper path, but this cannot always be done in the dense jungle. The head has often to be held down to avoid parasites, and the feet are often so entangled as to give a jerk, setting him off more quickly in his stupid course. I have been so firmly caught by a thick branch between the stirrup-iron and foot as fairly to hold my ox back (the stirrups being attached to the belt round his body), yet he pulled so as to bend the stirrup-iron and nearly break off my foot.

NO MORE OF ME

The plains adjacent to Loanda are somewhat elevated and comparatively sterile. On coming across these we first beheld the sea: my companions looked upon the boundless ocean with awe. On describing their feelings afterwards, they remarked that "we marched along with our father, believing that what the ancients had always told us was true, that the world has no end; but all at once the world said to us, 'I am finished; there is no more of me!'" They had always imagined that the world was one extended plain without limit.

TELLING THEIR CHILDREN

The villages are widely apart, and difficult of access, from the paths being so covered with tall grass, that even an ox can scarcely follow the track. The grass cuts the feet of the men; yet we met a woman with a little child, and a girl, wending their way home with loads of manioc. The sight of a white man always infuses a tremor into their dark bosoms, and in every case of the kind, they appeared immensely relieved when I had fairly passed, without having sprung upon them. In the villages, the dogs run away with their tails between their legs, as if they had seen a lion. The women peer from behind the walls till he comes near them, and then hastily dash into the house. When a little child, unconscious of danger, meets you in the street, he sets up a scream at the apparition, and conveys the impression that he is not far from going into fits. Among the Bechuanas, I have been obliged to reprove the women for making a hobgoblin of the white man, and telling their children that they would send for him to bite them.

A THOUSAND COMETS

Although Livingstone did declare at one point that he thought all rivers and hills "discovered" by Englishmen ought to have English names, he exercised considerable restraint: by 1857 he had given only one English name to a geographical feature, renaming the Mosioatunya, "the smoke that thunders", the Victoria Falls.

The side [of the chasm at the falls] over which the river precipitates itself is perpendicular too; but in three of the five or six parts into which the stream is divided at low-water, about 3 feet of the edge of the lip is bevelled off. Several pieces also having fallen in give this lip a serrated edge; but the water falls at once clear of the rock and becomes a fleecy mass as white as snow. The pieces of water, if I may so express myself, do not at once lose their cohesion, but give off streams of vapour, in their downward course, exactly as comets are represented on paper, or as a piece of steel when burned in oxygen gas. The beautiful mass thus resembles a thousand comets speeding on their course. On looking down into the fissure on the right of the island, where the largest quantity of water falls, nothing is seen but a dense white cloud with two bright rainbows on it. (It was about mid-day and the declination of the sun nearly the same as the latitude when we visited it.) An immense stream

Victoria Falls

of vapour rushes up from the cloud unlike anything I ever saw before. When about 300 feet high it loses its steam colour, becomes dark, and descends in a shower, exposure to which for a quarter of an hour wetted us to the skin. A few yards back from the opposite lip a dense unbroken hedge of evergreen trees stands. Their leaves are constantly wet from the consensed vapour, and from their roots several little rills run back into the gulf, but never reach the bottom, for the ascending columns of vapour literally lick them up off the perpendicular wall before they are half-way down. I have estimated the depth at 100 feet, but we cannot see what it is on the right of the island. On the left of the island a large piece has fallen in, and that lying on one side of the chafing river below enables me to form an approximation: my companions amused themselves by throwing stones down the falls, and wondering to see how small they became before they were lost in the cloud. In former days the three principal falls were used as places where certain chiefs worshipped the Barimo (gods or departed spirits). As even at low water there are from 400 to 600 yards of water pouring over, the constancy and loudness of the sound may have produced feelings of awe, as if the never-ceasing flood came forth from the footstool of the Eternal. It was mysterious to them, for one of their canoe songs says,

"The Liambai, – nobody knows
Whence it comes or whither it goes."

KINA BOMBA
Frustrated by the difficulties of the western route, Livingstone decided instead to follow the Zambezi east to the coast, to see whether it would offer a route for trade and Christian civilisation. He set off with 114 Kololo companions in November 1855.

The further we advanced, the more we found the country swarming with inhabitants. Great numbers came to see the white man, a sight they had never beheld before. They always brought presents of maize and masuka. Their mode of salutation is quite singular. They throw themselves on their backs on the ground, and, rolling from side to side, slap the outside of their thighs as expressions of thankfulness and welcome, uttering the words, "Kina bomba." This method of salutation was to me very disagreeable, and I never could get reconciled to it. I called out "Stop, stop! I don't want that;" but they, imagining I was dissatisfied, only tumbled about more furiously, and slapped their thighs with greater vigour. The men being totally unclothed, this performance imparted to my mind a painful sense of their extreme degradation.

An incident on the march.

THEY WISH SEED
Two weeks from Tete, on the Vunga range.

The people have several times invited my men to spend the night with their daughters. The object of this is to secure children for themselves. A man may come from another tribe to live with a young woman whom he fancies. He must perform obeisance to the mother-in-law every time he comes near her hut, and always keep her well supplied with firewood, not an easy matter along the river. Though his wife bear him many children he can claim none of them, and must depart at last to his own tribe childless. One of the Bastards has a child at Nyampungo's, but cannot claim it. They say they wish seed from my men who are able to kill elephants, as it must be good, but my party have hitherto been very wary and fear a snare.

IN A FIT OF RAGING THIRST
Dr Salis, the late physician of Mosambique, tried the curious experiment of curing fever by depriving the unfortunate patients of water except in very minute quantities. An officer in a fit of raging thirst crawled by night to a large pot of water and drank in long delicious draughts the whole, an enormous quantity between two and three gallons. After returning to his cot he commenced vomiting and purging copiously, and in three days left the hospital quite well. Thus ended the experiment, for no one else would submit to the doctor afterwards.

The more usual treatment for fevers along the Zambezi was to place bags of hot sand on the sufferer's body, especially the joints, feed him warm soup, and administer a purgative.

IS THIS THE WAY YOU GO?
The Kololo men who made the eastern journey were under orders from their chief not to turn back until they reached Livingstone's wife, Mary, – then in England – and to bring her back with them. Livingstone prevailed on most of them to go no further than Tete, but one, Sekwebu, was still with him when he arrived at the fever-ridden coastal settlement of Quelimane. Sekwebu, who was captured by the Ndebele as a child and grew up in the Tete district, had travelled along both banks of the Zambezi several times and knew the local dialect. Livingstone describes him as a man of "great prudence and sound judgement".

After waiting about six weeks at this unhealthy spot, in which, however, by the kind attentions of Colonel Nunes and his nephew, I partially recovered from my tertian, H.M. brig "Frolic" arrived off Kilimane. As the village is twelve miles from the bar, and the weather was rough, she was at anchor ten days before we knew of her presence, about seven miles from the entrance to the port. She brought abundant supplies for all my need; and £150 to pay my passage home, from my kind friend Mr. Thompson, the Society's agent at the Cape. The Admiral at the Cape kindly sent an offer of a passage to the Mauritius, which I thankfully accepted. Sekwebu and one attendant alone remained with me now. He was very intelligent, and had been of the greatest service to me; indeed, but for his good sense, tact, and command of the language of the tribes through which we passed, I believe we should scarcely have succeeded in reaching the coast. I naturally felt grateful to him; and as his chief wished *all* my companions to go to

England with me, and would probably be disappointed if none went, I thought it would be beneficial for him to see the effects of civilization, and report them to his countrymen; I wished also to make some return for his very important services. Others had petitioned to come, but I explained the danger of a change of climate and food, and with difficulty restrained them. The only one who now remained begged so hard to come on board ship, that I greatly regretted, that the expense prevented my acceding to his wish to visit England. I said to him, "You will die if you go to such a cold country as mine." "That is nothing," he reiterated; "let me die at your feet."

When we parted from our friends at Kilimane, the sea on the bar was frightful even to the seamen. This was the first time Sekwebu had seen the sea. Captain Peyton had sent two boats in case of accident. The waves were so high that, when the cutter was in one trough, and we in the pinnace in another, her mast was hid. We then mounted to the crest of the wave, rushed down the slope, and struck the water again with a blow which felt as if she had struck the bottom. Boats must be singularly well constructed to be able to stand these shocks. Three breakers swept over us. The men lift up their oars, and a wave comes sweeping over all, giving the impression that the boat is going down, but she only goes beneath the top of the wave, comes out on the other side, and swings down the slope, and a man bales out the water with a bucket. Poor Sekwebu looked at me when these terrible seas broke over, and said, "Is this the way you go? Is this the way you go?" I smiled, and said, "Yes; don't you see it is?" and tried to encourage him. He was well acquainted with canoes, but never had seen aught like this. When we reached the ship – a fine, large brig of sixteen guns and a crew of one hundred and thirty – she was rolling so, that we could see a part of her bottom. It was quite impossible for landsmen to catch the ropes and climb up, so a chair was sent down, and we were hoisted in as ladies usually are, and received so hearty an English welcome from Captain Peyton and all on board, that I felt myself at once at home in everything, except my own mother-tongue. I seemed to know the language perfectly, but the words I wanted, would not come at my call. When I left England I had no intention of returning, and directed my attention earnestly to the languages of Africa, paying none to English composition. With the exception of a short interval in Angola, I had been three and a half years without speaking English, and this, with thirteen years of previous partial disuse of my native tongue, made me feel sadly at a loss on board the "Frolic."

We left Kilimane on the 12th of July, and reached the Mauritius on the 12th of August, 1856. Sekwebu was picking up English, and becoming a favourite with both men and officers. He seemed a little bewildered, everything on board a man-of-war being so new and strange; but he remarked to me several times, "Your countrymen are very agreeable," and "What a strange country this is – all water together." He also said, that he now understood why I used the sextant. When we reached the Mauritius a steamer came out to tow us into the harbour. The constant strain on his untutored mind seemed now to reach a climax, for during the night he became insane. I thought at first that he was intoxicated. He had descended into a boat, and, when I attempted to go down and bring him into the ship, he ran to the stern, and said, "No! no! it is enough that I die alone. You must not perish; if you come I shall throw myself into the water." Perceiving that his mind was affected, I said, "Now, Sekwebu, we are going to Ma Robert [Mary]." This struck a chord in his bosom, and he said, "O yes; where is she, and where is Robert?" and he seemed to recover. The officers proposed to secure him by putting him in irons, but, being a gentleman in his own country, I objected, knowing that the insane often retain an impression of ill-treatment, and I could not bear to have it said in Sekeletu's country that I had chained one of his principal men, as they had seen slaves treated. I tried to get him

Kebrabasa

on shore by day, but he refused. In the evening a fresh accession of insanity occurred – he tried to spear one of the crew, then leaped overboard, and, though he could swim well, pulled himself down hand under hand, by the chain cable. We never found the body of poor Sekwebu.

OBLIGATIONS TO THE MADMEN
In 1858 the British government commissioned Livingstone to return to the Zambezi, this time as head of a full expedition with staff including an artist, a geologist, a botanist and his brother Charles. Part of its brief was to encourage the natives to "apply themselves to industrial pursuits and to the cultivation of their lands, with a view to the production of raw material to be exported to England in return for British manufactures". In 1855-6 Livingstone had followed the Zambezi for most of its course to the sea, and assumed it was fully navigable. Unfortunately, a detour upriver of Tete had meant he missed the Kebrabasa rapids, impassable to shipping – as he now discovered. Although the expedition then headed north and (wrongly) claimed European discovery of Lake Nyasa, it was rent by disagreements and petty quarrels, and Livingstone's wife, Mary, died near the coast after travelling out to join him.

The party pushed on at last without guides, or only with crazy ones; for, oddly enough, they were often under great obligations to the madmen of the different villages: one of these honoured them, as they slept in the open air, by dancing and singing at their feet the whole night. These poor fellows sympathized with the explorers, probably in the belief that they belonged to their own class; and, uninfluenced by the general opinion of their countrymen, they really pitied, and took kindly to the strangers, and often guided them faithfully from place to place, when no sane man could be hired for love or money.

SNEAKING ABOUT IN THE DARK
It is believed also that the souls of departed Chiefs enter into lions and render them sacred. On one occasion, when we had shot a buffalo in the path beyond the Kafue, a hungry lion, attracted probably by the smell of the meat, came close to our camp, and roused up all hands by his roaring. Tuba Mokoro, imbued with the popular belief that the beast was a Chief in disguise, scolded him roundly during his brief intervals of silence. "You a Chief, eh? You call yourself a Chief, do you? What kind of Chief are you to

215

come sneaking about in the dark, trying to steal our buffalo meat! Are you not ashamed of yourself? A pretty Chief truly; you are like the scavenger beetle, and think of yourself only. You have not the heart of a Chief; why don't you kill your own beef? You must have a stone in your chest, and no heart at all, indeed!" Tuba Mokoro producing no impression on the transformed Chief, one of the men, the most sedate of the party, who seldom spoke, took up the matter, and tried the lion in another strain. In his slow quiet way he expostulated with him on the impropriety of such conduct to strangers, who had never injured him. "We were travelling peaceably through the country back to our own Chief. We never killed people, nor stole anything. The buffalo meat was ours, not his, and it did not become a great Chief like him to be prowling round in the dark, trying, like a hyena, to steal the meat of strangers. He might go and hunt for himself, as there was plenty of game in the forest." The Pondoro, being deaf to reason, and only roaring the louder, the men became angry, and threatened to send a ball through him if he did not go away. They snatched up their guns to shoot him, but he prudently kept in the dark, outside of the luminous circle made by our camp fires, and there they did not like to venture. A little strychnine was put into a piece of meat, and thrown to him, when he soon departed, and we heard no more of the majestic sneaker.

A later traveller, Parker Gillmore, records a Shona man walking out into the darkness beyond a campfire, carrying only a burning brand, to berate a lion in similar fashion.

THE FISH SWIM

We had ample opportunities for observing the effects of this matokwane smoking on our men. It makes them feel very strong in body, but it produces exactly the opposite effect upon the mind. Two of our finest young men became inveterate smokers, and partially idiotic. The performances of a group of matokwane smokers are somewhat grotesque: they are provided with a calabash of pure water, a split bamboo, five feet long, and the great pipe, which has a large calabash or kudu's horn chamber to contain the water, through which the smoke is drawn, Narghillé fashion, on its way to the mouth. Each smoker takes a few whiffs, the last being an extra long one, and hands the pipe to his neighbour. He seems to swallow the fumes; for, striving against the convulsive action of the muscles of chest and throat, he takes a mouthful of water from the calabash, waits a few seconds, and then pours water and smoke from his mouth down the groove of the bamboo. The smoke causes violent coughing in all, and in some a species of frenzy, which passes away in a rapid stream of unmeaning words, or short sentences, as, "the green grass grows," "the fat cattle thrive," "the fish swim." No one in the group pays the slightest attention to the vehement eloquence, or the sage or silly utterance of the oracle, who stops abruptly, and, the instant common sense returns, looks rather foolish.

Smoking dagga – Livingstone's *matokwane* – through an earth pipe.

216

WITH EYES FLASHING FURY

A curious little blenny-fish swarms in the numerous creeks which intersect the mangrove topes. When alarmed, it hurries across the surface of the water in a series of leaps. It may be considered amphibious, as it lives as much out of the water as in it, and its most busy time is during low water. Then it appears on the sand or mud, near the little pools left by the retiring tide; it raises itself on its pectoral fins into something of a standing attitude, and with its large projecting eyes keeps a sharp look-out for the light-coloured fly, on which it feeds. Should the fly alight at too great a distance for even a second leap, the blenny moves slowly towards it like a cat to its prey, or like a jumping spider; and, as soon as it gets within two or three inches of the insect, by a sudden spring contrives to pop its underset mouth directly over the unlucky victim. He is, moreover, a pugnacious little fellow; and rather prolonged fights may be observed between him and his brethren. One, in fleeing from an apparent danger, jumped into a pool a foot square, which the other evidently regarded as his by right of prior discovery; in a twinkling the owner, with eyes flashing fury and with dorsal fin bristling up in rage, dashed at the intruding foe. The fight waxed furious, no tempest in a teapot ever equalled the storm of that miniature sea. The warriors were now in the water, and anon out of it, for the battle raged on sea and shore. They struck hard, they bit each other; until, becoming exhausted, they seized each other by the jaws like two bull-dogs, then paused for breath, and at it again as fiercely as before, until the combat ended by the precipitate retreat of the invader.

HE ANSWERED PROMPTLY

Sininyane was one of the group of Kololo who had accompanied Livingstone on his journey down the Zambezi valley in 1855-6 and, their numbers decimated by smallpox, had been waiting at Tete for the explorer's return. Most of them in fact chose to settle permanently in the area; only 20 elected to return to Linyanti with Livingstone.

Sininyane had exchanged names with a Zulu at Shupanga, and on being called next morning made no answer; to a second and third summons he paid no attention; but at length one of his men replied, "He is not Sininyane now, he is Moshoshoma;" and to this name he answered promptly. The custom of exhanging names with men of other tribes, is not uncommon; and the exchangers regard themselves as close comrades, owing special duties to each other ever after. Should one by chance visit his comrade's town, he expects to receive food, lodging, and other friendly offices from him. While Charles Livingstone was at Kebrabasa during the rainy season, a hungry, shivering native traveller was made a comrade for life, not by exchanging names, but by some food and a small piece of cloth. Eighteen months after, while on our journey into the interior, a man came into our camp, bringing a liberal present of rice, meal, beer, and a fowl, and reminding us of what had been done for him (which Charles Livingstone had entirely forgotten), said that now seeing us travelling he "did not like us to sleep hungry or thirsty." Several of our men, like some people at home, dropped their own names and adopted those of the Chiefs; others were a little in advance of those who take the surnames of higher people, for they took those of the mountains, or cataracts we had seen on our travels. We had a Chibisa, a Morambala, a Zomba, and a Kebrabasa, and they were called by these names even after they had returned to their own country.

I AM DEAD

The Kololo, having been away from home for over four years, here find themselves at last again within sight of the columns of vapour rising from the Victoria Falls, and hear the first reliable news from their home districts.

We were informed that, the rains having failed this year, the corn crops had been lost, and great scarcity and much hunger prevailed from Sesheke to Linyanti. Some of the reports which the men had heard from the Batoka of the hills concerning their families, were here confirmed. Takelang's wife had been killed by Mashotlane, the headman at the Falls, on a charge, as usual, of witchcraft. Inchikola's two wives, believing him to be dead, had married again; and Masakasa was intensely disgusted to hear that two years ago his friends, upon a report of his death, threw his shield over the Falls, slaughtered all his oxen, and held a species of wild Irish wake, in honour of his memory: he said he meant to disown them, and to say, when they come to salute him, "I am dead. I am not here. I belong to another world, and should stink if I came among you."

JOHN KIRK

Kirk was botanist and medical officer on Livingstone's Zambezi-Nyasa expedition in 1858-63. The young man's private journals, published for the first time in 1965, offer a revealing perspective on the leadership qualities of the doctor ("a man who takes small intense hatreds"), and his deteriorating relationship with brother Charles. Kirk survived the Livingstones and went on to enjoy a distinguished career in the service of the British government, ending as respected consul-general at Zanzibar.

MORE THAN ORDINARY ATTENTION

Kirk's terms of employment, penned by Livingstone before they set off.

Finally, you are strictly enjoined to take the greatest care of your own health and that of the Expedition. My own experience teaches the necessity of more than ordinary attention to the state of the alimentary canal, constipation is almost sure to bring on fever, and it would be well if you kindly explain to the different members, the necessity of timely remedial aid to overcome any tendency to it, especially if accompanied by dreaming, drowsiness, want of appetite or unpleasant taste in the mouth in the mornings. If quinine combined with a mild aperient be administered, this precautionary measure will often ward off an attack of this formidable disease. Feeling the fullest confidence in your zeal in the great cause of African civilisation and rejoicing in being associated with you in this noble work I heartily commit you and the cause in which you will, I hope, be an influential pioneer, to the safe keeping of the Almighty Disposer of events.

WITH THE BODY IN ITS MOUTH

This morning there was a woman taken off by an aligator about 300 yds. from the launch. She had been drawing water. All that we saw was a splash but afterwards we saw the beast swimming about with the body in its mouth. This is the sixth eaten this season at Senna. It is quite unsafe to stand near the water edge and the people ought to know that and do as many now do, dig holes in the sand and get the water filtered or make a stockade to keep them out but they think that the aligator won't take them unless they have done some ill. They also believe that they pass into lions, aligators and other beasts after death. How much the aligator actually eats of a person, I don't know but they tell me they find bodies of people with only small pieces taken out. When we are under steam, the aligator often takes us for some beast swimming and comes after us full speed. One enormous beast was shot the other day close alongside making at us. He got the ball in the head and sank and as it punched a hole in a fatal place, there would be small account of him again. When they catch a fish, they snap at it like a dog until it is well back in their mouth.

THROUGH THE UTERUS
Kirk shot a female elephant.

The height from foot to shoulder was 6 ft. 9 in. the circumference of the foot 42 ins. the ear in perpendicular 52$\frac{1}{2}$ ins. She was a young cow, not full grown, the hair was still on the chest and the height under double the circumference of the foot which it ought to be in the full grown beast. The teeth were small. The cutting up was soon begun and the skin was no joke to get through. It is spongy but calculated to deaden a bullet very much. When we got to the interior of her, we found the bullets had done their work well. One passed through the belly, through the uterus, the foetus and out nearby to the skin of the other side. Several others had gone a long way. My steel pointed balls had done splendidly but the steel was found separate from the lead. The uterus I secured. The placenta consists of a host of rounded bodies scattered over the interior. The cord divided in three portions. The foetus was well grown with hair, no signs of teeth. The Mammere are placed on the chest. This will be a glorious specimen for anatomists and Sharpey and Owen may fight over it. An Elephant with big teeth is nothing rare but with young is something worth coming for.

He tried to preserve the foetus in a salt and alum solution, but it rotted.

219

MOST IMPROPER EXPRESSIONS
An entry in November 1860.

Rain in the morning. The loss of my notes seems greater daily. In them I had compass bearings both on the way up and down, the geology also put down and lists of the most common plants. Besides these, the general history of our journey which has been rather a singular one for the quarrels between the two brothers and the use of the most abusive filthy and blasphemous language ever heard in that class of society. As these might have been asked for afterwards, as I was told they would, I noted down the expressions. The quarrels began before our setting out, about an old pillow which had rotted in the ship, like many better things. I could not easily see why the old pillow should raise Dr L's indignation but if I remember aright, it was over Mr C.L's reply. However it ended in a long altercation, Mr C.L. using most improper expressions to a superior officer, Dr L. saying [that] he had been a failure from the beginning and that the only mistake made was in bringing him out. On the way up near Manyerere hill, there was another dispute. Dr L had asked me to take time to his observations. Mr C.L. spoke of his service as the service of the Devil and that when he came out, he though he came out with a Christian gentleman. At Zumbo, the two made up the quarrel and went on lovingly until Sechele when they had another round but this was nothing. It began about grubb. The people told Dr L that they had had no meal when they returned home. The fact was they were the opposite of hospitable. They behaved in a very niggardly way. The grand row came off at Sinamanis about Mr C.L. kicking Lishovi, the head man of Makololo, with his boot. Dr L. remarked that Mr C.L. would not like to hear repeated what he had said of other members of the Expedition. The rain went off somewhat about 8 a.m. We marched on the path at the mouth of the Kebrabassa. It is as bad as anywhere else on the journey. Reached the outpost of the Portuguese Tete residents by afternoon.

TIED BY THE NECK
On the Shire River.

The soon-to-be-rescued slaves.

At 10.20.am. we arrived at M'bame's village, not the one however with which we were acquainted, as he had come much nearer to the Shire. On the way, Dr L. was taken sick with vomiting and purging, caused by the fatigue and wet of the first day.

About 1 pm. while we were in the huts, a gang of 84 slaves was marched into the village with a few drivers. On being spoken to, the latter ran off, not before 4 guns had been taken and all the gear they carried with them. The

220

bulk however of their goods being carried by the slaves remained safe also. One of them was Katura a slave of Sr. Tito who served as our cook and Steward at Tette. He was excessively afraid on being caught. He declared that he had been sent neither by Tito nor by his agent, Sr. Candido, but that they came off secretly.

The slaves were, most of them, tied by the neck with ropes, in gangs, some refractory ones had beams of wood as thick as a man's thigh and six feet long with a fork at one extremity in which the neck was secured by an iron pin.

The party consisted of women and children chiefly, with a few men. They began clapping their hands as soon as they knew that we were their friends, the English. The ropes were cut adrift and the sticks sawn off their necks, while the goods of the traders were seized by our men. Unluckily in the confusion the slave drivers were suffered to escape. The people of the village looked on during all this with great satisfaction. Before many minutes had elapsed, the slaves now free, were cooking what was their master's food with their own sticks which had served to fasten them and the women clothed with white calico. The atrocities committed on the march seem to have been very great. Two women were shot because they attempted to escape. This had been done to make an impression and prevent others from doing so. One woman who was unable to carry both her load and her young child, had the child taken from her and saw its brains dashed out on a stone.

BURNING LIKE FIRE

On the way, Rowe, the 2nd engineer got into a disagreeable mess from what he calls Botanizing! which he swears he will never do again. He had been unsuccessful in shooting a buffaloe and before returning sat down in the bush on a call of nature. In a dreamy state, he began amusing himself slicing up the branches of a tree *Euphorbia* which are heavy and when the Mosquitoes began to trouble him, he rubbed them off, his hands being covered with the milky juice. Soon after returning, he found himself burning like fire and the next 48 hours found him bathing with cold water, a certain part which now had left all human form and was covered with a multitude of small blisters. On the third day things got better but a considerable loss of leather ensued and he had to display himself in the Highland costume, sailors trousers not being well adapted for the interesting state he was in.

WILLIAM COTTON OSWELL

In 1849 Oswell, having led the first party of Europeans to Lake Ngami, decided to take home one of the extraordinary long-horned oxen that the local people bred. Though only three years old, the creature had a horn span a shade over four metres measured along the curve. Oswell hoped to get it back to England and a zoo. In many places the path cleared for the wagons through the bush on the journey up had to be widened for it to pass. When the lake was left behind, the grass was so short the beast could not feed, its horns hitting the ground before it could get its mouth down. It was practically impossible to cut enough fodder, and after 1,200 kilometres it had to be shot. Oswell, who had served as government elephant hunter in India, made five expeditions to the African interior between 1845 and 1851. Handsome, strong – at the age of 72 he could still hold up his end of a grand piano – generous and brave, he was described by a biographer as "a fine specimen of the muscular Christians produced by Dr. Arnold at Rugby". He was extraordinarily protective of David Livingstone, who although a mere companion on Oswell's expedition to Ngami, failed to mention Oswell's name in his initial report on the journey. In later years Oswell even destroyed sections of his own notebooks for fear that if they were published after his death, they would detract from the fame he felt Livingstone deserved. Of all the European sojourners in southern Africa, Oswell most clearly expressed a genuine love for travel "… the feeling, as you lay under your kaross, that you were looking at the stars from a point on the earth whence no other European had ever seen them; the hope that every patch of bush, every little rise, was the only thing between you and some strange sight or scene".

SELLING THE ALLIGATORS
Observations on native dogs at the crocodile-infested Zouga or Botletle River in central Botswana.

Three or four would wish to cross, either for better fare, or to see their friends on the other side; but though alligator is very partial to dog, dog is not so fond of alligator. Assembling on the banks, they would run, barking violently, a quarter of a mile up stream, in full view; halt, join in a chorus of barking, yelping and baying; suddenly pull up in the middle of the concert, dash at the top of their speed, absolutely mute, and out of sight on a lower level, to the point they had started from, and then jump into the water and swim across, thus selling the alligators, who, hungry after their "course of bark," were eagerly expecting their dinner at the spot where they had had the largest dose.

PUFFING MYSELF OUT
Hunting in Botswana, Oswell wounded an elephant bull in thick bush.

After a time the thorns thinned out and I caught sight of the wounded elephant holding a course of his own a little to the left of his fellows; and when he entered the tropical forest beyond I was in his wake and very soon compelled to follow where he broke a way. Lying flat on my pony's neck, and guiding him as I best might by occasional glimpses of the tail of my now slowly-retreating pioneer, I laboured on in the hope that more open ground might enable me to get up alongside of him. A most unpleasant ride it was; my constrained position gave me but little chance of using my hands to save my head; I was at one time nearly pulled from the saddle by the heavy boughs and at another nearly torn to pieces by the wicked thorns of the wait-a-bit, which although no longer *the* tree of the jungle, was intolerably scattered

The dogs and crocs on the Zouga.

222

through it. I have killed elephants on very bad ground, but this was the worst piece of bush I ever rode into in my life. A little extra noise from the pursuers caused the pursued to stop; and while clinging like Gilpin to the calender's horse, and peering at the broad stern of the chase, I saw him suddenly put his head where his tail ought to have been; the trunk was tightly coiled – an elephant nearly always coils his trunk in thick bush for fear of pricking it – forward flapped the huge ears, up went the tail, and down he came like a gigantic bat ten feet across. Pinned above and on either side, by dismounting I could neither hope to escape, nor kill my opponent. I therefore lugged my unfortunate animal round and urged him along. But I had not taken into account with what great difficulties and how slowly I had followed the bull. He was now in full charge, and the small trees and bush gave way before him like reeds, whereas I was compelled to keep my head lowered as before, and try and hold the path, such as it was, up which we had come. I was well mounted and my spurs were sharp. Battered and torn by branch and thorn, I yet managed a kind of gallop, but it was impossible to keep it up. The elephant thundered straight *through* obstacles we were obliged to go round, and in fifty yards we were fast in a thick bush and he within fifteen of us. As a last chance I tried to get off, but in rolling round in my saddle my spur galled the pony's flank, and the elephant screaming over him at the same moment, he made a convulsive effort and freed himself, depositing me in a sitting position immediately in front of the uplifted forefoot of the charging bull. So near was it that I mechanically opened my knees to allow him to put it down, and throwing myself back, crossed my hands upon my chest, obstinately puffing myself out with the idea of trying to resist the gigantic tread, or at all events of being as troublesome to crush as possible. I saw the burly brute from chest to tail as he passed directly over me lengthways, one foot between my knees and one fourteen inches beyond my head, and not a graze! Five tons at least! As he turned from chasing the pony, which without my weight and left to its own instinct escaped easily to my after-rider's horse, he swept by me on his way to rejoin his companions, and I got another snapshot at his shoulder. As soon as I could I followed his spoor, but must have changed it in the thick bush, for in five minutes I had run into and killed a fresh elephant in a small open space. The Bushmen found the first, next morning, dead.

Oswell said he suffered "night-elephants" for a month or more after this close shave.

WE EAT MEN
Sebetwane, warrior chief of the Kololo, met Oswell and Livingstone on the Chobe in 1851, and visited them alone one night when he "dreamily recounted the history of his life, his wars, escapes, successes and conquests".

Then he waved his hand westward and opened out a story of men over whom he had gained an easy victory, "away, away, very far from the bitter waters"; and to whom, when they asked for food, wishing to bind them with fetters of kindness, he sent a fat ox, and,

"would you believe it, they returned it, saying they didn't eat ox. 'Then what do you eat?' I asked, '*we* like beef better than anything.' 'We eat *men*,' said they. I had never heard of this before; but they were very pressing, so at last I sent them two slaves of the Macobas, the river people, who, as you know, are very dark in colour, but they brought them back, saying they did not like *black* men, but preferred the redder variety, and as that meant sending my own fighting men, I told them they might go without altogether."

Sebetwane died of an old wound a few weeks later, and was succeeded by his son Sekeletu, who we have encountered in Livingstone's writing.

FRANCIS GALTON

Before he left London in 1850 to go exploring and hunting in south-west Africa, Galton bought a shiny crown at a theatrical finery shop to place on the head of "the greatest or most distant potentate I should meet with". He travelled in the territory of the Damara (a "greedy, heartless set of savages"), northern Namaqualand, and Ovamboland, where he performed his coronation on a chief named Nangolo. Galton was not a patient man: he believed oxen were "essentially perverse and vicious", and thrashed local people and those of his servants not big enough to hit him back. He later achieved distinction as a meteorologist, a pioneer of the science of fingerprinting, an experimental psychologist and a statistician. Among his projects was a map showing the geographical distribution of beauty in Great Britain. He also applied his intriguing mind to the "science" of eugenics, using the theories developed by his distinguished cousin Charles Darwin to argue the practicability of supplanting "inefficient" races by better strains, and the duty on those strains to make conscious efforts to improve the human race.

THEY DID SO IN PAIRS

These savages were as ignorant of the country two days' journey off as an English labourer usually is. My friend, who told me of Omanbondè, told me also that I could get to the Ovampo by way of that lake, and he told me much more. He mentioned most particularly a remarkable nation, who were deficient in joints both at the elbows and knees. They were therefore

unable to lift anything to their mouths by themselves; but when they dined, they did so in pairs, each man feeding his *vis-à-vis*.

We had, after a long drought, a most terrific thunderstorm; the lightning flashed so continuously that I could read a newspaper by its light without stopping, my eye taking in enough words by one flash to enable me to read steadily on until the next one. It lightened in three different parts, and we were in the middle. There were some flowers in front of me, and the lightning was so vivid, and its light so pure, that I could not only see the flowers, but also their colours. I believe this is

224

a very rare thing with lightning. There were four savages running in a line, about one hundred yards off, on their way to
their huts: after one of the flashes, only three remained;
the other was struck dead. Mr. Hahn [a missionary]
and I picked him up. It is curious how little a negro's
features are changed by death; there is no paleness.
His widow howled all night; and was engaged to
be married again the succeeding day.

The Swakop ran violently after this storm, pouring vast volumes
of turbid and broken water for three days down what had hitherto been an
arid sandy channel.

Mr. Hahn's household was large. There was an interpreter, and a sub-
interpreter, and again others; but all most excellently well-behaved, and
showing to great advantage the influence of their master. These servants
were chiefly Hottentots, who had migrated with Mr. Hahn from Hottentot-
land, and, like him, had picked up the language of the Damaras. The sub-
interpreter was married to a charming person, not only a Hottentot in
figure, but in that respect a Venus among Hottentots. I was perfectly aghast
at her development, and made inquiries upon that delicate point as far as I
dared among my missionary friends. The result is, that I believe Mrs.
Petrus to be the lady who ranks second among all the Hottentots for the
beautiful outline that her back affords, Jonker's wife ranking as the first;
the latter, however, was slightly *passée*, while Mrs. Petrus was in full *embon-
point*. I profess to be a scientific man, and was exceedingly anxious to
obtain accurate measurements of her shape; but there was a difficulty in
doing this. I did not know a word of Hottentot, and could never therefore
have explained to the lady what the object of my foot-rule could be; and I
really dared not ask my worthy missionary host to interpret for me. I therefore felt in a dilemma as I gazed at her form, that gift of bounteous nature
to this favoured race, which no mantua-maker, with all her crinoline and
stuffing, can do otherwise than humbly imitate. The object of my admiration stood under a tree, and was turning herself about to all points of the
compass, as ladies who wish to be admired usually do. Of a sudden my eye
fell upon my sextant; the bright thought struck me, and I took a series of
observations upon her figure in every direction, up and down, crossways,
diagonally, and so forth, and I registered them carefully upon an outline
drawing for fear of any mistake; this being done, I boldly pulled out my
measuring tape, and measured the distance from where I was to the place
she stood, and having thus obtained both base and angles, I worked out the
results by trigonometry and logarithms.

SHE ATTEMPTED TO STAND
… leaving Andersson in charge, I took Hans, John Morta, and one of the
waggon-men, who spoke very good Dutch, and started for Jonker. I previously gave it out among the Damaras that I was gone to make peace
between the Hottentots and them. I packed up my red hunting-coat, jack-
boots, and cords, and rode in my hunting-cap: it was a costume unknown
in these parts, and would, I expected, aid in producing the effect I desired.
I started on the 16th of December. It was about a three days' ride; but as

none of us knew the road, we strayed a little, which made us longer. I saw a horrible sight on the way, which has often haunted me since. We had taken a short cut, and were a day and a half from our waggons, when I observed some smoke in front and rode to see what it was: an immense blackthorn three was smouldering, and from the quantity of ashes about, there was all the appearance of its having burnt for a long time: by it were tracks that we could make nothing of; no footmarks, only an impression of a hand here and there. We followed them, and found a wretched woman, most horribly emaciated; both her feet were burnt quite off, and the wounds were open and unhealed. Her account was that many days back she and others were encamping there; and when she was asleep, a dry but standing tree, which they had set fire to, fell down, and entangled her among its branches: there she was burnt before she could extricate herself, and her people left her. She had since lived on gum alone, of which there was vast quantities about; it oozes down from the trees, and forms large cakes in the sand. There was water close by, for she was on the edge of a river-bed. I did not know what to do with her; I had no means of conveying her anywhere, or any place to convey her to. The Damaras kill useless and worn-out people: even sons smother their sick fathers; and death was evidently not far from her. I had three sheep with me, so I off-packed, and killed one. She seemed ravenous; and though I purposely had off-packed some two hundred yards from her, yet the poor wretch kept crawling and dragging herself up to me, and would not be withheld, for fear I should forget to give her the food I promised. When it was ready, and she had devoured what I gave her, the meat acted, as it often does in such cases, and fairly intoxicated her: she attempted to stand, regardless of the pain, and sang, and tossed her lean arms about. It was perfectly sickening to witness the spectacle. I did the only thing I could: I cut the rest of the meat in strips, and hung it within her reach, and where the sun would jerk (*i.e.*, dry and preserve) it. It was many days' provision for her. I saw she had water, fire-wood, and gum in abundance, and then I left her to her fate.

A USELESS CUR

We were a good deal troubled for the want of water on our return; the little pool I mentioned was dried up, and we had taken no water with us, for want of a vessel to carry it in. Our Damaras, who drove the cattle, were quite knocked up under the excessive heat, and a Ghou Damup, whose charge it was to carry the iron pot, lay down somewhere altogether exhausted. At night we arrived, and all of us drank water till we were quite ill. I continued resolving to drink no more; and then rewarded my resolution with one more mouthful. One cannot help drinking, the water seems to have no effect in quenching the thirst. The next day we rode but a short distance, as we had to wait for the two men who were missing, and they might be badly put to it. However, they never came.

We thought the Ghou Damup had stolen the pot, and absconded in an old soldier's coat, with which I had just rewarded his fidelity. There was considerable doubt if we should find water for the remainder of the journey; and, as our stomachs had been thrown out of order, I hardly liked to go so far without taking some: I could not think what to use as a water vessel, when my eye fell upon a useless cur of ours, that never watched, and only frightened game by running after them, and whose death I had long had in view. Dogskin is the most waterproof of hides, so I despatched the cur and skinned him. His death was avenged upon me in a striking manner, for during the night a pack of wild dogs came upon us, scattered our sheep who were not well kraaled in, and killed them all.

They did not in fact make much use of the waterskin, for the day was relatively cool. "Being fresh from the animal it had to be used with the hair inside," Galton wrote. "It held the water very well, but gave a 'doggy' taste to it."

FULL IN HIS FACE

The Ovampo are, as all blacks and most whites, very superstitious; a particular fear seems to possess them of a stranger charming away the life of a person he may happen to eat with. Why dinner time should be the season when the charm has most power I do not know; but such is considered to be the case. Accordingly, counter-charms are used; sometimes one is in fashion, sometimes another; now, Nangoro, when a young man, being a person of considerable imagination, framed a counter-charm for his own particular use, and this being of course taken up by the court, is at present the fashion of the whole of Ovampoland, and it was to this counter-charm that I personally objected. The stranger sits down, closes his eyes, and raises his face to heaven; then the Ovampo initiator takes some water into his mouth, gargles it well, and, standing over his victim, delivers it full in his face. This ceremony having once been performed, all goes on smoothly, though I am inclined to think that, like vaccination, it requires to be repeated at intervals, as its effect dies away. Old Netjo yielded to my objections the day I dined in his house, as Chik had done when I first met him, and compromised the matter by rubbing butter between my eyes instead. But Nangoro's mind was not so easily satisfied; he was harassed with suspicions; and though he invited me to drink beer at his palace, yet he contrived to be out of the way when the beer was brought in, and made the three courtiers sit down with me instead.

ANIMALS OF UNACCOUNTABLE MANNERS

... not only the colour of our skin but the straightness of our hair was a constant marvel to the Ovampo. They wondered if we were white all over, and I victimised John Allen, who had to strip very frequently to satisfy the inquisitiveness of our hosts. Nangoro positively refused to believe in the existence of any country which was inhabited by whites alone. He seemed to consider them as rare migratory animals of unaccountable manners but considerable intelligence, who were found here and there, but who existed in no place as lords of the land.

On his return to England Galton wrote The Art of Travel, or Shifts and Contrivances Available in Wild Countries, *which included advice on how to ride an ox, lift a stranded schooner off the rocks, tie up a prisoner securely, use an umbrella to catch rain, and distribute the belongings of a dead companion. This is from the section on dealing with the hired help.*

Bearing towards natives. – A frank, joking, but determined manner, joined with an air of showing more confidence to the savages than you really feel, is the best. It is observed, that a sea-captain generally succeeds in making a very good impression on natives; they thoroughly appreciate good practical common sense, and are not half such fools as strangers usually account them. If a savage does mischief, look on him as you would on a kicking mule or a wild animal, whose nature it is to be unruly and vicious, and keep your temper quite unruffled.

EDWARD SHELLEY

Shelley, a relative of the poet, was a violent, unimaginative, hard-drinking military officer who made several hunting trips to the interior between 1850 and early 1854. A month after the incident described here he also shot one of his dogs which had annoyed him. The names in brackets are the horses he was riding.

AND HAD TO WALK HOME

MONDAY, 13TH SEPTEMBER. Went out shooting and saw nothing. (Toby).

TUESDAY, 14TH SEPTEMBER. Nothing particular.

WEDNESDAY, 15TH SEPTEMBER. Went out shooting this morning, but did not see anything. Some Balalas arrived, confirming the report about the Boers having attacked Sicheli, and likewise of their having driven off a lot of Lentue's [?] cattle. Sicheli is reported wounded in the arm. (Scrat.)

THURSDAY, 16TH SEPTEMBER. Nothing particular.

FRIDAY, 17TH SEPTEMBER. Went out shooting this morning and saw nothing. I don't think I shall ride out again from this water as it is only working the horses for nothing. (Blue Kop.)

SATURDAY, 18TH SEPTEMBER. Went out on foot to try and stalk a spring buck, but did not see anything.

SUNDAY, 19TH SEPTEMBER. As usual.

MONDAY, 20TH SEPTEMBER. As usual. Nothing particular.

TUESDAY, 21ST SEPTEMBER. Went out on foot to try and shoot something, but did not see any game.

WEDNESDAY, 22ND SEPTEMBER. Sent Webber and one of the boys out shooting on horseback, neither of whom have as yet returned.

THURSDAY, 23RD SEPTEMBER. Webber and Cupido returned rather late last night, having shot a couple of elands. Sent off a lot of Kaffirs and a Hottentot with a led horse to bring the meat to the wagons, none of whom have as yet returned. (The weather very boisterous).

FRIDAY, 24TH SEPTEMBER. Cupido returned late last night. The Kaffirs brought the meat of the elands during the day. The weather has been cloudy all the afternoon, threatening rain.

SATURDAY, 25TH SEPTEMBER. A little rain this morning accompanied with thunder and lightening.

SUNDAY, 26TH SEPTEMBER. As usual an infernally fine sunshiny day.

MONDAY, 27TH SEPTEMBER. Went out after three giraffes but could not come up to them. On my way home got a long shot at a spring buck but hit a tree.

TUESDAY, 28TH SEPTEMBER. Dick, I and an after rider went out after giraffes and managed to come to grief. In the first place Dick's horse could'nt go, so he was very soon out of sight. Then I rode against the bough of a tree, which did not turn out to be so rotten as I thought. I was consequently knocked off but not hurt. Could'nt catch my horse who, just as I was trying to get hold of the bridle, turned round and kicked at me and hit my bullet pouch, so after making several vain attempts to catch him I let drive and shot him, but fortunately it was only a flesh wound. I also broke my pet pipe and the end off my ramrod and had to walk home.

THOMAS BAINES

In a self-portrait painted when he was 38, Baines presented himself as a grand romantic: a wide black hat, an untrimmed black beard reaching down to a red-and-gold scarf flung carelessly around his shoulders, and dark eyes that gaze confidently into the distance. This was the man who circumnavigated Australia, travelled with Livingstone, accompanied British troops in the Eastern Cape as South Africa's first war artist, and was elected a fellow of the Royal Geographic Society. What the portrait does not convey is that Baines, who came to South Africa from England in 1842 to earn a living as a professional artist, remained impoverished to the end of his days, rarely got on well with his travelling companions ("Baines is a pig," wrote Charles Andersson, himself not the pleasantest of men), and suffered fits of depression. Yet he left a priceless artistic and historical legacy in the oils, sketches and eloquent journals of his travels in an African hinterland he saw as ripe for imperial expansion.

BY BLOWING INTO IT

Chapman tells me that the name "Swakop" is not from the Dutch Swart Kop or Black Hill, but is in the Hottentot tongue a somewhat coarse translation of "Fair round belly with good capon lined." Here we were serenaded by a kind of chirping lizard. Farther on is to be found a peculiar species of green and yellow bull-frog, which the epicures of the country clean by blowing into it till the entrails are forced so far toward the mouth that they can be drawn out by the insertion of a finger. The Damara mode of forcing an unwilling cow to give milk is, I dare say, efficacious, but hardly admits of description.

Chapman said Baines tried cooked frog near Lake Ngami, and that it was reported to be "savoury as it was delicate, the roe being considered the best part".

FLOCKS OF LOVELY BUTTERFLIES

Traversing a length of hill and dale, which now seemed wearisome enough, we passed the vlei, scarcely disturbing the wild fowl on its placid surface, and a few hundred yards beyond, came in sight of the gigantic carcase looming like a grey granite boulder above the bush. Of course I have seen elephants, but it has always been at my home, and not in theirs, and neither picture nor well-groomed black-skinned show specimen from India I had ever seen had quite prepared me to stand, for the first time, without a sensation of awe and wonder beside the mighty African, fallen in all his native grandeur in his domain. Masses of earth had been upturned by his broad feet; his column-like legs were stiffened in his tracks; the tusk upon the lower side was buried in the soil; the head and curling trunk were extended forward, leaving his broad forehead (flat, or even convex, and not channelled in the centre like that of the Indian, and as represented in all the pictures I have yet seen, those of Harris even seeming to have been influenced by his Indian experience) nearly in a line with his body. The ears, which in the African are of huge size, covered with their upper part nearly half the neck, the hindmost angle reaching to the death-spot behind the shoulder, and the lower descending nearly to a level with the chest. The rough grey side, deeply marked with wrinkles crossing each other like a network, destitute of hair, except a solitary bristle here and there, rose, more like a rock than the skin of a lately living animal, so high that I could barely see the head of a man beyond it – a dark purple stain upon the lower side of the chest alone indicating the manner of his death, the bullets having entered on the side now in contact with the ground. The sun was just beginning to be warm, and the carcase was not yet swelled; nevertheless the Bushman approached the intestine like a practised fencer, springing back with marvellous agility when he had made his blow; nor was his caution vain, for the discharge of a fire-engine was nothing to what followed: and I can easily imagine the ordnance-like explosions of which I have heard, when the body of an elephant that has lain all day under a vertical sun is pierced for the first time.

In a short time the fat and various pieces of the intestine were spread like blankets over every bush; titbits were broiled and eaten among the garbage in which the savages were revelling, taking apparently a special delight in wild songs, which issued in most sepulchral tones from the cavernous interior; but to me, I must confess, the most disenchanting sight of all was the flocks of lovely butterflies, with all their spiritual and Psyche-like associations, fluttering fearlessly among them, and feeding, greedily as they, upon the most offensive portions.

TRYING TO GET AN OBSERVATION

As last night was tolerably clear, I stayed up till about two this morning, trying to get an observation for the latitude. A heavy dew made everything wet and uncomfortable, rendering the stars also misty and dim: still I was on the point of securing α Crucis, when, just as the star was on the meridian, one of the dogs took it into his head that I must be the wolf that had been prowling round all the evening; it was therefore his duty to bark, the rest of the villanous curs, of course, gathering to the summons, making in less than no time a very Pandemonium all round me. β Centauri would have been good, but by accident I touched the tangent screw instead of the microscope in reading off, and so vitiated the observation. While thus engaged, a spectre-like form glided noiselessly through the gloom, and the wolf (i.e. hyena) stood within twenty yards looking at me. Fearing that the rush of the dogs, should they wake up, would capsize me and my quick-silver too, I drove him quietly away, and saw him, when I returned to my work, standing inquisitively in the same place as before. Arcturus and α Crucis passed the meridian within so short a time of each other that the lighting up of my candle, with everything wet around me, kept me trying to read off the one till it was too late to catch the other.

DRINKING THE MIRAGE

Everything looks cold and hard, the salt plain sometimes appearing like ice, and at others like a shallow muddy sea, with none of the mirage which yes-terday so perfectly and beautifully simulated long vistas of water between the distant islands, and tempted away our thirsty dogs in hot pursuit of the deceitful vision, which, receding as they advanced, led them away and away, till their arrival at the opposite shore dispelled the illusion, only to show them the watery cheat upon the plain they had just crossed. Tantalus and his cup was a mere nothing to a pack of dogs, with parched tongues and blis-tered feet, running hither and thither in hope of drinking the mirage.

ITS EYES ALREADY PECKED OUT
On the Vaal River, 1850.

On our way homeward we fell in with an unfortunate wildebeeste that had been shot in the flank by Bower and was now wandering about with its bowels protruding from the wound and hanging in a dried and blackened mass at its side – and its eyes already pecked out by the crows. We rode up and gave the poor creature a couple of pistol bullets, one through the head and the other through the body behind the shoulder, both balls coming out on the opposite side. A convulsive shivering of the body and a short gasp-ing for breath were the only effects of these apparently mortal wounds, and the poor blinded wretch followed our horses as we turned away, as if imploring us to end its misery, which, for want of another charge of ammuni-tion or even a pocket knife, we were unable to do.

WITH CONSIDERABLE INTEREST
Tuesday, 8th. Fried the remainder of the fish, and boiled the thermometer, a culi-nary process which was watched with considerable interest by one of the Hot-tentots.

The temperature of boiling water was used to determine altitude.

White shirts and trowsers
Visiting the Ndebele king Lobengula, successor to Mzilikazi, on a gold-prospecting trip to Matebeleland, 1870.

On Sunday, Mr. Lee told me that the rain makers objected to the flags, which we generally shewed on holidays, over our wagons, as they were likely to drive away the rain, and as no point of honour was involved I thought it best to humour him. We had a little conversation with the king, who was free from prejudice on the subject, but who very reasonably urged the impropriety of offending his people, while he was yet not formerly [formally] settled in his power. Subsequently, I found that only the white bordered union jack was objectionable; there was no harm in the red ensign so long as it hung quietly, and did not flutter in the wind. White shirts and trowsers also could not be spread out to dry, without frightening away the rain clouds, but dark clothing might be hung out *ad libitum*. We also discussed the supposed power of these rain-makers, and the king said he knew that neither the man nor the crocodile's scales, and other ingredients which he burned, could make rain; "But," said he, "this is our way of asking for it; just as you ask for it with a book."

Upon a bedroom candlestick
Returning to the town [Port Elizabeth], I took up my quarters at the hotel of Mr. Ure, where I was comfortably accommodated during my stay, albeit the revels of my fellow lodgers were not infrequently protracted to the small hours of the morning, and, to judge from the difficulty with which they gained their respective dormitories, mine host's bill must have been rather heavy. Feats of agility or sleight of hand that would not have disgraced an itinerant company of professional jugglers were occasionally exhibited at these convivial meetings, and I was told one morning that one of the company, after drinking all night, had balanced himself upon his head upon a bedroom candlestick at the imminent risk, should the rim give way, of driving the sockets into his brain, if such indeed he possessed.

Ivan Goncharov

IVAN GONCHAROV

When Goncharov entered the Russian civil service in 1834, he was already a published novelist. In 1852 he was appointed secretary to a naval mission to the Far East, an unsuccessful bid to thwart American attempts to open up trade with Japan. On his return to St Petersburg – a journey he undertook by land, via Siberia – Goncharov was appointed the state's first literary censor under a liberalised censorship regime. His celebrated novel Oblomov *followed in 1858. Here we join him in March 1853 during the voyage to the East; his vessel, the frigate* Pallada, *has anchored at Simon's Town, and he and his companions are exploring Cape Town and its surrounds.*

Just like snow
On the road the Malay attached to us as guide brought us

The Castle, Cape Town.

grapes. We returned all the way through gardens. Passing from gully to gully through huge oaks, we climbed a hill and after descending it found ourselves in the town. As soon as we entered the street, somebody said: "Look at Table Mountain". Everybody glanced up and stopped in amazement. Half of the mountain had vanished.

The cloud I mentioned had grown while we were passing through the gardens and in a thick layer just like snow had covered the whole top of the mountain densely and impenetrably and had descended the sides to an even level. That was the table-cloth being laid on the table. We walked downhill through the streets, looking about us all the time. The table-cloth continued to descend with unbelievable speed so that we hadn't reached the middle of the town before half the mountain was covered. I expected that there might be a storm, some of those impetuous winds that terrorise ships in the roadstead, but the Capetowners said that there would not. Table Mountain can muffle itself up completely in a shroud and they aren't afraid; the trouble is when the Lion puts his cap on.

YES, O YES, YES!
The "picture" is a reference to Caroline, attractive daughter of the widow who owned the hotel where the Russians were lodging, and who was in the habit of adopting poses where she would be elegantly framed by a window.

After dinner, we found a large company, augmented afresh. There was an old colonel in the East India service and his wife. Having served out his term in India he was retiring to England. He was a tall, gaunt man in a blue jacket, more like the skipper of a merchantman. His wife was tall, gaunt too, with a scanty pale-brown chevelure which she arranged almost hair by hair and parted nearly down to the brain. Beside me sat another old man, also returning from India. He was an important official, very well educated and quite grey. He could well have been the uncle who used to be

233

described in novels as returning from India with tremendous wealth just in time to help his nephew marry the poor girl. He was well and even fastidiously dressed, with a big ring on his finger – quite the uncle. For a long time he glanced occasionally at me and I at him. I saw that he was watching us Russians not without interest and that he would like to start a conversation and find out, perhaps, something about Russia. The port was in front of him and the sherry in front of me. At last the old man spoke.

"May I drink a glass of wine with you?" he said.

"With pleasure", I answered, and he poured me out a glass of port which I never drink and I poured him out a glass of sherry which he did not like. After that silence reigned. We munched. Again I saw that he was winding himself up to ask me something.

"What's the road like from Simonstown here?" he said at last.

"Very good", I answered and after that he asked me nothing more.

A very fat lady, about forty-five, was also sitting at table. Her big dark slow-moving eyes turned every minute to the Captain. She was tightly corsetted and her close-fitting dress exposed the round, massive shoulders, arms, etc., with which nature had so lavishly endowed her. She ate very little and took little tiny morsels of meat and vegetables into her mouth with the tips of her lips. There were also the previous day's two young people.

"Yes, yes!" the Colonel's wife continually affirmed when anyone was talking to her. Father Avvakum from boredom, in the interval between two courses, counted the number of times she said "yes".

"In seven minutes, thirty-three times", he whispered to me.

After dinner, the picture was again adorning its frame and with an addition. Beside Caroline was Alice, or Elis as our chaps called her, mimicking the English pronunciation. I approached them alone to ingratiate myself with them. The aim of the ingratiation was to wheedle a wax candle for the evening. For three days I had vainly asked for a candle and had even given money to Alice so that she might buy some. The ladies of the house sent the money back without the candles. Finally, they made up their minds to give me a candle that wasn't tallow. Having got what I wanted I went off to my room and had just sat down to write when I heard the voice of Father Avvakum shouting in the purest Russian:

"Is there no water here? Is there no water here?"

At first I paid no attention to his shouts, but then remembering that besides me and the naturalist there were no other Russians in the town I began to listen more carefully. His voice got nearer and nearer and expressed alarm.

"Is there no water here? Water, water, quickly!" he shouted, almost in despair.

I sprang from the table and looked out. He was running along the corridor straight to my room; in his hands were thunder and lightning and round him a foul-smelling cloud of smoke spread out. I was frightened. What could be happening?

"Is there no water here? Water quickly!" he kept repeating.

A whole thousand of matches had caught fire in his room and he had been so terrified that, forgetting himself, he had demanded water in

Russian although in all rooms, including his, a pitcher stood. The matches continued to sizzle and crackle in his hands.

"Here's some water!" I said, pointing to the washstand, " and there's water in your room too."

"I had no idea", he answered.

I began to call Alice to take away the remains of the fireworks and then gave full rein to my laughter.

"Don't call, don't call!" he interrupted me. "I shall be ashamed."

"Shame is not smoke, it won't eat your eyes out", I said, "and your smoke might make you faint."

Next day at lunch, we were again five or six; the Colonel and his wife, the obstreperous Englishman and we two. We lunched en famille. The Colonel's wife poured out tea and coffee. She spoke French and a lively conversation started between us. At first it was only about the previous evening's fireworks. I had already heard, on my way past the buffet, the obstreperous man asking Mrs. Welch what the foul smell was that had spread through the hotel the previous evening. Then he asked the Colonel's wife if she had smelt it.

"Yes, O yes, yes!" she agreed ten times in a row.

"Repulsive, unbearable", continued the obstreperous man.

"Yes, yes", the Colonel's wife said plaintively with a sigh.

"One, two, three, four!" Father Avvakum counted the number of "yesses".

"But do you know what this 'yes' means?" I asked him.

"It means an affirmation, our 'da'", he answered.

"That is so, but do you know what it affirms? That yesterday evening there was a repulsive smell of sulphur."

"What …?" he said, starting, and to conceal his agitation, helped himself to a whole omelette with his spoon.

"But did you smell it?" insisted the obstreperous man, turning to the Colonel and eyeing us.

"Wasn't it just as if there was a fire in the house?" he asked the Colonel's wife again.

"Yes, yes", she answered.

"Five, six", Father Avvakum counted mournfully.

Soon after she engaged in conversation with me about the frigate and our travels. Having found out that I had been in Portsmouth, she asked me vivaciously, if I knew St. Eustace's Church.

"Of course I do" I answered, although I did not know which church she was talking about. There are several of them. "It's a fine church", I added.

"Yes … oui, oui", she agreed.

"Seven", counted Father Avvakum, "and I shall reckon in 'oui' now["], he whispered to me.

CHARLOTTE BARTER

The frontispiece to Barter's book Alone Among the Zulus *shows her with at least ten attendants, but their black skins presumably disqualified them from being counted as companions. Barter learned Zulu in England before going to Natal, so*

Barter, alone, crossing a river.

that she could proselytize among the heathen; on this journey in 1855 she rescued her brother, who was incapacitated by fever during a hunting trip.

HIS LIFE WAS CHARMED

Encouraged by his success on this occasion, the driver sallied forth again with the gun, and after walking some distance he fell in with a rhinoceros. He managed to get near enough to shoot at it; the animal, being hit, turned furiously on his enemy, who adroitly climbed up into a tree, and waited till it passed again within bullet range, when he contrived, with the other barrel, to inflict a wound somewhere about the neck. The monster then started off at his full speed, and made for the plain beyond.

When this story was related over the evening fire to the people at the kraal, they told the disappointed hunter that he need not have wasted his ammunition, for that the beast which he had encountered was not a common rhinoceros, but a man named Matikilala, who, for some private reasons of his own, or possibly through the malice of some powerful sorcerer, wandered about in this form; that his life was charmed, and no bullet could hurt him; and that after being shot at, he invariably trotted away to his relations in the far country beyond, and amused them with the tale of his day's adventures. "The whole tribe," said they, "are probably laughing at you at this very moment."

JOHN COLENSO

A controversial theologian and even more controversial champion of Zulu rights, Colenso was appointed Anglican bishop of Natal in 1853. He found room for polygamy in the church, and agreed with Zulu converts that much of the Old Testament, including the account of Noah and the ark, was simple mythology.

WHERE IS MARITZBURG?

Here he and his horse are lost in the hills near Pietermaritzburg, on their way back from a visit to Richmond.

It was now, I suppose, about midnight, and all escape from my difficulties seemed hopeless until the morning. However, I mounted again, and, refusing to let the animal go down the stream any further, I gave him his head in any other direction. He took me straight up over a grassy hill, and brought me very soon to the entrance of a Kafir kraal. The dogs began to bark, and give notice of my arrival. All remained still, however, among the human inhabitants; and if I wished to be any the better for being brought into their vicinity, it was necessary that I should call into my service all the little stock of Kafir I possessed, and make the most of it. So I began with shouting, "*umFana! umFana!* – Young man! young man!" Presently, amidst the noise of the dogs, was heard an indistinct growl from the interior of the nearest hut; and, in a few minutes, the piece of wood or wickerwork, which served as a door, was removed, and out came a tall Kafir, just roused from his slumbers, and hastily wrapped in a blanket.

But, now that I had caught my hare, how was I to cook it? Very fortunately, Mr. Shepstone had once told me, that the Kafir name for Maritzburg was the same as that of Dingaan's old capital, which it replaced in importance – though not in situation – as the chief town of the district; and this I knew from my old Missionary readings was Umkunginghlovu. So, putting on a bold face, I began with my black friend, *"Ku-pi umKunginghlovu? – Where is Maritzburg?"* I suppose my Kafir question was perfect; for, taking up my words, *"Ku-pi umKunginghlovu?"* he forthwith proceeded with a long, and, I dare say, very exact description of the way to that young city, not a word of which, unfortunately, was intelligible to me. I shook my head, and tried another sentence: *"Bamba iHashe* – lay hold of the horse."* Standing at a most respectful distance, with outstretched arm and hesitating fingers, he took hold of the bridle, which I stretched out to him, and again delivered himself of a long address in Kafir, telling me, I fancy, that he was uncommonly afraid of horses, and would much rather have nothing to do with them. I thought Mr. Shepstone's great name might be of use, in procuring special attention to my necessities; so very solemnly pronounced the word, *"Somséu,"* his Kafir designation. The word took effect as I expected, but only to procure me another long speech, in which he coupled together the words Somséu and umKunginghlovu, and, I suppose, took the trouble to inform me that Mr. Shepstone was a citizen of Maritzburg, and when I got there I should find him. My case was getting desperate: but I began once more, *"inHlela kumKungighlovu? – the path to Maritzburg?"* Whereupon he stood up erect, and, with a majestic sweep of his arm, indicated the hills under which I was to take my way, and under which, in fact, I had been wandering up and down all the night. My object was, of course, if possible, to get the Kafir to go before me, and show me the path. So setting my horse in motion, I said, *"Pambile* – go in front,"* which he did, and stepped down the grassy slope, telling me all the while, I suspect, that "he was rather sick, and would much rather not go very far that night." It was useless to trouble him further; so I looked for sixpence for him. Alas! I had only half-a-sovereign, and two-pence. I gave him the latter sum, to which he growled, I am sorry to say, very unmistakeable Kafir; but I could only shake my purse at him, and exhaust my store of Kafir, by saying *"File! File!* Dead! Dead!"* I could hear him repeating, mournfully, the word, as I rode slowly away.

The hills around Pietermaritzburg.

THE GREAT BLACK HAND

Ngoza was headman to Natal Secretary for Native Affairs Theophilus Shepstone, and was described by Colenso as a person of considerable power, with a substantial number of followers.

About dusk I was told that Ngoza was waiting to pay his respects to me. I happened to be dressing at the time, and was naturally unwilling to keep any one waiting, so was

237

making what haste I could in donning my apparel. But I was told there was no necessity whatever for this – that, in fact, it would be quite the thing to keep him waiting for some time – he would, as a matter of course, expect it – time was of no consequence to him, and he would amuse himself, somehow or other, in the court-yard until I came out. In due time, I stepped out to him, and there stood Ngoza, dressed neatly enough as a European, with his attendant Kafir waiting beside him. I said nothing (as I was advised) until he spoke, and, in answer to a question from Mr. Green, said that he was come to salute the inKos'. "Sakubona," I said; and with all my heart would have grasped the great black hand and given it a good brotherly shake: but my dignity would have been essentially compromised in his own eyes by any such proceeding. I confess it went very much against the grain; but the advice of all true Philo-Kafirs, Mr. Shepstone among the rest, was to the same effect – viz. that too ready familiarity, and especially shaking hands with them upon slight acquaintance, was not only not understood by them, but did great mischief in making them pert and presuming. Accordingly, I looked aside with a grand indifference as long as I could, (which was not very long,) and talked to Mr. G., instead of paying attention to the Kafir's presence. Mrs. Green then came at my request, kindly to assist in communicating with him; and speaking in Dutch to her Kafir maid, who spoke in Kafir to Ngoza, she told him from me, that "I was glad to see him, and hoped to see him again at his kraal, under the Table Mountain, in about a month's time." – "He would be very glad indeed to see me," – with some words of special compliment. I bade him come for a blanket to-morrow, and then dismissed him with *"hamba kahle* – walk pleasantly," …

RICHARD RIDGILL

Ridgill, a Methodist minister, was on his way from Cape Town to southern Namibia in 1855 to take over the Warmbad mission.

LAUNCHED UPON THE AIR

13th. – A dark, rainy morning. One wagon stuck fast in the bank of a river, and had to be dug out. Pleasant occupation an hour before dawn.

We called at a farm under Piquetberg, hoping to see a countryman whose fame had reached us, and who, unfortunately, was from home. Joris possessed an inventive genius, and had set himself to solve the problem of aërial navigation. After long study and many experiments, the flying machine was completed, and a final trial was to be made. Assisted by his good wife, Joris conveyed it to the summit of a neighboring hillock, and having adjusted the complex apparatus, took his seat. With her vigorous arm, Kaatje gave the necessary impetus, and Joris and his machine were fairly launched upon the air. Alas, for the aëronaut and his hopes of fame! Down, down, still down the engine descended, until it dashed into the depths of a filthy pool, to the dismay of a host of ducks and swine congregated there. Half smothered with fetid mire, struggling and spluttering, Joris called lustily upon Kaatje, who rushed to the rescue of her luckless spouse. Thus ignominiously ended the aërial career of a very worthy man.

HUGO GUTSCHE

After the Crimean War ended in 1856, men from the British Army's German Legion were recruited to form a military settlement on the Eastern Cape frontier. Before they sailed, they attended to some preliminaries, explained here by King William's Town minister Reverend Hugo Gutsche. Gutsche was interviewed in 1919 by George Cory, who was Rhodes University's first professor of chemistry but is better remembered as a historian and author of the monumental The Rise of South Africa.

A COMPREHENSIVE WEDDING

With reference to the men: They were unmarried, or the much larger proportion of them [were]. So it was intimated that all should get married and find wives in England as soon as possible. The soldiers seem soon to have accommodated themselves at short notice. A comprehensive wedding took place at Browndown Church near Portsmouth. Two-hundred and eighty-one men and 281 women (or thereabouts) were joined together in Holy Matrimony *at one operation*. A German officer who was present pointed out to the parson, that in one case at least, a man had got hold of the wrong woman's hand. "It doesn't matter" said the parson (Rev. Wilman) "they can sort themselves out when they get outside." Then [they] went out and had a drink. Several of the young women disappeared afterwards.

Twelve years after, one of these men, a parishioner of [mine], came and said he had conscientious scruples with reference to the woman he had been living with. He did not think she was the women he had married in England. But nothing could be done to mend matters.

DAMMES HUET

While waiting to be accepted as a preacher by the Nederduitse Gereformeerde Kerk, Huet made a journey in 1857 to missions in Basutoland and the Orange Free State. His arrival in Winburg coincided with an abortive bid by Transvaal president Marthinus Pretorius to annex Jacobus Boshoff's young Free State.

THREE HUNDRED BRAVE MEN

The town that from afar had appeared to me so dead, I found in great commotion, as the *President* of the Free State with his *Commando* were expected back at any moment from their expedition against the *Transvaal Republic*. Indeed it was not long before the report of rifle and cannon shots made us aware of H.E.'s arrival. I went to the window to see the procession. It was a curious sight. First came a hundred men, mostly farmers, unshaven, ragged, seated on horses or skeletons of horses, and armed with rifles or pistols. Then came the trap of the *President*, that looked no less festive than, and made me think of, the sleigh in which NAPOLEON returned from his *Russian* campaign. And yet it was no defeat, but rather a triumphal parade. Next came another carriage, and after that a few ox wagons, with which the first procession was concluded. Salutes crashed; hurrahs resounded. And there was reason. For had not the two *South African* republics faced one another on the battlefield? Had not the three hundred

brave men of PRETORIUS dared to advance to a distance of 300 paces from the seven hundred of BOSHOF? Were not both sides ready for the fray? Was it not through the wonderful disposition of Providence, that the fuse, which was to ignite the cannon that would give the signal to attack, would not burn? And was it not because of that delay, that the *Transvaal* burgers got time to put up their little white flags (which they apparently carried with them in case of emergency) and offer peace? … Well does the suspicious world say that when the *Transvaal* heroes came up against an unarmed *Kaffer*kraal, whose children had aroused their covetousness, they would have been possessed of more resolution. Well does it say that some of those triumphant warlords that found themselves in the peaceful *dopper* section, at the moment that the battle was to begin apparently went to the ditch to drink water, and did not reappear till both thirst and danger had, at the same time, disappeared. However, one should not believe everything the world says. And whatever of this was true or false, the result of the campaign was glorious, achieved its goal, and this (according to the expression beloved by many) without any *innocent* blood shed!

KARL SCHERZER

Dr Scherzer was a scientist on a converted Austrian man-of-war, the Novara, *which spent more than two years circumnavigating the globe, unfurling the imperial flag in "climes where it had never before floated" and exploring outlets for Austrian commerce. The expedition, which reached home in 1859, amassed a scientific collection that included 100 human skulls "representing the craniology of almost all the races of the globe".*

THIS SINGULAR RACE
The aborigines whom Jan van Riebeck found, when, with three Dutch ships, he landed in 1652 at Table Bay, and in the name of the Dutch East India Company established a settlement, have now almost entirely disappeared from the capital. If anyone desires [to] see a veritable Hottentot or Bushman, he must undertake a troublesome journey, of weeks' duration, into the inhospitable interior. In Cape Town this singular race is only now and then to be met with in prisons or hospitals, and even then of a mixed breed.

At the Moravian mission Genadendal. The young pupils of the Seminary for Teachers, destined to be dispatched into the remotest districts of the colony as teachers and apostles of Christianity, were put through their paces for the Austrian visitors.

Genadendal

The examination commenced with a performance on the piano by a Mestizo lad of about sixteen, son of a Mulatto father by a Hottentot mother. This youth displayed a decided talent for music, coupled with truly admirable execution; and besides the piano, played the organ, the violin, and the violoncello. Next, a variety of questions in geography and history were put to the pupils present. These consisted chiefly of easy intelligible questions, principally relating to England. Those examined were surprisingly well acquainted with the history of Liverpool, London, Manchester, Dublin, &c., and could enumerate many particulars about the Thames and Westminster Abbey. What proved most disagreeable, was the singular custom that prevailed, of all the pupils answering at once, each hoping, by out-clamouring his fellow, to prove his intimate acquaintance with the subject under discussion.

JOHN PUMP

Railways were only at the plotting stage in South Africa when "John Pump" – a pseudonymous contributor to the Cape Monthly magazine – made his plea for sanity in 1857. "I have been reading the newspapers lately, and I see plainly enough that the newspapers and the Parliament are determined to ruin the country," he wrote. "It is time for a practical man to speak out, and I mean to do it."

EVERYTHING THAT IS RASCALLY

Introduce railways! What for? what do we want with railways? We kept the convicts out, and we want to bring in railways. Why – they are worse than all the convicts in the world, they are the main cause of all the wickedness in the world, the foundation of all the roguery, trickery, deception, thieving, embezzling, forging, eloping, and everything that is rascally. Who was Robson? A railway clerk. Who was Redpath? A railway clerk. Who was Sadlier? A railway speculator. Is not one mad, the other transported, the third a suicide? And do you want to introduce such fellows here? Don't tell me that railways did not make them rogues: I should like to know whether they could have done what they did without railways. I'm a plain man, and I should like a plain answer.

Is not the curse of Europe the spirit of speculation? Don't men of capital ruin themselves by it? Don't clerks rob their masters for it? Don't servants steal for it? Don't wives go into debt with their milliners and spend their pin-money on it? And what causes speculation? Railways!

Who stays at home now? Where do you ever find a man who can say "I was born in this town where you see me; I have lived all my life here, and

I mean to die here?" Does not everybody go gadding about, and flying all over the world at thirty miles an hour, and making a travelled monkey of himself, and get to fancying Frenchmen as good as Englishmen, and frogs as good as beef, and claret as good as beer? And what is the cause of all this? Railways!

Did you ever hear of an elopement at the Cape? No. Don't you hear and read of them every day in England and the rest of Europe? Don't wives and daughters constantly run away with popinjay scamps with hair on their lips and nothing in their pockets? And how do they run away? By railways!

Did you ever hear of thirty or forty people being smashed to death, and a hundred and fifty more with broken arms and legs, from travelling in a Cape wagon? Didn't you ever hear of it in England? Of course. Railways again!

But what *do* we want with railways here? We do very well without them. *I* have done very well without them. I began life with a wagon and a span of oxen, and now I have got about – never mind how much – a year. I am not going to satisfy your curiosity by telling you. And that, by-the-by, reminds me of another evil of these abominable railways; they encourage curiosity to a frightful extent. Men go rushing off to *see* things that they would never have troubled their heads to *think* about in the good old times.

JOHN MACKENZIE

Another emissary of the London Missionary Society, who joined Robert Moffat at Kuruman in 1858 and wrote a tedious book about his experiences.

KOM BINNEN!

It being winter, the weather was pleasant during the day, but bitterly cold at night. Mr. Philip's cart, which was our quarters by night and by day on the road, was just long enough for us to lie down comfortably in it, and broad enough to hold Philip and myself, provided the one who went in first turned on his side, when he was joined by his companion, and the cart-sail was shut from the outside by the servant. The luxury of undressing was reserved for more favourable circumstances. Wishing on one occasion to start at an unusually early hour, we had given the two "boys" or servants orders the night before to call us if they awoke first. Accordingly, a tap came to the side of our cart at early dawn. Half awake, and doubtless fancying himself in his study at Philippolis, Philip shouted out "Kom bin-nen!" – "Come in!" – awakening both himself and me with the earnestness of his hospitality. The impossibilities connected with any immediate acceptance of this invitation appeared with great force to the boys outside, who gave unrestrained expression to their amusement.

Right: John Mackenzie

ANONYMOUS

The queen here is Langazane, most influential of the widows left by Zulu king Mpande's father. The unidentified writer of this 1859 magazine article, who describes her as shrewd and intelligent, declined an offer of one of her daughters in marriage.

EVEN AS A LOOKING-GLASS

The following morning, after a frugal breakfast of mealie-meal porridge, and tea without sugar, I called again on her royal highness, and spent a few hours in her hut. The floor was a splendid piece of Zulu workmanship. Its substratum consisted of soil of ant-hills, finely pounded, and stamped down flatly. It had then been smeared over not only with cow-dung, but also with grease, and finally polished with small round stones. Under this process it becomes almost as smooth and even as a looking-glass, and its color a shining black or dark-green. This kind of work requires a great deal of attention, in order to avoid fissures, and takes several weeks for its completion. Yet the floor never becomes so hard as that the nails of a heavy boot would not leave an impression; and it is for this reason that the missionary, Mr. Schreuder, has received the name uMnyateli, the treader, in addition to two other names by which he is known throughout Zululand, viz.: u Yohanesi, *i.e.*, Hans or John, and u Mfudisi, or teacher, missionary.

CHARLES ANDERSSON

Illegitimate son of an English gentleman bear hunter and a Swedish country girl, Andersson was Frederick Galton's companion on his journey to the Ovambo. After Galton returned to England, Andersson completed a gruelling first-ever trek to Lake Ngami from the west. An ornithologist of note, he stayed on in Namibia to trade and mine copper. Setting himself up as a warlord with a following of Cape mercenaries and locally recruited Herero, he was crippled by a bullet in the knee when he led a raid on the Nama in 1864. A hard man, he died of disease during a trip through Ovamboland three years later. Andersson's mercenaries, the Otjimbingwe British Volunteer Artillery, had their own theme song:

Andersson on his ox.

> … *No rapture nor plunder we covet,*
> *No conquest have we in our view,*
> *But we'll rally round the flag of Old England,*
> *And die by the Red, White and Blue.*

AN AGREEABLE SENSATION

The morning before leaving Omutjamatunda a curious accident occurred to me. On lying down at night alongside a small fire, the air was quite calm; but, towards morning, a strong and cutting wind arose. To protect myself against the chilling blast, I was

243

obliged to pull the blanket over my head, and was thus slumbering in happy ignorance of everything. After a time, an agreeable sensation of warmth and comfort stole over me, and the most exquisite visions floated before my imagination. By degrees, however, this pleasant feeling was converted into uneasiness, and ultimately into absolute pain. I was writhing in agonies. By a violent effort, I roused myself out of the trance, and, starting to my feet, discovered that the coverlet was ignited. A spark had fallen on it, and, being composed of quilted cotton, it had for a long time been slowly smouldering, which accounted for the agreeable feeling I had at first experienced. On the fire coming into contact with my body-linen, however, the lulling sensation was changed into one of torment. Hans had had a similar accident at Schmelen's Hope, on which occasion almost the whole of the skins, &c., spread beneath him, were consumed before he was aware of what had happened. From that day forward, as may be supposed, I always made my bed far away from the fire.

NO LESS THAN EIGHT

To give the reader an idea of the immense quantity of game hereabouts, I may mention, that in the course of the few days we remained at Tunobis, our party shot, amongst other animals, upwards of thirty rhinoceroses. One night, indeed, when quite alone, I killed in the space of five hours (independently of other game) no less than eight of those beasts, amongst which were three distinct species. And it is my belief that if I had persevered I might have destroyed double the number. But I never took delight in useless slaughter. In our case – and I think I may say in all cases where I have been concerned in killing a great number of wild beasts – not a pound of flesh was ever wasted; for what we did not require for our own use, was devoured by the natives.

JAMES CHAPMAN

Chapman believed that after a flogging his Damara servants "generally did well for a few days", and he would administer as many as 20 lashes for more serious offences. The Damara certainly got the raw end of the stick in his travels: on his last journey, an abortive 1863 bid to open the mighty Zambezi to trade and navigation, he simply abandoned those who fell ill with fever, and 18 of them were killed by marauding Ndebele. Whatever his failings in the labour relations field, Chapman was a fine diarist. His original journals are a vivid account of 15 years as trader, explorer and elephant hunter. "A smart rider on a smart horse is frequently able to kill several elephants out of one troop," he noted in an essay on hunting, "and the writer once killed 7 in the course of an hour." He made several trips to Lake Ngami, and in 1853 through a stroke of ill fortune narrowly missed becoming the first white man to see what would be known as the Victoria Falls. Chapman carried a camera, and against awesome odds managed to produce images that included the first photograph of a welwitschia, and one of his travelling companion, Thomas Baines, presumably near the southern tropic in midsummer, titled "the man without a shadow".

Photography in difficult conditions.

THERE WAS NO INK

Having some business on a neighbouring farm, I asked for a pen and some ink. The lady of the house brought me a pen, but there was no ink, but she asked me to wait a little and she would make some. She sent for some fresh cattle dung, and putting it into a rag milked her own breast into it and, squeezing the contents through the rag into some fine gunpowder, produced ink and gave it to me without the least concern, while I was amazed.

I HAD TO RUN FOR IT

On returning, Fischer was with me and we fell in with a leguaan, an immense brute. I proposed we should kill it with stones, as I wanted to skin it. We made the attack, but it charged us furiously with tail erect and open mouth shewing very red inside, and forked tongue and blue cheeks. Fischer was obliged to run with the animal after him and I after the two of them for 300 yards, Fischer having thrown away his gun; I had [no] opportunity of shooting, as Fischer was always before it. He however chased it round an antheap at last and I came up. I was too much exhausted to shoot … and before I recovered it set sail after me and I had to run for it, also throwing away my gun. I ran back to where I had left the horses and mounted one, and so it laid down. Fischer then came up and, not having picked up his gun yet, threw a lucky shot with a stone and stunned him. We tried to kill it by stabbing to the heart, but all our endeavours were fruitless. It would not die, and so we left it.

WE HAVE GOT NO NEWS

Here his party have surprised a group of San near the Ntwetwe Pan, who notch arrows to their bows, preparing to sell their lives dearly, until Chapman's men assure them they have come "to kill elephants, not men".

Having recovered from their panic, a young girl approached our guide, and anointed and sprinkled him with a powder made from a red root, repeating some unintelligible words; this, we were informed, was a usual ceremony, which would act as a charm against Porrah, the evil spirit, doing him injury for having brought so great a surprise on his friends. This

245

ceremony being ended, another girl brought a dish of pounded sweet berries for our guide to eat, and several for ourselves, and, this done, he had to relate the news, which he did, as is usual, in a sort of rhythm consisting of measured sentences, each containing a certain number of syllables, to which the listeners made one and the same antiphonal response. The news related was addressed to the father of the family only, and then the respective parties greeted each other by clapping hands all round. Bushmen do not exchange this greeting until the news has been told, so that it may be understood from the intelligence given whether the errand is peaceful and friendly. No one dare give any information in the absence of the chief or father of the clan, and Bushmen and other natives never expect it, knowing their customs. In my early travels I have frequently met with young Bushmen who, when asked questions, made me no reply than "I don't know." Being better acquainted with their customs, I have never, of later days, asked them for news, but have inquired for their father, to whom I first tell my own news as well as I can, and then get his story. Travellers unaccustomed to their ways are apt to become impatient and uncivil. The first version of what a Bushman or any native has to say can never be relied on; whatever you ask him about, he invariably says first, "I don't know," and then promises to tell you all he does know. Ask him for news, and he says, "No; we have got no news," and shortly afterwards he will tell you news of perhaps great interest. Ask him for a pinch of snuff, he always says he has got none, but presently produces it.

The preliminary ceremonies being over, the Bushmen indulge in a bout of smoking from a rude clay pipe, which being passed round, each inhales one mouthful. A fit of violent intoxication ensues, the stomach distends, the breast heaves, the eyes turn their whites to view, a quivering motion seizes the whole frame, and they fall back in terrible convulsions; kicking and writhing, their faces assume the most hideous contortions, and the foam issues from their mouths, while the more hardened of the party try to restore the senses of their fellows by squirting water from their mouths on their faces, and pulling at a tuft of hair in the crown of their heads. This is one of the most disgusting spectacles that can be witnessed. It occasionally happens that some of them die in these convulsions; others, on recovery, say they have been in an ecstacy of delight, and desire a repetition; and it is every young Bushman's greatest boast to have been drunk from tobacco. When smoking alone, they frequently fall into the fire, and are sometimes burnt to death. In the course of my rambles, I have seen hundreds who have been injured by fire, into which they have fallen during this state of delirium; and they are too lazy or thoughtless to take any precautions before they commence these dangerous orgies.

San rock painting of a trance dance.

A PITCH OF EXCITEMENT
The "porrah" described here was a trance dance, a religious ritual which has been recorded in rock paintings throughout southern Africa. Blood from nasal bleeding had a magical significance.

246

Before parting with our Bushman friends, we witnessed illustrations of the passive and effeminate disposition of the men, in the revel accompanying the parting feast, for which we presented them some tobacco and a fly-bitten ox for slaughter. The men allowed themselves to be beaten by the women, who are in the habit of belabouring their husbands in order to keep them in subjection. The men got broken heads, and one had his nose, another his ear, nearly bitten off. We were pleased to see them all happy and enjoying their last night with us. I witnessed the Porrah, or Devil's Dance, when they worked themselves up to a pitch of excitement, fell to the earth and writhed in agony, and foamed at the mouth till relieved by letting of blood. It was a wonder that some who fell were not suffocated with the dust the rest raised as they danced in a circle round the fallen to the time of one, two, three, and twisted their bodies, arms and legs. The men carried fans of gnu tails, plumes of black ostrich feathers waved on their heads, and moana seed pods encircled their ankles as rattles. The women clapped hands and stamped loudly to keep time.

SOME UNCOUTH GESTURES
The original Hottentot, or Namaqua dance, somewhat resembles that of the Bechuana and Bushmen, a monotonous singing, stamping, and clapping of hands, together with some uncouth gestures. The dance got up for my edification is chiefly memorable for the extreme inelegance of its figures, and the vulgar attitudes which the women delight to place themselves in. About a dozen of these followed one another in a circle, in a hop-skip-and-jump sort of manner, singing, clapping their hands, and lifting one leg high in the air, throwing a bitter melon through under it for the next following to catch, and so on. The vulgarity and unseemliness of this dance are much increased by the almost nude forms of the women, whose enormous pendant bosoms dangle about in a most disgusting manner.

BOX ON THE EARS
A Nama settlement at Gobabis.

The church bell here being cracked, a koodoo's horn is blown to call the inhabitants to prayers or meeting. They seem rather fond of going to

247

church, and soon after the signal are to be seen coming from all directions, bearing little cross-legged veldt-stoeljies over their shoulders, the women wearing prints and shawls of the gaudiest of colours. In church a good many behave with becoming decorum; others are in the habit of going to sleep during the service: and in order to check this propensity a *bode* or messenger, otherwise called the *corporaal*, moves about from one end of the building to the other, and, on finding a delinquent, arouses him or her, without distinction of person, by a most unmerciful box on the ears.

EYELID TO EYELID

It often happens that from one to a dozen oxen faint and die on the road under the exertion, and we have to lie awake all night and watch, for fear of losing some of our loose cattle and sheep. The journey must be accomplished during the hours which intervene between 3 or 4 o'clock in the afternoon and early sunrise on the following morning – it being absolutely necessary to give up all thought of farther progress by the time the sun is an hour above the horizon, otherwise your oxen are done for, and your people likewise. By dint, however, of sharp and constant driving, when the load does not exceed 2000 lbs. it can be done well enough, but we have to keep strict watch on our men, who, notwithstanding that they generally put pieces of stick across their eyes – from eyelid to eyelid – to keep them open, will sometimes drop down overcome with fatigue, or even fall asleep while walking. Their bleared eyes, when thus pegged out with sticks, and their dust-covered hair and faces, seen by the light of our wood fire, look truly diabolical.

FOR AN IGNORANT SAVAGE
On the Zouga River, east of Lake Ngami.

We met here a personage I had often wished to see, a native conjurer. Report had long made us familiar with the marvellous performances of this man, but we were glad of an opportunity of having ocular demonstration. This person was a remarkably fine specimen of a Bayèyè (Makoba, or boatman), and by the careful manner in which his toilet was made and his body anointed, he evidently had some pretensions among his countrymen to being a dandy. He had no ears; but, with a smiling and pleasant expression of countenance, he possessed all the robust proportions, activity, and muscular development of his tribe. As he could not perform any of his prodigies during the daylight, we invited him for the evening, when he punctually appeared. He was evidently under some apprehensions that his secrets were known and could be exposed by the white man; but we gave him a fair chance, though scrutinizing his actions during his performance very severely, and we must do him the justice to say that his tricks, which were all sleight-of-hand, were, for an ignorant savage, remarkably clever, and equal to what I have seen performed by celebrated wizards. One of his tricks was burning a bunch of beads tied in a bundle of grass in the midst of our little circle, and making them appear again uninjured; also pounding certain things to pieces and restoring them to their shapes. All his tricks are performed after invoking Morimo (God) by holding his hands up in a supplicating attitude. He attributes everything to his influence with God, and is quite stubborn on that point. His ears, he told us, also were with God, but we shortly after learnt a very different story, which was that the chief had taken them off, in order to try and cure him of an unconquerable love of displaying his ingenuity upon sundry little properties of the chief, which, by his sleight-of-hand, were conveyed from the chief's residence to his own.

CRUNCHED A TEAPOT
A skerm is a brushwood shelter, used for lying in wait for game.

At a waterhole.

On the following afternoon, while Baines's dinner and his blankets were lying in readiness for him at the skaarm, without anybody to look after them, a wolf (hyena) made free with his sketch-book and one of the blankets, which it tore and partially devoured, ate off the horn handle of a table-knife, and crunched a teapot, but could not appreciate our style of cookery, for it left the cooked viands untouched.

INTO THE MIDDLE
The Damara cattle do not appear to be so hardy as colonial oxen when water is scarce. They become dreadfully thirsty an hour or two after their usual time for drinking, and though they drank yesterday forenoon, it was ridiculous to hear them bellowing, and to see them scampering at full speed, with tails up, like so many panic-stricken buffaloes, to the water when they smelt it. Here were upwards of 100 head of cattle in the rush, and 200 sheep and goats, many of which unfortunate creatures, being the weaker, were knocked down and jumped over, and so trodden or nearly squeezed to death in the crush. When the cattle reach the water it generally happens that, greedy and over-nice as they are, the foremost at once dash into the middle, and then the hindermost try to pass them, not satisfied with the water that has been disturbed and rendered muddy by the foremost. Thus the rear rank takes front rank in regular skirmishing order, until they have gone right through, and then the stupid animals come back to look for that which they formerly discarded, but which they now find is still more muddy. They continue walking round and round in the middle of it very disconsolately for an hour, sipping an occasional but reluctant mouthful, while the sheep and horses have long ago taken their drink very peacefully on the very margin of the pool, and are now grazing contentedly.

I HELD THE STUMP
April was one of Chapman's servants.

13th December. – April returned from Chuma-Chukeroo, whither I had sent him to engage porters: he brought two miserable wretches, mere skeletons, with the promise of a further supply of this questionable article on the morrow. Next day, conceiving it a duty incumbent on him to feed the poor hungry fellows, April went out, of his own accord, to hunt. At night, after I had retired to bed, one of our people arrived in great distress, having been sent by April to ask assistance. His gun had burst, and injured his hand, and the poor fellow was so weak from loss of blood that, being unable to walk any farther, he had lain down under a tree about 10 miles off. I called up all the men to go to his assistance, taking with them food and water. I feared lest the lions and wolves, which are very abundant, and even now roaring about us in great numbers, should devour him; but Shapatani insisted that he should not be able to find the place again in the dark. It was indeed pitch-dark, cloudy, and drizzling. I tried hard, however, to get them to go off at once, as April had no fire, and it would be a miracle if the lions were to miss a wounded and bleeding man: but all to no purpose.

15th December. – In the evening April was brought back on a stretcher, carried by three men. The rest of them did not forget to bring the quagga which April had shot; and Jem had killed two rhinoceroses with one shot from my big gun. I have never heard of such an achievement before. Poor April's hand was in a frightful state: the thumb gone, and all the fingers smashed, and a large piece of iron had evidently gone through the palm. It presented, indeed, a horrid spectacle, and, seeing that there was no remedy but amputation, I had it dressed for the present, and sent him to bed after a good mess of milk and porridge, the first thing he has eaten.

Next morning, after a restless and anxious night, I rose early, for the purpose of taking April's hand off. The poor fellow made no objection. I could not perform the operation without John's assistance. He did not like the cutting, but I made him take the knife while I held the stump, put back the integuments, and caught hold of the arteries, while the hand was severed from the wrist. John did his best, yet at best it was but a clumsy job, as may well be imagined, for neither of us had ever seen anything of the kind done before; and when I had, with much difficulty, secured the arteries, which were constantly slipping, the ligatures could not be found. However, we were not ten minutes about it, bandaging and all, and there were not two tablespoonfuls of blood lost. The poor fellow bore it all very patiently, and that was a great matter. It may easily be imagined what I felt, especially as my nerves are at best not very strong, and I was now very ailing myself. But it was a case of emergency, and my sense of duty carried me through.

STUCK IN HIS OPEN JAWS
The oxen found a few melons in the night, and 4 [of] them each got a melon stuck in his open jaws, like a potato in the mouth of a sucking pig, in which painful predicament they travelled 7 miles, nor would they allow us to relieve them.

THOMAS MACLEAR

Governor of the Cape Sir George Grey was a deceitful and egotistic man, and his neurotic wife, Eliza, was not the most pleasant person either. The interplay of their personalities reached a dramatic climax in 1860, when they were returning to the Cape from England after Grey had narrowly escaped being sacked. The couple were travelling on the flagship of Admiral Sir Henry Keppel, who was going to take up an appointment as commander-in-chief at Simon's Town. The three of them had adjoining cabins with interleading doors, and it soon became clear that Eliza found the naval man's company more attractive than that of her husband. Keppel taught her to drink whisky, and installed a double bed in his cabin. Grey's version of events was subsequently recorded at the Cape by his friend the distinguished astronomer Thomas Maclear.

Two letters dropped out

One morning he [Grey] went to her door & found it locked; he rapped, no answer, he rapped again & again louder & was then let in by her. Her face was flushed or blushing; her head was dressed as if she was going to a ball, hair covered with jewelled net work, she was in slippers & the remainder of her dress a light deshabile. She appeared confused & after a little hesitation said "George, I could not let you in before, I was there" pointing to the direction of the W.C.

George Grey

Another morning at breakfast time, K's servant came to the table & reported that he had been to his door which was locked, he rapped & called but received no answer & was afraid something had happened. Cap^n T [Turnour, captain of the ship] jumped up & went to the door & was also unsuccessful. They began breakfast & after a time he appeared & said "I was so deeply interested in the book you lent me (Lord Dundonal's life) that I could not answer when called."

G now became miserable & he determined to act with vigor.

In the evening she was sitting as usual on the upper deck with K on a sopha. He went up at 11 o'Clock & requested her to come down: she refused; but came down some 15^m after. Next evening he went up at 11 o'Clock & requested her to retire, she refused; he then ordered her to retire, she disobeyed. He went down to her cabin & took up a book, as usual with his feet on a rest to relieve his hip [an old injury]. In about 10 minutes she came down & drawing her seat close in front to his & putting her face close to his face she addressed him "so you are jealous of K, why don't you call him out you coward", disgusted, G suddenly put down the book & pushed the rest from his feet, the book touched the side of her head in lowering it, she said you have struck me, he replied "Eliza I did not touch you intentionally", she persisted in her assertion which he persisted in denying then called her attention to the gulf before her, to the notorious profligate lebertine she was dealing with in K. That night he knelt by her bedside for the greater part of the night begging & praying of her to think of the future & of herself, & using every argument he could think of to rouse her honour: but seemingly with little effect.

None of his servants had spoken to him on the subject, & he was unwilling to condescend to watch her, yet he was in doubt whether it was not his duty to discover if she was guilty with this man. "A voice within me told me it was my duty!" "I prayed to another Power for advice & arrived at the same conclusion." "My future happiness & honour were at stake."

The Venetian bars as usual on Shipboard do not admit of seeing into cabins, but between the upper bar & the timbers there was sufficient space for seeing into hers. A similar space was above the bars which separated her cabin from K's. On discovering this, G waited on the night following the scene last mentioned until (L.G.)'s maid left her cabin, &, when all was still he looked through the crevice. To his disgust he saw (L.G.) in *her night dress* mounted up on something with a note in each hand, moving them about in the space as if to direct attention to them. He instantly set his foot against the door with all his might to break it open for the purpose of securing these notes, but the lock held fast: the violence of the blow produced a thundering noise; in a second or two she opened the door. He demanded the letters she had in her hand the moment before. She denied having any letters: he insisted[,] she denied; turning to her bed he jerked off the clothes & the two letters dropped out, which he seized & put into his jacket. He went to her writing table & there discovered another unfinished. She ran at him & tried to get them from him telling him he had no business with her letters. He ran out, took a hasty glance at them, then went to the outside door of K's cabin, the door was open & there stood K with only his shirt & dressing drawers or petticoat on. She rushed bye G screaming, & placed herself close to the side of K still in her night dress.

G pushed her away from K, the latter said you may abuse me as much as you please but you shall not abuse the Lady. He could scarcely finish the sentence however before G seized him by the throat & would have strangled him if he had not been pulled off, & kept back. G looked at K & pointing up his hand desired him to "go above", meaning to the upper deck. K refused instantly K [sic, apparently in error for G] dashed forward and knocked him down, he reeled under one of the guns. G stepped back & again desired him to "go above". He refused & before G could be prevented he felled him again with a violent blow. When he got up he looked like an idiot, his shirt torn & otherwise disfigured. He was led away to one of the officer's cabins, while G half frantic retired with Cap^n T to the latter's cabin. Maddened & desperate he told Cap^n T to put about for Rio or Buenos Ayres or he would jump overboard, he did not care what became of him. T went to K & returned stating that the vessel should not be put about. G said that he was determined he gave 20 minutes & if the vessel was not about for Rio within that time, he would take other measures. T went off & G armed himself with a cutlass. T returned with an offer to put them on board another vessel or on shore at [blank]. G replied you have now only 15 minutes to put about for Rio or Bu – A. I am determined, I have taken a resolution, I have secured a cutlass. T returned again with a negative answer. Then G told him if the vessel is not about within the time mentioned I will address the ship's Company. You know who I am, they know who I am, I am on board this vessel by Her Majesty's Command; the men will not sanction this outrage upon me. T said you surely won't do that. "I am determined".

The ship was put about for Rio within the time mentioned.

Grey dumped his wife in Rio to make her way back to England on the mail packet. The notes he had found were one from Keppel "expressed in warm terms & stating that he must *see her". The other was from her saying she would see*

252

Keppel "when all was safe". In 1896, when Grey was in his dotage, Eliza unexpectedly announced that she thought it her duty to return to him. Their brief reunion – they both died two years later – was marred for her by the discovery that he had much less money than she expected.

JOHN BISSET

Sir John Bisset, veteran of three frontier wars, was invited to accompany Queen Victoria's son Alfred on a hunting tour in 1860, and was thoroughly impressed by the young prince's pluck and manliness in the field. Other writers estimated that thousands of animals, rather than the 600-plus mentioned by Bisset, perished in the massacre he describes here: several black beaters were trampled to death by a charging herd of zebras.

RED UP TO THE SHOULDERS

The extensive plains in the Free State are intersected here and there by belts and cross-belts of mountains, with only gaps between, through which the countless herds of large game pass from one plain to another. For days before we arrived the natives had been concentrating from distant points towards Reit Vley, leaving men in the "several necks," as they passed on, to prevent the game from escaping back to the plains, from which they were being driven towards a common centre.

Early on the morning of the 24th His Royal Highness and the shooting party of twenty-five guns in all started for Mr. Baines' farm, which caused us to diverge nearly six miles from our route. We reached Reit Vley about eight o'clock, and were provided with a sumptuous breakfast. During all this time we saw masses of game closing in from all directions.

Our first sport was, however, to have been a Lion, and we made for a hill where it was supposed the monarch of the plains would be found; but I am sorry to say we were disappointed; he had managed to escape from his lair during the night; and as time was precious, we had to give up the lion for less noble game. Herds upon herds of large game (all of the antelope species) were passing us, and the battue commenced by the Prince bringing down a great wildebeast, or gnu. This ferocious-looking beast turned on His Royal Highness on being wounded, and received a second ball, which rolled him over. This was the signal for a general onslaught.

The hunting party advanced up the plain in extended order, a few yards

Alfred and fellow hunters.

apart, and masses of game kept breaking through as the pressure of the coming streams of antelopes, quaggas, zeebras, bles-boks, eelands, ostriches, hartebeasts, wildebeasts, koodoos, &c. &c. came pouring on towards us, and, checked by our fire, commenced to whirl. The plain in which we were was of vast extent – I dare say nearly a hundred miles in circumference – and the whole of

this extent was one moving mass of game. The gaps between the mountains on all sides of this plain were stopped by a living line of men, and we were in the midst of this whirling throng firing at great game at not twenty-five yards' distance as fast as we could load. The Prince fired as fast as guns could be handed to him, for Currie rode on one side and I on the other, and we alternately handed guns to him as he discharged his own. As the circle narrowed there really was considerable danger from the game breaking through, for when a stampede took place so much dust arose that you were in danger of being trampled to death. It became very exciting to see great beasts larger than horses rolling over from right and left shots not ten paces from you, and also charging down with their great horns lowered as if they were coming right at you and then swerving to one side or the other.

All this time we were working back towards Bloom Fontein, as it was Sir George Grey's intention to move on a stage on the journey the same afternoon. During the great slaughter of the day the circle of natives was closing in; and the mass of game became so dressed [pressed] together at last, that the Prince and Currie took to their hunting hog-spears and charged into the midst, driving home the "Paget blades" into the infuriated animals. It was at this point of the battue that Sir George Grey rode up and directed us to desist. He was a keen sportsman himself, and had been committing great slaughter up to that moment. This great destruction of 600 head of large game was no wilful waste of God's creatures; some thousands of natives had been employed to drive the masses together, and they had brought 600 pack-oxen to carry away the carcasses for their winter supply of food. Their mode of preserving the meat is to cut it into thin strips, about the size of your finger and to hang it over bushes or on strings supported by sticks; the sun and rarefied air up-country will dry it in a day or two; you can then pack it away in a dry place, and it will keep for months or even years, the meat retaining all its nutriment.

We selected some of the choicest of the game to be carried back to our wagons, and many trophies of heads, horns, tails, and skins were also reserved. All these were intended by Mr. Baines to be preserved for His Royal Highness; but I am sorry to say they never reached the Prince, although they were sent to England in charge of a South African traveller.

Six hundred head of large game were shot on this day, besides numbers speared by the natives, and most of the sportsmen looked more like butchers than sportsmen, from being so covered with blood. His Royal Highness and Currie were red up to the shoulders from using the spear. I cannot myself boast of many trophies, as I generally handed my double gun to the Prince as fast as I could load it; nevertheless I could not resist now and then bowling over a couple of great antelopes as they whirled past me. It was a very exciting day, and were His Royal Highness to live for a hundred years I do not believe he could ever see such a scene again, for the game in South Africa is fast disappearing.

LUCY DUFF GORDON

Duff Gordon, who counted Charles Dickens, Lord Tennyson and William Make-
peace Thackeray among her circle of London friends, sailed to the Cape in 1861 to
recuperate from a bronchial condition. She stayed there eight months, keeping in
touch with her husband and other family members through a string of witty and
observant letters. But her lungs worsened on her return to England. She eventual-
ly sought relief in the dry air of upper Egypt, and, often painfully short of breath,
lived out her last years with a maid in a home in the ruins of a temple at Luxor.

SLAPPING HER BLACK BOY
On the voyage out.

The humours of our company would make you angry. The *naif* display of
selfishness and absurdity on many hands is wonderful. Mr. and Mrs.
Polson have fought the Captain on every point. They want meals in their
cabin at separate hours, fresh water *ad libitum*, candles, and cooking lamps,
le diable à quatre; and she is now prostrate after fits of hysterics (temper)
such as I could not have believed in. She found some relief in slapping her
black boy and her German maid, but still suffers severely. He modestly
asked me to use my "extraordinary influence" with the Captain to have the
uprights which help to support the maindeck (where I sleep) sawn in two
because they creak tremendously!! I could not keep my countenance at
such a *saugrenu* idea.

I WAS A DISGRACE
Here she describes a New Year bisley at Caledon where, she wrote to her husband,
she was beginning to feel much better. "The glorious African sun blazes and roasts
one, and the cool fresh breezes prevent one from feeling languid … On Christmas-
eve it was so warm that I lay in bed with the window wide open, and the stars blaz-
ing in. Such stars! they are much brighter than our moon."

Lucy Duff Gordon

It was a very amusing day. The great tall Dutchmen came in to
shoot, and did but moderately, I thought. The longest range was
five hundred yards, and at that they shot well; at shorter ranges,
poorly enough. The best man made ten points. But oh! what figures were there of negroes and coloured people! I longed for a
photographer. Some coloured lads were exquisitely graceful, and
composed beautiful *tableaux vivants*, after Murillo's beggar-boys.

A poor little, very old Bosjesman crept up, and was jeered and
bullied. I scolded the lad who abused him for being rude to an
old man, whereupon the poor little old creature squatted on the
ground close by (for which he would have been kicked but for
me), took off his ragged hat, and sat staring and nodding his
small grey woolly head at me, and jabbering some little soliloquy
very *sotto voce*. There was something shocking in the timidity
with which he took the plate of food I gave him, and in the way
in which he ate it, with the *wrong* side of his little yellow hand,
like a monkey. A black, who had helped to fetch the hamper,

suggested to me to give him wine instead of meat and bread, and make him drunk *for fun* (the blacks and Hottenots copy the white man's manners *to them*, when they get hold of a Bosjesman to practise upon); but upon this a handsome West Indian black, who had been cooking pies, fired up, and told him he was a "nasty black rascal, and a Dutchman to boot", to insult a lady and an old man at once. If you could see the difference between one negro and another, you would be quite convinced that education (i.e. circumstances) makes the race. It was hardly conceivable that the hideous, dirty, bandy-legged, ragged creature, who looked down on the Bosjesman, and the well-made, smart fellow, with his fine eyes, jaunty red cap, and snow-white shirt and trousers, alert as the best German Kellner, were of the same blood; nothing but the colour was alike.

Then came a Dutchman, and asked for six penn'orth of "brood en kaas", and haggled for beer; and Englishmen, who bought chickens and champagne without asking the price. One rich old boer got three lunches, and then "trekked" (made off) without paying at all. Then came a Hottentot, stupidly drunk, with a fiddle, and was beaten by a little red-haired Scotchman, and his fiddle smashed. The Hottentot hit at his aggressor, who then declared he *had been* a policeman, and insisted on taking him into custody and to the "Tronk" (prison) on his own authority, but was in turn sent flying by a gigantic Irishman, who "wouldn't see the poor baste abused". The Irishman was a farmer; I never saw such a Hercules – and beaming with fun and good nature. He was very civil, and answered my questions, and talked like an intelligent man; but when Captain Davies asked him with an air of some anxiety, if he was coming to the hotel, he replied, "No, sir, no; I wouldn't be guilty of such a misdemeanour. I am aware that I was a disgrace and opprobrium to your house, sir, last time I was there, sir. No, sir, I shall sleep in my cart, and not come into the presence of ladies." Hereupon he departed, and I was informed that he had been drunk for seventeen days, *sans désemparer*, on his last visit to Caledon. However, he kept quite sober on this occasion, and amused himself by making the little blackies scramble for halfpence in the pools left in the bed of the river.

ELIZA M.

In 1863 the matron of St Matthew's Mission at Keiskammahoek in the Eastern Cape went to Cape Town for a holiday. She took with her two of the "Kafir scholars" from the mission; an unnamed boy, and a girl recorded only as Eliza M. Eliza kept a journal of her visit, from which this description of Cape Town is taken.

THE EARTH SEEMED TO MOVE
There are not many trees in the town; in some places there are not many at all, but in one place it is like the bush; it is pleasant underneath the trees; there are stools to sit on when a person is tired. That path is very long; I saw two Newfoundland dogs. I did not know that I should ever come to see them when I heard them spoken of. They are dogs with large heads and great long ears; the hair is like sheep's wool, and they have great claws; they are suited to assist people. It seemed as if it could swallow me without

chewing; I was very much afraid, but one was not very big, it was about the size of the dogs of black people, when it barks, it say so with a great voice. Also, I saw sheep rather unlike others, in the tail here it was very large, the head was small, and the body was large and fat.

I have forgotten to mention something which I ought to have said before; when I came out of the ship and walked on the land the earth seemed to move, and when I entered a house, it seemed to imitate the sailing of a ship, and when I lay down it seemed to move.

I saw an ox-wagon here, but I had not imagined that I should see a wagon.

We go to a very large beautiful Church; I don't forget the people who sing, the English; the prayers are said with thin voices as if it were singing; but the chief thing done is singing frequently, all the while there is continually singing, and then sitting. There is a Kafir school here; I went one day, they were reading; they can read well; there are also carpenters &c.

There is another place besides that which I said is like the bush, and in that place there are trees and flowers, and two fountains; a thing is stuck in, and the water comes out above. I saw the date-tree when it is young; it is one leaf, yet when it is grown, it is a very large tree. In that place there are wild birds, doves are there, and those birds which the English call canaries, and a very beautiful bird, its tail is long, its bill is red.

Yesterday the soldiers had sports, the music-band played, and when they finished playing they fired. They were many, and they fired together. And as we were walking, they fired; I was very much startled and afraid. And to-day they are playing the music. It seems to-day it exceeds in sweetness, I mean its sound.

There came a person here who is a Kafir. I rejoiced very much when I heard that he too was one. He asked me what I had come to do here; I said "I am only travelling." He asked whether I was a prisoner, and I said "No." He said he was very glad, he had thought I was a prisoner. I told him that

257

I was going away again, and he said "May you go in peace, the Lord preserve you well till you arrive whence you came." I never saw a person like him of such kindness; he said he had come here to learn, he came from where I did; but I should not have known him to be a Kafir, and he did not know that I was one.

There are creatures which are eaten; they come from the sea, their name is called crawfish, they are frightful in appearance, yet their flesh is very fine and white.

The person of this house is a dyer of clothes, the white he makes red, and the red green, and the brown he makes black. I saw the wood with which they dye. Soap is cut in pieces, and put in water, and heated and boiled well, and continually stirred. This thing – dyeing clothes, – is a great work. Water is even in the house; I don't know where it comes from, a person turns a thing, and fresh water comes out as if it were of a river.

There are also carts for selling meat, and for selling bread. I saw the fire-wagon. I did nothing but wonder. I did not know that it was such a big thing. It is long, with many wheels, they are not so large as those of an ox-wagon; people sit in places inside. The wheels run on metal; I say I could do nothing but wonder very much. I had not thought that it was such a great thing. And when it is about to proceed it says "Sh!" I don't know whether it is the boiling of the water; it hastens exceedingly, a person would be unable to notice it well, yet now some people say that this is a small one which I have seen. If it treads on anything, it must smash it, it is a very great thing. I shall never forget it. Where I saw it, the place was fenced on both sides, and I beheld it from the outside. I entered it another week after I had seen it; we went to Somerset West and slept one night. In the morning we returned by it; when I was inside, the earth seemed to move; it is pleasant to ride inside. I end now although this is not all the news about it. When I was in it, I saw a sugar plant; it is not a large plant, it is short with red flowers. I saw other trees at Somerset which I had never seen before.

One day I saw people going to a burial, the carriages were black, but that people should wear black clothes is done also among the natives where a person has died; there were stuck up black feathers, and on the graves were placed stones with writing; the name of the person was written, and the years of his age, and the year in which he died.

JAMES BOWKER

Driven to cannibalism by the travails of the Mfecane, groups in some areas of Basutoland may have carried on eating humans even after the crisis passed. The detritus in the "cannibal caverns" near Thaba Bosiu offered grim evidence for this. Bowker, a soldier, administrator and authority on South African butterflies, visited the site in about 1869.

BOILED RATHER THAN ROAST

Upon our arrival at the mountain above the cavern we left our horses in charge of a native, and descended a steep and rugged foot-path (or rather I should have said, a *hand*-and-foot-path, for the hands have quite as much

to do in travelling this precipitous path as
the feet), and by dint of holding on to tufts of
grass, shrubs, projecting rocks, &c, &c, and
by slipping, sliding, and scrambling, we at
length arrived upon a grassy ledge, in the
face of the cliff, where we could stand without the necessity of holding on. On turning to
the right of this ledge the scene opened out in
all its grandeur; and certainly, in all my life and

wanderings, I have never beheld a more savage looking place. The cavern
is formed by the overhanging cliff, and its entrance, a long, rugged, natural arch, extends along the whole face of the cavern, or nearly so, which is
in length about one hundred and thirty yards, and its breadth about one
hundred. The roof of this place, which is lofty and arched, is blackened
with the smoke and soot of the fires of the savages who formerly inhabited
it, and its floor, strewn with the remains of what they had left there, consisted of heaps of human bones, piled up together or scattered about at ran-
dom in the cavern, and from thence, down the sloping face of the rock, as
far as the eye could reach, the clefts and small level spots were white with
the bones and skulls of human beings; skulls especially were very numerous, and consisted chiefly of those of children and young persons. These
remains told too true a tale of the purpose for which they had been used,
for they were hacked and cut to pieces with what appeared to have been
either blunt axes or sharpened stones; the marrow-bones were split into
small pieces, the rounded joints alone being left unbroken. Only a very few
of these bones were charred by fire, showing that the prevailing taste had
been for boiled rather than roast meat.

You may guess the feelings with which I wandered about this gloomy
sepulchre, and examined its various places of interest. One spot was pointed
out to me, with rough irregular steps, leading up into the interior of the cavern to a gloomy-looking natural gallery, and in this place, I was informed,
were stowed away the unfortunate victims not required for immediate consumption. From this place it was impossible to escape without passing
through the middle of the cavern, which they could not do without being
detected.

Horrible as all this must appear, there might be some excuse made for
savages, driven by famine to extreme hunger, for capturing and devouring
their enemies; but with these people it was totally different, for they were
inhabiting a fine agricultural tract of country, which also abounded in game;
but, notwithstanding all this, they were not contented with hunting and
feeding upon their enemies, but preyed much upon each other also, for many
of their captures were made from amongst the people of their own tribe, and
even worse than this, in times of scarcity, many of their own wives and children became the victims of this horrible practice. If a wife proved lazy, or
quarrelsome, she was speedily disposed of; or a crying baby would in like
manner be silenced, and any member of the community showing signs of
sickness, or bodily infirmity, would not be allowed to linger or to fall off in
condition. Such were the horrible practices of this degraded people, and
although it is now commonly reported that they have for many years entire-

ly given up this diabolical way of living, I saw, while at the cavern, unmistakable evidence that the custom has not been altogether abandoned, for amongst the numerous bones were a few that appeared very recent; they were apparently those of a tall, bony individual, with a skull as hard as bronze; in the joints of these bones the marrow and fatty substances were still evident, showing but too plainly that not many months had elapsed since he had met his fate.

EDWARD MOHR

Mohr dedicated his account of his 1869 journey to the Victoria Falls to German chancellor Otto von Bismarck. He travelled with a German flag, displaying it with firmness at crucial moments, and wrote that the people of Pietermaritzburg were convinced he was a political agent come to annex the Transvaal to Germany. However, he himself had no illusions. "My own private opinion," he wrote, "… is that sooner or later the whole of South Africa, from Cape Agulhas to the Zambesi, will belong to the great power which already owns the Cape Colony."

THEY WERE SCHMART FELLOWS
Here he is at Sandspruit in northern Natal, with a knee so agonisingly rheumatic as to make any travel impossible. He had just sent off a note to an English doctor at Ladysmith when by chance a "travelling doctor" arrived at the hotel. Desperate for relief, Mohr agreed to see him.

Dr. Martin wore a broad-brimmed hat adorned with a dozen large grey, white, and black ostrich feathers; a blue sailor's shirt, a leather belt, in which was stuck a six-barrelled Colt's revolver, leather breeches, and wellingtons reaching up to the knees.

"You are a German," he began, "and in me you find a fellow-countryman." During his long residence in Africa, his language had become a kind of conglomerate of German, English and Dutch. He was no longer able to keep the three idioms distinct, but mixed them up in his talk in chaotic confusion. He examined my knee, heaved three heavy sighs, making a kind of snorting noise like a young hippopotamus when it is wounded, portentously shook his feather-crowned head, observed that the matter was serious, very serious, and the examination was over.

By this time I had become highly suspicious of the fellow, and I therefore put a few questions to him, inquiring, for instance, to what university he had been. He at once replied to St. Petersburg. There he always handed the instruments to the doctors, and had himself put on bandages, prepared plasters, etc., etc., so that he learnt to do all the doctors did, even the most skilful "Yerman" ones – meaning German, I suppose – "They were schmart fellows, those Yerman doctors."

He added with an air of the greatest assurance, "I can cure your knee in three days, but of course all depends on what you mean to pay. I am well-known in Natal and amongst the Boers of the Free State and Transvaal Republic; everybody knows me. I cure everything that comes in my way." I think Goethe must be right when he says, "only trust yourself, and other people will trust you too." At all events, I placed my case provisionally in Dr. Martin's hands, and agreed to pay him twelve dollars down.

He laid on a warm poultice of camomile flowers, wrapped it round with flannel, and most earnestly recommended me to take a stiff glass of grog as hot as I could possibly swallow it every half hour, offering moreover himself to superintend the carrying out of his prescription. Nay, he even shared this internal treatment with me in the most sympathetic manner, taking three doses to my one; so that when I had safely got through the fourth glass, he had already disposed of a dozen. Soon afterwards an irresistible drowsiness came over me, and I fell asleep, whilst my doctor retired to the adjoining room to enjoy a hearty meal and continue his libations – all at my expense, of course!

It must have been about 8 o'clock in the evening when I was awoke by a confused noise at my door. The next moment Dr. Martin staggered into the room, his face deeply flushed, his eyes staring and unsteady, and a surgical knife in his hand. He gave me the reassuring information that he had come to perform a little operation, just to make a few incisions in my knee. With this end in view he rolled towards my bed, and I, with my revolver, which I always kept under my pillow, ready in my hand, awaited his onslaught, when, fortunately for all parties, Smith and Machlapean came in, and without ceremony whisked my Æsculapius out of the room, forbidding him on any account to enter it again. After some noisy resistance he laid down to rest, and quite early the next morning saddled his horse, disposed of two leather bags containing pills, salves, and medicines for the Boers about his own person, and rode across the neighbouring frontier at full speed, evidently unwilling to meet the doctor from Ladysmith, who would doubtless have had him up at once before the next magistrate for unlicensed practising.

IF WE HAD STAYED AT HOME

… on the 23rd, when, owing to the dampness of the ground, we had encamped upon a grassy plain without a tree or shrub upon it, we were overtaken by a gale of wind, accompanied by heavy and bitter cold rain. The fires, which had been lit under great difficulties, owing to scarcity of wood, were soon extinguished, and I at once set to work, with the aid of my Kaffirs, to erect temporary shelters with the aid of the tents, canvas mats, everything we could lay hands on, in short. In one tent we placed the horses; in another, Kaffirs, sheep, goats, and dogs were huddled together as best they could; whilst some of the men crept under the carts, sheltering themselves in hammocks hung beneath them. The poor oxen, however, were left entirely unprotected, exposed to all the fury of the wind and rain.

Under these circumstances, Hübner and I shared the dry shelter of the carts with one Kaffir each, thus leaving more room to the others. My companion was my former servant, Machlapean, who had been with me on my expedition to Zululand in 1866, and was especially useful, as he could speak English fluently and correctly. In the excitement of the moment I was foolish enough to lie down in my trousers, which were wet through with the rain, a piece of thoughtlessness for which I had to do penance soon enough; at the time, however, I found myself perfectly comfortable beneath my woollen wrapper, and now, whilst the storm raged and the rain poured down without, the following conversation took place amongst the Kaffirs in their tent:

"We Kaffirs certainly are stupid fellows, always to let ourselves be talked over by the whites. Wherever the foreigner wanders, we must needs march behind; we are like apes, like injis (dogs), who follow their master directly he leaves the court. If we had stayed at home, might we not now be sitting chattering by the fire in the kraal dry and warm? The women would bring us mabele (Kaffir grain), meat, and amasi (sour milk); but here it's about as dry as the middle of a river, and 'ki nai inchlala' (I am hungry)."

Now Machlapean, lying beside me, looked upon all this as treason to his master, and he replied with all the vehemence natural to Kaffir eloquence:

"Now just listen to me, you fellows down there. You think yourselves men and warriors (majachas), and you've no more spirit than the little boys of my native Zululand. Have you forgotten how you told your wives that you meant to go with the white man, to eat his meat, to earn his money, and to see and observe everything which happened on the journey, so as to talk about it for a whole year afterwards? Didn't you sing and dance and roar like imbubes (lions) for two days beforehand? and now you can only howl like impisis (hyenas). You're miserable fellows; your mothers didn't give you milk enough!"

Then arose a storm of opposition, and everybody agreed that as Machlapean was lying warm and dry in the cart with his master, he had no right to have any voice in the matter.

WITH THE CLOSEST ATTENTION

Early the next morning the chief's people arrived, and then ensued all the noise, chattering, and bargaining which are inseparable from transactions with the natives.

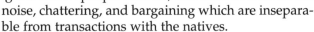

To get their business done quickly was by no means the chief consideration with the Makalakas; they wanted to stay by the cart as long as possible, to stare at all the wonderful things going on there. To the little natives, especially the boys, who were about the place from sunrise to sunset, and had never heard of such a thing as school, the chief event of the day was seeing the white man eat his dinner. To enjoy my meal in peace, I had a thick hedge of brambles thrown up opposite my table; but for all that they still came in crowds, pressing as near as they could, watching everything with the closest attention, and greeting any slip of the spoon on its way to my mouth with a roar of laughter. The use of knives and forks, which they called little assagais (javelins), especially amused them.

262

LIKE A WILD ANIMAL IN THE DESERT

In the night a meteor of the size of a skittle-ball dashed across the sky from the north-north-west to the south-south-east, and approached the stars Aldebaran in Taurus and Antares in Scorpio, leaving a trail of phosphorescent light behind it. About two minutes after its disappearance a dull report rang out in the stillness, like the distant firing of some heavy piece of ordnance.

The men lying near me on the ground were very much frightened at the appearance of this splendid phenomenon, and talked about it in an excited manner with many gesticulations. Presently, however, as Cluley, who understood them better than I did, explained, their conversation took a fresh turn, and they wondered how many people I had killed in my own country that I was obliged to wander about like a wild animal in the desert, adding that it was very childish to be always looking at the sun, the moon, or the stars; one could have that pleasure just as well at home.

EVEN A POCKET-KNIFE

With infinite fatigue and trouble I managed to reach the Kumala with my exhausted oxen, arriving on its banks on the 31st of September. A few showers had already fallen, and the ground was so soft that I was obliged to halt for a few days. Here the Jennings met me on the 3rd of October, bringing with them eight young ostriches, only six days old, which they presented to me. The Kaffirs soon made a big cage of branches, which was fastened across the back of the cart; and in a very short time the birds became quite tame and affectionate. They travelled with us in their cage, and when we halted we let them out to graze on the tender grass shoots which were now beginning to spring up everywhere.

Although ostriches are amongst the wildest and most timid of living creatures, they can be completely tamed when taken quite young. My pets soon learnt to know me from the Kaffirs; and when I went for a walk they would run after me like house-dogs. At four weeks old they ran so fast that none of my people could keep up with them; and when we were encamped on the Mangwe they sometimes remained away for the whole day, but they always came back to the tent in the evening with the oxen and goats. I rewarded them for their faithfulness, on their return, by strewing a spoonful of coarse salt on the ground, which they picked up eagerly. As they grew older their digestive powers increased, and they swallowed down whole chops, bones and all, maize, cooked buffalo's flesh, goat's ribs, and, on one occasion, even a pocket-knife with three blades, belonging to Ziesmann, without any ill-effects whatever. Four of them must have travelled more than one thousand three hundred miles with me altogether; and as they grew bigger they became as accustomed to the noise of firing as old grenadiers. If I wanted to call them back when they were out with me, I had only to let off my gun, and they would come running up at once.

On his return journey, Mohr was hauled up before a magistrate in Potchefstroom and fined for allowing his birds to disturb the peace in the town: they trod on a small boy, panicked a span of oxen and indirectly caused the death of a foal.

CHAPTER SIX

1870 to 1890

In which we encounter an elephant hunter
who also plays the zither, a greedy bulldog
named Nelson, some useful advice on
safety pins, a screw from the Ark
and a man with a hole chopped in his head.

//KABBO

//Kabbo, whose name translates as Dream, was a member of the /Xam San, proba-
bly a shaman, from the Strandberg in the northern Cape. Convicted of stock theft
in 1869, he was sent to Cape Town, where as prisoner number 4628 at the
Breakwater Prison he was to labour on the breakwater then under construction at
the harbour. Governor Sir Philip Wodehouse gave the philologist Dr Wilhelm Bleek
permission to keep //Kabbo at his Mowbray home until his sentence expired, on
condition that he was locked up at night. Dia!kwain, quoted at the beginning of
this book, was handed over under similar conditions. Bleek realised that the San,
who for generations had been hunted like animals, also faced cultural genocide, and
wanted to record their language before it was too late. //Kabbo arrived in Mowbray
in February 1871 and stayed almost three years, sharing his kukummi – *his own*
stories and those of his people – with the doctor and his sister-in-law Lucy Lloyd,
and providing what is today an invaluable record of a vanished culture. Patient
though he was, he longed for the day he could go home.

San at the
Breakwater Prison.

WATCHING FOR A STORY

The Flat Bushmen go to each other's
huts; that they may smoking sit in front
of them. Therefore, they obtain stories at
them; because they are used to visit; for
smoking's people they are. As regards
myself I am waiting that the moon may
turn back for me; that I may set my feet
forward in the path. For, I verily think
that I must only await the moon; that I
may tell my Master, that I feel this is the
time when I should sit among my fellow
men, who walking meet their like. They
are listening to them; for, I do think of
visits; (that) I ought to visit; (that) I

ought to talk with my fellow men; for, I work here, together with women; and I do not talk with them; for, they merely send me to work.

I must first sit a little, cooling my arms; that the fatigue may go out of them; because I sit. I do merely listen, watching for a story, which I want to hear; while I sit waiting for it; that it may float into my ear. These are those to which I am listening with all my ears; while I feel that I sit silent. I must wait (listening) behind me, while I listen along the road; while I feel that my name floats along the road; they (my three names) float along to my place; I will go to sit at it; that I may listening turn backwards (with my ears) to my feet's heels, on which I went; while I feel that a story is the wind.

WAITING FOR THE BOOTS

... I must sit waiting for the Sundays on which I remain here, on which I continue to teach thee. I do not again await another moon, for this moon is the one about which I told thee. Therefore, I desired that it should do thus, that it should return for me. For I have sat waiting for the boots, that I must put on to walk in; which are strong for the road. For, the sun will go along, burning strongly. And then, the earth becomes hot, while I still am going along halfway. I must go together with the warm sun, while the ground is hot. For, a little road it is not. For, it is a great road; it is long. I should reach my place, when the trees are dry. For, I shall walk, letting the flowers become dry while I still follow the path.

CARL MAUCH

Mauch was a short-tempered German geologist who claimed to be the first white man to visit Great Zimbabwe, which he reached in 1871. He fathered the enduring myth that it was built by the Queen of Sheba in imitation of the temple of Solomon. For the benefit of other travellers, he recorded the equipment he took on his journey, which included this intriguing selection of clothing.

I CHOSE THE THICKEST FLANNEL

I could not very well follow the demands of elegance or fashion, not even the demands usually required for man to clothe himself according to the season. I had to consider it far more practical to travel with one suit only, probably for several years. Durability is the foremost reason and, therefore, I clad myself with the exception of underwear, in leather. Coat, vest and trousers were suitable made of tanned, softly treated buckskin and supplied with many roomy pockets each of which had to hold its particular object. A tough leather cap covered the head with two shields to keep the sun-rays from the face and neck. The lower extremities rested, without socks, in strong boots. These had a triple sole and were, moreover, studded with heavy iron nails. I chose the thickest flannel I could find for my underwear. This costume was certainly well-wearing, but with the proverbial African heat, its weight was at first almost insupportable. Bye and bye one gets accustomed to it and though one is inclined to call the weight of the clothing a mistake, it is however compensated by various advantages. The leather garment is made so loose and comfortable that there is a layer of air between it and the body which nearly always retains the same temperature, be it hot as at noon or cool as at night. Moreover, the surface is smooth so that, in case a naughty buffalo or a short-tempered rhinoceros should suddenly force the wanderer to seek his safety in flight through dangerous thornbushes, only a few points of contact are offered on which could occur any of those well known rectangular tears the like of which we can observe on ordinary clothing material when we want to push quickly through rosebushes or blackberry shrubs.

A LUCKY THROW
Out in the bush, Mauch would go beyond the circle of firelight after dark with a sextant to fix his position by sighting a star.

Vega 59° 44', error + 22". Lat. 21° 29' 22" S.
During the observation I was suddenly hit on the back of my head by a burning log, so that the glowing embers shot past on both sides. One of my men who was fetching water mistook me for a large carnivore and made a lucky throw.

WILLIAM GUYBON ATHERSTONE

A man of many parts, Dr Atherstone was one of the first surgeons outside Europe to operate with an anaesthetic, using ether to amputate a leg of the deputy sheriff of Albany. He named the first dinosaur ever collected in South Africa, from a site south of Grahamstown. He also made the first identification of a diamond in the region – a 21-carat pebble found near Hopetown. In 1871 the Cape government asked him to investigate the discovery of a two-and-a-half-ounce gold nugget in the Koup, just north of the Swartberg. After visiting the site, he concluded the nugget was not from the area, and was likely dropped there by someone. But while the gold proved a disappointment, he had already found other treasures by the wayside. The Bain with him was probably Thomas, son of fellow palaeontologist Andrew Geddes Bain.

A SCREW OF THE ARK

Next morning, at early dawn, we trotted along, parallel to the range, over Devonian shales and sandstones, towards the upper end of Boschluis Kloof. Here, halting suddenly, Bain exclaimed: *"There lies the Gouph!"* and a scene burst upon us I shall not forget in a hurry. Breathless I gazed down the valley on the boundless sea of blue mountains, cones and peaks, table tops and jagged lines of hillocks, tingled with the faint blush of early morn – the huddled groups of hills in the mid-distance, still in deep shadow; with the aloes and crassulas, and fantastic rocks of the Zwarteberg on our right, and the road winding down the steep sides of the Little Zwarteberg, whose topmost crags were just painted by the glowing rays of the unseen sun. What a wild charm thrown over the distant labyrinth of hills in the soft glow of early morn! What glorious anticipations! What impatient yearning for exploration! What visions of unknown gold that first glimpse of the Gouph called up! Nuggets of the Gouph! Yes, there they lay; painted in all the glorious colours of the rainbow; a grand chromatic blending of gold and crimson and azure with the grey tints of the deep kloofs; untouched by the magic rays of sunrise, reflected from the light canopy of faint thin clouds above on the distant landscape.

"Do you see," whispered Bain, interrupting the silence, when he saw that I breathed freely again (for I must confess the unexpected view fairly took the breath out of me) – "do you see that slaty bend in the road below us, half-way down? 'Twas there some two years ago I found orthis and spir-ifers – Silurian fossils, in fact – not known by my father." Hurriedly sketch-ing the scene and the road winding down through the graves of myriads of extinct creatures of this old continent, I jumped in after him, and down we glided along an excellent road – (they all are excellent in the West) – keep-ing a sharp look-out with both eyes for fossils; and before very long, the kloof resounded with blows and shouts. "Hurrah! Hurrah!" re-echoed by Bain some distance below me; "Haw! *Haw!*" re-echoed the baboons from the mountain above us. "Goud – *now* is dat die ware goud!" shouts Hendrik, the driver, further down still, leaving his cart and bewildered horses, to hammer on his own account. What a scene of excitement! No time to breathe! Hammer and chisel, and echoing shouts of indignant baboons – trilobites, encrinites, orthides, &c. I'll not bother you, dear reader, with the romantic names of all those queer "creatures before the Flood". The sun rose higher and higher. The drops grew larger and larger, trickling down *every-where.* Paper collars "no good" for geologists, according to Hendrik; but they got stiff again, dry and crumpled. Suddenly I felt a "presence" – shad-ow overspread me. Could it be that of a vulture? No cloud was visible. I looked up from my knees, with hands full of fossils. "Wat bedui' dit" ("What does this mean?") drawled out a tall tan-coloured Boer, bending over me, with a bundle of hay which he was taking to his sick mare lower down. I looked up into his big, vacant, meaningless face. "Zoek yulle goud?" ("Are you hunting gold?") A smothered laugh almost choked me; but, dashing the big drops off that I might see the gifted stranger more clear-ly, I handed him a bit of rock with a beautiful orthis, and some small perfect trilobites, red on the grey rock. "Wat voor een ding is dat?" ("What is that?") *"Versteende bosluis"* (a fossil bush-louse), said I. "Myn magtig! en *dit* is Bosluis Kloof!" (and this is Bosluis Kloof) he wonderingly exclaimed. *"Of course,"* said I; "that is why they gave it the name. Look! here are hundreds, thousands in the rock. Here, break them out for yourself, you unbeliever!" "I see them with my eyes," he remarked; "but how did they get in the rock?" Here Bain came up and joined us. *"Jou ongeloofige schepsel!"* said he. "Don't you read your Bible? and don't you know all about the Flood and the *dieren* that were in the ark? Here, what is this?" – showing him a beautiful cast of an encrinite two or three inches long, the most perfect representation of a rusty screw that I ever saw. "That must certainly be a screw of the ark!" said he; "but magtig! *how rusty!*" "Think of the *time* elapsed since then," urged I, hammering another out of the stone for him. "Ja, dit's waar! It is wonderful –

truly incredible. Really, gentlemen, if I had not seen it with my own eyes, I would *never* have believed it!"

And off he strode with his bundle of hay.

HIS LIVING COVERLET

Atherstone undertook a winter journey to the Vaal River to examine the new diamond diggings there for himself. He was left "rather reeling and unsteady" by the extraordinary energy being expended on the search for the stones. This is an incident on the way up.

An hour before daylight I awoke, and found Britz, jun., who had shot the three springboks, melting bullets for more to convert into biltong, so I sat by the fire till daylight, listening to the story of his life, past and present, and his views of the future, and then went out in the crisp hoar-frost, white as snow, to look for our driver. I found him asleep in the sheep kraal, in the open air, a friendly angora ram lying on his chest and warm-hearted merinos cuddling over and round him! He jumped up from under his living coverlet, and began to dress. "What; take off your clothes on a night like this!" said I, perfectly astonished. It was really the fact; he had used *them* as a pillow, so the sheep got the warmth of *his* body and he got *theirs*, as he lay on his "hotbed" in the warm sheep kraal like a very cold cucumber.

WITH AN AUDIBLE CRACK

At the Du Toit's Pan diggings, just south of what was to become the Kimberley mine.

I jumped off my table just before sunrise (I sleep on the shop-board on a bale of blankets). On opening the door, a grand Russian snow scene astounds me, the sun rising pale through the lurid frost-haze, everything looks jaundiced and ghastly. A frozen flag, trying to fly, snaps in two with an audible crack in the wret[c]hed attempt; my vapoury breath obscures my sight; the basin is frozen all over in my iron bedroom, and ice an inch thick floats in the casks outside. A black fellow passing tells me the vlei is all solid; he has just run over it (he comes, he says, from the 'bovenland,' and has never seen solid water before: "Machtig, dat's wonderlyk"!) The digger heaps look like snow hummocks – frosted and frozen; the disselbooms, sides, and tents of the wagons opposite, and the beards of the burly Boers, their quaint red night-caps and thick warm wraps, and everything else, all sparkle with minute frost icicles; and fellows in cosey karosses, and

shivering females grouped round the fires, with the steam of the viands seeming as if it would freeze before leaving the dish, but no smoke visible! The scene to the south is still more extraordinary: the glassy lake, or 'pan,' and the vlei and indistinct trees, looking like smoke through the haze and the lurid glare of the frost-fog. Far colder inside these iron houses than out, for the sun is out and blinking, so I run outside to warm and watch the digger world melt down in the sunshine.

A DESERTER

This document was found among the papers of a British army colonel, Henry Stabb, when he died at Pietermaritzburg in 1888. It is a copy in his own hand of what purports to be a letter written by a deserter from the 32nd Light Infantry, to a friend in the regiment. Stabb would likely have seen the original when he was a captain in the 32nd, stationed in the Eastern Cape in the early 1870s.

I LAUGH NOW

On board the royal mail packet roman for Southampton St. Helena Dec 12 1871 Dear Companion I take the opportunity of writing to you which I have almost been afraid to do before for obvious reasons. I presume that you got the benefit of the doubt when you deserted with me.

I am very sorry that you had not the good luck to come the second time with me and share the good fortune that I am sharing now. I will just give you a brief outline of my career as near as possible.

Deserted from King W[illiam's Town], tramped up to the Vaal river, had no money or friends when I got there and had no money to start anything. I got sick and in with bad company chiefly deserters from the same corps. Tracked away from the Vaal river on the 4th of January along with Duffield, Haslitt and Wakefield. I was sick with the deysentery, hungry, dirty, ragged, penniless and lousey, the remainder ditto. Joined the Jackobsdal police on the 7th of January, the three others went on, that is the last I saw of any of them.

I could see that honesty would never prosper so I determined to dispense with that altogether. I got the name of been steady and industrious during the two months I stopped there and the shopkeepers would trust me to any amount. I run up a debt of £21 then I cleared out with my 2 months wages and all the money I had earned as well at well sinking and brickmaking. I deserted of[f] beat with a fine Colts revolver and a buls eye, and let a Kaffir out prison to carry my blankets. £20 reward was offered for my apprenison but it was all no use. I walked a hundred miles across a flat to a place called Sivonelle, commenced digging but had no luck, got charge of a veld at Sivonelle to ride about on horseback and put all the stray cattle in the pound and I got so much a head for them. Rode off altogether with the horse and 12 fat oxen into Alhama district, Waterboer's terrytorry and exchanged them for sheep. Sent the sheep to the fields for sale. Spent the money digging at Cawoods hope, no luck, tramped about the Free State, took a well to sink for £50, worked at it a fortnight. The family went away 80 miles to what they call knockmoll [nagmaal] at Boshoff. As soon as he had gone I jamped 16 of his best horses and rode them 4 hundred miles up in the Transvaal and sold them at very fair prices, and I never looked behind me since. Now I am clearing out with at the least 5 thousand pounds when all my diamonds is sold. I am a first class passenger on board the roman. You will see my name in the papers on board the roman Mr. Goddard. I took your name that is all I got belonging to you. I got some portraits took in Wellington on purpose to send you and I have lost them out of my portmanteau, but Ill get some more took in England or America where I am going shortly and send them to you.

I have improved in health as much as in wealth. I am over 13 stone now and my head is not swelled so much as it was. I laugh now and say to myself no more third watches along with bet, no more bad soup dinners, no more linering cots with Ohara, no more running home to barracks at eight with my trowsers unbuttoned after giving a girl the last four pence and not a penny left for butter in the morning, no more clean shirt parades on Sunday morning, no more paradeing again at retreat for not clean shave, no more pack drill for going sick without a cause when your half dead. I am thinking at spending a few summer months in America at some flash watering place. I have been very lucky digging of late, I have found nearly a 100 diamonds the largest 30 carats …

REPORT OF THE SELECT COMMITTEE

This committee of the Natal legislature was set up to look at the question of native labour from beyond the borders of the colony. It reported back in 1872, proposing measures to make the overland journey less hazardous, and to regulate transport by sea from Delagoa Bay. The committee also expressed the view that it was a Good Thing for members of a "barbarous community" to have contact with civilisation as labourers, as it would elevate their ideas, and those of their tribes when they returned home.

BY LAND AND BY SEA

It happens with most countries that when the necessity for additional labour arises, the source of supply is distant, and the means of procuring it both tedious and expensive; but Natal is a remarkable exception to this general condition, because it is almost surrounded by native tribes, and the area of its chief labour supply, outside of itself, extends from its northern boundary to the Zambezi River.

3. The inhabitants of this immense region are estimated at several millions, and among them all, the Government and the people of Natal are held in the highest respect.

4. We know from the testimony of European travellers, and from such of the natives themselves as are enterprising enough to seek, unaided, a field for their industry in this Colony, that among large masses of this population, there exists not only willingness but anxiety for the opportunity of earning money in Natal; and if further evidence were wanted on this subject, we have it in the fact that considerable numbers of them do come annually to Natal, both by land and by sea, of their own free will, and that after a stay of one-and-a-half or two years, they leave with the results of their labours, to return to their homes. We also know that no inconsiderable proportion of those who make the attempt over land, with their scanty sup-

ply of food, and still more scanty covering, die annually on their way to Natal from starvation and exposure.

5. There is also the significant fact that parties of these people return to the same masters after two or three years' of absence, and that they are sometimes found to have carefully preserved, and to bring back with them, the passes which those masters gave them when they started on their journey homewards; showing that, in their experience at least, those unofficial and legally valueless papers were useful in contributing to their safe conduct; and no one can estimate the importance this shows to be attached to such documents, who are ignorant of the trouble it costs to preserve from speedy destruction a piece of paper in a native hut on the East Coast of Africa.

6. Then we have the recent and still more remarkable development that on the expiration of their term of service, parties of laborers sometimes select two or three of their number, and entrust them with the bulk of the earnings of the whole party in gold, to return with it by ship, while the main body finds its way home overland.

EMIL HOLUB

Holub, a Czechoslovakian doctor, ethnographer and naturalist, had been stirred since boyhood with a desire to explore Africa. He set up a medical practice in Kimberley to finance an expedition that took him as far as the fever-ridden upper reaches of the Zambezi. He returned to Europe in 1879 with a collection including 18,000 insects, thousands of dried plants, fossils, skulls and horns, bird skins, mineral and marine specimens, various "anatomical or pathological curiosities", and live animals including small buck, tame jackals, a baboon, a lynx, two eagles, a secretary bird and a vulture. In addition, he had artefacts from about 30 tribes, including San rock engravings from the northern Cape. A second venture six years later, with the aim of traversing the continent from the Cape to Cairo, ended north of the Zambezi when two of his European companions died of malaria, his porters deserted, and local people destroyed his camp and 14 of his 32 volumes of journals. Holub still made it back to Europe with another 130 cases of specimens. He spent the last years of his life battling malaria and sciatica, and bitter about what he thought was a complete lack of understanding of his work. He died in poverty in 1902.

Holub: "Easter Sunday in the Vaal River."

SUCH A TREMENDOUS POKE

Holub is here paying a call on the Kwena chief Sethšele, whom the hunter Frederick Selous, after being served tea from a silver pot and china cups a year earlier, described as "the most completely civilised Kafir that I had yet seen". Sethšele had been Livingstone's only convert to Christianity, foreswearing all wives but one to qualify as a true believer. Livingstone was devastated when he discovered the chief had lapsed, and that one of the abandoned women was pregnant. Sethšele showed Holub and his companions into a

271

drawing room furnished with chairs and couches of walnut with red velvet uphol-
stery, then to an adjoining room for the tea ceremony.

The dining-room table was handsome, and covered with a white cloth. Tea was served in cups shaped like little bowls. The king swallowed at least a quart. The sugar basin, cream-jug, and the rest of the service were placed upon a side-table; they were all of silver, being, as I understood, a present from the merchants who made periodical visits to Molopolole. The tea was good, and the cakes unexceptionable.

There was now a renewal of the conversation that had commenced in the drawing-room, and I was catechised about the proceedings of the English Government in the diamond-fields, and those of the Dutch Government in Pretoria and Bloemfontein. The queen clearly had no interest in these subjects, and gradually resumed the nap which had been interrupted by our arrival. Sechele appeared a little vexed at her breach of etiquette, and attempted to rouse her by some spasmodic coughs, which became more violent at each repetition. Failing, however, to awaken her from her slumber, which every moment grew more sonorous, he stealthily gave her such pushes with his elephantine foot that I had the hardest matter to keep from bursting out laughing.

Controlling myself as well as I could, I said, "Morena, when I was only thirteen years old, I read your name in Nyaka Livingstone's book. I little thought that I should ever see you and speak to you: far more surprising is it to me to find myself drinking tea in your palace."

The king, although he still practised rain-magic, had become familiar with some passages of Scripture, and said, with a sanctimonious air, "His ways are past finding out."

But while Mr. Williams had been interpreting what I said to him, he had kept one eye fixed on his wife; and, observing to his disgust that she was almost falling from her seat in her drowsiness, he only waited until he thought I was not watching him, to give her such a tremendous poke, that she had a narrow escape of knocking her cup off the table with her forehead.

OUR AMAZEMENT WAS GREAT
At the Victoria Falls.

On the evening before our departure we had an adventure with a lion, which terminated in a way that was somewhat amusing. I had returned from an expedition to the falls, and was followed by Walsh, who was coming back from one of his bird-hunts; he came in rather excited, declaring that in crossing a meadow on his way towards the river, he had seen a lion. The spot which he described was only about three-quarters of a mile away, and it did not require a very long consultation before we resolved forthwith to commence a lion-hunt. I confess I was not a little concerned when I heard that the ladies proposed to accompany us; but my objections were soon overruled, Mrs. Francis urging that she had already seen several lions killed, and Mrs. Westbeech, the bride of a few months, insisting that her husband should not go without her.

The greater part of the Zambesi valley is thickly wooded, but as I have described, there are occasional tracts of meadow, almost bare of trees, bordered towards the stream by hedges of saro-palms. It had been in coming over one of these that Walsh had seen the lion spring from behind a tree, and disappear into the palm-thicket. On reaching the tree we found another tree close beside it, only about fifteen feet high, against the stem of which a pyramidal ant-hill had been erected.

We lost little time in making our arrangements; we divided into four detachments, the first including Westbeech, Francis, Walsh, and myself; the second, Oppenshaw, Bauren, and two of the Cape servants; the third, two more Cape servants, and two Matabele with guns; whilst the fourth was made up of the rest of the servants, who were armed with assegais, kiris, and sticks. The three former detachments were to march upon the thicket from opposite directions; the fourth was to remain at a distance outside to give warning of any movement they should see.

Hardly had we gone ten yards towards the assault, when the ladies' voices brought us to a stand; they had come to the conclusion that they were unsafe beneath the tree, and requested their husbands to help them on to the top of the ant-hill.

Again we started, proceeding very slowly and with much caution. Just as we got within a few feet of the palm-bushes we were startled by a tremendous roar, sonorous enough to try the nerves of the most experienced hunter, and to make him realize the essential difference between a *felis leo* and a *felis domestica*. The hero of the forest was so close to Francis, that it might easily have pounced upon him before we could render any assistance.

We stood still and gazed upon the bush, but no lion could be seen. Some one suggested it might be prudent to retire a little, and everybody seemed ready enough to act upon the suggestion; accordingly, with our guns cocked and our eyes fixed upon the spot from which the roar had proceeded, we stepped gradually backwards; still no signs of the lion; we resolved to fire, but we fired in vain; we determined to set light to the bush, but all to no purpose; the lion had escaped.

On turning round to look for the other detachments, we discovered that the sound of the roaring had thrown them into a state of dismay; some of them had disappeared entirely; the whole of the fourth company had climbed up into the trees.

The lion expected.

Just at this moment our attention was arrested by another cry from the ladies; the wind had fanned the flames of the bushes to which we had set light, and the smoke was driving so densely towards them that they were in danger of being choked; we soon rescued them from their unpleasant situation, and were all but agreed to give up the chase, and to go back again to our camp.

Westbeech, however, made the proposition that the hunt should be continued higher up the river; he was an experienced and daring hunter, and perhaps

273

was a little anxious to exhibit his capabilities to his young wife. In order to carry out the proposal, it would be necessary to cross the meadow over which Walsh had been passing when he first saw the lion. After some hesitation it was settled that the party should undertake a second chase, with the exception of Mrs. Westbeech, who was left in charge of some of the Matabele servants, who were quite content to undertake so pleasant a part of the enterprise.

But although we crossed the meadow, we did not arrive at the bushes; startled by a cry of distress we looked back, but no trace of Mrs. Westbeech could be seen. Our amazement was great; Westbeech himself was the first to recover his composure, and started back with all speed to ascertain what had happened; we followed after, but what was our surprise, when all at once found that he too had disappeared! We did not notice that the Matabele were in fits of laughter, nor for a while could we understand what Francis, who had run on some way in front, could mean when he turned round and threw his gun upon the grass before our feet, and bade us stop. In another moment Westbeech emerged from under ground, and directly afterwards Mrs. Westbeech reappeared after the same fashion. The explanation of the mystery was not hard to find. The natives had dug pitfall after pitfall to catch game; having no guns, they make great holes in the ground, sometimes ten or twelve feet long and nearly as many deep, so much narrower at the top than at the bottom, that it is impossible for any animals to get out when once in. Into one of these Mrs. Westbeech had had the mischance to fall, and Mr. Westbeech, in his eagerness, had run into another.

Beyond a few scratches, the lady happily had sustained no injury, but the *contretemps* naturally had the effect of making us abandon all further thought of the chase.

As for the lion, we were informed by some Batokas who came to visit us as usual in the evening, that it was quite true that one was lurking in the neighbourhood; but it was so accustomed to human beings that it gave no cause for anxiety, and the natives were not afraid to pass it, even at night.

SUFFICIENTLY STARTLING

Finding that the Limpopo was only three feet deep just below its confluence with the Marico, I determined to make my way across. We felled several

stout mimosa stems, and made a raft; but the new wood was so heavy that under my weight it sank two feet into the water. Convinced that my experiment was a failure, I was springing from one side of the raft on to the shore, when a crocodile mounted the other side – an apparition sufficiently startling to make me give up the idea of crossing for the present.

I MAY RECOMMEND A FEW LOCUSTS

I had an opportunity during our short stay here of tasting the favourite national dish. Some Batlapins were passing through the place, and were roasting some locusts over red-hot ashes. As soon as they were sufficiently cooked, a good many of the men took them and devoured them entire; others pulled off the feet and the wings; the more fastidious stayed to take out the insides, and it was in this condition that they were offered to us. After partaking of the luxury, I think I may recommend a few locusts to any *gourmand* who, surfeited with other delicacies, requires a dish of peculiar piquancy; in flavour I should consider them not unlike a dried and strongly-salted Italian anchovy. It is only the true South African locust that is available for the purpose of food. I found that I could make a good use of them as fishing-bait, and that they answered much better than earth-worms.

Andrew Smith said roasted locusts tasted like "a piece of half-burnt paper".

TRULY FEARING THE WORST
An episode recounted to Holub by a Rolong chief whose name the explorer gives as "Shebor".

A party of natives were on their way from Maraba, in the Makalaka country, to the diamond-fields, a distance of 800 miles. It was by no means unusual for such parties to quit their homes with simply a hide and an assegai, quite prepared, during their long and arduous journey, to live on nothing but roots, wild fruit, and occasionally a small head of game. The spectacle they would present to any traveller who might meet them was very piteous. Sometimes they would be almost destitute of food of any sort for days together, and be reduced well-nigh to skeletons. Their progress would become more and more painful; and they would endeavour to mitigate the pangs of hunger by drawing in the waist-bands which with a strip of hide formed clothing. The ordinary custom was for them to travel in single file, the strongest first, then the less robust, followed by the weakest; so that an invalid would often be quite by himself, a long way in the rear. In the party of which the chief was speaking there were two brothers, one of whom, on account of his feeble condition of health, had for more than a week been obliged to take his place last in the procession. Arriving at the bank of the Sitlagole, the party halted to search for some roots, not unlike turnips, which were known to grow there, and which they hoped to cook and enjoy for supper. They found the roots in such abundance that it was resolved to spend the night on the spot, and they kindled a fire to prepare their meal. On closing in, it was soon ascertained that the sick comrade was missing. They looked at each other with much perplexity; but the brother of the absent man, without losing a moment, snatched up his own and his brother's share of the roots that had been gathered, fastened them to a strap upon his shoulder, seized his assegai, and started off. The rest drew closer in, enjoyed their supper, lighted up several additional fires as a protection from attack, and laid themselves down under the bushes to sleep.

The missing Bechuana was a Batloka, and the evidence went to show that the poor fellow had been compelled to rest so often and so long from his weakness, hunger, and sore feet, that he had fallen far into the rear, and, missing his way, had strayed into a rocky valley full of bushes that were notoriously the haunt of lions. Here no doubt he had been pounced upon and killed, for the brother had not gone far before he could trace the spot where the

A second victim.

proper path had been left, and proceeding onwards he soon observed a lion's footprints in the sand. Instead of turning back, he had apparently caught sight of his brother's stick, straw hat, and gourd bottle, lying on the ground, and, trusting to his assegai, had resolved to venture on alone.

"But what was an assegai," exclaimed Shebor, "in the face of a lion who had just tasted human blood?"

It was clear that before he reached his brother's corpse the lion had sprung from its concealment, and secured him as a second victim.

Finding next morning that both the men were absent the whole party was in consternation, too truly fearing the worst. They applied for help at a Barolong farm close at hand, and, following the tracks, were not long in discovering the two mangled bodies close to each other. The marks on the ground were quite distinct, and left no doubt that a lion had just quitted the spot. Probably it had only been scared away by their own approach, and they determined to continue their chase. After they had made their way for about 500 yards along the bank, they caught sight of a tawny object in a thicket just ahead. They hardly dared to hope that it was the creature of which they were in pursuit; but simultaneously a number of them fired, and great was their triumph when they discovered amongst the bushes the carcass of a huge lion pierced by six bullets.

ANDREW ANDERSON

Anderson was a well-meaning soul – he once put a frog out of its misery after hearing it give "almost a scream" as it was impaled on a thorn by a butcher-bird – but his 1887 book Twenty-Five Years in a Waggon *is sadly uninspired. He was at one time a magistrate at the Cape.*

HOT AS CAN BE WISHED
In the colony it is open; no trees, scanty grass, and an immense open rocky country, so that the stones become so hot that they destroy the boots. I have frequently made my tea by placing the kettle with water on a stone for half an hour; then put in the tea, let it stand a few minutes, and it is as strong and hot as can be wished.

FREDERICK SELOUS

Selous, son of a chairman of the London Stock Exchange, began hunting ivory north of the Limpopo in 1872 and led the pioneer column that spearheaded white settlement in Rhodesia. A true colonial visionary, he wanted to see Mashonaland become a "rich and prosperous portion of the British Empire", and believed the

276

Shona should be carefully protected "for they are the people who will supply the native labour that will be so necessary in the future development of Mashunaland". At the end of his book A Hunter's Wanderings he devotes five pages to lists of the animals he shot. Some people, he acknowledges, might consider this a "dreadful record of slaughter", but he says it has to be remembered that he was often accompanied by not only his own employees, but a "crowd of hungry savages", all of whom depended on him for food. One of his own favourite dishes was roast elephant's heart "nicely salted and peppered". Selous realised what relentless hunting was doing to the herds, but was unable to turn back. "Elephants are … now so scarce, that one cannot afford to leave even smallish ones alone," he wrote in 1878. Recalling his shooting of two white rhino in 1882, he says they were probably the last of their kind he would ever see. "Some few white rhinoceroses no doubt still survive, but it is not too much to say that long before the close of this century the white rhinoceros will have vanished from the face of the earth. I hope my readers will pardon this long digression, but the subject of the extinction of this huge quadruped has a melancholy interest for me, when I remember that, twenty years ago, it was a common animal over an enormous extent of country in Central South Africa." Surviving a trampling from an elephant cow in the same year, and service in the Ndebele War of 1893 and the "rebellion" of 1896, he was killed in 1917 during a First World War engagement with German forces in East Africa, where, at the age of 65, he was serving as a lieutenant in the British army.

THAT'S NO HYMN
When I first went out to South Africa I used to play a little Bavarian instrument – the zither – and I kept up my playing for many years, and when travelling through the Transvaal my musical talents used to keep me in butter, milk, and eggs. When we outspanned near a Boer farm, Edwin Miller, a young colonist who was usually with me, and who was thoroughly at home with the Boers, used to go up to the house, and in the course of conversation ask the goodwife if she was fond of music, and then tell her about my little instrument, when of course I was asked to play, and my pathetic Bavarian airs used to be much appreciated, and the old illustrated Bible was usually brought down, and the drawing of the "Harp that David played" compared to my zither; and then I was offered milk, eggs, butter, and fresh bread if it was baking day. Miller, at my suggestion, always brought up an immense bucket for the milk, with many apologies because we had nothing smaller; for the goodwives in the Transvaal do not care about parting with much fresh milk as they want it for butter-making. However, if you bring up a big bucket, they are obliged to pour a good deal in to make any kind of show at all. Once we came to a farm on a Sunday morning, and Miller at once tried to open negotiations for obtaining milk and fresh butter. The ladies were most anxious to hear the music, but the old Boer had scruples of conscience, it being Sunday, and it was only when Miller pointed out that my zither was the same instrument as the harp that David used to play that he consented to have it brought up to the house. When I had tuned it up he insisted that nothing must be played but hymns; so I played him the Danube Waltz, and noticing his astonishment, assured him that it was a French hymn. He seemed puzzled, but only muttered that it did not sound like a hymn. I then played him "Il bacio," when he jumped

277

up, and striking his hand on the table, said, "Nay, verdommt, daats geen Psaum niet, daats en yodlepijp" ("No, damn it, that's no hymn, that's a horn-pipe"). With the help of the ladies of his family we persuaded him that it was an Italian hymn, and he took all the rest quietly, and his wife and daughters set us up again in butter, milk, and eggs.

Kafirs walk in front
Along the banks of the river about here we found that the natives had dug a great number of pitfalls, about ten feet in depth, to entrap hip-popotami, elephants, or buffaloes, which, being always placed in the pathways made by these animals, and neatly covered over with dry grass, are most difficult to detect, even when one knows there are such things about; but the unconscious traveller, ignorant of anything of the sort, is almost sure to be engulfed in one of them sooner or later. This happened to two of our party, neither of whom, luckily, was in any way hurt, after which we adopted the plan of letting one of the Kafirs walk in front, who gave us due notice of their whereabouts, by either uncovering them with an assegai or falling into them, an example which we were, of course, careful not to follow.

Torn in three pieces
Selous' companion Clarkson encountered a herd of nine elephant bulls and shot three, but one of the African gun-bearers did not return to camp that evening. Selous recounts what followed in Clarkson's words.

"At break of day I left camp, and riding straight to where I had shot the first elephant, took up the spoor of the tuskless bull, and had followed it for maybe two miles when I came to a place where he had stood under a tree amongst some dense underwood. From this place he had spun suddenly round, as the spoor showed, and made a rush through the bush, breaking and smashing everything before him. Fifty yards farther on we found Qabeet's gun, a little beyond this a few odds and ends of skin that he had worn round his waist, and then what remained of the poor fellow himself. He had been torn in three pieces; the chest, with head and arms attached, which had been wrenched from the trunk just below the breast-bone, lying in one place, one leg and thigh that had been torn off at the pelvis in another, and the remainder in a third. The right arm had been broken in two places and the hand crushed; one of the thighs was also broken, but otherwise the fragments had not been trampled on." There is little doubt [says Selous] that the infuriated elephant must have pressed the unfortunate man down with his foot or knee, and then twisting his trunk round his body wrenched him asunder.

THE HORRORS OF THAT JOURNEY
According to Selous, Lobengula sent two cattle-raiding expeditions across the for-biddingly arid country east of the Kalahari to Lake Ngami – a 1,300-kilometre round trip, for those who made it back. The raids seem to have been carried out in the 1880s.

The second expedition sent by Lo Bengula to Lake Ngami was a most disastrous one. The Batauwani got information concerning the impending attack from some Bushmen, and had time to remove all their women and children, and to drive all their cattle to beyond the Botletli river. They then lay in ambush amongst the reeds which fringed the river's bank, and awaited their foes, and when they appeared gave them a very warm reception with their breech-loading rifles. Many of the Matabili were shot, including Pulinglela, one of the king's brothers, and many other men of note. Many more were drowned in trying to cross the Botletli, on a bed of water-plants, which grew so thickly on the surface of the river in one place that they thought it would support their weight. Possibly the thickly-growing vegetation might have supported the weight of a few men at a time, but as the bold attempt was made by a large number at once, their united weight broke through the bed of weeds, and they were all precipitated into deep water, where many of them being unable to swim were drowned. Baffled and beaten, the marauders had now to commence their retreat to their own country through four hundred miles of desert, under the most disadvantageous circumstances. As is usual, they had only brought with them a sufficient number of cattle to serve as food during the time occupied by the journey from Matabililand to Lake Ngami. Once there, it was their business to capture and take back to their king the flocks and herds of their enemies – a certain number of which would have been slaughtered every evening for their consumption. On this occasion they did not capture a single animal, and with starvation staring them in the face, commenced their long march homewards.

The horrors of that journey have often been described to me by survivors. A few head of game were shot, and a few Bushman encampments were looted, but many hundreds of Lo Bengula's fiercest warriors died from starvation, thirst, and exhaustion on their return from this disastrous expedition. Towards the end of the journey ever-increasing numbers died daily round every pool of water on the line of march. Parched with thirst, and exhausted with starvation and fatigue, they would lie flat down and drink their fill, and day after day, I have been told, numbers died in this position. Only the remnant of the army got back to Matabililand, and of the fine regiment of the "Intembi" but few survived to tell the tale of their unsuccessful raid to Lake Ngami.

AS IF CARVED IN STONE
Elephant spoor.

I had followed it for some distance, and had got about a hundred yards beyond a sort of pass, between a rocky ridge on the one hand and a mass of large granite boulders on the other, when I came face to face with one of the elephants, a large cow, coming straight back towards me on the spoor

279

of the herd she had left. The forest was very open about here, and she saw me as soon as I saw her, and, raising her head and spreading her ears, charged forthwith, screaming loudly. Turning my horse I galloped back for the rocks, but the stallion would not put out any pace, and I could tell from the screams that the elephant was gaining rapidly upon me.

Hastily turning my head I saw she was getting very near, and knew she would soon catch me; so I resolved to dismount and run for the rocks. My stallion was, in some respects, a perfect shooting horse, and immediately I leant forward and seized his mane he stopped dead. I was off and in front of him in an instant, and running for the rocks, which were not twenty yards away. As I got round the first rock I turned, and this is what I saw. The horse was standing absolutely still, with his head up and his fore feet planted firmly in the ground, as if carved in stone, and the elephant, which had then ceased to scream, and was making a curious rumbling noise, was standing alongside of him, smelling about with her trunk. In front of my saddle was tied a leather coat, with a red flannel lining – a present the preceding year from my friend poor Montagu Kerr – and I suppose that the elephant must have touched the horse with her trunk, as he suddenly gave a jump round, throwing the red-lined coat into the air. He then walked slowly to the rocky ridge behind him, and again stood still about fifteen yards away from the elephant. All this time I had been afraid to fire, for fear of exasperating the elephant, and causing it to kill my horse. I now, however, determined to do so, and was thinking of firing for her brain, for she was very near me, when she raised her head and ears and came towards the rocks screaming like a railway engine. She must have got my wind, I fancy, suddenly. However, she could not get at me without going round the other rocks; and as she did so, she gave me a splendid chance at a distance of not more than fifteen yards. I fired into the centre of her shoulder, and immediately the bullet struck her she stopped screaming, and, dropping her ears, swerved off. She only ran a hundred yards or so, and then fell over dead, shot through the large blood-vessels of the upper part of the heart.

FRANK OATES

Oates was a wealthy young English traveller and amateur naturalist who journeyed to Matabeleland in 1873. He reached the Victoria Falls on the last day of 1874, but died of fever only weeks later. His natural history collections were given to the British Museum and Oxford University. They included six skulls that Oates collected with some difficulty from the site of an Ndebele massacre of San. His posthumously published journals include a detailed scientific paper by an Oxford anatomy professor on the skulls, with useful observations such as that their average capacity was 1,285 cubic centimetres "as against 1485 cub. cent. obtained by Professor Flower for the cubage of seven Caffres and Zulus".

MEETING A SMALL TORTOISE

As we travel through the bush Indian file, returning to the waggon, Echle (the chief hunter I have with me), meeting a small tortoise, picks it up, spits on it, and puts it to his forehead. He says this is lucky when you want to get elephants, and he says, however large the tortoise is, this is done. He is then allowed to walk off.

SUCH A WOUND

… the dogs began to bark late one night, and a man appeared at the fire in a miserable plight. He was a rebellious induna, or headman, whom the king had ordered to be killed. There are a certain number of indunas, who have certain districts given them to rule over under the king, and if they presume too much on their authority they are put to death without much trial. Some of them would be insufferable in their conduct to white men if the king did not keep them in order. This particular man, I believe, the king had given fair warning to, and told him to take a horse and fly the country, but instead of taking one he took two, and he was brought before the king, who thought it best to make an end of the matter. They took him outside the town, and hacked him with their axes, leaving him for dead. What must have been intended for the *coup de grâce* was a cut in the back of the head, which had chipped a large piece out of the skull, and must have been meant to cut the spinal cord where it joins the brain. It had, however, been made a little higher than this, but had left such a wound as I should have thought no one could have survived. It is wonderful, however, how hard Kafirs are. When I held the lanthorn to investigate the wound I started back in amazement to see a hole at the base of the skull, perhaps two inches long and an inch and a half wide, and I will not venture to say how deep, but the depth too must have been an affair of inches. Of course this hole penetrated into the substance of the brain, and probably for some distance. I dare say a mouse could have sat in it.

His voice was weak, but he evidently enjoyed his supper and the warmth of the fire. My boys said he was a "wolf" – the term applied to outlaws – and that he ought to be killed or driven away. He told me that it was five days since he had been set upon; and that, after he had been left for dead, he got up and ran away on coming to himself. He wanted to go under my protection to the Zambesi, an honour, however, which I declined, but I gave him a blanket and some things to buy food with, and told him he must go next morning, and advised him to make for Mungwato. He asked for a pipe, and for a drink of brandy, which reminded me of Old King Cole; and if he had been given to amusing himself by listening to the violin, I have no doubt he would have asked for a tune, as he seemed disposed to take things very philosophically. I poured some arnica and water into the hole, and when he lifted up his head a perfect stream of it ran down

his back. He said if he was not killed he should see me at Mungwato when I returned. I believe he did reach Mungwato alive, but I don't know whether he remained there.

The induna was seen the following year living near Rustenburg in the Transvaal, apparently in perfect health.

GUSTAF DE VYLDER

De Vylder was a Swedish draughtsman and self-taught naturalist who at the age of 43 managed to raise finances for a collecting trip to present-day Namibia. One of his aims on the expedition, which began in March 1873 and lasted two years, was to "get a Bushman child". This wish was fulfilled when a trader at Omaruru in Namibia gave him an orphaned boy, about seven years old, for whom he had bartered a rifle. The child had been renamed Joseph, and the next day De Vylder was already referring to him as "my son" and sewing European-style clothing for him. A month later he turned down an opportunity to buy a San girl of the same age from a Herero. "[He] wanted me to buy her for a double-barrelled gun, but I wanted to give only a rifled musket," he said. De Vylder took his adored Joseph back to Sweden, but the child contracted tuberculosis on the voyage and died five years later. De Vylder's own parents divorced when he was only about six years old, and his father died when he was 12. He never married.

DO YOU COME TO DESTROY US?
The "natives" were Khoikhoi on the banks of the Orange River.

In the afternoon we looked at natives dancing to the music of reeds into which they blow. The women sing and the words, translated, mean: "My friend, from where do you come? Do you come to destroy us? From where do you come?"

BUT HE IS AN ENGLISHMAN
De Vylder's mounting irritation with the English trader Bingle and his bulldog was spread over three months of entries, which I have condensed here. Bingle was taking a load of goods to Ovamboland, and De Vylder agreed, sight unseen, to accompany him. Bingle was not in a good mood when he arrived at their rendezvous in Otjimbingwe. During the trip up from Walvis Bay he had quarrelled with Basters living along the way, one of whom had almost bitten off his thumb.

18 July 1873, Friday
... Our first goal is Omaruru, a journey of 4 days. Our equipment for several months on the road where there will not be anywhere to buy provisions

is a leg of mutton, some bottles of sauce, various jams, a little rice and flour, as well as sugar, coffee, and tea. When I remarked that we should have taken sheep and goats for slaughter, Mr Bingle replied that we did not need any provisions as he was going to shoot so much large game that we would have plenty to eat …

6 August 1873, Wednesday
… We left this watering-place at 9 o'clock after Mr Bingle had shot a dove, his first kill since our departure from Otjimbingwe. We stopped at 1 o'clock to prepare our midday meal and continued our journey at 2 o'clock. In the afternoon we saw first a flock of guinea-fowl but one of the men missed; shortly afterwards a steenbok came within range and Mr B. wanted to take it, but instead of shooting, he started to run after it and thus frightened it away. When I asked him why he had not shot, he said that he had only one cartridge along and therefore wanted to come within closer range …

7 August 1873, Thursday
… Still further on I saw four ostriches, one male and three females, but I thought it best to wait for the wagon. It soon came and the people were sent out, and set about it so well that they killed a female and chased the others towards the vicinity of the wagons where all three passed at a distance of 50 paces from Mr B. but, as with the buck the previous day, instead of standing still and shooting he started running after them …

13 August 1873, Wednesday
… We halted for the night. Mr B. had seen and, as usual, had missed a couple of gemsbok.

14 August 1873, Thursday
… We have in part merely crossed the veld without following any track and made a new track on the advice of the Bushmen. This departure from our plan is because some Hottentots have led Mr B. to believe that the Bushmen have many feathers that he can get at a good price. I am convinced that this is just one of their usual tricks, and I have told Mr B. this, but he is an Englishman and because of that he does not understand anything. Mr B. has a filtering apparatus but now that we need it, he cannot find it. During the first day's hunting he also lost all his keys. I am already starting to regret that I accompanied him on this journey as it now seems that the entire undertaking will become a big farce …

24 August 1873, Sunday
… Mr Bingle, Mr Brooks, and Grote Klas rode ahead to do the shooting. Mr Bingle first missed a crane. Then they chased two gemsbok and Mr Bingle became so excited that he did not hear what the others said to him. He rode right up to the gemsbok, so close that he said he could have put his rifle right against them, but to be sure he dismounted, and while doing so the gemsbok ran away. Now he fired and a peculiar thing happened – the bullet went exactly between the two gemsbok …
  On Saturday one of our Hottenots had shot a steenbok which was hung

in a tree after it had been skinned. In the night a strange dog came and took the buck, which had been hung too low. Mr Bingle's bull-dog Nelson woke up and chased away the strange dog. Now Mr Nelson considered the buck to be his by rights as he had saved it from the jaws of the thief, and started to eat it. People sleeping close by woke up and wanted to retrieve the buck, but Nelson chased them away also, and in the morning there were no more than a few bones left. Our dogs have literally nothing to eat and we and our people do not have much more …

31 August 1873, Sunday
… Mr Bingle has been unwell since we entered the land of the Bushmen. He spends most of the time lying in the wagon and taking medicines, now one, now another, without knowing what his illness actually is or what effect the medications will have. This way of using medicines is utterly English …

3 September 1873, Wednesday
… We left Sissekab at midday. Mr Brooks and Mr Bingle went ahead to hunt and Mr Brooks shot a "pou", the skin of which I received. When they returned, I wanted to take the shot out of Mr Bingle's breech-loader so that there should not be an accident because he throws his gun down anywhere, but found that his gun was not loaded. He had been hunting all afternoon with an unloaded gun …

17 September 1873, Wednesday
… In the afternoon one of our Hottentots shot a zebra and Mr Hake shot another one. Mr Bingle accompanied them on horseback, fell off the horse just as he came within range of a herd of zebra, fired three shots at them and missed, his horse ran away with the zebras, and he returned on foot later on and looked very abashed. Thus ended the hunt.

RECOVERED SO WELL
The return journey from Ovamboland was not easy. This entry is from a Sunday, when the travellers were resting after a 23-hour trek made in a desperate bid to reach water. The women mentioned here were travelling with the wagons in the hope of sharing the spoils of the hunt.

Since last evening when we came on to the Okasima Plain, we did not see our Damara women until this afternoon. On arrival at the plain one of them had given birth to a boy and this was why they had dropped behind. The mother had recovered so well that she could walk across the plain carrying a child on her back and a quite heavy load on her head.

THE HUNTER DISMOUNTS
It is considered that a good horse will be able to run down ten ostriches in the hunting-season; if you wish

to shoot the ostriches, you can kill still more while on horseback. Generally the bird is not shot while on horseback, but you let it run until its strength is exhausted and it falls down, unable to rise again when the hunter rides up to it. It lies with its neck stretched out on the ground, the hunter dismounts, and gives the ostrich a blow on the head with the thick end of his riding-crop, which kills the bird. He then cuts off its wings and tail, pulls off the skin from back and stomach, then ties the back and stomach skins, wings and tail to his saddle, and returns with his booty. The carcass is generally left where the bird has fallen. Neither horse nor man can endure to kill more than one ostrich a day. By running down the ostrich in this manner, you avoid getting the feathers bloody which always reduces their value.

I WAS NOW UNBENDING

At this moment one of my herders came and sat down on the wagon without having his rifle with him. I asked him where it was, and he said that he had taken a servant for himself who carried his gun and looked after the cattle. I immediately gave him a cuff, which in a trice removed him from the wagon, after which I ordered him to go to the animals, to take his gun and guard them, or leave my service at once. I further told him that he did not require a servant because he was himself in service, and he should first have ascertained that he had food to give a servant before engaging one; now he had none unless he planned to steal food from me. His servant came to the wagon and told me that the Hereros so often killed people of his tribe at Otjozondjupa that he wanted to leave the place. I felt sorry for the boy and had he initially come directly to me I would perhaps have engaged him, but to set an example I was now unbending, otherwise every one of my servants would soon take a servant for himself, and these again others, and in the end I would have a whole commando to support while nobody wanted to do any work.

WILLIAM MORTON

Morton, an American doctor, visited the diamond fields in 1874, when Kimberley was still largely a town of tent-cloth, corrugated iron and wood, and its streets teemed with activity.

SIMPLY A GUN

A stream of foot passengers lines the side-walks, while along the centre of the streets crowds of naked negroes, often singing their weird songs, go to and fro from their work. Or perhaps a gang of "raw" natives, just down thousands of miles from the countries to the North, dusty, thin as skeletons, foot sore, dirty and strange, with barbaric utensil and ornament, thread their way along, hooted at, and pelted with dirt and stones by their better initiated countrymen. This reception of the neophyte is of daily occurrence, and the ear can readily follow the direction pursued by the entering band by listening for the succession of derisive yells which greet it at each step of its progress.

The negro – certainly at first – attracts the newly-arrived traveler's attention. And once and for all, it is well to banish from the mind the idea that the negro of South Africa looks like the black man as known to us here in America. Our former slaves are descended from a much inferior race. The native at the diamond mines belongs to a superior and dominant type called, in general, Kaffirs, who have overrun and conquered the territory south of the Zambesi river from Hottentot and Bushman. They are, physically, splendid specimens of humanity – walk erect and with careless freedom and grace – go quite naked, except for the waist-cloth, and swinging blanket for cool nights. Their simplicity and good nature is refreshing, while their bravery, even against well-disciplined troops, is a matter of history.

Everything the white man wears is to them in the light of ornament, and it is a study to watch the merry crowd file along. One stalwart fellow wears only a vest; another has found and put on an abandoned tall hat. One wears a gaiter-boot, or old shoe, picked up by the road-side, or a long stocking and no boot, or simply a shirt. Another struts proudly by in the bright-buttoned uniform of a soldier's coat, his brown legs in marked contrast to its bright red. Every cast-aside paper collar is seized and donned, and all this soberly and demurely, and in ignorance of its comicality.

The native laborer comes mostly from a region of teeming population, between 16° and 22° of south latitude – that is to say, from the country between the Zambesi and Limpopo rivers, beyond the northern border of the Transvaal Republic. As a fair sample of the tribes represented, I quote the returns of the Native Registry Office, at Kimberley, for the month of March, 1876: Mahowas, 1,086; Makalakas, 19; Batlapins, 170; Basuts, 186; Baralong, 5; Bechuana, 85; Shangans, 142; Colonial, 4; Griqua, 3; Zulu, 123; Koranna, 4 – Total, 1,827, registered for a month. However, the number registered is, as a rule, probably not more than one-half, as the law requiring registration has never been possible to enforce.

These natives have been pouring in crowds into the diamond fields for seven years, at the rate of 30,000 a year; each gang of from thirty to forty men, after a journey on foot often of 1,000 miles, during which many of them die from starvation and cold, remaining and working only just long enough to supply each member of it with gun and ammunition – *i.e.*, about three months – and then returning to their land. They carry back no money, but simply a gun; and they come for nothing else.

The English Government permits the sale of guns to them indiscriminately; and it is a well-established fact that 300,000 have been thus disposed of.

These natives declared war upon the Transvaal Government a few months ago; and we now see what all this preparation meant.

HENRY MACDONALD

A horrifying echo of the Abeona *disaster. The* Cospatrick *left Gravesend for New Zealand in mid-September 1874. Most of the 479 people on board were emigrants. She caught fire on the night of November 17, in open sea some 1,600 kilometres southwest of the Cape. The crew's attempts to extinguish the blaze were hampered by panic-stricken passengers, who mobbed the boats. Some were killed by burning wreckage, while others jumped into the sea, where they either drowned immediately or clung to debris until they lost strength. MacDonald, the second mate, made it into a boat with 30 other people. With neither compass, food, nor water, they headed for Cape Town.*

AWAKENED BY THE MADMAN

About 11 days out, Sunday, 22d, weather dull and a heavy swell on. Thirst began to tell severely on us all. A man named Bentley fell overboard while steering and sank. Three men died, having first become mad in consequence of drinking salt water. We threw their bodies overboard. Monday, 23d. – Blowing hard, and a high sea running, which kept us continually baling water out. We tore seats and stern sheets out and made a drag, which caused the boat to lay easier; but it only being fastened with strands of painter, we lost it. Four men died the same as the others, but we were that hungry and thirsty that we drank the blood and ate the liver of two of them. We lost our only oar this day by the man steering falling asleep. Tuesday, 24th. – Strong gales; rigged another drag, fastened with braces and belts and clothing of the dead. Six more deaths to-day. Wednesday, 25th. – Light breeze and awfully hot; some more died, and we were reduced to eight, three of these out of their minds; we all felt very bad that day. Early on the morning of Thursday, the 26th, it not being daylight, a bark passed close to us, running. We hailed, but got no answer, which made us lose all hope. One more died. Light, fine weather. We kept sucking the blood of those that had died. Friday, 27th. – Squally all around, with light showers, but we never caught a drop of water. We threw one overboard, but were too weak to lift the other. We were five, two A.B.'s [Able Seamen], one O.S. [Ordinary Seaman], myself, and passenger, who was mad, and attempted to drown himself three times. We were all fearfully bad, and had all drank sea-water. We were all dozing, when, being awakened by the madman biting my feet, I saw a vessel bearing down on us. The vessel proved to be the British ship British Sceptre, of Liverpool, from Calcutta for Dundee. We were (five in all) taken on board and treated with every kindness; but two, Bob Hamilton, A.B., and the passenger, name unknown, died, and Thomas Lewis, A.B., Edward Cottes, O.S., and myself were brought to St. Helena and landed.

They were the only survivors.

ROBERT BALLANTYNE

Ballantyne was the quintessential author of Victorian boys' adventure stories. Twentieth-century critic Naomi Lewis noted that his most popular yarns followed the formula of a young white male going to some remote spot and, backed by "a sort of trinity of God, gun and empire", joyfully killing as many of its animals as the pages allowed. "With luck, a few black natives, usually cannibals, are bagged as well," she wrote. "Only dogs, loyal servants to man, are exempt from gunshot; cats too may be rescued from bullies." Ballantyne visited the Cape in 1876; his Six Months at the Cape, *from which this extract is taken, came out three years later and was still being reprinted 30 years after that. I have been unable to identify the chiefs who were passengers with him on this voyage from Port Elizabeth to Cape Town.*

IN DIGNIFIED SILENCE
We were to have started on a Saturday afternoon, but a gale said "no," and we left on Sunday morning. Even then, although the gale had abated, a surf so magnificent was rolling into Algoa Bay that no ship's boat could approach the jetty. This obliged the passengers to go off to the steamer in a surf-boat. Of course the boat could not approach nearer the dry sand than fifty yards or so. There she heaved about in oceans of boiling foam, while naked Kafirs carried us on board one by one. For the males among us this was fun – in regard to the females, it was at all events funny. The Kafirs bore the latter in their strong arms as children are carried, and put them over the gunwale tenderly, but the gentlemen were made to sit on their shoulders, as one sits on horseback, and were treated with less ceremony. A giant in ebony carried me off, and trotted as he went, to the delight of some of his comrades; but I was accustomed to riding, and patted his black head approvingly.

The boat was full of men, women, and children; white, black, and brown; clothed and semi-naked. There were a number of Kafir men (passengers) who would gladly have dispensed with clothing altogether, but the laws of the Colony forbid this in the presence of civilised life – except in the case of those who have to work in the surf. The laws, however, were not strictly carried out. One man, being carried on board by a brother-black, stepped down into the bottom of the boat with his trousers over his arm. He had taken them off for coolness as a man throws off his coat!

While standing on a commanding point in the stern, a fellow-passenger directed attention to a group of Kafirs who tried to keep apart from the others, and looked dignified. These, he told me, were a party of native princes, chiefs, and councillors, who had been brought fresh from their wilderness home – with their own consent, of course – and were being taken to Capetown for the purpose of being impressed with the wealth, power, grandeur, and vast resources of the white man. The other Kafirs, of whom there was a large gang, were common fellows, who chanced to be going by the same steamer as navvies to work on the Western railways. The difference between the navvies and their nobility was not great. Personally there was scarcely any, and the somewhat superior cloth of the robes worn by the latter made no great show.

The big boat was hauled off by a rope through the surf, the sail set, and we were soon alongside the ocean steamer whose iron sides rose above us like a city wall. There was nothing but an iron ladder, flat against this wall, by which to ascend. The heaving of the surf-boat was great. It approached the ladder and retreated from it in the most irregularly spasmodic manner. Only active men, accustomed to such feats, could get upon it. Kafirs, although active as kittens, are not accustomed to the sea, or to the motion of ships and boats. For them to ascend was a matter of great difficulty; for the women and children it was impossible.

But the difficulty had been provided for. Presently we saw a great cask like an overgrown hogshead swing over the side and descend into the boat. It was caught by our sailors and placed on the stern-sheets. Several tars from the steamer descended to assist. The cask was large enough to hold three or four women besides a child or two. Amid much giggling and persuading it was filled, a signal given, steam applied, and the party was whirled aloft with a scream, and lowered on the vessel's deck in safety.

The cask was again sent down. Meanwhile some of us had scrambled up the ladder, and a few of the Kafir navvies followed our example, but the most of them required a good deal of encouragement, and some strong persuasion, while others refused flatly to attempt it. All this time the black aristocrats looked on in grave silence. If I remember rightly there were a young prince, an old councillor, and two or three chiefs.

When those navvies that could be persuaded, or kicked up the ladder, had been disposed of, the sailors turned upon the timid ones and bundled them into the cask, neck and crop, four and five at a time. There was necessity for speed, and sailors are not wont to be delicate when this is the case. At last the aristocracy were approached. Whether the sailors knew who they were I cannot tell; it is probable that they did not, but judged by the "outward appearance." They were "niggers," that was enough for Jack.

"Come along, old boy," said one, grasping the old councillor; but the councillor held back; Jack therefore gave him a powerful shove and he went into the cask head-foremost. Another man had seized the young prince at the same moment. That potentate – who in his own land possessed the power of life and death – turned round with dignity, and in doing so afforded an unlooked for opportunity to the sailor, who pushed him gently till he tripped against the cask and went in backwards, squeezing the old councillor almost flat.

"That's your sort, Bill, fetch another!" cried Jack, as he packed the prince down.

One chief was quick-witted enough to submit and stepped in of his own accord. Another half-stepped and was half-thrust in.

"Hoist away!" shouted Bill.

At that moment a forgotten navvy caught Bill's eye, he seized him by the neck; Jack helped; the man was thrown on the top of all, and went up next moment like a spread-eagle cover to the cask.

When this "lot" was lowered four or five of the Jack-tars on deck, who greatly enjoyed the fun, turned it suddenly over, and thus it was emptied of its human contents.

Even at that moment of humiliation the savage chiefs were true to themselves. They rose from the deck in dignified silence, the prince merely saying, sternly, to the gentleman who had charge of the party, "Was *this* what you brought me here for?"

It is but just to add that the gentleman in charge of these noble visitors did his best to prevent the outrage, but it had occurred suddenly, in the exuberance of "Jack's" spirits, was over in a few seconds, and could not be undone.

These Kafir chiefs were afterwards feasted and fêted by the governor and gentry of Capetown, but I have my doubts whether they will ever forget or forgive the treatment received on that occasion in Algoa Bay.

In truth, being transferred in this way was seldom dignified: Fanny Barkly, daughter of a bishop, describes how she was put in a basket to disembark at Durban, and then to her surprise had an actress dumped on top of her. "I was rather glad to emerge from my friendly basket, as I found my fellow-traveller heavy, she being a young woman of ample proportions. Not only did she almost reduce me to a state of pulp, but she also screamed loudly all the time, although she certainly had much the best of it."

ROWLAND ATCHERLEY

Atcherley spent just under a year in South Africa in 1877-78 exploring opportunities for a "trading and colonizing" company, hunting, and prospecting for gold in the eastern Transvaal. He was tempted by the proposal of Colonel Weatherly, a retired dragoon officer, that he help raise a troop of horse for the expected Zulu war, but declined. "You know," Weatherly told him, "In fighting niggers, one incurs no personal danger, as is the case in a European or civilized war. It is either a case of cover-shooting or badger-drawing." Weatherly was last seen wading on foot into a mass of Zulu warriors at Hlobane, sabre in one hand and the body of his dead son clasped with the other. Here Atcherley is en route to Durban, watching 35 tons of cargo being transferred from his boat to lighters in the open sea off Port Alfred.

LIKE A WET SACK

The cargo had to be lowered by the steam-winch from the deck into the lighter alongside, and as the sea was pretty rough, it may be imagined that this was no easy matter. At one moment the lighter would be almost on a level with the ship's deck, at another down in the trough of the sea, some fifteen feet lower. The bumps that lighter gave the ship's side were numerous and hard. I do not think that one single package went through the ordeal of transhipment without damage. Many were visibly smashed to pieces, others dived into the sea between the lighter and the ship's side and were crushed to splinters. A case said to contain a tombstone, and labelled "with great care," was smashed in two, one-half falling into the hold of the lighter and the other plunging into the sea. At one upward surge, the mast of the lighter caught our derrick, and was snapped off like matchwood, bringing down all the rigging, and seriously injuring a man. How they stuck to the decks of that lighter was to me a marvel, as she was actually being whisked about like a cockle-shell. But the most exciting part had yet to come. The cargo having been transhipped, a small hatch was opened on the lighter by two of the hands, and a woman, in a perfectly unconscious state, was dragged forth, brought to the edge, and held out like a wet sack to be caught up. Three times the lighter rose up to the level of the deck, and as many times was the woman missed being caught; but a fourth and mightier wave, however, brought her up again, and then, seizing their opportunity, the men stationed in the gangway clutched the poor, insensible

Landing in a south-easter at Port Elizabeth.

291

creature, and, after a moment's dangling in mid-air, safely landed her on board, amid the cheers of the lookers-on.

MY USUAL PLACE
North of Newcastle, heading for the Transvaal.

That evening at the outspan I had something of a treat. The waggon being rather too crowded for comfort, I preferred sleeping underneath it, and had, as was my custom, comfortably ensconced myself in my usual place. Awaking at about six in the morning, I found to my utter astonishment that I was alone, and that the waggon, together with everything else connected with it, had disappeared. It was evident that I had been sound asleep at the time of inspanning, and that the Kafirs, not having noticed me, had actually trekked on, and would probably now be eight or ten miles ahead. So I had nothing for it but to take up my bed and walk, and console myself with a vow to make it lively for those Kafirs when I came up to them. After a five-mile trudge with my heavy rugs and rifle, I fell in with Cecil and Sydney, who had returned to meet me, and now assisted me with my traps on to camp, another three miles further. I kept my vow, and the Kafirs never omitted to wake me after that.

ANONYMOUS

This unnamed traveller's account of a journey from Grahamstown to Port Elizabeth was published in the Cape Times in 1877. He and a friend were obliged to travel by horse cart as far as Sand Flats, where they met the railway and had time for a hurried meal before the train arrived.

FREE UNDER THREE
Here we took a second-class ticket – my companion and I – and were shortly joined by two mothers, each with three children under three. What a number of youngsters there seems to be when one travels by train – no end of them both here and in England; and I rather enjoy seeing railway companies done in this fashion. It is a convenient rule 'all children free under three,' which is an age they never reach until they get quite beyond a size that places deception altogether out of the question. Who is to judge of 'under three?' The porter is generally a young man who would rather pass a pretty little mother if she looked slily at him, even if she said she had *six* youngsters under three. Besides, what do those boys know of children's ages; a porter ought to be a man who has enjoyed the blessing of having had 'his quiver full of them.' Before the train started another mother appeared with three more youngsters under three. Mothers seemed to have made a dead set at our compartment, and already it began to feel warm. At last the train crawled away, and soon got on to its fullest rate – about 6³/₄ mile an hour. At the next station, lo and behold! another mother with three children under three joined the happy throng; it got warmer, but fortunately none of them were afraid of the fresh air, and so we were able to have both windows open, and thus secured a fine draught right through

the compartment. Probably a dozen additional children were found to have the whooping cough next day. I fancied we had now escaped all further additions to our interesting and lively party, but 'there's many a slip,' &c., for arriving at Commando Kraal Station (by-the-way, who gives the names to the stations?), excited and breathless, we observed two mothers rushing in with six more children, carrying kettles, cups, and saucers, tea-pots, sugar, and milk in bottles. Recognizing a face they knew, in they tumbled, bag and baggage, into our unfortunate compartment. It was terrible work to squeeze in, but we managed it – something like thirty in all. I never saw so many babies in arms, but very good babies they were. We learnt from the last party who favoured us with their presence that they were in the bush having a picnic when they heard the railway whistle. Everything was gathered up in a hurry, but the mothers had the presence of mind not to throw away the boiling water, and so when they found themselves in the train, they finished their tea making, and passed a cup all round; and they had all taken their cup of tea and carefully packed away the cups and kettle before the train again moved on. Such is railway travelling to the Bay!

FREDERICK BARBER

Barber was born in Grahamstown, and like so many other pillars of South African society, did his schooling at St Andrew's College there. He tried his hand at diamond mining, ostrich farming and gold prospecting in the eastern Transvaal, where he and his brother Harry gave their name to Barberton, before moving on to the Witwatersrand. There he sank the first shaft into the reef and became a director of several gold mining companies. The brothers were keen hunters, and Fred once held the world records for several antelope heads. These pieces are from an 1877 trip, when they intended to go to Lake Ngami to hunt ostriches and collect wild chicks for sale in the colony. However the Tswana chief Khama refused them permission, so they detoured to Lobengula's territory to try their luck with ivory. They must be the only people ever to have gone elephant hunting with ostrich incubators in their baggage.

LOOKING DOWN THE MUZZLE

A case of lynch law of a very drastic nature also occurred during our stay here. A party of natives passing during the night had stolen some pumpkins and mealie cobs from one of Loben's huts in the lands. The executioner, Mavonya, was sent in pursuit. They were spoored to Umganen, a neighbouring kraal, where they were found and summarily strung up on the nearest trees.

Later we had the pleasure of being introduced to Mr. Mavonya. He was a sprightly, cheerful little chap, and told us many interesting anecdotes of his experiences as sheriff and hangman.

He was very proud of a Colt's revolver which the King had given him, [and] carried it slung over his shoulder beneath his blanket. He said it was a beautiful instrument, so small and yet so effective, and saved so much trouble. Before he had it, he used to have so much trouble in getting malefactors killed. Some of them objected to being knocked on the head, and if they were strong he had to take men with him, and sometimes chase them for long distances, and kill them in a slovenly manner with axes, assaigais, and knobkerries. But now he had as a rule very little trouble. He would walk about with a light stick, meet his victim, ask him for snuff, and while pleasantly chatting, would whip out his handy little gun and blow their brains out before they suspected anything. Sometimes he would show them his little gun, and while they were innocently admiring it, or looking down the muzzle, he would let it off in their faces, and there was an end of them. These and many other pleasant tales he told, with an air of utter contempt of human life that was quite refreshing. He showed us his little gun, but we were careful not to look down the muzzle.

A GRAND CHANCE

We had some very fine Boer dogs in camp. Neither the Drakes, Vermaak, nor myself had ever used them on our elephant hunts, and we had often discussed the question as to whether any good would result from the use of them. So one day we all went out together, taking with us our pack of mongrels. We expected great things. The dogs would chase the elephants, who naturally would become excited and retaliate, and while they were engaging each other's attention, we would have our innings and shoot them down with impunity.

We had the good fortune to find the spoor of a troop of cows with calves. Here was a grand chance. The dogs would hunt the calves, and while the anxious matrons are busy protecting their children, we would shoot them. As usual, they made for a thick synanga and then commenced feeding. We did not want to find them here, so [we] moved slowly and cautiously forward, keeping the dogs well back. And very lucky for us that we did not [find them there], as it turned out, for, overtaking them just as they had left it, and we had got into the outskirts, we saw the troop crossing some open bush to another [synanga] some distance off. Our dogs now spotted them and gave chase at full speed, came up to them and made for the calves who, terrified at the sudden onslaught, made a great noise, trumpeting and squealing. The cows, disturbed by the unusual commotion among their offspring, came tearing back to the rescue [and] hunted the dogs with maledictions shrill and high, who in turn fled to their masters for protection, closely followed by the enraged and anxious matrons.

Here was a sight for gods and men! Elephants trumpeting and charging like Mohawk Indians on the warpath, calves and dogs mixed up, squalling, screaming, yelping, and barking; branches of trees, bark, and dust flying; the whole mixed mob bearing down upon us at the rate of about forty thousand miles an hour, necessitating a hasty skedaddle. We cleared out right and left, and gave them space to pass back into the thick bush from which they had come, and into which we did not care to follow such a set of vicious, ill-tempered, cantankerous old dames again. At any rate, we blazed away into them as hard as we could, and several were sent to their last account. At any rate, we had had enough of hunting elephants with dogs, and didn't try it again.

WILLIAM NELSON

Nelson came out from England in 1877 and secured a job as overseer on the diamond fields, charged with "watching the niggers" to stop them swallowing stones they uncovered during sorting. He began putting together a collection of curiosities, and after a year made a trip north to the Soutpansberg, trading for weapons and other artefacts, and collecting rocks, plants, birds, insects and snakes. He was probably partly inspired by Emil Holub, who had been exhibiting in Kimberley prizes from his own travels that included the complete skeleton of a black man "picked up in the wilds". Nelson in later life settled at Booysens south of Johannesburg, where he established a reputation as a nurseryman.

NOVELTIES OF INTEREST
From a letter to his parents, written soon after he arrived on the diamond fields.

I have forwarded the following samples – One tin of the diamondiferous soil from our mine, set with crystals, and a piece of jasper from Vaal river. The soil must be kept from the air, or it would quickly fall to powder. One tin of rubies and river crystals. One tin and one bottle of Vaal river stones. One box of carbon, iron pyrites, etc. One box agates from Vaal river. One tin of topaz and Delagoa Bay shells. One packet Porcupine quills. One box dried grasses. One packet of cones of a conifer growing on Baines' Kloof, which will probably prove to be Retinospora. One packet of three tins and two boxes birds' eggs. One box of falcon's eggs, and kaffir hair. One packet of crystals and mica. One tin of shells and kaffir curiosities, kaffir knife, spoons, and Dutch

egg cup. Two kaffir pillows, such as are used by our "boys", kaffir corn, kaffir chair, and one packet of "imfe" or sugar cane. One bottle containing a snake, velvet spider (probably the Acteriopus Æddificatorius), Millipede (Onicus), a species of woodlouse, Salamander, etc. Two tins pineapple and Cape gooseberry jam. One parcel of "Biltong", or dried flesh of the antelope, which is cut up in thin slices and eaten without cooking. Ten karosses, or rugs of animals' skins, – some of these I have taken off the floor – namely, two jackals, one spring-boc, one meerkat (Cynictis Steedmannu), one lynx, one rabbit, one hartebeest, one wild cat, and one duiker-boc (Antelope Grimma), most of which will be novelties of interest to you.

THE ONLY WHITE MAN

On his trip to the north, Nelson was accompanied by a young coloured man who had worked with him on the diamond claim, son of a Cambridge-educated Englishman and a black woman from Natal. Though he criticises the Boers here, when it came to blacks Nelson was in fact as prejudiced as the next white man.

Although many of the Boers are extremely illiterate, it would be impossible for you to conceive the profoundness of their hatred of those whom they are pleased to designate the "coloured trash". They especially pride themselves upon being the aristocracy of this part of the world. Even my companion, who is coloured, is never asked into their houses on that account, though I can assure you, in this matter of education and refinement, he is very far in advance of the best of them. This distinction, as you may readily surmise, is far from agreeable to me, but such is the fact notwithstanding. During the whole of our journey hitherto, he has not entered a single Dutchman's habitation. As I am the only white man in our party, I am regarded as the sole "Baas" (proprietor) of the concern, whilst he, although having an interest in our speculation, is considered by those people, and is often mentioned as my "boy", my "kaffir", and sometimes even as my "hottentot". This is very irritating and extremely annoying to me personally, but I have thus far avoided the slightest manifestation of disapproval to these prejudiced people, and by this means I have secured many more of the necessaries, I may almost say luxuries, for his use than would have been possible had they treated him more kindly, and this I have done at their expense, although without their knowledge.

KATIE STUART

Stuart was the eldest of 12 children of a wealthy Fraserburg merchant and a niece of the writer Olive Schreiner, though she shared neither her aunt's literary ability nor political beliefs. Stuart survived a difficult adolescence and the deaths in quick succession of a husband and child to establish herself as a formidable campaigner for temperance and moral purity. She travelled to England in 1899 to lend her weight to the pro-war party, and was instrumental in establishing the Victoria League, an empire-wide organisation of patriotic women. One member of London high society described her as "copious, impracticable, well meaning and infinitely comic".

MOTHER AND HOME

At the age of 12 Stuart was sent off to school in Cape Town, which then – about 1874 – involved a six-day journey by Cape cart to the railhead at Wellington. For the trip, she was entrusted to the care of an "elderly gentleman" who was taking his own granddaughter to school.

Parents, brothers, and sisters accompanied us for some miles (*half-pad* – half-way, as we say in South Africa), and we partook of tea and cakes in the veld as an *affscheids* (good-bye) meal. So delightful to me was the prospect of school life and of the new world before me that I had but few tears to mingle with those of my loved ones, though a lump arose in my throat as I relinquished baby, who had been nestling in my arms during the drive, and gave mother and father the last kiss. Of holiday reunions there was no prospect in those days of immense distances, with a railway extending only to Wellington, and the farewell was one for some years.

Our first outspan on the journey was at a comfortable farm. Despite the warnings of a darkening sky, the rumbling of distant thunder, and a small preliminary shower, we foolishly, after but a short outspan, and having partaken of coffee, pushed on, and had scarcely started when the rain came down in torrents.

We crossed a small *spruit* already swollen from the rainfall higher up, and a few hundred yards further on we came to a second spruit, now a roaring and impassable torrent of angry, muddy, swirling waters.

Turning back, to our dismay we found the first spruit had in the few minutes that had elapsed since we crossed it become impassable too – so there we were – stranded between two angry streams, in full view of the comfortable Boer homestead we had so foolishly quitted against its owner's kind advice. The angry waters steadily rose on both sides, until ere long we were forced to seek refuge on a slight rise, where fortunately for us a small plot of ground about twelve yards square remained comparatively dry all night.

We two girls obtained what sleep we could in the cart, whilst the old gentleman and the driver bivouacked beneath. Our terror at the situation when darkness fell was not alleviated by our driver's suggestion that we must look out for snakes which might be driven in self-preservation like ourselves to higher ground. The afternoon's hopes and courage had disappeared *in toto*, and I yielded to a passionate storm of weeping and craving for mother and home, which had never seemed so precious before. By the morning the waters had abated, and we were able to pursue our way.

HARRIET ROCHE

The authoress of On Trek in the Transvaal *devoted five pages of her 1878 book to the process of leaving her Hertfordshire home, and apologised for what at first sight might not seem to have much to do with the rest of her narrative. "But, in truth, it has a good deal to do with it," she explains. "If we had not left 'home,' how could we in the nature of things ever have finally got to the Transvaal?"*

BIG SAFETY PINS
I strongly advise all who may contemplate a visit to South Africa, whilst they avoid superfluities, to be well provided with necessaries, compactly packed. Let them bring a light macintosh – a lady's should be silk lined; a folding india rubber bath (one not requiring inflation is best); an expanding macintosh basin, with a bag to hold it, the soap, towel, &c., too, with loops to hang it by, and above all, a hammer and nails with which to make their own little extra tidinesses after everything is supposed to be duly arranged by the wagon outfitter; a good stout ball of string, needle, thread, spare buttons, and tapes. All such sundries, common sense would suggest, but a reminder can do no harm. Tinned food for travelling is most requisite; and so is a spirit-lamp, wherewith to heat your coffee or tea when the cruel veldt fails to supply you with any fuel more lasting than a wisp of dry grass, or the pitiful leavings of the old camp-fire of some one who has gone on before you, and who has been in as great need as yourself of the wherewithal to make a blaze. Bring big safety pins! when your canvas bags begin their mad dance against the sides of the wagon, or your hat takes a flying leap from the peg upon which you have placed it, or your curtains persist in gaping apart – bring out your store of precious "safetys," and thank me for the hint.

FANNY BARKLY

Barkly's husband was appointed magistrate of Thaba Bosiu in Basutoland in 1877, and the family travelled out from England with a Sotho servant named Maria, who had been taken abroad by a colonial official. Here they are making their way by ox-wagon from Durban to what Barkly said was known as "Advance Post, Cannibal Valley".

The nurse Maria was a great amusement to us. She was the most civilised savage that I ever came across. Perfectly black, with woolly black hair, large brown eyes, beautiful teeth, and a good figure, she was quite a beauty in her way. She boasted that when she was in the service of Lady Broome, she had the honour of being spoken to by Her Majesty the Queen of England, besides having been "presented" to several duchesses, and had had many presents given to her – amongst others a travelling bag, fitted up, and a great many smart costumes. When arrayed in a large Gainsborough hat, velveteen dress, long suède gloves, and a silver chatelaine, she was indeed a wonderful sight, and caused much excitement along the route. Whenever we stopped she was at once surrounded by native women, who screamed with envy at the gorgeous vision. I am sorry to say that on one occasion, having indulged rather freely in Kaffir beer *en route*, brought to the waggon by some of her friends in large clay bowls, manufactured by the Basuto women, who use them for everything, the admiration of her fellow-countrywomen, combined perhaps with other causes needless to mention, were too much for Maria, who suddenly jumped out of the waggon and rushed up a mountain, screaming and yelling that "the moon had gone up hill." She was speedily brought to her senses, however, by being pursued by a number of baboons who were playing and dancing on the top of the mountain, and promptly made a rush for Maria, who managed, fortunately, to get back to the waggon, or it would certainly have been her last journey.

Soon after arriving at the post Maria abandoned job and European finery in favour of marriage to a local headman, skins, beads and cosmetics of oil and red clay. Barkly found herself faced with the challenge of cooking, ironing, washing clothes and making bread, none of which she had done before.

Dorsland trekkers.

JAN ALBERT COETZEE

Between 1874 and 1905 several groups of Transvaal Boers made gruelling "Dorsland" treks through the Kalahari to Namibia and Angola. Coetzee, who gathered first-hand accounts from those who had taken part, said the initial group left for no reason other than an "irresistible longing to trek". Those that followed, however, were impelled by dissatisfaction with the government of the liberal President Burgers and the British authorities who succeeded him. The 128-wagon trek described here left the headwaters of the Limpopo in 1877, under the command of Louw du Plessis. It included 480 people, of whom at least 37 died of fever and other causes. Coetzee, who went to Angola in 1924 as a teacher, reported approvingly that although the Portuguese – with the exception of the "better classes" – continued to cross-breed with the natives, the Boers "have not only kept religion and nationality pure, but also their blood, and will undoubtedly also do so in future". An ardent Afrikaner nationalist, Coetzee in 1957 formed a committee which oversaw the repatriation of almost all the Boer descendants still in Angola.

TO THE CLOUDLESS HEAVENS

The second day, after the wagons arrived at the Motloutsi, the Commandant summoned a meeting, to consult over the manner in which they would tackle the desert. Twice the Commandant sent a young man specially to invite Jan Greyling to attend the gathering and share in the deliberations. But the final answer from the former leader was:

"Tell Lou Plesie, this is not the time to hold meetings. It is now time for every man to stand squarely on his own feet, and press forward to get through the Thirst, and I say, tomorrow, when the day breaks, I will inspan and trek with a will, and those who love me, follow me!"

When the next day broke, Jan Greyling and his party trekked with all their wagons, – between ten and twenty in number – and stock in a westerly direction, following the road from Damaraland, into the desert.

At sunrise the big lager of du Plessis sent their loose stock into the "Thirst", on the wagon tracks of Jan Greyling. This was about six thousand head, herded in groups by old and young. Behind every group of cattle was a wagon with food and water (a severely restricted quantity) for the herders. Also on the same day the families who had not gone ahead with the supply-wagons, left the water and followed the stock.

A few hours from the Motloutsi Jan Greyling and his people arrived at the sand wells of Tlabala, where they obtained a little water and moved on, after the stock had trampled the wells closed. Three days after that they came to the well of Inkowane, and all this time the poor oxen had to trek without water! However there was not any water at Inkowane either, and

they then harnessed the oxen two teams to a wagon, left half the wagons standing there with the baggage, and hastened further westward with the families on the other wagons.

A little further the loose cattle began racing ahead, because they smelled water (the west wind was blowing). The following morning they outspanned near a couple of sandhills, just this side of a pan, in which as they understood, there was still a small amount of drinking water, and drove the oxen thither. At the same time thousands of cattle rushed past the sandhills from the rear and towards the west. These were the animals that entered the "Thirst" after Jan Greyling. It was hopeless for the herders to try to head off the thirst-crazed creatures. The pan, in which there had indeed initially been a little water, was in a few hours turned into a mud-puddle, trodden so sticky, that you could have built houses with it. Jan Greyling and the other fellows brought those of their oxen which had not died from the mud (which they had eaten), back to the wagons at the sandhills and the trek continued, leaving behind one wagon with an old greybeard and a number of young girls. Some women walked ahead with little jugs and bottles and small buckets.

Terrible now was the suffering of man and beast. All sorts of methods were used just to get enough moisture to wet the throat, but without success, so that some people became half demented.

A young man, from one of the provision-wagons, who came from behind, collected a tin full of mud at the pan to steam it out, as it was hoped in this way to obtain some moisture. When he reached the two wagons at the sandhills, one of the girls raced to him with open arms and called out in delight that her prayer had been heard. How great was her disappointment when she upended the tin over her thirsty mouth, and no water came out! The girls accused the young man of concealing water for them in his wagon, and in a half-crazed way they searched his wagon, without success. Then they ran around, called for help from On High, and only the following day did they also follow with little jugs on Jan Greyling's wagon tracks. The old greybeard climbed into a tree, held his open mouth up to the cloudless heavens in the hope that rain would fall, then climbed down from the tree, took his Bible, lay under the wagon, opened the Bible, glanced briefly in it, threw away the Book and thereupon told the girls, that he would not die of thirst but that they would, because they had brought him to this suffering.

About the fifth day, after they had entered the "Thirst", Jan Greyling and his people arrived at the wells of Tlakane, where they could obtain drinking water.

For the stock that left Motloutsi at sunrise, there was no water at Tlabala, although some people were able to get a little for themselves, after they had dug out the wells, but even this small quantity was muddy and foamy. Herds of hundreds of cattle passed by Tlabala one after another and disappeared in the terrible dust, which rose on high from the brush-covered ridges of sand. On the third day the people discovered everywhere along the road sacks of flour, ploughs, bellows and other heavy goods, which had been thrown off the wagons of Jan Greyling's people, and those who were trekking with the provision wagons behind the stock, were by this time themselves obliged to lighten their wagons. The oxen could no longer pull the wagons through the thick sand in the burning rays of the sun, and some collapsed in the yoke. The oxen had grown unusually fat on good grass and a lack of work beside the Crocodile River, and for this reason their resilience was seriously reduced. From about the second day on, that they were in the desert, they could also no longer graze because of thirst, although there was enough sweet grass under the trees. Many people were accordingly obliged to abandon their wagons with all the heavy stuff, such as food, clothing, tools etc., and to harness from different wagons the oxen that were not yet weak, before one wagon, to flee in it with the women and children. Some merely pushed out the tail-ends of the wagons and proceeded on those.

But the "flight" went extremely slowly in the heavy sand, in which the wagons' wheels sank at times by half a spoke or deeper still. Day and night they travelled, just to reach water.

At Inkowane the foremost herders dug out the well after they had removed the dead cattle one by one, and as the other people arrived there, they could at least drink a little, but there was so little water in the well, that it happened, that a man would from the evening to the morning scoop with a spoon the trickle of water that seeped through, and in that time fill only five bottles!

Some of the stock-herders and provision wagons in the lead did not even stop at Inkowane, but pressed ahead as swiftly as possible, so swiftly even that they caught up with Jan Greyling and his people, before they and their wagons left the sandhills at the Modderpan.

At Inkowane there was before long again a terrible confusion of men and animals at the water. Groups of people were still leaving the well; some wagons were so full, that the women and children had to stand and many had to go on foot. In some wagons there were other people lying sick from the fever, which they had picked up at the Krokodil River.

The people who left the Motloutsi after the stock, soon joined up with those who had driven the stock, and it is difficult to imagine greater suffering and despair than that which occurred from Inkowane on. When the cattle got to the west of Inkowane, they stampeded in groups with a fearsome bellowing and disappeared in all directions into the sandy desert. A multitude rushed one after the other into the Modderpan (also named Haakdoringpan), ate the mud and ran off mad into the veld. Before long many animals lay dead alongside the mud. However between Inkowane and the Modderpan a Bushman exchanged water in an ostrich eggshell with people, and he was asked to bring still more to barter. He was watched and in this way it was discovered how he sucked the water from the ground with a reed, and spat it into the eggshell. It was a stopped-up well, which was then dug open and provided refreshment for many people.

More places were discovered where reeds protruded from the ground and these were not stopped-up wells. The Bushmen bound a small bundle of grass around the bottom end of the reed, or rather hollowed-out branch, and buried it in the earth. When they sucked on the reed, a bit of water came after a while. People who dug at such a place then arrived at a layer of rock. More than one Dorsland trekker sucked on such a reed, because it would not have helped to search for the well.

Even before they arrived at the Modderpan, some mothers cut the throats of sheep to give the blood to their crying children; and pressed the stomach contents through cloths into a basin, so that, after it had cooled a little, it could be used to ease the terrible thirst. This did not however contain much liquid.

Some people ate the pan's mud; one boy half-deliriously slid into the mud on his belly, ate of it and called out: ["]Ah! the water does taste good!"

The sand was so hot by day, that it burned right through the soles of shoes, with the result that people were often obliged to seek shelter under trees; driven by thirst, they often used these occasions to dig roots from the earth and chew on them, although some were bitter and some could have indeed possibly been poisonous.

Some people's horses were good and in this way they could race ahead to Tlakane and then return with small amounts of water to relieve others, who were still struggling in the sand. Because fortunately even in the wild flight of thirst there was no lack of wonderful examples of self-sacrifice, heroic courage and acts of love and humanity.

ANTHONY TROLLOPE

Trollope wrote with his watch in front of him, to ensure that he produced 250 words every quarter of an hour. By 1877, when he made a five-month visit to South Africa, this system had already produced some 50 works ranging from his novels to plays and travel books. He completed the last chapter of his South Africa – a *two-volume mix of travelogue and political analysis – as his ship made its way home across the Bay of Biscay. "Our duty to the Kafir of course is to civilize him," he concluded. "Work alone will civilize him, and his incentive to work should be, and is, the desire to procure those good things which he sees to be in the enjoyment of white men around him." Here he meets Xhosa chiefs in King William's Town.*

YOU AND THE TROUSERS

On the morning appointed about twenty Kafirs came to me, clustering round the door of the house in which I was lodging, – but they declined to enter. I therefore held my levee out in the street. Sandilli was not there. The reason for his absence remained undivulged, but I was told that he had sent a troop of cousins in his place. The spokesman on the occasion was a chief named Siwani, who wore an old black coat, a flannel shirt, a pair of tweed trousers and a billycock hat, – comfortably and warmly dressed, – with a watch-key of ordinary appearance ingeniously inserted into his ear as an ornament. An interpreter was provided; and, out in the street, I carried on

my colloquy with the dusky princes. Not one of them spoke but Siwani, and he expressed utter dissatisfaction with everything around him. The Kafirs, he said, would be much better off if the English would go away and leave them to their own customs. As for himself, though he had sent a great many of his clansmen to work on the railway, – where they got as he admitted good wages, – he had never himself received the allowance per head promised him. "Why not appeal to the magistrate?" I asked. He had done so frequently, he said, but the magistrate always put him off, and then, personally, he was treated with very insufficient respect. This complaint was repeated again and again. I, of course, insisted on the comforts which the Europeans had brought to the Kafirs, – trousers for instance, – and I remarked that all the royal princes around me were excellently well clad. The raiment was no doubt of the Irish beggar kind but still admitted of being described as excellent when compared in the mind with red clay and a blanket. "Yes, – by compulsion," he said. "We were told that we must come in and see you, and therefore we put on our trousers. Very uncomfortable they are, and we wish that you and the trousers and the magistrates, but above all the prisons, would go – away out of the country together."

THE FISH WAS LUGGAGE
Adventures on the regular coach from Durban to Pietermaritzburg.

We were apparently quite full but heard at starting that there was still a place vacant which had been booked by a gentleman who was to get up along the road. The back carriage, which was of the waggonette fashion, uncovered, with seats at each side, seemed to be so full that the gentleman would find a difficulty in placing himself, but as I was on the box the idea did not disconcert me. At last, about half way, at one of the stages, the gentleman appeared. There was a lady inside with her husband, with five or six others, who at once began to squeeze themselves. But when the gentleman came it was not a gentleman only, but a gentleman with the biggest fish in his arms that I ever saw, short of a Dolphin. I was told afterwards that it weighed 45 pounds. The fish was luggage, he said, and must be carried. He had booked his place. That we knew to be true. When asked he declared he had booked a place for the fish also. That we believed to be untrue. He came round to the front and essayed to put it on the foot-board. When I assured him that any such attempt must be vain and that the fish would be at once extruded if placed there, he threatened to pull me off the box. He was very angry, and frantic in his efforts. The fish, he said, was worth £5, and must go to Maritzburg that day. Here Apollo shewed, I think, a little inferiority to an English coachman. The English coachman would have grown very red in the face, would have cursed horribly, and would have

304

persistently refused all contact with the fish. Apollo jumped on his box, seized the reins, flogged the horses, and endeavoured to run away both from the fish and the gentleman.

But the man, with more than colonial alacrity, and with a courage worthy of a better cause, made a successful rush, and catching the back of the vehicle with one hand got on to the step behind, while he held on to the fish with his other hand and his teeth. There were many exclamations from the folks behind. The savour of the fish was unpleasant in their nostrils. It must have been very unpleasant as it reached us uncomfortably up on the box. Gradually the man got in, – and the fish followed him! Labor omnia vincit improbus. By his pertinacity the company seemed to become reconciled to the abomination. On looking round when we were yet many miles from Pieter Maritzburg I saw the gentleman sitting with his feet dangling back over the end of the car; his neighbour and vis-a-vis, who at first had been very loud against the fish, was sitting in the same wretched position; while the fish itself was placed upright in the place of honour against the door, where the legs of the two passengers ought to have been. Before we reached our journey's end I respected the gentleman with the fish, – who nevertheless had perpetrated a great injustice; but I thought very little of the good-natured man who had allowed the fish to occupy the space intended for a part of his own body. I never afterwards learned what became of the fish. If all Maritzburg was called together to eat it I was not asked to join the party.

Alexandre De Serpa
Pinto

ALEXANDRE DE SERPA PINTO

Major Serpa Pinto made his first acquaintance with Africa as part of a military force crushing resistance to Portuguese rule in Moçambique. In 1877 he was commissioned to survey the Angolan hinterland for the Portuguese government. When he had put some 600 kilometres between himself and the coast, he decided to carry on walking. Having survived the usual hazards of fever, hostile locals, hunger, unreliable bearers and dangerous animals, the travel-worn and penniless explorer arrived in Pretoria just over a year after setting off. He was promptly invited to dinner with the Transvaal government treasurer.

To touch up the seams

That gentleman had invited several guests to meet me, which compelled me to pay some attention to my toilet. My trousers, which bore but little semblance to their original aspect, and which had been subjected to more than one patch at my own hands (although my talent for tailoring had never been brilliant), were carefully cleansed from the dust and mud splashes of twenty different countries. I found a pair of stockings which had been most neatly darned by Madame Coillard, and which were therefore sure to give satisfaction. My iron-heeled boots, a product of Tissier of Paris, were blacked for the first time, and really did not look at all bad. My coat was the article which most troubled me, for it had been furnished with leathern pockets, once black, but which were now, alas! worn into an extraordinary colour. Mr. Turner's ink-stand, however, was handy, and by the aid of a quill pen I managed to touch up the seams and all the exposed portions, so that I thought it would pass muster at night, although by day the artifice might perhaps be a little too apparent.

Having then well brushed and combed my long beard and still longer hair, I set out for the house of the Treasurer of the Transvaal.

On entering the drawing-room I was completely dazzled.

The ladies in full dress, the men in their well-fitting black coats, the servants in livery, the bright yet harmonious colours of the silken upholstery, the carpets, the mirrors, all those things, indeed, to which I had been so long a stranger during the hard and savage life I had been leading, produced in me, at first, a perfect bewilderment of brain.

I felt as a blind man may be supposed to feel when the bistouri of the skilful oculist removes the cataract which has condemned him to months of darkness, and sight is suddenly restored to him.

My greatest difficulty was what to do with my hands; they seemed ever in search of something to lay hold of, and missing the customary feel of the rifle, they were dreadfully in my way.

Dinner was announced. I took in the lady of the house, and when I was seated I began to be conscious that my very old clothes were dreadfully shabby.

The appearance of the table awakened in me fresh surprise. The glass, the china, the silver, the wines sparkling in their cut decanters, attracted me in turn and the sight of the *menu*, written on an elegant card, had for the moment all the fascination of an ancient manuscript.

I must have committed many absurdities, but I have no recollection of what they were, for the whole scene appeared to me as a delightful but uneasy dream.

The dinner over, we repaired once more to the drawing-room, where my attention was soon attracted by the sound of music; a lady had sat down to the piano, and was playing in charming style one of Chopin's Nocturnes.

It was like a new sensation to listen to the notes and watch the fingers flying over the ivory keys. The harmony penetrated to my very soul, and made me giddy with emotion. I was in quite a state of feverish excitement when I returned to my Café, where I found prepared in a corner of the saloon a regular bed furnished with blankets, sheets and pillows.

I was about to lie down as I stood, but recollected in time that civilised people were accustomed to undress before they did so. But I got no sleep. My impressions of the day had been too full – my mind was disturbed by too many things, and the sheets bothered me.

EDWARD SANDEMAN

Lollipops, according to Sandeman, were often more effective than money in persuading Boers to part with milk, eggs or butter. Supplies for his eight-month hunting safari through Natal and the Transvaal in 1878 included 30 pounds of sweets and ten of chocolate, as well as good quantities of preserved lobster and salmon. The Royal Hotel was – and still is – in Durban.

MOST ENORMOUS COCKROACHES
The Royal Hotel did not hold out any inducements in the way of comfort for us to remain longer than necessary. Like most colonial hotels, it consists of a two-storied stone building containing some eight or ten rooms, and adjoining this, behind is an heterogeneous mass of outbuildings, which are used for the greater part of the bed-rooms, kitchen, offices, bath-room, and stables. The whole hotel is overrun with the most enormous cockroaches, some a couple of inches long; and our veracious landlord, without a smile on his countenance, assured me that he had seen a couple of them catch, kill, and devour, a half-grown chicken. But as he afterwards also informed us that these same cockroaches were the chief ingredient in Worcester sauce, I will not vouch for the accuracy of either statement.

I ATTEMPTED TO HIT IT
I had a long ride after a blesse-bôk in the afternoon. With my first shot I had wounded it slightly, and as my horse was fresh I soon rode into it; but on putting my hand into my pouch for a cartridge, I found it was empty. I then rode right alongside, but my horse took fright and sheered off each time I attempted to hit the bôk's head with the butt end of my carbine. At last the bôk laid down, and I got off to try and compass its death with carbine and knife combined; but the instant I dismounted, the bôk rose up and limped slowly, but still faster than I could keep up with on foot. A dozen times I attempted to hit it from the saddle, but with no success, and a dozen times the bôk laid down and got up again before I was near enough to touch it on foot. There was not a stone far or near; and at last, much disgusted at my carelessness in leaving the waggon with an empty pouch, I had to leave the bôk, for darkness was coming on. I sincerely hope the poor beast recovered from his wound, but most probably the vultures benefited by my loss.

PARKER GILLMORE

Gillmore is said to have served in the British army in the Crimea and China, and he tried unsuccessfully to raise a native labour corps during the Anglo-Zulu War. He travelled extensively in southern Africa in the 1870s, hunting, trading in ivory and gold, and producing a stream of wordy books on his experiences.

WHAT DO YOU CALL THEM?
North of Colenso in Natal.

At sunrise I crossed the ferry, and at first traversed a very pretty country, afterwards a most dismal one. Who knows the stretch of old Scotland that extends from Seutra Hill, beyond Blackshiels, as you go to the town where is reported to have lived bonnie Maggie Lauder? After you have got a mile or two over the ridge, halt, and look to all the *airts* of the wind – moor in front, moor behind, and moor to right and left. Such is the land through which we are now passing. At length I arrive opposite a tavern, with "hot meals" announced in the window.

Can it be possible in such a place as this? I cast my eyes up, and see over the door a gorgeous painting of sunset, all red herrings and Findon haddocks, and over it, in large characters, the name of the house, "The Rising Sun." Calling to mind the old proverb enforcing us not to judge by appearance, I enter. In a suave, bland voice I ask, "What can I have?" "Some nice fish, sir," says the host. "How long before they are ready – twenty minutes or half an hour? for I wish to look after my cattle first." "Say thirty minutes," replied the host. "Very well," meekly I answered, and made my exit forthwith, and attended to the wants of my four-footed beasts, anticipating the meal. Fish – only think! fish – which I had not eaten for ever so long.

At the appointed moment I found myself entering the house with fish on the brain. On being shown into the dining-room, I discovered a dirty towel spread on the table, a loaf of very doubtful bread, a plate, and a small box of sardines. "Ah! an appetiser. This fellow understands the secret of living!" mentally exclaimed I. So I sat down and ate the sardines, and vociferously knocked on the table for the waiter to bring the *pièce de resistance*.

The host entered.

"Those sardines were very good. It was very thoughtful of you to provide them. I will now, if you please, have the fish – the *poisons*;" for I thought to make a facetious joke.

The landlord stared; so did I. At length he gasped, "You have eaten the fish."

"You don't call those fish?" I cried out furiously.

"Well, what do you call them?" he answered.

I seized the empty sardine-box. He retired rapidly, and closed the door between us.

Vowing vengeance on the perpetrator of such a joke – for I do not like jokes when I am the victim – I pondered over my disappointment, and lit my pipe to help me to think. At first I considered myself a very ill-used man; then that I had been grossly deceived; and before I left the table I asked myself the question, Are sardines not fish?

GUARDIAN OF THE NIGHT
The moon, wherever seen from this earth, would be supposed to look exactly the same; but such is not the case in South Africa, for not only does the guardian of the night look double her preconceived size, but her radiance

seems increased many fold also. To read ordinary type by her light is easy; to distinguish the hours on your watch not difficult; and I have before now, in that country, sewn on a button or mended a rent in my clothes by her rays, without the assistance of lamp or candle.

MARY BARBER

Barber, mother of Fred and Harry whom we have encountered in the Matabeleland bush, was a remarkable woman. Married to an Eastern Cape farmer and sometime diamond miner, she developed a wide-ranging interest in natural history. She published scientific papers, discovered and had named for her a variety of insects and plants, corresponded with one of the most distinguished botanists of the age, Joseph Dalton Hooker, and influenced Darwin's work on the origin of species. She was also a keen amateur archaeologist, an artist of considerable talent, and a poet. These two pieces are from her journal of a trip from the Kimberley diamond fields to Cape Town, then by boat to Durban. There she holidayed with her brother, the retired James Bowker who wrote the account of the "cannibal cave" quoted earlier in these pages.

RESIGNED TO HIS FATE

The Umgeni railway line is very picturesque, winding through the partially wooded hills and vallies near Durban, and on round the spur of the Berea to several stations in the neighbourhood. It was in this vicinity, while awaiting the arrival of the train one day, that we witnessed rather an amusing incident. I will tell it, so that the mothers of Natal may thereby become aware of the lessons in patience and resignation which their children (unknown to them) are being taught.

A Kafir girl near one of these stations, was in charge of a little boy about twelve or fourteen months old, when suddenly, some of her friends called to her from the opposite side of the hill. The girl, after having answered their call, took a nice soft piece of twine out of her pocket (which had evidently been used before for the same purpose) and deliberately tied the little fellow up to the stem of a tree, not very far from the station. Poor little boy! he was used to it, and appeared to be quite resigned to his fate. He sat down, and without crying or uttering a word of complaint commenced playing with the stems of a plant; whilst away went his nurse at full speed to join her friends on the hill side: he appeared to possess full confidence in her return.

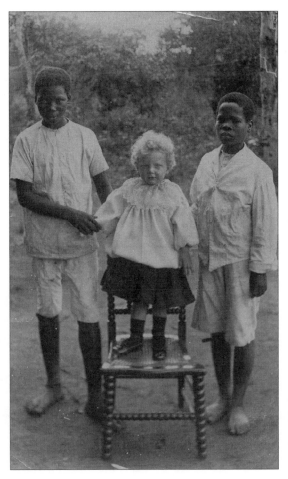

JUST LIKE THE GOVERNMENT
Still in Natal.

In this neighbourhood a Dutchman turned up who was chatting with my brother. They evidently knew each other very well. The Dutchman was complaining bitterly of the long continued seasons of drought, and regretting the days of his youth, at which time, he said, heaven dealt more leniently with the farmers; that the thunderstorms occurred at shorter intervals to gladden the face of nature and the growing corn. My brother, wishing to have a little joke with him, remarked that it was all very well when electricity was abundant, "but now", said he, "the most of it is required for the electric telegraph". His friend failed to see the joke in this, and, firing up in a moment, declared that he had never thought of this before, but of course it sufficiently accounted for the deficiency of thunderstorms, – "it was just like the government," he said; "it was always doing stupid things, always oppressing the people, and ruining the country", and away he went, vowing vengeance against the government, and declaring that "if a telegraph pole was planted on his farm he would immediately have it chopped down". We could not explain, he was too angry to listen to reason.

DAVID KENNEDY

The writer was a member of "the Kennedy family of Scottish vocalists"; while two other brothers studied singing in Milan, he, his father and two sisters toured South Africa in 1879. They performed to appreciative audiences in venues such as the courtroom in Fauresmith, where people brought their own chairs, and a general dealer's store in Alice, where they borrowed a piano for the occasion. At the nearby Lovedale mission they attended a church service, and were overwhelmed by the sound of 300 voices pronouncing Xhosa clicks in unison, and by the bass they achieved. "These Kafirs actually were singing down to C below the stave," Kennedy noted in amazement. The Kennedys planned to visit India the following year.

Diggers on their way to the diamond fields.

MY POOR MURDERED QUEEN
We found in South Africa, even more markedly than in Australia, that English and other nationalities highly appreciated Scottish song. We met with several instances of how enthusiastic Scottish feeling exists in the midst of colonial life, which, with its prosaic features and struggle after material wealth, is not always the best conserver of national sentiment. This feeling is apt to become eccentric, as

was the case with the Scotsman of King William's Town, who had a portrait of Mary Queen of Scots hung in his bedroom, and who, every morning on rising, stretched his hands towards it, crying, "Oh, my poor murdered queen!"

THE BIGGEST HOLE
At Kimberley, then only nine years old, the Kennedys performed at the Theatre Royal, and ate cabbages that cost 7s 6d each.

We made it our first business to go and see the world-famous mine, only a few minutes' walk from the hotel; for the town is built close to the edge of the mine. You come to the end of a street, and see a slight rise – all that remains of the old Colesberg "koppie." A few steps further, and you stand on the clear-cut brink of the biggest hole that man has ever dug. A vast crater suddenly yawns at your feet. It is shaped like a bowl, has sloping sides of light-coloured rock, stretching down to the blue diamondiferous soil at the bottom. Such is the expanse of the mine, that in the first hasty glance you may actually fail to note for a few moments that it is alive with human beings; but there are more men down there than would people half-a-dozen villages. You see thousands of blacks working in the claims at the bottom, and dotted like ants on the sides. You see every nook and corner, every man in the mine, every one of the many interests that centre here, all displayed at once. The claims lie clearly spread out beneath you like a map, – an expanse of small blocks, which do not look to be thirty feet square. These present great irregularities, as some of the claims are being worked faster than others. If a claim stands idle, the adjoining workers, digging

The Kimberley mine.

311

down on either side, leave it standing like a square tower; but there is a law which compels a man to work, if his claim is becoming dangerous to those around him. You see the blacks busily toiling round sheer clay battlements at one place, shovelling on the edge of steep precipices here, climbing up naked pillars of earth there, the column being marked with tiny holes, the only foothold of the daring worker. Square pools of water gleam in several places, and walls of dark blue clay cross and re-cross the whole bed of the mine. Round the margin of this deep bowl circles a fringe of steam machinery, working the buckets that run up and down on wires, and convey the "blue," as the diamondiferous soil is called, to the surface. These wires converge from all sides into the bottom of the mine. They are not very large, but very numerous. They stand out like threads of silver, when struck by the sun's rays; but in some lights, or when viewed against the darker side of the mine, are not visible at all. The mingled hum of voices rising from the seething mass of labour below, the whirring of the many buckets flying through the air, the Æolian murmur of the wind playing over the web of wires, the far and near rumble of vehicles running round the edge of the mine, – are every whit as wonderful to the ear as the sight is strange to the eye. At one place there has been a shaft sunk by Baring, Gould, & Co., so as to do away with an ærial tramway; and at another, a tramway has been run down through a narrow cleft, cut deeply into the lip of the mine, in order to diminish the gradient.

Once we saw the mine late in the afternoon, when the men were leaving work. The spectacle was extraordinary. Out from the depths of the mine the Kafirs were swarming, like bees from a disturbed hive. Some were crawling up the steep slopes; some skipping along narrow tracks, where, from our distant standpoint, we could see no foothold; some jumping from ledge to ledge; here and there a couple of them coming up in a bucket, with other Kafirs hanging on to the bottom of it by the runners, flying through the air on such a lengthy journey that you could scarcely believe a man could suspend himself by the arms so long. On all sides the Kafirs were scrambling up to the surface – laughing, shouting, and singing, as merry as boys released from school. A dense continuous file of Kafirs was all the time walking up the tramway: Kafirs half clad, Kafirs in old great-coats, Kafirs in jackets made out of sacks, Kafirs in shirts, Kafirs in corduroy. Large numbers of them, too, had on old soldiers' coats, which generally showed up in bright red specks all over the workings. As the men were dispersing, the blasting operations commenced. A bell is supposed to ring, as the signal for the firing; but on this occasion several shots were fired before the warning rang out, and before the mine had been emptied of its dusky labourers. The charges are lit by one or two of the "boys" belonging to the different claims, while the proprietors look down from the brink. One claim-owner standing near us wished he had an opera-glass, so that he could see if his Kafir was lighting the fuse properly. Every few moments a quick puff of smoke burst from the floor of the mine, followed by a dull rumbling sound, and an immense mass of rock would heave slowly over with a grinding crash. When a more than usually good shot went off, the Kafirs clapped their hands and hurrahed, the mine echoing and re-echoing with their shouts. Frequently the hard clay would fly up viciously, and everybody ducked their heads behind the edge, though there seemed little fear of fragments reaching us at such an elevation. It was most exciting to see two or three blasts simultaneously – the whole crater-like mine seeming in volcanic convulsion, and the Kafir stragglers, in a state of scare, leaping behind clay walls, running into holes, or dashing excitedly up the sides. We overheard a claim-owner remark, rubbing his hands gleefully as he saw the flying pieces of rock: "Aha! that shot has landed a rich lump on *my* claim!" In a few minutes, the huge basin, so lately a scene of busy life, was as silent as an open grave. Soon the sunlight faded away from the opposite brink, and the dark blue of twilight gradually settled down in the bottom of the mine.

SHE'S A PRISONER

My father and I paid a visit to the Kimberley gaol. Among gaols it is unique. The buildings lack, of necessity, the massiveness and seclusiveness that prisons have in England – what can be done with sun-burnt bricks, wood, and corrugated iron? – and the general business of the gaol is managed in an off-hand, amateurish way that contrasts strangely with the sharp routine and dignity of an old-country gaol. We remember it as seeming like a lot of white-washed out-houses scattered round two rough back yards, while the warders, not having any uniform, might have been judged from their clothes and general air to be plasterers, or plumbers, or anything, in short, rather than gaolers. In the prison-yards were Zulu policemen, squatting in picturesque groups on the ground. In company with the energetic visiting-doctor we made the round of the cells. In the first were two native chiefs, who suffered the indignity of having to put out their tongues to the doctor. Next cell contained a number of coloured criminals, crouching round the wall, who were all adjudged in good condition. A sort of general inspection of health then took place about the court-yard, our friend the doctor thoroughly but deftly disposing of the various cases. Here there was a treadmill, the criminal power of which is utilised for the noble purpose of turning a washing-machine. I stepped on the wheel and trod for a few revolutions, the Kafirs on the mill looking as if they thought me an

Kimberley jail.

egregious fool. Close by was a large cell, containing a most unusual spectacle: a tribe of bushmen, not criminals, but starving refugees from the war in Secocoeni's country, far to the north of Griqualand. There they were, all herded together – men, women, and children. Dwarfish, yellow, ugly-visaged people they were; the race who, in their native state, live in mountain-caves, shoot with the poisoned arrow, use the flint and steel, and smoke their native opium; whose forefathers painted those marvellous pictures on the rocks, which have ever been the wonder of

ethnologists. This huddled crowd of emaciated beings was a sight which, once seen, could not be forgotten. One could never dream that hunger and privation and savage life would lower man so near to the level of the brute; and yet there was the bushwoman "skelping" her squalling child, just like any fond British mother. In a room not far from this we were introduced to two ladies, one of them the matron of the gaol. My father invited her to come and hear our concert; he could not do less than proffer a ticket to the decent old lady who sat knitting beside her. "She's a prisoner," whispered the matron. "Ah, Mr Kennedy," said the decent old lady, "here they put people in the gaol for things they would never dream of at home." We were not long in discovering that she was Mrs —, a notorious buyer of stolen diamonds!

MRS HUTCHINSON

Mrs Hutchinson, whose book does not reveal her first name, penned a spirited account of a nine-month sojourn in South Africa. Her husband George, an officer in the Perthshire Volunteers, was ordered to Natal in 1878 as war with the Zulu loomed. She accompanied him to Durban on a troopship. His unit was ordered to Utrecht in the Transvaal; she persuaded him that they should buy a horse so she could go too.

OH, THAT RIDE!

My husband's consent, however, was only half the battle, and that the least important half by far; for on the morning of the day on which he was to begin his march, I received a note, in which he said that he was unexpectedly detained at the barracks, and that unless I felt up to going into the market and buying the horse myself, I should have to be left behind after all.

Of course, I felt up to it. In the face of such a contingency, I would as soon have set out to buy a balloon as a horse – and, in fact, am about as competent a judge of the good points of the one as the other. Accordingly to the horse auction I went, and should probably have got into sad difficulties if it had not been for the extreme kindness of some of the gentlemen staying in the hotel, who volunteered to help me in making so important a purchase; and, to cut the matter short, I found myself, by the afternoon, the possessor of a dark-brown mare, not bad looking, sound in wind and limb, together with a saddle and bridle and all other equipage appertaining.

The bargain was not completed till some time after my husband had been compelled to march his party out; but as I had taken the mare, or rather she had taken me, for a pretty successful trial trip down the street, I felt no uneasiness at being left to come out alone to the camp in the cool of the evening.

Oh, that ride! It is the one recollection connected with South Africa that will recur to me with laughter till my dying day. I may as well say at once that, though I am accustomed to driving, I know about as much of riding as of navigating a ship, but my dignity would not suffer this to appear; so I scrambled into the saddle with any amount of assurance, and as (I suppose from looking at other people) I found I was able to assume a fairly square seat, I produced upon the party assembled to see me off a far better impression of my skill than I either pretended to or deserved.

The mare, however, was not to be taken in. Before we had gone fifty yards from the door, the intelligent creature set off at a smart trot, evincing a desire to get over the ground with which I fully sympathized. The trot, however, quickened into a canter, which became faster and faster; and by the time we had got into the principal street of Durban, we were dashing along in fine imitation of the great Gilpin, avoiding collision with the carriages and great ox-waggons by what appeared to be either a miracle, or some extraordinary talent for judging distances on the part of the mare. It was not that I would not have stopped if I could. I twisted the reins round my arm, round the pommel, and even thought, impelled by phaeton experiences, of trying to get them round my leg, and pulled with all my might, first this way, then that, then all together. But I did not know then, what I now hear to be a notorious fact, namely, that a Cape horse has, as a rule, a mouth like the trunk of a tree, and that, once set going, nothing short of a dead wall ahead, or his own disinclination to go on, will stop him. It was the latter which brought the mare to a standstill at last, on the pavement, amongst a crowd of people. A friend who had witnessed our struggles now came up, and implored me, as I valued my life, not to attempt to go any further.

"I must go on," I said, "to Maritzburg. Indeed, I cannot stop." Which was true enough, as, some one having led the mare into the road and pointed her head in the required direction, we were off again, and only stopped when we reached the level crossing, of which the mare insisted on making a careful examination before taking me any further. Being now out of the town, I thought it was safe to give vent to the indignation I had been smothering all the way; and as her head seemed to be the only part where she had any feeling, I fell upon her, and belaboured her soundly about the ears, which she took in such very bad part that she made a rush for a ditch full of nettles, landed safely on the other side in about ten inches of sand, and there remained with her head towards the bush, and nothing that I could do would bring it round.

I know of no reason why I should not have been there still, if it had not been that a gentleman, in passing, was struck with my forlorn situation, and offered to escort me a few miles on the way to Roy Koppas, where our camp was to be pitched. I need not say that I gladly availed myself of his kindness, and the rest of the journey was made in comparative comfort, with the exception of the last two or three miles, when I had to go on alone and give battle to the mare in the dark.

DANCING WITH RAGE

As soon as the column came down the hill, the tug of war began. The commissariat officer, who is young and energetic, had made up his mind that we should make the halt for breakfast on the further side of the river; the master of the wagons, glorying in his independence, "concluded," as Yankees say, to stop on this. The contention was carried on with great spirit on both sides, and was an edifying spectacle to us who were privileged to sit round on the grass, dying with hunger, while we watched this battle of the gods. While the tumult was at its highest, we attempted another adjournment to the hotel, but were speedily called back to our duty, with-

out having had time to swallow a mouthful of anything more satisfying than soda-water. We were now at the end of the sixth hour, and matters were still at a dead-lock, all of us who constituted the rank-and-file of the opposing armies beginning to look exceedingly grim, and to display a certain amount of tartness in our conversation with one another.

Our young officer, who made up in spirit and resolution what he may have lacked in years and previous experience, evinced every determination to face starvation for himself (and the rest of us) sooner than give way; but as her Majesty's troops must on no account be included in this inconvenience, the men were all transported across the water in the ferry-boat, and sat down to a comfortable meal on the other side.

"There shall be an account rendered for this conduct," said our officer, whose dignity had received unpardonable affront at being publicly bearded by this insolent official. "The man will never have another contract with Government again, I will take care of that."

"My oxen are outspanned, and he may get them in again if he can," announced the other, on the step of the hotel, appealing to Mrs. Chose and myself as the nearest audience. "What do I care for his contracts? Tell me that! The oxen are mine and the wagons are mine. I'm a Natalian, I am. Oh, yes, I'm a Natalian!"

"You're not," said I, mistaking the sound. "Whoever heard of an *Italian* called Dickens? Don't talk such stuff!"

This turned the vials of his wrath upon us.

"I tell you I am a Natalian!" he shouted, absolutely dancing with rage. "I never was so insulted before."

"And we never were so hungry before," we retorted, with pardonable asperity, as we resumed our prowl round the baggage-wagon, in search of something to devour.

/HAN≠KASS'O

Son-in-law of Wilhelm Bleek's San informant //Kabbo, /Han≠kass'o lived at the Bitterpits south of Kenhardt. He had also served time in the Breakwater Prison. After the death, within months of each other, of Bleek and //Kabbo, /Han≠kass'o returned voluntarily to Cape Town in 1878 to continue the work, with Lucy Lloyd, of recording San kukummi. This was not without cost: his wife and an infant son died on the journey to the Cape, and though he was a gentle and kindly man, the two years he spent with Lloyd, cut off from his own people, were very lonely. He returned to the northern Cape in December 1879: his fate is unknown. Here is his account of the ceremonials on Cape Town's Grand Parade organised for the return of governor Sir Bartle Frere, architect of the Anglo-Zulu War, from a trip in early 1879 to the Transvaal. While in Pretoria, where he had been negotiating with Boers chafing against the British annexation of the territory two years earlier, Frere was formally censured by the home government for his conduct of the Zululand campaign. However, public opinion at the Cape was firmly behind him, and his journey back to Cape Town turned into a triumphal procession, with flag-decorated streets, escorts, triumphal arches and banquets in the towns he passed through. His reception on the Parade was no less enthusiastic.

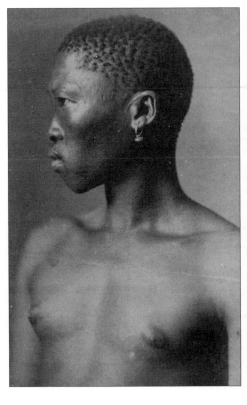

/Han≠kass'o

AMONG THE PEOPLE, PEOPLE

The people were turning about; they were turning about! They stood still, stood in rows. The other people stood together. They watched what the people were doing. The children gathered themselves together; they looked at what the people were doing, looked at the people who arranged the people in lines, so that the people might stand quietly, keeping in lines, the people standing behind. The children stood upon the parade because they did not have place where they could stand. They stood upon the parade because they did not have a place where they could come to stand. Therefore, when the cannon fired, the people who had been where the train stops came running. They ran, coming among the people who had been standing. They also stood.

A dog came in among the people; it looked about for a place through which it could go. It went in among the people; it went among the people, people, people, people. It went in among the people, went through the people and came out yonder, behind the people. And then he came back again, because the children frightened him back: he came back again to the people. He went in among the people. He came out on this side of the people. Then he took the road. He seems to have returned home, for I did not see him again. When the great white man was passing along between them, the people went forward, while the people felt that they were following the great white man. And the people who were riding followed the people who were red (i.e. the soldiers). And other people followed them in the middle of the street, the people with white caps (i.e. the volunteers). And the people who played, followed them. The people whose caps were white, they were those who went in front (of the volunteer cavalry and band), because they were those who followed the great white man. The people who were riding (the volunteer cavalry) followed them. And the people who played, they too followed them. And the people went forward altogether; the people were no longer there.

BERTRAM MITFORD

Mitford came to South Africa from England in 1882 specifically to visit all the battlefields of the Anglo-Zulu War. He recorded several first-hand accounts by Zulu warriors who took part in the campaign, and a Union Jack fluttering at Isandhlwana, scene of one of colonial Britain's most humiliating military defeats, moved him to verse:

> *... fitter monument ne'er crowned the fallen soldier's grave,*
> *Oft upon blazoned fold unwound floating o'er land and wave,*
> *Emblem of Britain's might renowned, watching o'er her brave.*

Some 1,500 troops and at least 2,500 Zulus died in the battle and its immediate aftermath, which included a frenzied and bloody pursuit of fleeing remnants of the imperial forces.

LITTLE HEAPS OF STONES
One morning I started from Isandhlwana to explore the line of retreat to "Fugitives' Drift," as it is now called, accompanied by one of the mission clergy, who had kindly offered to act as guide. Riding over the camp ground we crossed the waggon road on the "neck," and struck into the narrow path running along the base of "Black's Kopje" down into the ravine.

Isandhlwana: after the battle.

Heaps of *débris* lay about – bones and skulls of oxen, belt buckles, sardine tins, shrivelled-up boots, the nails falling out of the rotting soles, odds and ends of clothing, old brushes – in fact, rubbish of all sorts; while every ten or twenty yards we would come upon sadder traces of the flight in the shape of little heaps of stones, through the interstices of which could be seen the bones of some unfortunate buried underneath. The track is smooth enough for three or four hundred yards, and then the trouble begins; as we get among the thorns the ground is seamed with deep dongas yawning suddenly before us, rendering riding anything but safe. Now we are on the brink

Fleeing from the Zulu.

of one of these chasms; then the track suddenly diverging, takes us along a narrow razor-like ridge with a fall of some fifteen or twenty feet on either side. I pictured to myself what long odds were against a lot of men riding for their lives over such ground, all crowding upon each other, and the savage enemy behind rushing in among them with unearthly yells, driving the maddened horses into the dongas and stabbing their riders – and many seemed to have come to grief here, judging from the traces. At the bottom of one of these fissures lay the fragments of an ammunition train, which had evidently taken a regular "header," the shattered skeletons of four horses or mules in a heap together, and thinly covered over with stones those of the two unfortunates who presumably were with the team. Among twisted-up ends of old straps and harness, ammunition boxes splintered and broken were strewn. I found the rope handle of one of these intact, and very hard I had to saw at it before I could get it off. Pretty good this, after three years of exposure to weather. On all sides were traces and remains of the flight; here and there one would come upon significant heaps of earth or stones, or a rag of clothing fluttering on a bush just as it had been torn from some fugitive. After crossing the stream at the bottom of the valley the ground is open, but fearfully rough and stony, and so it continues the whole way. The bulk of those who fled must have been killed within the first couple of miles, according to the signs.

FLORENCE DIXIE

After spending six months exploring Patagonia, Lady Florence Dixie had been planning to cross Alaska and the Bering Straits with Indian guides in order to spend a winter on the "mystic Arctic shores of far-off Tuski land". However she changed her mind at the last minute, volunteering instead to nurse wounded British soldiers in South Africa, where the independence-seeking Transvaal Boers had humiliated Sir George Colley's forces at Laing's Nek. The Morning Post *appointed her its correspondent, and although the war ended in March 1881, before she reached the front, she covered the ensuing negotiations on the status of the*

*Transvaal for the newspaper, thus becoming the first official woman war corre-
spondent. In later years she campaigned for the deposed Cetshwayo's restitution to
the Zulu throne, home rule in Ireland, and equal rights for women, including par-
ity of dress between the sexes. Brand, the owner of the mules that Dixie encounters
here at a hostelry below Laing's Nek, was president of the Orange Free State, and
had been mediating between the Transvalers and the British.*

PRESIDENT BRAND'S MULES

The stable accommodation was not of the best, but I managed to secure a
snug corner, into which I put the horses and mules; and within a short time
after our arrival I was gratified to find them all eating heartily, and making
a good meal off oats, hay, and Indian corn. While watching them I was
somewhat surprised to see a mule-driver lead in six fat, well-to-do mules,
and proceed to eject mine. As soon as my astonishment had in a measure
subsided, I made a dash for the man, and angrily inquired what he was
about. In very broken English he replied that he was making room for
President Brand's mules.

"What do I care whose mules they are?" I answered; "mine are not to be
moved from here."

"But dese are de President's," gasped the Kaffir, gazing at me in astonishment.

"Well, and if they are, what of that?" said I, defiantly; "mine are as good
as the President's any day; so make off at once and find room elsewhere."

A smile stole over the Kaffir's face as he heard me compare his well-fed,
sleek, and pampered mules to my thin, wretched-looking animals. The comparison was doubtless hastily made, and in the heat of dispute; as I made the
assertion I felt that the strictest truth was not being adhered to, and I could
hardly keep from laughing myself. How the matter would have ended I do
not know, had not President Brand at this juncture made his appearance, and
ordered his man forthwith to obey me. The Free State mules were relegated
to other quarters, and my poor tired animals left in peace.

WILLIAM CLARK RUSSELL

Russell was author of a small armada of maritime works, including Sailors'
Language, *a dictionary of sea terms, and* The Wreck of the "Grosvenor", *an
account of the loss of a fictitious vessel on the way to the Bermudas. He travelled
to the Cape by steamer in the mid-1880s, and his book* A Voyage to the Cape *was
written to enlighten readers on the inner workings of these "powerful iron sea
palaces". It includes nine pages on modern and old-fashioned ways of taking depth
soundings, and a diatribe against the presence of pianos on long voyages.*

A RATHER SERIOUS THING

The plum-pudding was a failure. There was a curious rumour that the singular sloppiness of it had provoked some tears from one cook and dark
threats from the other. Plum-pudding is all very well on Christmas Day at
home when, snow or no snow, the indications of the thermometer serve as an
apology for dyspepsia. But plum-pudding heavy, dark, and on fire within a

few hundred miles of the equator, when the light of the sun has a distinct sting in it, and when gentlemen who undertake to eat the dish go to work upon it in duck trousers, no waistcoat, and faces inflamed with perspiration, is a rather serious thing. It is like hot pea-soup and the smoking roast leg of pork, not to mention the iron-like sausage and the liver and bacon – the bacon all lean, and cut in stout steaks – which they will insist upon serving up when the sun stands right overhead, and the following breeze leaves the atmosphere on deck a dead and scarce breathable heat.

FRANK FILLIS

Fillis was a showman whose travelling circus became a household word in South Africa in the 1880s and '90s. He bankrupted himself with a tour to England that included a Zulu chief who had been at Isandhlwana, President Kruger's ex-coachman, five elephants and a crack-shot Boer who wore a silver skullcap to cover a bullet wound received in action against the British.

NOG EENSLAG!
One day our horses got knocked up, and it became evident that we could not proceed much further – a serious state of affairs in a sparsely populated country with not too many houses of accommodation or hotels. Soon however, we came to a farmhouse, and we decided to enquire whether the farmer and his good wife could put us up for the night. None of us knew Dutch, but got a boy to act as interpreter, and he made our request known to the farmer.

Frank Fillis

"No," replied the latter in a gruff and decided tone, and speaking, of course, in the *taal*, "you must trek on."

Now it was all very well to say trek on, but here was I with a cart load of ladies, two horses knocked up, and the only house of accommodation twelve miles distant. A nice how-d'you-do indeed. I told the farmer that we would pay him well, but he was obdurate, and finding all my entreaties of no avail, I told the boy to inspan and determined to make the best of it.

Now I am sure I don't know why I did it, but being a little lively – though there seemed small enough occasion for such a feeling – and by way of an innocent diversion, I suddenly commenced to turn somersaults in the field in front of the Boer's house. The effect was electrical. The old man leapt to his feet, for he had been sitting on his stoep smoking his pipe, and stared at me in sheer amazement. Presumably he had never seen a man turn a somersault before.

321

"Nog eenslag!" ("again") he shouted out. Thinking to please him, and bring him round to a more hospitable frame of mind, I repeated the performance. "Alle machtie!" cried the old Boer, and he rushed into the house to fetch out his good *vrouw*.

A stout old lady made her appearance, and once more the command went forth.

"Nog eenslag! Kijk die schepsel!" ("Look at this.") I repeated the performance. The farmer straightway stopped the boy from inspanning the horses, sent them into his best stable, placed the best rooms in his house at the disposal of the ladies, and gave us all a right royal reception and entertainment. He lent us sound horses in place of our sick ones, and the following morning sent us on our way rejoicing; nor would he accept a penny of payment. But I may tell you that in another way I paid pretty dearly for our night's accommodation. For by the time we had finished supper, the old Boer must have had in his house generations of kinsfolks – sisters, brothers, uncles, aunts, and cousins in dozens from the whole country round. And as each new arrival appeared on the scene that awful word was dinned into my ears, "Nog eenslag!" ("Do it again.")

MARIANNE NORTH

The only continent not visited by this extraordinary woman was Antarctica, and she probably would have found a way of getting there had she been told it offered botanical specimens worth painting. She took her sketchbooks to the highlands of Brazil, painted towering gums and pink cockatoos in Australia (where she went at the urging of Charles Darwin), climbed a volcano in Java, and in California lamented the fate of the vanishing redwoods. North's last journey, in 1884-85, was to paint auricarias in Chile. In her autobiography she quotes an apocryphal story about a fellow globetrotting female artist, who was asked if she would like to go to New Guinea. Oh yes, she replied, but she was married now, and it was not the sort of place one could take a man to. North herself never took a husband: the world is probably the richer for it. Her works are displayed in a specially constructed gallery at Kew Gardens. This extract finds her on a day trip to Van Stadens gorge, outside Port Elizabeth, in 1882. Sparaxis pendula is a dainty member of the iris family, with masses of pink bells hanging from a reed-like stem.

I WAS SURE YOU WOULD DO THAT

Just where the water bubbled out purest and freshest were quantities of a small pink and white disa and lovely droseras. We returned over the windy downs on the other side of the hills amidst acres of protea bushes of different sorts, and huge everlasting-plants standing a yard

322

or two above the ground, with white velvety leaves round a thick stalk, surmounted by a cauliflower head of white petals and yellow stamens. These looked like tombstones at a distance. A gentleman who had been also to the gorge cut one of the great things down, and carried it home over his shoulder for me to paint, for which I was grateful, for it was no small weight. One of the proteas had a deep dahlia-carmine centre and pink bracts edged with white ostrich feathers, the leaves exquisitely tinted with lilac, like the bloom on plums. After leaving those downs, we came to a marshy hollow, and saw the *Sparaxis pendula* for the first time. Its almost invisible stalks stood four or five feet high, waving in the wind. These were weighed down by strings of lovely pink bells, with yellow calyx, and buds; they followed the winding marsh, and looked like a pink snake in the distance, making me scream with joy when I first saw them. "I was sure you would do that," said my guide contentedly.

JOHN KNOX BOKWE

Known to his fellow Xhosa as Umdengentonga, one whose stature is out of all proportion to his diminutive size, Bokwe was a product of the Eastern Cape's Lovedale College. The college was founded by the Glasgow Missionary Society as a centre for Christian education. He was ordained as a Prebyterian minister, published a collection of hymns and a biography of the early convert Ntsikana, and briefly partnered J Tengo Jabavu on the weekly newspaper Imvo Zabantsundu. *In 1884, while on the Lovedale staff, he travelled to Cape Town with a consignment of the institution's products for the Cape Industrial Exhibition. The Lovedale stall, with wheelbarrows, handiwork, furniture, ironmongery, bookbinding, printing and agricultural produce, was reportedly a great success. Bokwe lodged at a boarding house in the city centre, carrying the address on a scrap of paper in his pocket in case he forgot it. He attended the theatre, promenade concerts and several churches, travelled to Robben Island to visit a Xhosa man jailed for life for killing a policeman in the 1877-78 frontier war, and visited the colonial education office. In a letter to Lovedale principal James Stewart after Bokwe's visit, Superintendent-General of Education Dr Langham Dale said the exhibition proved what the "native" could do while guided step by step by a European. The question now was whether he could "go it alone", without supervision.*

John Knox Bokwe

"I believe it will take another generation's persistent schooling and training, before the native has acquired that directive intelligence, self-reliance, moral steadiness, and modest self-measurement, which are necessary alike to the honest citizen and the useful workman," said Dale.

UP WENT THE BOTTLE
We join Bokwe, still a generation away from directive intelligence and moral steadiness, in the train on his way to the exhibition.

323

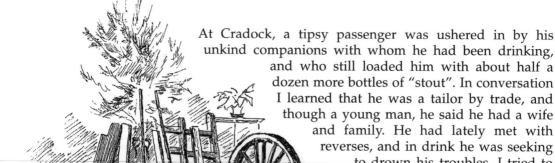

At Cradock, a tipsy passenger was ushered in by his unkind companions with whom he had been drinking, and who still loaded him with about half a dozen more bottles of "stout". In conversation I learned that he was a tailor by trade, and though a young man, he said he had a wife and family. He had lately met with reverses, and in drink he was seeking to drown his troubles. I tried to advise the poor fellow as to the right source where comfort could be found. He confessed the sorrow he had that he should give himself so much to drink, and thus break his old mother's heart, and cause discomfort to his family; but, he said, drink had such a hold of him that it was difficult to free himself, and his companions did not discourage his weakness for it. I felt he was a likable fellow, and noticed that all along the line he was pretty well-known. If he could only be separated from his companions, he thought, with God's help he might keep sober, or, at any rate, lead a better life. He made a vain resolve to turn over a new leaf; and mostly the whole of that day kept to his promise. Several times in his sober moments, I noticed tears falling down his cheeks. We were not alone at that time, as other passengers came in at De Aar. I could only lift my soul in prayer to God to help the poor man now suffering. One of the gentlemen in our carriage was unfortunately a *moderate* drinker, and the other an abstainer though not a pledged one. By and bye the moderate drinker produced from his pocket a flask of brandy, and took a sip. With longing eye I noticed how our weak brother watched the replacing of the bottle in its corner; the sight of the sparkling but cursed liquid, brought back the craving so ruinous to his life. War was within his breast whether he should ask for a drop, or keep to his resolution of only a few hours ago. In a moment the word was out of his mouth – "Please sir, I should thank you for a little from that bottle of yours." I reminded him of his promise, and tried to prevent his taking the drink. He excused himself by saying that it was to take away the stupefying effects of last night's over-indulgence. Up went the bottle, down rolled the drop, and the unhappy craving was raging anew! At the next station he got more drink, and later on brought a bottle into the carriage. To save him I pitched it with its wretched contents out of the window, but it was now of no use. At Beaufort West he was well-nigh left behind, for he had contracted new companions in the bar, and got more drink. When we reached Cape Town at 1 p.m. on Wednesday, 24th September, I bade my fellow-traveller goodbye, with one farewell warning to desist from the ruinous course he was following, and

The Lovedale stand at the industrial exhibition.

thought I had seen the last of him. But next morning I met him at the Telegraph Office, with a companion, and he was as drunk as the night we met at Cradock.

ROWDIES AND LOW CHARACTERS
In Cape Town.

It appeared to be the custom with some to powder the hair and paint the face, thus giving it a very ghastly and unnatural expression, and then sing to the people in the Exhibition. At first I could not make out what was wrong, but by and bye I saw the whole cause. On enquiry, I was told that this is the fashion of ladies or gentlemen, who act or sing on the stage. At once I determined to go to the Theatre and judge as to what kind of a place it is. Accordingly on Friday night, 3rd. Oct., while you in the Literary Society were profitably discussing the lives of John Bunyan and John Milton, I was among the rowdies and low characters of Cape Town, who had gone to pass their time in the gallery of the Theatre Royal. All ages and conditions of men and women were represented in the assemblage, from an infant in her mother's arms, to a grey-haired grandfather. Coming up the flight of stairs, previous to entering the Theatre, I passed no less than two *Bar-rooms* for the sale of liquor, and belonging to the Theatre Company. I thought within myself, – if the approaches to this place are of this nature, the good intended to those who frequent it must be of a doubtful character. My conclusion, – when I went in and saw the exciting scenes of the actors, and the spirit of the place, – was, that with the majority of those present, the lower the tone of the play the better it took; and the higher the tone was raised, I fear the less paying it would become to the managers; and that one's morality would not improve by frequent visits to theatres, if all are the same as the Theatre Royal, Cape Town.

WILLIAM HUNT

Hunt was an American cattle rancher, showman and adventurer who adopted the stage name Farini the Great after becoming the second man to walk a tightrope across the Niagara Falls. He imported a group of San to exhibit at Coney Island, and, his interest aroused by accounts of their homeland and the possibility of finding diamonds there, travelled in 1885 through the Kalahari to Lake Ngami. His equipage included 37 rifles, 12 mouth organs and a concertina. Hunt's colourful account of his experiences included the discovery of what has become known as the lost city of the Kalahari, an alleged collection of stone ruins which no subsequent travellers – including 20th-century expeditions – have been able to locate. No mean botanist, he was also the author of the work How to Grow Begonias.

GOTT HAT UNS NICHT VERLASSEN
Hunt discovered that the nubile hospitality offered to Andrew Geddes Bain extended far beyond Pondoland. The Kert here is Gert Louw, a hunter who acted as interpreter for the Coney Island San, while Fritz Landwer is a trader who also formed part of the expedition.

Chief Mapaar and his wife.

Two attendants at once showed us the way to the hut which was to be my home for the next week. At the entrance stood two old women, but on entering I was somewhat surprised to find standing in the middle of the floor, which was covered with skin mats, a young woman who was evidently expecting us, and who made no sign of an intention to retire. Kert explained that the height of hospitality among the Balala was to provide a visitor with a wife *ad interim*, and that the dark beauty in question had been allotted to me by the thoughtful consideration of Mapaar. I must at least make a pretence of satisfaction, and accept the favour in the spirit that prompted it, if I did not wish to offend the whole village.

Here was I, in the interior of the Dark Continent, a wanderer on the face of the earth, far from home, relations, and friends, suddenly provided with a home, and a wife, all ready, without trouble, expense, or ceremony. This beats the matrimonial agency business hollow. How many men would be glad to have some of the customs of Africa acclimatized in Europe and America, and marriage made easy *à la* Bakalahari!

And how many more men would be happy if divorces were as quickly arranged as in the Kalahari desert, which certainly carries off the palm from America in this respect!

"The dark beauty hath an exceeding strong aroma, very different from that of Rimmel's shop!" I urged.

"Oh!" interposed Fritz, who evidently read what was passing in my mind, if he did not quite understand my words, "dat is noddings; gif she to me, und I vill vatch dat. One so nice as half is good for me enough. I would not my nose up turn eef I her in Jarmany see. I am glad eef I find anodder so half as young."

But I felt it would not do to humour Master Fritz at the risk of offending Mapaar; so making semblance of being pleased, I sent for my blankets and took possession of my own domicile.

Towards evening, going over to the waggons to see how my followers were doing, I found a number of women about, making themselves quite at home, and asked Fritz who they were.

With unfeigned satisfaction beaming from his face, he replied, "Gott hat uns nicht verlassen; die Frauenzimmer sind unsere Weiber."

The other men were all equally happy, with plenty of meat, and wives to cook it for them; they were quite resigned to their fate, and for once I envied them. I could not accommodate myself to circumstances so easily; so staying out for a time to reflect how best to act, I returned to my hut just before dark, and, with an air of great fatigue, threw myself on my blankets and feigned sleep, to avoid offending my dusky bride, who presently stole out of the hut, attracted by the singing and revelry going on among our neighbours at the waggons. As the sun rose she returned, bringing some milk and mealies for my breakfast, and seemed quite pleased when I partook of her fare. I motioned to her to join me, but she drew back, shocked at the idea, which the tribe will not countenance, of a woman eating with a man – even though he were her husband!

AND HAD WOKE UP DEAD
Hunting ostriches on foot in the southern Kalahari, Hunt went further from camp than he intended, and found himself faced with a solitary night on the sands.

After plucking the best feathers, I lay down beside the bird, and casting care to the winds – though taking care to have my gun within reach, in case of a night attack – was soon fast asleep. The barking of the jackals and hyenas woke me two or three times; but with that exception I never slept more soundly. At dawn I woke, and was rubbing the sand out of my eyes, not feeling quite sure

Augrabies Falls

where I was, when my eyes lighted on a human face, only a few yards off, its gaze steadily fixed on mine. I seized my gun, but the being, whoever he was, did not flinch, and I thought I must be mistaken, and rubbed my eyes harder, but the only effect was to drive the sand more firmly in than ever. There, straight in front of me, was a human being – a Bushman by his colour – staring and grinning at me, all but his head and shoulders concealed behind a bush, or beneath a slight covering of sand. I approached and called out, but the being answered not, nor moved. It would never speak again. It was the dead body of some poor Bushman who had perished miserably while out hunting, for at his side lay his gun, and on the bush was hung a bunch of ostrich feathers – somewhat weather-worn, but still worth perhaps £20. The desert winds had performed the last office of burial, covering his body with a light pall of sand, leaving only his head exposed. Not an animal had molested this grave – a sure sign that the man had died of thirst; at least so the natives held, asserting that nothing will touch the body of such a man.

There was no doubt that the man had lain down to rest beside the bush, overcome with fatigue, thirst, and hunger, and had woke up dead. A shudder went through me as I reflected that my own fate might not be so very different, and that, had it not been for my trusty water-bottle, my bones might already have been keeping his company. Looking round at that moment, what was my dismay to see the bottle lying empty on the place

where I had slept! I had omitted to close it overnight, and now I was many hours away from home, and not a drop of water left. Still it was no use crying over water spilt in the desert: I must make the best of it, even if I had to carry my spoil all the way back. So I skinned the ostrich, and was tying my feathers up in a bunch with those of the dead Bushman, when I thought I would take the mummified skull of the man away as a memento. It was with some difficulty that I severed the vertebræ; but at last I succeeded, and then, gathering up my miscellaneous assortment of trophies, shouldered the Bushman's gun on one side, and my own on the other, and began my weary tramp back to the waggon.

This was not the end of the drama: Hunt claimed he then chewed some bulbs for moisture, which proved poisonous, and that he collapsed under the blazing sun, unable to see, speak or move. One of the expedition's dogs tracked him down.

Hunt's desert safari: "The first bath for many months."

HOUSES FOR HORSES

So we stayed where we were that night, and next morning moved on in an opposite direction, presently falling in with a gang of Bastard hunters – old friends of Kert's, who gave them a long account of the sights he had seen in England. He had seen the Queen, he said, who had asked him for a lock of his hair, and made him captain over the Bastards, telling him to take great care of the people for her sake. Then he described the number of people in England as being beyond all calculation: as thick as the ants and grasshoppers were on the veldt, to say nothing of the animals.

"What sort of house does the Queen live in?" asked one.

"Ah, you should see it! It has thirty-five windows one above the other; like thirty-five houses put one on the top of the other; and there are as many more under the ground."

"He! oh!" was the only remark his listeners made; but when he went on to say that there are no oxen, but "the horses and waggons are so thick that you can hardly cross the road," they gave vent to audible expressions of doubt, and I had to be appealed to, to verify these statements. This being done to their satisfaction, Kert continued, –

"You can walk for a day without seeing grass, nothing but stone roads and houses;" but he was pulled up short with a chorus of –

"Ha, Kert! we cannot believe that: how can all the horses live when the people outspan, if there is no grass?"

This was a poser, and Kert had to appeal to me; and when I explained that the horses had houses to sleep in,

Right: "Kert"

328

and that the grass was gathered a long way off and dried, and brought to them in their houses, they would hardly believe me.

"Houses for horses to live in and no grass?" one of them said inquiringly to Jan.

"Oh, yes; it's so," said Jan.

"Have you seen it?"

"Yes," he replied. "I have seen the same at the Diamond Fields, and at Cape Town, and I have seen cows which never go to the veldt, but live in houses which are cleaned and washed every day."

"The English must be fond of work to do this," was the philosophical reply. "Our way is much better; we can sit and drink coffee and smoke while the cattle feed themselves."

Kert then described how he had been to a circus, saying, "All the animals talk in England, and are taught to do all kinds of things like people. The Englishmen have lions in waggons, and go in amongst them and play with them, and the lions never kill them, but are afraid of them."

This they utterly refused to believe, even when Jan put in his spoke in support of Kert, and when, on appeal, I corroborated the statement. Their experience of lions was so completely at variance with this that they could not believe such a thing.

ANONYMOUS

The pessimistic John Pump's warnings in the 1850s on the dreadful consequences of railways went unheeded. From a pocket-sized 1887 guide to Grahamstown and Port Alfred titled Pleasure: Advice and Information to Those in Search of it.

LEAPING OVER THE SLEEPERS

Port Alfred is situated forty-three miles from Grahamstown by the railway. Trains at present leave the city every Monday, Wednesday, Friday, and Saturday morning at 8.30, arriving in Port Alfred at 11 o'clock, leaving the Port on the same days at 3 p.m., arriving in the city at 6.30 p.m. The fares are 5/6 third class, 7/6 second class, and 11/- first class; return fares – a single fare and a half. In holiday time there is usually an increase of trains and reduction in fares.

When the line was first used for traffic, before it had been properly consolidated and the arrangements perfected, some amusing incidents occurred. De-railing was of frequent occurrence, but never attended with any serious result, and it was always

taken as a matter of course. When any passenger felt by the bumping of the coach that the wheels were leaping over the sleepers, he would project himself from the window, swing his arms frantically and gesticulate violently, when the train was stopped and the coach put on its proper track. Likewise, if a passenger's hat blew off he would repeat the signals, and the obliging officials would stop the train and allow him to get out and pick it up. Cutting up live stock that strayed on the line was not at all an unusual business. Playful natives used to place large stones on the line and sit down alongside to watch results; but a careful look-out was always kept, and the result was invariably an exciting chase after the unsophisticated aborigine by the indignant passengers. On one occasion an excursion train proved too heavy for the engine to haul up an incline, so the male passengers alighted, put their shoulders to the wheels, and with a vigorous, united, and continued shove, pushed the train out of its difficulties. Another story is that the supply of coal running short, the train was halted while the driver and stoker went into the bush to chop wood. But those days of romance are now over, and the traffic is conducted like any other red-tape-tied concern.

RAMADEEN, AN INDIAN

Testimony in an official inquiry into the indenture system that brought thousands of Indians from their homeland as cheap and often badly treated labour for the burgeoning sugar plantations of Natal. The Indian Immigrants Commission sat from 1885 to 1887 under the chairmanship of supreme court judge Walter Wragg.

What can I say

I am going back to India. I was born in the district of Baraitch in India, which is one month's walking journey from Calcutta. When I left India, the nearest place, where the railway was from my place, was eighty miles. I can count twenty. It is ten years since I came here. I was ten years on Mr. Shires

Cane cutters.

estate (Milkwood Kraal). I came to that estate first, indentured. I have been nine years with the same master. I was two months with Mr. Binns, and two months at my house; after that I was at Mr. Kennedy's (Zee Cow Lake) eight months. I did not stay longer than nine years with Mr. Shires, as I did not care to go to the Umtshezi (Estcourt) where Mr. Shires was sending coolies. During these nine years I was treated well; my master never had occasion to punish me during that time. I have no fault to find with my master. I have not been in hospital. Mr. Shires employed many coolies – about two hundred. Mr. Shires takes good work and gives good wages. His coolies are contented. I am taking home £17 sewn up in a patch at the top of

330

my trousers at the back. I have some loose silver for the expenses of the way. I shall not have to unstitch my trousers for money before I reach Calcutta. When I step ashore at Calcutta I shall have the £17 clear. I do not think that if I had stayed at Calcutta I should have had £17 in hand. I have also lived well and spent much, and I might have saved more. I have no wife here. I have no children. I have had nothing to do with any woman here; but my brother died in India, his widow and child came here. She has not been living with another husband, but she has lived with me as my wife. She is not going back with me. While I am away she will live on money which I have given her for her expenses for a whole year; after that time I intend to come back. I have left with her, as money for such expenses, £8. I have bought for her jewellery – three bracelets, armlets, bangles, a necklace, anklets, nose-rings of gold, a pair of earrings; the whole are worth £9 6s. 9d.

During my ten years stay here I have not remitted money home to India through the office of the Protector of Immigrants.

I have been to Pietermaritzburg. I shall return from India in a year. I intend to go home to see my father and brothers and sisters; if they are alive I shall stay with them, if not, I shall shorten my stay and come back here. Here, I have eaten with the different people and broken my caste, my friends in India will not even eat with me, so I must come back. When I go back I will ask my mother to cook, but I will tell her what I have done; she will cook, and I will eat outside; she will not allow me to eat inside where she and my relatives are. No fine could bring me back my caste, being a Brahmin. Just before coming away my last offering to the Ganges was that of the holy thread: I was not worthy to wear it any longer. When the coolies come here, they lose all caste, even the Brahmins intermarry with the Shamars. What is to be done? In our own country if a Brahmin goes even for a call of nature, he must put a thread round his ear.

In my country we burn our dead. What can I say, being single? Burning the dead has never been done here. What is the use of saying anything?

HERMAN DAVIS
AND
EBEN LOOMIS

In October 1889 the United States government, under authority of a special Act of Congress, dispatched a scientific expedition on board the USS Pensacola to Cape Ledo in Angola to observe the total solar eclipse which was to occur on December 22 that year. The expedition had 12 tons of astronomical instruments, a gaggle of scientists that included experts in anthropology, terrestrial physics, language and botany, and a guard of marines to prevent any local cannibals eating the scientists. The instruments were operated by a pneumatic organ-valve system developed in New York. The scientists reached the site two weeks ahead of the event and set up camp. Davis, an assistant astronomer, takes up the tale.

HOW VAIN ARE EARTHLY HOPES

By hard work on the part of all, and for which thanks are especially due to the officers and crew of the Pensacola, we succeeded in getting our heavier apparatus in place, and in making a change of twelve inches in the length of our 40-foot telescope tube when at the last moment it was ascertained to be too short(!) and gave no well-defined image on the plate.

By 3 A.M. Sunday, Dec. 22, everything was fixed as well as possible under the circumstances and we retired to rest until sunrise.

At 5.30 the eastern sky became of a ruddy tinge, showing prospect of a beautiful day. At 6 it was a little obscure and remained so till 11.45, at which time the sky cleared and the sun came out very bright, raising the temperature exceedingly. During all our stay at Cape Ledo the characteristic of the weather was rain all night, cloudy mornings with rain occasionally and a very bright sun in the afternoon. Seeing it therefore become so clear at noon as usual, our hearts grew light. At dinner nearly all looked happy, but weary. The officers and men detailed to help us arrived from the ship, and while we were still eating the Pensacola steamed out to sea, to lie in the path of totality twenty miles off shore.

With "cannibals" at Cape Ledo.

We felt that the critical moment was drawing near. The eclipse was to begin according to calculation at about 1.30 P.M., and totality at 2.56, lasting 3 minutes 9 seconds, the eclipse itself ending at 4.12. At 1.15 every man was at his post. Prof. Todd, assisted by Messrs. Wright and Carbutt, took charge of the double-polar axis and the eighteen instruments erected on it. Mr. Jacoby, in addition to winding our chronometer, which was sure to stop every four minutes unless constantly rewound, had charge of the 74-foot Brashear mirror. Prof. Abbe with a corps of naval cadets took his position on the beach prepared for meteorological work and for sketching the corona. Prof. Bigelow assisted by myself was stationed at the 40-foot direct photo-heliograph which was to be in operation during the entire eclipse while the others were to run only while total darkness lasted.

Alas! how vain are earthly hopes even when centred on celestial objects. During totality the sun and moon were entirely obscured by clouds, shutting from our gaze all that beautiful halo of light – the corona – which flashes out around the dark moon and can be seen only during a total eclipse.

The *Pensacola*.

Yet of the various phases we obtained 110 photographs, which, however, I fear, owing to the clouds, will be of no scientific value. Thus, however hard it may be to do so, we must pronounce the Expedition a failure so far as astronomical results are concerned – even when considered as merely experimental, save in so far as failure is profitable.

Very soon after the eclipse we saw the Pensacola making her way slowly back, to report clouds where she had been.

STRUNG WITH FIRE AND GOLD
After the Angolan anticlimax, the ship headed south to Cape Town. Davis visited the leper colony on Robben Island, and the diamond mine at Kimberley. Loomis, the expedition botanist, found some consolation in the vistas of the Karoo, where he could experience the "sweet mystery of distance".

The day had been very hot. Thunder-storms had been passing around the horizon all day. I counted eight separate and distinct showers at one time, though none of them happened to reach the spot where I was. As the sun neared the western horizon, it was gradually obscured by an enormous, lurid-purple thunder-cloud. In the dark gorges and misty ravines of that vaporous floating mountain, incessant flashes of lightning scattered a quivering gleam of palest yellow. In the bosom of

333

this brooding cloud lurked the yet chained forces of a destructive tornado, ready at any moment to burst its bonds and descend earthward on its course of terror and desolation. But another force was there, – a milder, more beneficent, yet far stronger power, before whose advance the black vapor with its incipient tempest retreated, broken and disordered. On the misty boundary between cloud and plain, a thin line of sky, brilliant with sunshine, broke through the blackness, separating the heavy cloud from the horizon, and through this narrow opening topaz-shafted arrows of sun-light smote the threatening cohorts of the storm, and they vanished. Driven upward by the sun-god, the torn shreds of flying vapor, no longer threat-ening, no longer lurid, but transfigured by the chastening of defeat, caught splendor from their conqueror, and glowed with rose and gold and crim-son. By a strange chance the clouds which twined and wreathed them-selves into forms grotesque, fantastic, and beautiful, took at one time the exact shape of a mighty harp strung with fire and gold. Lying distinct and vivid against the lucent sky, its form was so perfect, even to small details, that I actually expected to hear throbs of divinest music fall from those glowing chords and thrill the sunset air with a wordless song of celestial sweetness. But the fingers of the wind, toying carelessly with the instru-ment, shivered string of gold and frame of fire, and spun the dismembered fragments into other forms of wondrous beauty, and changed and shaped and re-shaped them again and yet again, until the mind was bewildered in endeavoring to follow the infinite succession of form and color.

The sun, by this time below the horizon, shot up into the sky great shafts of light, illuminating every wreath of mist, every mote and dust-speck in the air, until the west was a fountain of flame which leaped in chords of beautiful color to the very keystone of the heavenly arch, and dashed itself into a glory of crimson spray on the silvery shore-line of a cirrus cloud which spanned the heavens from north to south through the zenith.

CHAPTER SEVEN

1890 to 1900

Wherein Mohandas Gandhi is thrown off a train,
a maniac dies of an overdose of hair-wash,
we visit the site of phallic festivities and
learn about the Ovambo dog sacrifice, and
despite all his precautions, poor Mr Theal
is dismembered by a lion.

LIONEL DECLE

*Decle was a journalist who had already travelled widely in other parts of the world
when he received a commission from the French government to study the ethnolo-
gy and anthropology of southern and central Africa. Travelling with a revolver at
his side, threatening violence to those who crossed him, he came to the conclusion
that African blacks were barely removed from animals, incapable of gratitude,
affection, or of measuring time, coupled "exactly like a beast" and lived almost
wholly for the purpose of eating. But he said that if it was possible to breed desir-
able traits into apes over successive generations, "then such a development must
be even more practicable in the case of the negro". Here Decle has arrived at the village of Palapye in what is now Botswana, in 1891.*

THE SAME ACCIDENT

Half an hour later the waggons
arrived, mine minus its awning,
which had been torn away by the
projecting branch of a tree.
Hundreds of waggons have to pass
this place – many have met with
the same misfortune – but not one
of the drivers who has gone by has
ever thought of cutting this branch
down. I have seen many a place of
the same kind in South Africa;
either it is a branch that carries
away the awning of a waggon, or a
tree against which all the waggons
will bang themselves, doing great
damage. The accident over, the
drivers deplore it and go on. Time

after time they will pass the same spot, meet with the same accident, spend a lot of time in repairing its consequences; but they would not dream of exerting themselves for five minutes in order to remove the cause, and so save others, or even themselves on their return journey.

A STAGNANT OOZE

It was with deep anxiety that I left Mesa. I knew that the next water was nearly sixty miles distant, and I wondered how the oxen, in their miserable state, would ever manage to cover this distance; on the 20th September we had already been forty-eight hours without water. The beasts were a pitiable sight, and I began to be very much afraid, as our chance of relieving them seemed still very distant. First one would fall and then another, and, once they were down, we had great difficulty in getting them to rise again. I sent one of my party foward to reconnoitre, and he returned reporting water about twenty-five miles distant. At last, after having been sixty-seven hours without water, I reached Mathlalamabedi with one waggon and the double team, the other waggon having been "left till called for."

But here again there was not enough for the oxen to drink, so I unyoked them, intending to send them forward a march of about three hours, to where I heard there was a large well. But I had hardly got them "out-spanned" when they rushed off at full gallop in the direction of the water, which they could now smell. Our difficulty then was to prevent them getting there, for the well is dug out to a depth of about thirteen feet below the level of the ground, and is only about fifteen feet in diameter; if they all arrived at the same time, there was great danger that they would knock one another about, and that some of them would get suffocated and trampled on. Already the first relay, to the number of sixteen, which had been sent on first, had escaped from their driver and rushed ahead, and had managed to crush one of their number, which I found afterwards lying in the water unable to rise. After an immense amount of trouble we hauled him out by means of "reims" attached to his horns and legs, but even then we could

not get him to his feet. At Mesa an ox had fallen exhausted, but I succeeded in getting him up by administering to him about half a bottle of brandy. I tried this method once more here, but without success at the time, although two hours later the beast managed to get up. We ourselves were dying of thirst, but the water was so terrible that even the "boys" had not the courage to touch it. Imagine a mass of blackish mud, upon the top of which was a stagnant ooze of liquid animal manure. Covered with this layer of filth, it gave forth a putrid odour which completely impregnated you if you touched it. I fished up a pailful, and having thrown some alum into it I filtered it over and over again, and having well boiled it made some coffee and determined to try it. The coffee was bitter, with a distinct ammoniacal taste, and in the evening I was seized with violent vomiting. But if I had the courage to drink it, I was not bold enough to wash in it, the smell was too dreadful.

SORROW FOR HIS FRIEND
The next day we came to the usual outspan, and there I witnessed a most amusing scene of animal intelligence. My donkey Jack used to follow the waggon like a dog. When we started he had probably been in search of some dainty morsel, and a few minutes after we had outspanned, he came along. Seeing a waggon he cantered towards it and stopped. This was not my waggon, but one belonging to Mr. Lloyd, a missionary, who has since written a book to refute what I said about Khama in a London paper. Jack began to examine it – the waggon, not Mr. Lloyd – and soon discovering his mistake, came to his own lodgings. In the middle of the patch of swamp close to which we stood, several horses were grazing. For a few minutes Jack looked at them, then, after braying in the most desperate fashion, started at a mad gallop towards a white pony some two hundred yards off. When he got to it he rubbed himself against it; both animals began to lick one another, then rolled down together and lay literally in one another's arms. I discovered afterwards that this was a pony that had belonged to a man I had travelled with, and had always been Jack's particular chum. They had not seen each other for months, but Jack had at once spotted his old friend. But the most curious part of the performance was to come. After lying down together for a few minutes they got up, and Jack began to examine in an inquisitive fashion the head of his friend, then started licking him on the eye, soon braying in the most heartrending fashion. I discovered afterwards that the pony had had an eye put out since we last saw him, and there is no doubt that the donkey expressed his sorrow for his friend. This donkey was the most intelligent animal I ever had in my possession.

DAVID DE WAAL

De Waal, a member of the Cape Legislative Assembly and one-time mayor of Cape Town, was a close friend of Cape premier Cecil Rhodes. De Waal accompanied the Cape-to-Cairo visionary on three trips to what was to become Rhodesia, then newly chartered to Rhodes' British South Africa Company. Rhodes, who could have been reading Galton, believed the divine purpose behind evolution was to produce an ideal race of men who would dominate the world and secure peace, justice and liberty for all. Some of that clearly rubbed off on De Waal.

WHAT EXCELLENT LABOURERS
From an 1890 trip to the Tuli area of southern Matabeleland.

We passed the night there, as did also a large number of Kafirs who were *en route* to the goldfields. These men kept themselves remarkably quiet that

night: they sat around the fires they had kindled not far from our waggons, and, though there were about a hundred of them, they hardly made themselves as much as heard. Early the following morning they again took up their march. We followed a little later and soon overtook them. It was a pretty sight to see them march – all in faultless step and every one dressed in white cloth. They were young, tall, strong Matabele, with beautifully shaped bodies. As we passed them each one politely saluted us. Again I thought, "What excellent labourers these men would make for the white man!" If Kafirs only knew the advantages of serving under white masters, they would gain more civilisation in one year than they do from missionaries in fifty; selling wives as slaves would cease, polygamy would die out, and they would have a fair opportunity of hearing the Word of God, for wherever the white man is, there also are churches and preachers. As it is, there is now a general scarcity of labourers: Kafirs can live so cheaply and earn their living so easily that they decline to be dependent on the European. They are, however, beginning to recognise their degraded position, and some of them already know the privileges to be enjoyed by being servants to the white man.

PREJUDICIAL TO HIS DIGNITY
An 1892 journey to Mashonaland with Rhodes via Portuguese territory on the east coast, checking gold reefs as they went.

At eleven o'clock we passed a Portuguese Lema, or Governor, with a train of Kafir attendants. The Lema, resting most comfortably in a litter, was being carried by four Kafirs and followed by about fifty others. At regular intervals fresh hands had to take up the litter, whilst the "big Portuguese man," lying upon his back with a book in his hand, troubled himself about nothing; if he wanted anything, he had simply to order and there it was. When the Lema's train of natives saw us they all halted and stared with amazement at us and our horses. Some of them, I dare say, had never before seen a horse, much less a man upon one; for, if I may trust what I was told, no horse had ever before within living memory passed that way. The Kafirs were much taken up with the sight. They placed the Lema down and clapped their hands at us – their usual form of welcome-bidding. The word "Englishman" I heard more than one whisper as they stood beholding what must have been to them an impressive spectacle. The Governor looked very annoyed at the conduct of his servants in putting the litter down until we had passed; I suppose he considered such an act prejudicial to his dignity.

SAFEST OF THE THREE
The tragic tale of Mr Theal, a trader from Mutare in Zimbabwe's eastern highlands.
As night set in, he lay down with a Kafir attendant on each side of him, naturally thinking that in case a lion should tackle them during the night he would be the safest of the three. It was a quiet night, and no lions were to be heard, except a few a long distance off. The Kafirs slept soundly till the morning broke, when they awoke and missed their master, not having the slightest idea as to what had become of him. Later in the morning they met some fellow-Kafirs, *en route* to Massi-Kessi, who told them the shocking tale that they had passed on their way the head and feet of a white man. The horror-stricken Kafirs went to see, and they found and recognised the head of their master, Mr. Theal!

IN HONOUR OF THE PHALLUS
They visited the Great Zimbabwe complex in the company of Frederick Selous, on the way passing spots where, according to De Waal, "the ancient Phoenicians built

their huts". As they arrived in their mule cart, they were surrounded by a ring of several hundred Shona, and noted with concern that they were all armed "and that every eye was fixed on us with unusual gravity". It emerged that the locals had been warned that the "great master" of the land had arrived and that he intended killing all males and taking their wives and children into captivity. Rhodes and his comrades reassured them by offering to surrender their guns for the duration of their stay. "We have only come to see the temple that former white men had built and occupied," they told the Shona, who were probably too relieved at being spared to worry about the visitors' odd take on the history of the ruins.

After taking coffee we went in one company to see the remains of old Simbabe. We did not at first sight think the ruins nearly so gigantic as on viewing them more closely we found them. Dr. Jameson and I climbed up the massive but elegantly-built walls, which at some parts are between twenty-five and thirty feet high, and we walked on them almost right round the ruins. We were much interested in the Phallus or Phalli, the Phœnecian god, the top part of which had fallen in. Inside the temple there grew a large wild tree, the branches of which bowed about thirty feet over the walls.

At sundown we returned to our cart.

The country round about the ruins exhibits most picturesque scenery. Look where you will, all is green and beautiful.

There being no waggon in which we could sleep we spread our beds on the ground and, though numbers of hideous centipedes were creeping there, and though our beds were almost as hard as stone, we tried to sleep. Mr. Rhodes lay in the cart. It was a quiet, cool night; nothing but the night-bird broke its silence. As I lay there with everything appearing so gloomy and solemn around me, it was strange to me to think that the place, which was now as desolate and quiet as a churchyard, was once the abode of thousands of white men, and a place at which, in all probability, great festivities had frequently taken place in honour of the Phallus.

CHARLES ALFORD

Alford was a mining engineer who apparently came to the Witwatersrand in about 1889, where he worked for a firm in Simmonds Street. By 1893 he had established himself at Mutare.

Charles Alford, a self-portrait.

Muriel, in England, was his only child, and she treasured this and four other illustrated letters from him all her life. This letter was written in November 1892 from Macequece, a few kilometres east of Mutare.

MY DEAR MURIEL
My dear Muriel …

I had a very long journey here – first I tried a "muchillo" which is a thing like this but I could not get enough men to take it in turns to carry me, so the next thing I tried was this, but on the second day the poor donkey got sick and so at last we had to walk all the way. I had thirty black men to carry my things and we all went in a row like this

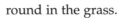

24 more →

and so we went along for 130 miles – when I came to a river I crossed it like this

… and every night I pitched my tent and had my dinner and went to bed in the tent with all the kaffirs sleeping round in the grass.

One day we killed a big

six feet long and one day it
rained so heavily that we had all to get underneath a large palm tree and
sit there nearly all day and we got all the
provisions wet which was the worst
thing of all – I did not see any lions but I
saw lots of wild buffalo and zebra and
many different kinds of buck and on
the Pungwe river I saw a great fat
hippopotamus put up his nose out of
the water to breathe, and on

the trees on the banks of the river there were little monkeys –
It was awfully hot and is so here now – some-
times the thermometer is above 90° – I am living now in an old fort – there is a dwelling
house and a kitchen and some storehouses and
a wall all round with gates and two little
Towers at the corners. The house is built of
stone and thatched with a great thick roof of
grass to keep out the heat of the sun and there is no glass
in the windows but calico instead and no boards for
floors but earth with mats spread over it … All the
Kaffirs – the black people who live in this country live in huts like this, and when a
number of huts are togeth-
er it is called a "Kraal".
The women
work in the
fields and carry
their babies in
baskets on their
backs …
Father.

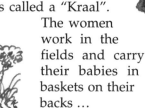

ROSE BLENNERHASSETT

Blennerhassett was a Welsh nurse who spent two years doing pioneering work in a mission hospital she co-founded at Mutare. This is from her homeward voyage in 1893.

USED THE TOOTHBRUSHES

We had another interesting traveller on board, in the shape of a madman. This unfortunate was shipped on board the *Kaiser*, at Durban I think, and soon proved very troublesome. He wandered all over the ship; chiefly frequenting the cabins of the second-class passengers, amongst whom he travelled. He ate the soap, drank hair-wash and eau de cologne, used the toothbrushes, and picked up any stray coins he could find. Every now and then he was searched and his unlawful acquisitions taken away from him. When we asked why he was not shut up in a cabin and taken out under supervision, we were much amused at being told that it was because he was an Englishman. "If he were German," said the Captain, "I would lock him up; but he is a bold man who locks up an Englishman." The poor madman never reached home; between the diet of soap and hair-wash, and the heat of the Red Sea, his health gave way. He had an apoplectic seizure, and died without recovering consciousness.

Gandhi outside his office in Johannesburg, 1905.

MOHANDAS GANDHI

After completing his training as a lawyer, Gandhi sailed from Bombay in 1893 to tackle a complex financial dispute between members of the Indian business community in South Africa. Disturbed by the mounting legal costs and acutely aware of his own ignorance of accounting, he persuaded the two sides to accept arbitration. Gandhi was so appalled by the conditions of Indian indentured labourers in South Africa that he stayed on after the case to fight for them. In the decade that followed, the future mahatma helped establish the Natal Indian Congress and conceived the idea of satyagraha, *or passive resistance, that won India her independence from imperial Britain half a century later. Despite his sympathies for the Boer cause, Gandhi also founded and served in an Indian ambulance corps, which served on the British side at the battle of Spion Kop during the Anglo-Boer War.*

I HAVE A FIRST CLASS TICKET
A week after his ship docked in Durban, Gandhi took the train for Pretoria, where the

343

court case was to be heard. Dada Abdulla Sheth was the wealthy Durban busi-
nessman who had hired Gandhi.

A first class seat was booked for me. It was usual there to pay five shillings extra, if one needed a bedding. Abdulla Sheth insisted that I should book one bedding but, out of obstinacy and pride and with a view to saving five shillings, I declined. Abdulla Sheth warned me. "Look, now," said he "this is a different country from India. Thank God, we have enough and to spare. Please do not stint yourself in anything that you may need."

I thanked him and asked him not to be anxious.

The train reached Maritzburg, the capital of Natal, at about 9 p.m. Beddings used to be provided at this station. A railway servant came and asked me if I wanted one. "No," said I, "I have one with me." He went away. But a passenger came next, and looked me up and down. He saw that I was a "coloured" man. This disturbed him. Out he went and came in again with one or two officials. They all kept quiet, when another official came to me and said, "Come along, you must go to the van compartment."

"But I have a first class ticket," said I.

"That doesn't matter," rejoined the other. "I tell you, you must go to the van compartment."

"I tell you, I was permitted to travel in this compartment at Durban, and I insist on going on in it."

"No, you won't," said the official. "You must leave this compartment, or else I shall have to call a police constable to push you out."

"Yes, you may. I refuse to get out voluntarily."

The constable came. He took me by the hand and pushed me out. My luggage was also taken out. I refused to go to the other compartment and the train steamed away. I went and sat in the waiting room, keeping my hand-bag with me, and leaving the other luggage where it was. The railway authorities had taken charge of it.

It was winter, and winter in the higher regions of South Africa is severely cold. Maritzburg being at a high altitude, the cold was extremely bitter. My overcoat was in my luggage, but I did not dare to ask for it lest I should be insulted again, so I sat and shivered. There was no light in the room. A passenger came in at about midnight and possibly wanted to talk to me. But I was in no mood to talk.

I began to think of my duty. Should I fight for my rights or go back to India, or should I go on to Pretoria without minding the insults, and return to India after finishing the case? It would be cowardice to run back to India without fulfilling my obligation. The hardship to which I was subjected was superficial – only a symptom of the deep disease of colour prejudice. I should try, if possible, to root out the disease and suffer hardships in the process. Redress for wrongs I should seek only to the extent that would be necessary for the removal of the colour prejudice.

So I decided to take the next available train to Pretoria.

The next morning Gandhi telegrammed a protest to the railway's general manag-
er in Durban, who also received a visit from Abdulla Sheth. When the evening
train arrived, there was a berth reserved for Gandhi. At Charlestown on the

Transvaal border, where the railway ended and passengers had to transfer to a stage-coach for Johannesburg, Gandhi had another unpleasant encounter when the white man in charge refused to let him sit inside with the white passengers. On the train from Johannesburg to Pretoria, Gandhi again took his place in a first class compartment – and was grudgingly allowed to stay.

On public footpaths
In Pretoria.

A very stringent enactment was passed in the Transvaal in 1885. It was slightly amended in 1886, and it was provided under the amended law that all Indians should pay a poll tax of £3 as fee for entry into the Transvaal. They might not own land except in locations set apart for them, and in practice even that was not to be ownership. They had no franchise. All this was under the special law for Asiatics, to whom the laws for the coloured people were also applied. Under these latter, Indians might not walk on public footpaths, and might not move out of doors after 9 p.m. without a permit. The enforcement of this last regulation was elastic so far as the Indians were concerned. Those who passed as "Arabs" were, as a matter of favour, exempted from it. The exemption thus naturally depended on the sweet will of the police.

I had to experience the effect of both these regulations. I often went out at night for a walk with Mr Coates, and we rarely got back home much before ten o'clock. What if the police arrested me? Mr Coates was more concerned about this than I. He had to issue passes to his Negro servants. But how could he give one to me? Only a master might issue a permit to a servant. If I had wanted one, and even if Mr Coates had been ready to give it, he could not have done so, for it would have been fraud.

So Mr Coates or some friend of his took me to the State Attorney, Dr Krause. We turned out to be barristers of the same Inn. The fact that I needed a pass to enable me to be out of doors after 9 p.m. was too much for him. He expressed sympathy for me. Instead of ordering for me a pass, he gave me a letter authorizing me to be out of doors at all hours without police interference. I always kept this letter on me whenever I went out. The fact that I never had to make use of it was a mere accident.

ALICE BALFOUR

In 1894 Balfour and three companions made a leisurely wagon trek from Mafikeng through Matabeleland and Mashonaland to Moçambique. She was a sister of Arthur Balfour, who would later become prime minister of Britain, and her party was given the use of Cecil Rhodes' mansion in Cape Town, and of the Free State president's coach in Bloemfontein. At a village in the Shurugwi area of Mashonaland one of her companions, a Mr Grey, ordered a chief to fetch him a calabash of beer. After a look at Grey, the chief complied "while the rest of the natives stood gazing at us", she wrote. "I didn't half like it, but I expect it is right to impress them with our 'moral superiority'." At the end of the five-month journey she lamented that she had seen neither lion, crocodile nor hippopotamus.

The Balfour expedition: camping north of Fort Victoria.

I THWACKED HIM

The town [Palapye] is built on the slope of a hill, and there is a lovely view of blue hills to the north, which augurs well for the future of our trip. I wanted to sketch this view, so Mr. Grey procured one of the police horses for me to ride up to the place. The animal was very lazy, and I thwacked him so hard with my umbrella that I broke the stick in two. (Do not imagine that I was cruelly urging him to unheard-of exertions: my ambition was only to make him keep up with Mr. Grey who was walking on foot!) As Bechuanaland stores do not boast of such rarely required articles as umbrellas, and as it was absolutely necessary for me to have one to shade me when sketching, my broken stick was given to a native to mend. It came back most artistically spliced with brass wire in ornamental patterns. The only drawback is that now the umbrella can neither be opened nor shut.

ON THIS SIDE

We reached the Shangani River early on the morning of the 11th, and when we woke up I called to John, our special "boy," to know on which side of the river we had outspanned, to which his lucid reply was "On this side."

346

BEST AND WILLIAMS

Workers from Moçambique headed for the Witwatersrand.

Messrs Best and Williams tried unsuccessfully in 1894 to sell the Witwatersrand Chamber of Mines a scheme for recruiting black workers on the east coast and railing them through a central depot to the Reef. In this way, they calculated, they could secure more than 20,000 labourers a year. Part of their written proposal was a description of the problems encountered by men obliged to make the whole journey on foot.

EVIDENCES OF THIS EVIL
Obstacles to natives en route. – The greatest and most dreaded of these are at the Transvaal borders, and for the succeeding hundred miles. In the first place, scarcity of food and shelter; from the borders to the Rand, on all the main foot-paths, can be seen the evidences of this evil; skeletons of those who have died are frequently seen, and at almost every store and dwelling near the road can be found those whom sickness or fatigue has compelled to give up the road and to either find a friend or perish. Secondly, many travel without a pass, not having the necessary shilling to buy one, and are forthwith taken by touts and agents (often assisted by the useful veldcornet), and forced to work for their greatest foes, the Boers and the railway construction contractors, who do not, we are told, scruple to use the sjambok freely, and often refuse to pay the natives even after three or four months' service. In addition to these general evils, the Inhambanes and Chobis are often cruelly treated by Mangonis, a class of Shangaans, on their way through the Shangaan country; this alone prevents all but the very bravest from leaving their homes.

FERDINAND ROTHSCHILD

Baron Rothschild was born into a banking family of legendary wealth, and spent his life enjoying it. He entertained kings, queens and emperors at his country estate in Buckinghamshire, and amassed a superb collection of art, books and rare objects. During a flying tour of South Africa in 1894-95, he stayed at Cecil Rhodes' home in Rondebosch amid a mess of unhung tapestries and Old Masters, and was a guest

347

of the De Beers Company at Kimberley. His Three Weeks in South Africa *was published the following year for private circulation, with an engraving of Cape Town's Standard Bank as frontispiece.*

VOLUMES OF WATER
An incident on the voyage out.

Yesterday was marked by a most distressing event. I had just finished my luncheon on the upper deck, was reading a book and smoking comfortably ensconsed in a snug corner on deck when Mr. Ohlson shouted to me to move away at once. I could not make out what he meant and stayed in my corner, but when he was joined by A.M. and others who vociferously called on me to move, I reluctantly left my seat – only just in the nick of time. A tremendous wave had broken over the bows, sending volumes of water along the deck. Fortunately I had secured a safe place on the hatch and at first was much amused at seeing a stampede of stewpans, boxes of provisions and various cooking and other utensils whirling along on the torrent. Bare-legged sailors came fishing for our tables and chairs, my book, in which I was much interested, eluded their grasp and perished in the deluge. But my mirth was soon checked on seeing a man covered with blood carrried past me to the dispensary. He was immediately followed by a second victim of the flood. We then heard that several third-class passengers had been knocked down by the wave. One had been severely cut about the face, another had his thigh seriously injured, and a third had been killed on the spot, his head having been dashed against the anchor. The poor fellow was a boatman from Algoa Bay, and helped to support his mother who has a small laundry at Plymouth. He is to be buried at sea – in fact, as I write these very words the engines are stopped and his body is being committed to the deep.

CHILDREN TO THE END OF THEIR LIVES
At the De Beers compound Rothschild found some 1,300 migrant workers all "contented, happy and merry", despite being kept virtual prisoners there for the duration of their contracts. It was Christmas Day, and the mine management had organised some festive activities, starting with a greased pole balanced across the water tank in the centre of the compound.

A few only of the Kaffirs ventured along the pole, none reached its end; they fell into the tank with a great splash amidst the roars and shrieks of the crowd. When walking the pole had come to an end, a hundred at least of the dusky spectators threw off their scanty accoutrements and jumped into the tank. Mr. Gardner Williams, Mr. Robinow, and other gentlemen connected with the Company were provided with bags full of shillings which they threw into the water. A wild scramble ensued. Up and down the black men bobbed in the water, diving, fighting, and splashing, groaning hideously and shouting vociferously; their long arms extended like snakes, their feet occasionally coming up like huge toads. It was a prehistoric scene in its every aspect and feature; it was a grotesque and picturesque but loathsome exhibition of uncouth savagery; it was a nightmare in broad daylight.

Before bidding a final adieu to the Kimberley Kaffirs let me say a word in their favour. They may be ignorant, they may be incapable of the same education as the white man, they may remain children to the end of their lives, but they are modest and moral, they enforce the most stringent laws against adultery in their natural condition, they are scrupulously clean in their habits, and with very few exceptions gentle, docile, good-tempered and easily managed. They always retain these characteristics unless they are brought under some bad European influence, which is chiefly exercised by inducing them to partake of alcoholic drink, especially the poisonous "Kaffir smoke" which even if only imbibed in small quantities has a vio-

lently intoxicating effect and drives the black man for the time being raving mad. In the compounds no alcohol is allowed, and with the money which the Kaffir saves, on returning to his kraal he purchases cattle, which in turn are exchanged, according to the amount, for a wife or several wives, who do all the work while he leads a life of happy idleness and contemplation.

PETER AUGUST MÖLLER

Möller was a Swedish army officer who went on to serve as an administrator in the Congo. He also travelled in South America, East Africa, and, in 1895-96, by ox-wagon through southern Angola and northern Namibia to Walvis Bay. These pieces are from this seven-month hunting trip.

LIKE A MURDERER

After this interlude we continued into the veld and only at about 11 o'clock did we discover the first tracks of a large herd of zebra. I had been walking the last hours to rest my horse, as I knew it would be strained during the strongest midday heat. We soon reached a vast, open grassland strewn with small groves of trees; here, but at a fairly great distance, we discovered a long row of zebra slowly moving away from us. They had not yet stopped for the midday rest and as I wanted to study them closer, I followed them at a distance below the wind until they entered a grove and came to a stop inside and round it. I stalked closer with the horse behind me, in the end I was close to a hundred metres from them and was just enjoying the interesting view of the animals in liberty and the beauty of the wilderness, when some dark object dashed out of the grass between me and the zebra – it was a herd of wildebeest that had been lying there and had now got my scent. At the same moment all the zebra were on their legs,

349

storming away at full speed, followed closely by the wildebeest. I had already rapidly mounted my good hunting horse that, pricking up its ears and stretching its neck at full gallop, as eager to hunt as I, pursued the fleeing animals of his own accord, while I had only to bend down for trees and branches and look out for holes in the ground made by hyenas or porcupines, that often caused falls and somersaults during such hunts on horseback. We flew along at lightning speed, soon I passed the wildebeest following the zebra and slowly I gained on the latter. Suddenly the animals swung round and stopped for a moment; I almost caught up with them and then the chase continued faster than before. In the herd of about 150 animals there was a large stallion which I had selected as my prize; he was constantly in the lead and encouraged the others to follow him by repeating "qoa-qoa-qoa-qoa".

I now had the wildebeest following behind me, capering about and kicking out as if they thought this was an amusing dance, I was now riding past the zebra mares and foals, having them on either side of me a few paces away; I was in the middle of the herd and was gaining on the stallions that kept in a small group in front. Soon I had all the mares behind me and, giving the horse a light touch with the hippo whip, I made a final effort to catch up with the stallions that also increased their speed and kept their distance well. I had been riding in a thick cloud of dust all the time, my eyes were almost clogged up and it did not even help to rub them with my hand. As I saw that I could not gain much more on them, I laid the gun across the withers of the horse, reined it in a little, jumped off and in a kneeling position fired two shots close to each other – I had a repeating rifle – at the big stallion. I thought I heard a strike home but the stallion continued with the others, therefore I quickly mounted and continued the chase anew. The animals were now far ahead and I lost sight of them but the dense dust-cloud showed distinctly where they had passed. Another gallop at full speed for a while and my horse suddenly threw itself to the side – there, behind some high grass, lay my zebra stallion with life just extinguished in the blue-shimmering, large eyes. I almost felt like a murderer – although we are once and for all obliged to live on animals …

EAT OF THE MEAT

Möller explained that the Ovambo had several kinds of sacrifice, some involving cattle or fowls, but one using a dog, and another with a bean standing in for the dog. The porridge mentioned here was served in lumps, which presumably made the process of eating the things stuck in it less messy. The aasisi *are the spirits of the dead.*

The dog that is to be sacrificed is not slaughtered, but its head is crushed to bits with a kerrie. A small stick wrapped with palm fibres is dipped in the blood running from the crushed head and it is stroked on the ill person's forehead, chest, arms and legs. After this the liver, heart and kidneys are roasted on the fire and porridge is made.

The sacrifice to Aasisi is made in the same way as described above and while saying the same words. A piece of the roasted parts is put into the porridge for the ill person and after having again sacrificed to Aasisi [by repeatedly throwing meat and porridge to Aasisi], the ill person must eat of the meat that he may not touch with his hands, but must bite off a piece sticking in the porridge. During this the Omutomisi [person performing the sacrifice] says the following strange words: "Eat your ohula [sacrifice], it is killed for you!"

The rest of the dog is now cooked and eaten by those present.

THE MARK OF A CURSE
In the Etosha area of Namibia.

The veld became more and more desert-like, we drove over quite bare, flat rocks. At sunrise we could glimpse the blue outlines of the Damara highland far on the horizon. Later in the day it started sloping slowly downwards and this was fortunate as the heat was terrible. Below us spread a wide plain that sloped from all sides towards the centre; there stood two lonely, tormented and withered camel-thorn trees and some goats were seen round them – that was the watering place Akahakana which we reached at about midday.

It is not encouraging to arrive at a place like this, in scorching heat, with exhausted draught-animals and tired yourself. The waterhole consisted of a couple of small holes in the rock with a little stinking, brack, green water, with a stinking, half-rotten tortoise-shell lying in the well and used by the Bergdamara for scooping the water. The small, half-dead acacias could not provide any shade and grass for the starved oxen was almost completely lacking; neither did they get enough water before the well was empty. Now they stood dejectedly round the wagons and did not want to look for food in the terrible heat of the sun. Never have I experienced such fantastic heat as at the bottom of this basin, never have I seen a more barren and sterile landscape; it was as if the mark of a curse had been imprinted on it. At two in the afternoon the heat became quite terrible, there was not a breath of wind, the air stood quivering, the ground was burning hot, underneath the wagons the thermometer climbed to over 40°C and in the sun it was over 50°C. To sleep was impossible, we lay panting in the heat, waiting for the evening. If the country was destitute and barren, so were the inhabitants, some few Bergdamara, thin and starved. Towards the evening they came down to water their goats and to fetch water, of which, since we had come, there was just nothing left. They begged for "tabakka" and good-naturedly let themselves be photographed without objection, in contrast to the aggressive people to the north. A whole family with women and children had come to drink and now squatted down to look at the strangers. Now and then they took out of their skin bags a dried locust that they seriously and thoughtfully stuck into the mouth and ate, sharing with the children whose swollen stomachs, thin limbs and hollow eyes indicated a starvation diet.

REASON TO BE JEALOUS
The Bushman appears to be shy and uncommunicative. The white man has generally nothing to fear from him as long as he is not wronged. In particular he must not be given reason to be jealous because they are very careful about their women; the bones of many white hunters are whitening in the desert where the arrow of the revengeful Bushman had struck him.

LIKE A CAT
One of my people, a Hottentot, once crept up to within range of a gnu that stood alone on a bare plain in the shade of an acacia, the only tree in the vicinity. Nobody could have thought of trying to creep up close to such a watchful animal on an open plain without any protection at all. But not so my Hottentot. Like a cat he started creeping along the ground towards the animal. It had seen us – we kept still at a distance of about 1000 metres – and was already disturbed, pricking up its ears and stamping its forefeet on the ground, but it obviously was not keen to leave the shade under the tree in the midday heat. My hunter creeps closer

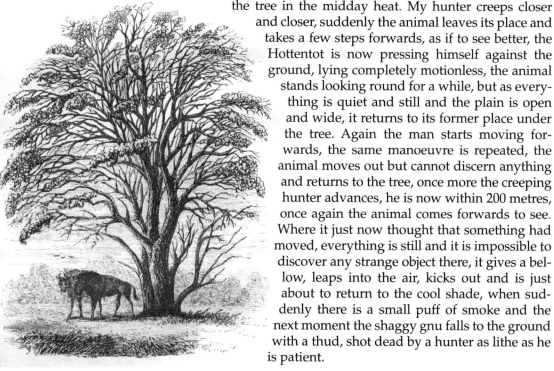

and closer, suddenly the animal leaves its place and takes a few steps forwards, as if to see better, the Hottentot is now pressing himself against the ground, lying completely motionless, the animal stands looking round for a while, but as everything is quiet and still and the plain is open and wide, it returns to its former place under the tree. Again the man starts moving forwards, the same manoeuvre is repeated, the animal moves out but cannot discern anything and returns to the tree, once more the creeping hunter advances, he is now within 200 metres, once again the animal comes forwards to see. Where it just now thought that something had moved, everything is still and it is impossible to discover any strange object there, it gives a bellow, leaps into the air, kicks out and is just about to return to the cool shade, when suddenly there is a small puff of smoke and the next moment the shaggy gnu falls to the ground with a thud, shot dead by a hunter as lithe as he is patient.

352

VIATOR

The pseudonymous Viator's 1896 pamphlet The Transvaal of Today *was a send-up of the travel books produced by visitors who had only the briefest acquaintance with South Africa. "Having now completed an extended tour of the Transvaal and northern districts of the Colony of Natal, covering a period close on eight days, I think it right to give the public the benefit of my experiences … feeling, as I do, that I am now thoroughly conversant with what is termed the situation, mining operations, speculation, and the future of the country," he wrote.*

I THINK IT'S THE RINDERPEST

I did not look round the town [Johannesburg] that night, I was worn out; so was shown to my room, and after ringing the alarm bell instead of turning on the electric light (which did not cause the slightest consternation), the two nobs being side by side – I am not used to the electric light – turned into bed. I had a comfortable room and a nice bed, but had a fearful bad night, experiencing in my dreams all the trials of my journey over again, quite apart from the fact that people in the hotel did not stop going to bed until about three o'clock in the morning, which does not have a soporific influence on a man who *has* gone to bed.

I awoke early the next morning, the 23rd, and after calling waiter, boy, umfaan, without any result, save that a tolerably good tenor voice had changed from baritone to deep bass, hastily dressed and proceeded to the dining rooms, when, by-the-bye, I found out that it was not early, that I had overslept myself.

The room was densely crowded with people partaking of breakfast. I was fortunate enough to find a seat at a table, and a very civil waiter, who at once placed matters on a comfortable footing by saying "Good morning, sir; just arrived, I presume."

I cannot make out what there was about my personal appearance to lead this waiter, and afterwards several other persons, to suppose that I was a new arrival, as I had taken some trouble to acquire the expression of a thoroughly-experienced resident – an expression indicative of the most perfect indifference to everybody and everything.

I may here relate a rather amusing incident which occurred at the breakfast table, which caused me to drop for a few moments "the most perfect indifferent expression."

I had already partaken of something or other, I forget

Johannesburg

353

The Simmer and Jack cyanide plant.

what, when, on glancing over the bill of fare, I ordered a mutton chop. The waiter brought it to me, but it was so hard I could not get my fork into it. Knowing the hotel was famous for its good cookery, and possessed French cooks, German cooks, Italian cooks, and cooks from other parts, I naturally asked the waiter for an explanation. I said, "This is curious, seeing what good professors you have in the cookery line. This chop is uneatable."

The waiter thought for a few minutes, then bent down and whispered in my ear, "Sir, I think it's the rinderpest."

I did not order anything else.

A CYANIDE DOG
Visiting a gold mine.

The manager kindly undertook to take me down a shaft. I had to decline on the excuse that I was thoroughly conversant with the undermining process, apart from the fact that my time was short – a man (a native) had just been brought up with a broken leg!

I saw only three animals on the mine (though, I believe, there were more), a compound cow and calf, and a cyanide dog.

The terms compound and cyanide do not refer to any particular class or breed; the compound cow and calf were so designated because they belonged to the compound manager, and the cyanide dog was simply a pup, prematurely aged, who had located himself outside the cyanide works.

Poor compound cow, I am afraid I must have seen the animal at its worst, as, owing to the

354

scarcity of green food, it presented the appearance of a cow that had supported itself on tailings, who took no interest in life, not even in the existence or subsistence of its near relative, the compound calf, whose appearance I decline to describe; it baffles description. I am inclined to think it will never reach mature age.

Poor, very poor, cyanide dog, I shall remember you for a long time. I can only describe you as an old pup belonging to the "any other class" breed, thin and emaciated.

I am told by gentlemen who have been employed on the cyanide works that it is injurious to the throat and chest. This must have affected my canine friend. There he sat all day amongst the broken pieces of quartz, not barking, but coughing at regular intervals. I hope to meet the animal again some day, but I am afraid, at least judging by his appearance, that long before I am able to pay another visit to the mines he will be amalgamated. I hope I may be pardoned using mining terms, but it becomes a habit after you have been some time on the mines.

Slocum greeting the full moon at sea.

JOSHUA SLOCUM

American mariner and first person to sail solo around the globe. He accomplished this extraordinary feat in an 11-metre sloop, the Spray, *under the mystic guidance of the pilot of Christopher Columbus' Pinta, whom he encountered in a vision after a surfeit of cheese and plums at the Azores. He had no corporeal companions except, briefly, a tree crab from the Keeling Islands, and a goat taken on board at St Helena, which ate his chart of the West Indies and his straw hat. At Samoa, his explanation that he sailed alone was greeted with scepticism. "I don't believe that. You had other mans, and eat 'em," said a woman. Slocum broke his circumnavigation to spend four months in South Africa in 1897-98, travelling around the country on a free rail pass provided by the colonial government. He tried to repeat his round-the-world feat in 1909, but disappeared without trace in the Atlantic.*

CURVES WITH MY HANDS
It sounds odd to hear scholars and statesmen say the world is flat; but it is a fact that three Boers favored by the opinion of President Krüger prepared a work to support that contention. While I was at Durban they came from Pretoria to obtain data from me, and they seemed annoyed when I told them that they could not prove it by my experience. With the advice to call up some ghost of the dark ages for

355

research, I went ashore, and left these three wise men poring over the *Spray's* track on a chart of the world, which, however, proved nothing to them, for it was on Mercator's projection, and behold, it was "flat." The next morning I met one of the party in a clergyman's garb, carrying a large Bible, not different from the one I had read. He tackled me, saying, "If you respect the Word of God, you must admit that the world is flat." "If the Word of God stands on a flat world −" I began. "What!" cried he, losing himself in a passion, and making as if he would run me through with an assagai. "What!" he shouted in astonishment and rage, while I jumped aside to dodge the imaginary weapon. Had this good but misguided fanatic been armed with a real weapon, the crew of the *Spray* would have died a martyr there and then. The next day, seeing him across the street, I bowed and made curves with my hands. He responded with a level, swimming movement of his hands, meaning "the world is flat." A pamphlet by these Transvaal geographers, made up of arguments from sources high and low to prove their theory, was mailed to me before I sailed from Africa on my last stretch around the globe.

Slocum later met Kruger in Pretoria; the president reacted "rather sharply" when he was told the American was on a voyage round the world. "You don't mean round *the world," he said. "It is impossible! You mean* in *the world. Impossible! Impossible!"*

THOMAS HARKER

Harker and a companion toured the southern Cape and lower Karoo on bicycles in 1898. Thanks to their use of strong inner tubes, in combination with the Dunlop Tropical Roadster Tyre, they suffered no punctures. Harker was however holed in the leg by a dog in Knysna.

NOTHING BUT LAUGH

After cycling easy for about eight miles, we encountered a farmer and his family sitting by the roadside. They had evidently been gathering flowers – perhaps for some near wedding – as they had clusters of them in their hands. I rode past at good rate, shouting out "Goede morgen" (good morning), and dashed through a rivulet which intersected the way. My friend, who was following me, jumped off his machine, and addressing the farmers humorously asked them (in Dutch) whether they had seen a mad cyclist pass. He declared to them that he had been chasing one for three days, that he (the cyclist) did nothing but laugh during that period, and was as mad as a cycling-hatter could be. The Boers replied that they had observed a "rooinek" flying past and that they thought he had fallen into a river close by with machine and all. We afterwards enjoyed the joke, but I imagine the report of the mad cyclist has by this time been circumstantially circulated through the Boer families; and no doubt it will be handed down from generation to generation.

HILDAGONDA DUCKITT

Queen of Cape cookery writers; not as weighty as Mrs Beeton, but she more than makes up for that with delightful local flavour. Hilda's Diary of a Cape Housekeeper, *published in 1902, three years before her death, has appendices on locust destruction and killing animals mercifully – with a diagram on how precisely to insert a stiletto into a crab's brain. Following the recipes for Mayonnaise Sauce and St Lucia Pudding is a section on tortoises, apparently at their best in September and October. "The tortoise is most nourishing, and scalloped with bread-crumbs, butter and lemon and salt, is most appetizing." To kill a tortoise: scratch its back, and when the head emerges, chop it off.*

A SUSPICION OF WHITE ONION

Well, shall we go to Cape Point for a week during the Christmas holidays? We all agree it will be delightful! The gentlemen of the party make arrangements with a farmer living at Simonstown over Red Hill to provide a tent-wagon and good span of oxen. We also take a small tent for some of the party to sleep in, the rest will sleep in the wagon; for each, rugs, a light gutta-percha mattress that folds up, a pillow. All this tidily strapped up goes down by train to Simonstown.

The ladies look after the hampers, as there are no shops at Cape Point, and only the lighthouse-keeper (who by the way is generally most hospitable and kind). We must not forget anything – least of all the gridiron.

We will take a piece of nice corned beef, which should be boiled slowly for four or five hours and pressed, putting a weight on a plate turned over it. This is a nice *pièce de résistance*, and a leg of mutton turned into sasaties. (See *Hilda's Where is it* for recipe.) Or we take the leg of mutton with us, and when we outspan cut it into chops to be cooked on the gridiron or pronged stick over the flame. Of course, one caters in proportion to the size of the party.

Some cold roasted chickens and cold frickadel keeps well, wrapped up in sandwich-paper.

Here is a good dish for picnics. Cut any pieces of mutton or beef (uncooked) in tiny shreds. Whisk up an egg or two with some finely-shred bread-crumbs, a little nutmeg, pepper, some hard-boiled eggs chopped up, a little parsley, a suspicion of white onion finely chopped. Mix all well together. Butter some paper and put a spoonful in each paper, folded *en papillote*, and fry in a pan in boiling fat, lard, or dripping. This is very good, and a nice dish for such occasions.

Then we generally can get fish. A nice "Hottentot" fish, or a galjeon – both are equally nice done on coals, just *broiled* with the scales on them. We also take down a few dozen mutton patties, which, when home-made, will keep for two days. A tin canister contains a few sponge-cakes, buns, moss bolletjies, some turn-overs, and any fruit that is in season, apricots, green almonds. In another basket we pack some cups and saucers, tea-pot, essence of coffee (*Hilda's Where is it*, p. 35). Milk we buy from the people living on the hills. The kettle for boiling the water is generally tied under the wagon, to economize space; and as we walk along we collect dry pieces of wood, which always is rather a scarce article; then if we have walked a good bit, and gathered lovely heather and other wild flowers as well as wood, we "Wait for the wagon, and all take a ride," and so we go on slowly but merrily, singing and laughing and talking; and at last Cape Point is reached, and oh, how grand and beautiful it looks!

The tired oxen are outspanned; the tent is pitched, and every one is busily engaged, and we are determined to have a very happy time.

FREDERICK FINDLAY

Frederick Findlay

Findlay was a nephew of Olive Schreiner, who, in a contribution to his turn-of-the-century book on his big-game shooting, condemned the "reckless and entirely wanton" destruction of African wildlife and urged the establishment of a vast game reserve. Findlay, whose book is peppered with photographs of himself surrounded by mounds of dead animals, agreed: it was, he said, "marvellous" how the great herds that once roamed over the rolling plains had been practically exterminated.

I DID NOT SHOOT HIM
Early next morning, accompanied by three of the young Boers, we set out in our cart for the flats, where they told us we should be sure to find wild ostriches and springbuck. On reaching the crest of a slight rise, one of the Boers sitting on the front seat of the cart suddenly shouted out, *"Daar is de vogelstruisen!"* ("There

are the ostriches!"), and we all scrambled out as fast as we could, rifle in hand. A dozen birds were standing about two hundred and fifty yards away, three cocks among them. For a moment they stood, and then, with half-spread wings, showing their beautiful white plumes, sped away at a great pace. *"Bang, bang, bang, bang, bom"* went our rifles and Piet Theron's old muzzle-loader, and a cock bird fell. Several voices shouted, *"Ik het hom geschiet"* ("I shot him"), and away we all rushed, as if we thought ownership

could be established by being first at the side of the prize. Young Andries Theron, who was soon going to marry a fair Karoo maiden, had been very anxious to shoot an ostrich, to secure some white feathers for her. He now shouted louder than the rest as he ran along, *"Ik het hom geschiet; Ik het mijn kogel hoor klap"* ("I shot him; I heard my bullet strike"), and reached the carcass first. Seizing one wing he lifted it to examine the plumes, then suddenly let it drop again, jumped back a pace or two, and said, *"Ik het hom nie geschiet nie"* ("I did not shoot him"). His sudden conversion was explained by the fact that there was a "D du T" brand in large letters on the fleshy part of the left leg. In a moment it flashed across our minds that we had shot a domesticated bird belonging to old Danie du Toit of Gemsbokfontein. There was no longer a claimant to the honour of having shot it. One remarked that he had seen his bullet strike the ground beyond the ostrich, another said he had not fired at a cock bird, and so on. We were, however, assured that the affair could be arranged with Oom Danie, which was evidently the case, for we heard nothing more about it.

TRANSVAAL GOVERNMENT

Pass laws of various description, all aimed at ensuring a supply of cheap black labour, had been around in South Africa for hundreds of years. But in 1896 the Transvaal Volksraad approved a law specially designed to trap men for the insatiable appetite of the gold mines. This is from an even harsher 1899 amendment.

With or without lashes
Article 16. – Any native who is found in a labour district without a district pass, according to Form "A," of that labour district, without a travelling or employer's pass, or with an elapsed travelling pass, or any trespasser according to Articles 5 and 8, shall be liable to a penalty of not less than £5, and not more than £10, or imprisonment, with or without hard labour, for not less than six weeks, and not more than three months, with or without lashes, not exceeding 25.

Any native sent by his employer, or wishing, with permission of his employer, to travel within the labour district in which he resides, must be provided by his employer with a special permit, describing the circumstances, and the object of his mission, date of issue, and the time for which

the pass was granted. This permit shall, however, in no case be issued for longer than three consecutive days.

Any native sent by his employer out of the district in which he works, must provide himself with a printed shilling permit; but, in case such native should travel together with his master, this permit shall not be required; and, in case of travelling by rail, the ticket shall be issued to the master only of such native, who shall furnish proof that the native is bona fide in his service by producing the native's monthly pass for the current month.

Any native found in a labour district without this permit, and not in possession of a district pass, under which he is seeking work, shall be punished in accordance with the penalties set forth above in this article.

NDUKWANA KA MBENGWANA

Ndukwana was the historian James Stuart's most important informant, yielding a wealth of detail on Zulu traditional custom and belief. A member of the Mtetwa clan, he would have been more than 60 years old when he spoke to Stuart in 1900: his father was thrown over a cliff on the orders of Dingane, who was himself killed in 1840. Here he talks about the land before the white man came.

No such things
Paths, private or public, slightly used and greatly used, traversed the country in all directions. There were no such things as *roads*, for there were no waggons. In no place could a man be said to be trespassing; there was freedom or right of way in all directions.

Sources

Major Roland Raven-Hart died in Durban in 1971, having in his lifetime travelled over 20,000 miles by canoe on the rivers of the world, capsizing only twice. An odyssey of a different sort was his journey through the accounts of early visitors to the Cape, locating them, translating them into English (he read and wrote 13 languages), and, most importantly, making them accessible to less talented individuals like myself. So, a word of gratitude to the gifted Raven-Hart, and to all the other historians without whom I would not have been able to produce this manuscript.

I also owe a particular debt to the Van Riebeeck Society, which has been so generous in allowing me to use material from almost a century of fine publications. In compiling the introductions to each entry in the text, I have borrowed liberally and without specific acknowledgement from the Dictionary of South African Biography, *the* Standard Encyclopedia of Southern Africa, *the forewords to modern editions of the travellers mentioned below, the admirable* Quarterly Bulletin of the National Library of South Africa, *and the now-defunct* Africana Notes and News.

My gratitude to those who gave permission to use copyrighted material. Every attempt has been made to trace copyright holders: I apologise for omissions or errors, and would be happy to rectify this in future editions.

Most of the pictures in this book were sourced from the collections of the National Library in Cape Town. Charles Alford's illustrations are reproduced courtesy of the Harold Strange Library of African Studies in Johannesburg; the San trance dance is from a shelter in the Eastern Cape. The originals of the portraits of Robert Gordon and Anne Barnard are in the William Fehr collection at the Castle in Cape Town.

Sources are listed here by the narrator named at the top of each extract in the text.

A deserter: in Edward Tabler, "A Deserter's Progress", *Africana Notes and News*, vol. 16 no. 5, March 1965.

Alexander, James: *An Expedition of Discovery into the Interior of Africa*, 2 vols., Henry Colburn, London, 1838.

Alford, Charles: "Letters from Africa to 'My dear Muriel'", Hilary J. Bruce and Carol Leigh (editors), *Africana Notes and News*, vol. 28 no. 5, March 1989.

Anderson, Andrew: *Twenty-Five Years in a Waggon*, 2 vols., Chapman and Hall, London, 1887.

Andersson, Charles: *Lake Ngami or Explorations and Discoveries, During Four Years' Wanderings in the Wilds of South Western Africa*, Hurst and Blackett, London, 1856.

Anonymous ("A real monkey-business"): "Historische Verhael vande tre-ffelijcke Reyse, gedaen naar de Oost-Indien ende China", in Isaac Commelin, *Begin ende Voortgangh van de Vereenighde Nederlantsche Geoctroyeerde Oost-Indische Compagnie*, 4 vols., Facsimile Uitgaven Nederland, Amsterdam, 1969. A facsimile reprint of the 1646 two-vol-ume original. My translation is based on the version in Roland Raven-Hart, *Before Van Riebeeck*, C. Struik, Cape Town, 1967.

Anonymous ("Even as a looking-glass"): "A visit to a Zulu Queen Dowager", *Cape Monthly Magazine*, vol. 5, 1859.

Anonymous ("Free under three"): *Cape Times* May 25, 1877. Thanks to Peter Coates, who discovered this piece.

Anonymous ("It was amazing"): "Journal, briefly describing a journey undertaken by the Commissary Cnoll ... to a place called the Warm Bath", in Colin Graham Botha, *Collectanea*, Van Riebeeck Society, Cape Town, 1924.

Anonymous ("Leaping over the sleepers"): *Pleasure: Advice and Information to Those in Search of it*, H. Guest, Grahamstown, 1887.

Anonymous ("Making a pretty harmony"): *A Journal of the First Voyage of Vasco da Gama*, edited by E.G. Ravenstein, The Hakluyt Society, London, 1898. Prof Eric Axelson says it has been established that the journal was "almost certainly" written by Álvaro Velho.

Anonymous ("Pretty good breakfasts"): Typescript, MSB 744, packet 1, document 45, National Library of South Africa, Cape Town.

Anonymous ("She made a hole"): "The shipwreck of the great galleon, the 'São João'", in Charles Ley (editor), *Portuguese Voyages 1498-1663*, J.M. Dent and Sons, London, 1947. For more on this and other wrecks along the South African coast, see Malcolm Turner's *Shipwrecks and Salvage in South Africa*, C. Struik, Cape Town, 1988.

Anonymous ("The salute was fired"): "Dagverhaal van de Landrijse, door den WelEdelen Gestrengen Heer Mr. Joachim Baron van Plettenberg ...", in George McCall Theal (editor), *Belangrijke Historische Dokumenten*, vol. 1 of 3 vols., Van de Sandt De Villiers and Co., Cape Town, 1896.

Anonymous ("They disappeared together"): *Narrative of the Loss of the Abeona*, Chalmers and Collins, Glasgow, 1821. The verse quoted is on a sheet titled *Elegy To the Memory of the unfortunate Sufferers on board the Abeona transport*, "printed for the booksellers", probably in Glasgow in 1820.

Arbousset, Thomas: *Missionary Excursion into the Blue Mountains*, edited by D. Ambrose and A. Brutsch, Morija Archives, 1991, for "Tree of the skirts", "Pleasant memories" and "And an umbrella".

— and Francois Daumas: *Narrative of an Exploratory Tour to the North-East of the Colony*, A.S. Robertson, Cape Town, 1846, for "Oh! my white men".

Atcherley, Rowland: *A Trip to Boërland*, Richard Bentley and Son, London, 1879.

Atherstone, William Guybon: "From Graham's Town to the Gouph", *Cape Monthly Magazine* (new series), vol. 3, 1871, for "A screw of the ark".

— "My Trip to the Diamond-fields", *Cape Monthly Magazine* (new series), vol. 3, 1871, for "His living coverlet", and the second instalment in the same volume and year for "With an audible crack".

Baatjoe of Samboua: Council of Justice records, CJ354, p. 459, in the state archives in Cape Town. I found the reference in Robert Ross' work on slavery, *Cape of Torments*, Routledge and Kegan Paul, London, 1983.

Bain, Andrew Geddes: *Journals of Andrew Geddes Bain*, edited by Margaret Lister, Van Riebeeck Society, Cape Town, 1949.

Baines, Thomas: *Explorations in South-West Africa*, Longman, Green, Longman, Roberts and Green, London, 1864, for "By blowing into it", "Flocks of lovely butterflies", "Trying to get an observation" and "Drinking the mirage".

— *Journal of Residence in Africa*, edited by R.F. Kennedy, 2 vols., Van Riebeeck Society, Cape Town, 1961 and 1964, for "Upon a bedroom candlestick", "Its eyes already pecked out" and "With considerable interest".

— *The Gold Regions of South Eastern Africa*, Edward Stanford, London, 1877, for "White shirts and trowsers".

There are several fine modern works on Baines and his art, one of which is Jane Carruthers and Marion Arnold's *The Life and Work of Thomas Baines*, Fernwood Press, Cape Town, 1996. There was a time the reading room of the National Library of South Africa in Cape Town was hung with Baines paintings. They were removed about the same time notices were put up warning users their bags and cellphones were about to be stolen.

Balfour, Alice: *Twelve Hundred Miles in a Waggon*, Edward Arnold, London, 1895.

Ballantyne, Robert: *Six Months at the Cape*, James Nisbet and Co., London, about 1909.

Barber, Frederick: *Zambezia and Matabeleland in the Seventies. The Narrative of Frederick Hugh Barber (1875 and 1877-8) and The Journal of Richard Frewen (1877-8)*, edited by Edward C. Tabler, Chatto and Windus, London, 1960.

Barber, Mary: "Wanderings in South Africa by sea and land, 1879 by Mary Elizabeth Barber", *Quarterly Bulletin of the South African Library*, vol. 18 no. 1, September 1963.

Barkly, Fanny: *Among Boers and Basutos*, Remington and Co., London, 1893. Maria's first employer, Lady Broome, gives more information on her protégé in *Colonial Memories*, Smith, Elder and Co., London, 1904.

Barnard, Anne: *The Cape Journals of Lady Anne Barnard*, edited by A.M. Lewin Robinson, Van Riebeeck Society, Cape Town, 1994. Not to be confused with a 1973 edition of letters and journals also edited by Lewin Robinson. For "Skin and all", "To lick his hand", "No business of mine", "Something very revolting", "Stinks of every description", "Laugh'd at by my friends" and "A clear good hand". On this last entry, see also *The India Guide*, George Gordon, printer, Calcutta, 1785, supposedly by an Emily Brittle but more likely written by a man.

— *The Cape Diaries of Lady Anne Barnard 1799-1800*, edited by Margaret Lenta and Basil le Cordeur, 2 vols.,Van Riebeeck Society, Cape Town, 1999, for "So choicely good", "Will you nothing take?", "Men of the Sea" and "To look at the stars".

Barros, João de: "Extracts from Da Asia: of the deeds which the Portuguese performed in the conquest and exploration of the lands and seas of the east. By João de Barros", in George McCall Theal (editor), *Records of*

South-Eastern Africa, vol. 6 of 9 vols., printed for the government of the Cape Colony, London, 1898-1903.

Barrow, John: *An Account of Travels into the Interior of Southern Africa, in the Years 1797 and 1798*, 2 vols., printed by A. Strahan for T. Cadell and W. Davies, London, 1801-1804. For a modern view of Barrow, see "Scratches on the face of the country, or what Mr Barrow saw in the land of the Bushmen", in Mary Louise Pratt's *Imperial Eyes: Travel Writing and Transculturation*, Routledge, London, 1992.

Barter, Charlotte (writing as "A Plain Woman"): *Alone Among the Zulus*, Society for Promoting Christian Knowledge, London, 1879.

Bergh, Olof: E. Mossop (editor), *Journals of the Expeditions of Olof Bergh and Isaq Schrijver*, Van Riebeeck Society, Cape Town, 1931.

Best and Williams: Witwatersrand Chamber of Mines, *Sixth Annual Report, For the Year Ending 31st December, 1894*, Argus Printing and Publishing Co., Johannesburg, 1895.

Beutler, August: "Reis van den Vaandrig Beutler", in George McCall Theal (editor), *Belangrijke Historische Dokumenten*, vol. 2 of 3 vols., Van de Sandt De Villiers and Co., Cape Town, 1896.

Bisset, John: *Sport and War*, John Murray, London, 1875.

Blank, Jan: "Extracts from the Journal of Commander van Riebeeck" for October 4, 1652, in Donald Moodie (editor), *The Record*, A.S. Robertson, Cape Town, 1838 to 1841.

Blennerhassett, Rose, and Lucy Sleeman: *Adventures in Mashonaland by Two Hospital Nurses*, London, Macmillan and Co., 1893.

Bokwe, John Knox: *Two Weeks' Trip to Cape Town*, Lovedale, 1884.

Bowker, James: "The Cave Cannibals of South Africa", *The Anthropological Review*, vol. 7 no. 25, April 1869.

Bucquoi, Jakob de: "Aanmerkelyke ontmoetingen in de zestien jaarige reize naa de Indien ...", in George McCall Theal (editor), *Records of South-Eastern Africa*, vol. 6 of 9 vols., printed for the government of the Cape Colony, London, 1898-1903.

Burchell, William: *Travels in the Interior of Southern Africa*, 2 vols., printed for Longman, Hurst, Rees, Orme, and Brown, London, 1822.

Butler, Henry: "A Glimpse of the Frontier, and a Gallop Through the Cape Colony", *United Services Journal*, vol. 77 nos. 307 and 308, 1846.

Cabreya, Joseph de: "Wreck of the Ship Nossa Senhora de Belem", in George McCall Theal (editor) *Records of South-Eastern Africa*, vol. 8 of 9 vols., printed for the government of the Cape Colony, London, 1898-1903.

Campbell, John: *Travels in South Africa*, Black and Parry, London, 1815, for "As if we had all been dead", "Temporary relief" and "Things of no use".

— *Travels in South Africa ... Being a Narrative of a Second Journey*, 2 vols., Francis Westley, London, 1822, for "The idea of washing", "So much of it", "With a loud voice", "Stars upon it", "Pieces of dirty paper", and "Without a bullet".

— Typescript of his journals, MSB77 in the National Library of South Africa, Cape Town, for "Heart of stone" and "He forgot his trousers".

— *Voyages to and from the Cape of Good Hope*, Religious Tract Society, London, 1840, for "He gently tapped his nose".

Camyn, Petronella: "Uittreksel van een Reisverhael van een Kaapsch meis-je", *Het Nederduitsch Zuid-Afrikaansch Tydschrift*, no. 6, December 1824, printed for the editor by the government printer, Cape Town. Her iden-tification as Camyn can be found in the newspaper *Die Burger*, November 20 1961. My thanks to Dr Stephen Craven for giving me access to a translation by Mrs D.C.J. Jongens-Jörg.

Casalis, Eugene: *My Life in Basuto Land*, The Religious Tract Society, London, 1889.

Castanheda, Fernão Lopes de: "Extracts from the history of the discovery and conquest of India by the Portuguese, by Fernão Lopes de Castenheda", in George McCall Theal (editor), *Records of South-Eastern Africa*, vol. 5 of 9 vols., printed for the government of the Cape Colony, London, 1898-1903. English translations of the other versions of D'Almeida's death, by Gaspar Correa and João de Barros, can be found in volumes 2 and 6 of the *Records*. There has been a suggestion that D'Almeida met his end at Hout Bay rather than on the shore of Table Bay: the debate on this claim reaches a climax of a sort in the *Quarterly Bulletin of the South African Library*, vol. 45 no. 1, September 1990. I have leaned heavily on Theal's three-volume *History and Ethnography of Africa South of the Zambesi*, Swan Sonnenschein and Co., London, 1907, in put-ting together the introduction to this and several other extracts.

Chalezac, Guillaume de: in Randolph Vigne (editor), *Guillaume Chenu de Chalezac, the "French Boy"*, Van Riebeeck Society, Cape Town, 1993.

Chamnan, Ok-Khun: in Pere Tachard, "Shipwreck at Cape Agulhas", *Cape Monthly Magazine*, vol. 1, 1857. See Michael Smithies' *A Siamese embassy lost in Africa: the odyssey of Ok-Khun Chamnan*, Silkworm Books, Bangkok, 1999.

Chapman, James: *Travels in the Interior of South Africa*, 2 vols., Bell and Daldy; Edward Stanford, London, 1868, for "We have got no news", "Some uncouth gestures", "Box on the ears", "Eyelid to eyelid", "For an ignorant savage", "Crunched a teapot", "Into the middle" and "I held the stump".

— *Travels in the Interior of South Africa*, Edward Tabler (editor), 2 vols., A.A. Balkema, Cape Town, 1971, © Swets & Zeitlinger Publishers and used with permission, for "There was no ink", "I had to run for it", "A pitch of excitement" and "Stuck in his open jaws". Read this rather than the 1868 work.

Coetsé, Jacobus: "Relaas, gegeven ... door den burger Jacobus Coetsé Jansz", in E.C. Godée Molsbergen (editor), *Reizen in Zuid-Afrika in de Hollandse Tijd*, vol. 2 of 4 vols., Martinus Nijhoff, The Hague, 1916-1932.

Coetzee, Jan Albert: *Dorsland-Trekkers*, Dirk Pons, Potchefstroom, 1926.

Cole, Alfred W.: *The Cape and the Kafirs*, Richard Bentley, London, 1852.

Colenso, John: *Ten Weeks in Natal*, Macmillan and Co., Cambridge, 1855.

Collins, Richard: "Supplement to the relations of a Journey into the Country of the Bosjesman and Caffre People", in Donald Moodie (edi-tor), *The Record*, A.S. Robertson, Cape Town, 1838 to 1841. For a more detailed account of the *Meermin*, see Jose Burman's *Great Shipwrecks off the Coast of Southern Africa*, C. Struik, Cape Town, 1967.

Couto, Diogo do: "Extracts from Asia: of the deeds which the Portuguese performed in the conquest and discovery of the lands and seas of the East. By Diogo de Couto," in George McCall Theal (editor), *Records of South-Eastern Africa*, vol. 5 of 9 vols., printed for the government of the Cape Colony, London, 1898-1903, for "Nothing to eat".

— "Narrative of the Shipwreck of the Great Ship São Thomé", in Charles Boxer (editor), *The Tragic History of the Sea*, University Press for the Hakluyt Society, Cambridge, 1959, for "This abominable cruelty".

　　Both extracts come originally from Do Couto's *Decada*, a magisterial continuation of the Portuguese history begun by João de Barros. Expressing the disillusionment of authors down the ages, Do Couto lamented to his princely patron Francisco da Gama that of 300 copies of an early volume of the *Decada*, he did not sell more than 30. "And to cap everything, although I sent presentation copies to the viceroy, to the archbishop, and to every captain of a fortress, none of them gave me in return so much as a jar of marmalade. I tell you this, that you may see how bad is this occupation nowadays."

Crew of the *Stavenisse*: "Extracts of a Despatch from Commander Simon van der Stell and Council to the Chamber XVII, April 15 1689", in Donald Moodie (editor), *The Record*, A.S. Robertson, Cape Town, 1838 to 1841.

Cumming, Roualeyn Gordon: *Five Years of a Hunter's Life in the Far Interior of South Africa*, 2 vols., John Murray, London, 1850.

Davis, Herman: *A Seven Months Cruise*, reprinted for private circulation, 1890. The second extract is from Eben Loomis' *An Eclipse Party in Africa. Chasing Summer Across the Equator in the U.S.S. Pensacola*, Boston, Roberts Bros., 1896.

Davis, John: *The Voyages and Works of John Davis the Navigator*, edited by Albert Markham, printed for the Hakluyt Society, London, 1880.

Decle, Lionel: *Three Years in Savage Africa*, Methuen, London, 1898.

De Grevenbroek, Johannes: "An Elegant and Accurate Account of The African Race", in Isaac Schapera (editor), *The Early Cape Hottentots*, Van Riebeeck Society, Cape Town, 1933.

Delegorgue, Adulphe: "Voyage dans L'Afrique Australe", in John Bird (editor), *The Annals of Natal*, vol. 1 of 2 vols., P. Davis and Sons, Pietermaritzburg, 1888.

De Vylder, Gustaf: *The Journal of Gustaf de Vylder*, edited by I. and J. Rudner, Van Riebeeck Society, Cape Town, 1998.

De Waal, David: *With Rhodes in Mashonaland*, J.C. Juta and Co., Cape Town, 1896. For a more recent exposition of the Phoenecian phallus theory, see A.C. Bruwer's breathtakingly single-minded *Zimbabwe: Rhodesia's Ancient Greatness*, Hugh Keartland, Johannesburg, 1965.

Dia!kwain: "The Relations of Wind, Moon, and Cloud to Human Beings After Death", in Wilhelm Bleek and Lucy Lloyd, *Specimens of Bushmen Folklore*, George Allen and Co., London, 1911. See also under "//Kabbo" below.

Dinya ka Zokozwayo: in C. de B. Webb and J.B. Wright (translators and editors), *The James Stuart Archive*, vol. 1 of 4 vols., Killie Campbell Africana Library manuscript series, University of Natal Press, Pietermaritzburg, from 1976.

Dixie, Florence: *In the Land of Misfortune*, Richard Bentley and Son, London, 1882. The copy in the Mendelssohn collection is inscribed by the authoress to the British general Redvers Buller.

Duckitt, Hildagonda: *Hilda's Diary of a Cape Housekeeper*, Chapman and Hall, London, 1902.

Duff Gordon, Lucy: *Letters from the Cape*, edited by Dorothea Fairbridge, Oxford University Press, London, 1927.

Dugmore, Henry: *The Reminiscences of an Albany Settler*, Richards, Glanville and Co., Graham's Town, 1871.

Eliza M.: "A Kafir account of Capetown", *King William's Town Gazette and Kaffrarian Banner*, 10 September 1863. It was rediscovered by Christopher Saunders, and is reprinted in full as "Eliza's Cape Town" in *Quarterly Bulletin of the South African Library*, vol. 35 no. 2, December 1980.

Ensor, Edward: "Edward John Ensor at the Cape in 1852", *Africana Notes and News*, vol. 20 no. 3, September 1972.

Ewart, James: *James Ewart's Journal*, C. Struik, Cape Town, 1970.

Fernandes, André: "Letters from the first missionaries of the Society of Jesus in the country south of the Zambesi", in George McCall Theal (editor), *Records of South-Eastern Africa*, vol. 2 of 9 vols., printed for the government of the Cape Colony, London, 1898-1903.

Fillis, Frank: *Life and Adventures of Frank E. Fillis*, Stafford and Co., London, 1901? See also Floris van der Merwe, *Frank Fillis: Die Verhaal van 'n Sirkuslegende*, FJG publications, Stellenbosch, 2002.

Findlay, Frederick: *Big Game Shooting and Travel in South-East Africa*, T. Fisher Unwin, London, 1903.

Fleming, William: in P.H. Butterfield, "A military Nimrod in mid-19th century Natal", *Africana Notes and News*, vol. 29 no. 6, June 1991.

Francken, Jacob: "Rampspoedige Reize van het O.I. schip *De Naarstigheid* …," in George McCall Theal (editor), *Records of South-Eastern Africa*, vol. 6 of 9 vols., printed for the government of the Cape Colony, London, 1898-1903.

Fynn, Henry Francis: *The Diary of Henry Francis Fynn*, edited by James Stuart and D. McK. Malcolm, Shuter and Shooter, Pietermaritzburg, 1950. The *Diary* is a heavily edited version of Fynn's already dubious version of events; historian and critic Dan Wylie has described it as "a tool for the preservation of an idealised settler face". See Wylie's *Savage Delight: White Myths of Shaka*, University of Natal Press, Pietermaritzburg, 2000.

Galton, Francis: *Narrative of an Explorer in Tropical South Africa*, Ward, Lock and Co., London, 1889, for "They did so in pairs", "She attempted to stand", "A useless cur", "Full in his face" and "Animals of unaccountable manners".

— *The Art of Travel*, John Murray, London, 1856, for "Keep your temper".
    For Galton's theory of eugenics and his beauty map, see his *Memories of my Life*, Methuen and Co., London, 1908.

Gandhi, Mohandas: *An Autobiography: The story of my Experiments with Truth*. Phoenix Press, London, 1949.

Gardiner, Allen: *Narrative of a Journey to the Zoolu Country*, William Crofts, London, 1836.

Gillmore, Parker: *The Land of the Boer*, Cassell, Petter, Galpin and Co., London, 1881. This is an edition of his *The Great Thirst Land* under another name. For "What do you call them?".

— *Days and Nights by the Desert*, Kegan Paul, Trench and Co., London, 1888, for "Guardian of the night".

Godlonton, Robert: *Journal of his journey by sea from Port Elizabeth to Cape Town*, typescript, Mendelssohn collection, Library of Parliament, Cape Town.

Goncharov, Ivan: in N.W. Wilson (translator) with notes by D.H. Varley, "A Russian View of the Cape in 1853", *Quarterly Bulletin of the South African Library*, vol. 15 no. 2, December 1960, for "Just like snow"; vol. 16 no. 1, September 1961, for "Yes, O yes, yes!".

For an account in English of the entire voyage, see Wilson's translation of Goncharov's *The Voyage of the Frigate Pallada*, The Folio Society, London, 1965.

Gordon, Robert: *Robert Jacob Gordon: Cape Travels, 1777 to 1786*, edited by P.E. Raper and M. Boucher, The Brenthurst Press, Houghton, 1988. (For all the extracts except the ones mentioned below.)

— Cullinan, Patrick: "Robert Jacob Gordon and Denis Diderot: The Hague, 1774", *Quarterly Bulletin of the South African Library*, vol. 43 no. 4, June 1989, for "Run to me".

— Cullinan, Patrick: "Colonel R.J. Gordon: The Dias Padrão at Kwaaihoek, the Heritage at Mossel Bay", in *Quarterly Bulletin of the South African Library*, vol 37 no. 2, December 1982, for "To make women fertile". The original is a partly illegible letter by Gordon to the French astronomer and politician Jean-Sylvain Bailly, which can be found in facsimile on pages 140-141 of VC595 in the state archives, Cape Town.

Also worth reading: Cullinan's *Robert Jacob Gordon*, Struik Winchester, Cape Town, 1992; and Eric Axelson's fascinating account of how he rediscovered the Kwaaihoek *padrão* in 1938 in *Congo to Cape*, Faber and Faber, London, 1973.

Graham, John: Item 10/88 on microfilm reel 119/5 of the Graham of Fintry papers, British Record Office, London.

Gutsche, Hugo: "Conversation with Rev. H. Gutsche", in J.M. Berning (editor), *The Historical 'Conversations' of Sir George Cory*, The Graham's Town Series, published for Rhodes University by Maskew Miller Longman, Cape Town, 1989.

Haafner, Jacob: *Lotgevallen en Vroegere Zeereizen*, Johannes van der Hey, Amsterdam, 1820.

/Han≠kass'o: "Kum 18, Sir Bartle Frere returns to Cape Town", in J.D. Lewis-Williams (editor), *Stories that Float from Afar*, David Philip, Cape Town, 2000. Whence also my note on pronunciation of the clicks.

Harker, Thomas: "A Cycling Tour in South Africa", *Cape Illustrated Magazine*, vol. 9 no. 4, December 1898.

Heeremans, Cornelis: "Voyage gedaan in den jaare 1688 den 19 October met het galjoot de Noord ..." in E.C. Godée Molsbergen (editor), *Reizen in Zuid-Afrika in de Hollandse Tijd*, vol. 3 of 4 vols., Martinus Nijhoff, The Hague, 1916-1932.

Herport, Albrecht: in Roland Raven-Hart, "New East-Indian Journey, by Albrecht Herport", *Africana Notes and News*, vol. 17 no. 3, September 1966.

Herschel, John: in David Evans, "Sir John Herschel to Captain Smyth", *Quarterly Bulletin of the South African Library*, vol. 25 no. 1, September 1970.

Hill, Pascoe: *Fifty Days on board a Slave-Vessel*, London, John Murray, 1844. For other equally sobering first-hand accounts of the horrors of the slave trade, see Robert Conrad's *Children of God's Fire. A Documentary History of Black Slavery in Brazil*, Princeton University Press, Princeton, 1983.

Hodgson, Thomas: *The Journals of Rev. T.L. Hodgson*, edited by R.L. Cope, Witwatersrand University Press, Johannesburg, 1977.

Holman, James: *A Voyage Round the World, including Travels in Africa, Asia, Australasia, America, etc. etc.*, 4 vols., Smith, Elder and Co., London, from 1834.

Holub, Emil: *Seven Years in South Africa*, 2 vols., London, Sampson Low, Marston, Searle, and Rivington, 1881.

Hubberly, William: "Journal and Evidence of William Hubberly", in Percival Kirby (editor), *A Source Book on the Wreck of the Grosvenor*, Van Riebeeck Society, Cape Town, 1953.

Huet, Dammes: *Reisjournaal*, edited by Karel Schoeman, South African Library, Cape Town, 1987. The library holds a rare copy of the first publication of the *Reisjournaal*, in the journal *Elpis* in 1857.

Hunt, William (writing as Gilarmi Farini): *Through the Kalahari Desert*, Sampson Low, Marston, Searle and Rivington, London, 1886. For subsequent attempts to find his desert ruins, see Fay Goldie's *Lost City of the Kalahari*, A.A. Balkema, Cape Town, 1963.

Hutchinson, Mrs (George William): *In Tents in the Transvaal*, London, Richard Bentley and Son, 1879.

Isaacs, Nathaniel: *Travels and Adventures in Eastern Africa*, 2 vols., Edward Churton, London, 1849. For a possibly more accessible version, see the two-volume set of the same title edited by Louis Herrman for the Van Riebeeck Society, Cape Town, 1936 and 1937. Dan Wylie (see the entry for Fynn above) describes *Travels* as a "mendacious, neo-fictional work". I have drawn on Wylie's work for my introductory section.

Janszen, Leendert: "Remonstrantie", in Roland Raven-Hart (editor), *Before Van Riebeeck. Callers at South Africa from 1488 to 1652*, C. Struik, Cape Town, 1967.

Jong, Cornelius de: *Reizen Naar de Kaap de Goede Hoop*, 3 vols., Francois Bohn, Haarlem, 1802.

//Kabbo: "//Kabbo's Intended Return Home", in Wilhelm Bleek and Lucy Lloyd, *Specimens of Bushmen Folklore*, George Allen and Co., London, 1911. See also Janette Deacon and Thomas Dowson, *Voices from the Past: /Xam Bushmen and the Bleek and Lloyd Collection*, Witwatersrand University Press, Johannesburg, 1996; and Pippa Skotnes (editor), *Miscast: Negotiating the Presence of the Bushmen*, University of Cape Town Press, Cape Town, 1996.

Kay, Stephen: *Travels and Researches in Caffraria*, John Mason, London, 1833.

Kennedy, David: *Kennedy at the Cape*, Edinburgh Publishing Co., Edinburgh, 1879.

Khān, Abū Tālib Ibn Muhammad: *The Travels of Mirza Abu Taleb Khan*, 2 vols., Longman, Hurst, Rees and Orme, London, 1810.

Kindersley, Jemima: *Letters from the Island of Teneriffe, Brazil, the Cape of Good Hope, and the East Indies*, J. Nourse, London, 1777.

Kirk, John: *The Zambesi Journal and Letters of Dr. John Kirk*, edited by Reginald Foskett, 2 vols., Oliver and Boyd, Edinburgh, 1965.

Kolb, Peter: *The Present State of the Cape of Good-Hope*, translated by Mr Medley, 2 vols., printed for W. Innys, London, 1731.

Langhansz, Christoffel: in Roland Raven-Hart, "The New East-Indian Journey of Christoffel Langhansz", *Quarterly Bulletin of the South African Library*, vol. 19 no. 4, June 1965. The original work is Langhansz' *Neue Ost-Indische Reise*, Leipzig, Verlegts Michael Rohrlachs, 1705.

Le Blanc, Marcel: in A.M. Lewin Robinson, "A Voyage to the Cape in 1687", *Quarterly Bulletin of the South African Library*, vol. 4 no. 4, June 1950. De Béze's brief account can be found translated into English in Edward Strangman's *Early French Callers at the Cape*, Juta, Cape Town, 1936.

Leguat, Francois: *A New Voyage to the East-Indies*, printed for R. Bonwicke and others, London, 1708. It has been suggested that Leguat's book is largely the product of his imagination. See "Francois Leguat – Fact or Fiction?" by A.H.S., *Africana Notes and News*, vol. 4 no. 6, December 1946.

Le Vaillant, Francois: *Travels from the Cape of Good-Hope into the Interior Parts of Africa*, 2 vols., London, William Lane, 1790, for "It was always Saturday".

— *New Travels into the Interior Parts of Africa by the Way of the Cape of Good Hope*, 3 vols., G.G. and J. Robinson, London, 1796, for "An absurd custom", "Such insupportable pain", "An intractable animal", "An extraordinary shot", "Without wasting time" and "This faithful servant".

   Further reading: J.C. Quinton and others, *Francois le Vaillant, Traveller in South Africa*, Library of Parliament, Cape Town, 1973; and Jane Meiring's *The Truth in Masquerade*, Juta and Co., Cape Town, 1973.

Lichtenstein, Heinrich: *Travels in Southern Africa*, 2 vols., Van Riebeeck Society, Cape Town, 1928 and 1930. A caveat: this 19th-century translation from the German original has been described as "worthless as a source for historical research". See "A Vague Equivalent", by A.H.S, *Africana Notes and News*, vol. 17 no. 5, March 1967.

Livingstone, David: *Missionary Travels and Researches in South Africa*, John Murray, London, 1857, for "You speak like a chief", "The great sow", "His cold wet nose", "As large as life", "No more of me", "Telling their children", "Kina bomba" and "Is this the way you go?"

— "Explorations into the Interior of Africa", *Journal of the Royal Geographical Society*, vol. 27, 1857, for "A thousand comets".

— and Charles Livingstone: *Narrative of an Expedition to the Zambesi and its Tributaries*, John Murray, London, 1865, for "Obligations to the madmen", "He answered promptly", "Sneaking about in the dark", "The fish swim", "With eyes flashing fury", and "I am dead".

— *Livingstone's African Journal 1853-1856*, edited by Isaac Schapera, 2 vols., Chatto and Windus, London, 1963, for "Slap his nose", "They wish seed" and "In a fit of raging thirst".

— *Livingstone's Private Journals 1851-1853*, edited by Isaac Schapera, Chatto and Windus, London, 1960, for "No chin at all".

   For critical examinations, see Tim Jeal, *Livingstone*, Heinemann,

London, 1973; and Dorothy O. Helly: *Livingstone's Legacy; Horace Waller and Victorian Mythmaking*, Ohio University Press, Ohio, 1987.

Loomis, Eben: See under Herman Davis.

Low, Harriet: "An American Girl at the Cape in 1834", *Quarterly Bulletin of the South African Library*, vol. 23 no. 3, March 1969. The original is Katharine Hilliard (editor), *My mother's journal: a young lady's diary of five years spent in Manila, Macao, and the Cape of Good Hope*, Boston, George H. Ellis, 1900.

Lucas, Gould: S. O'Byrne, "Lucas's Account of the Wreck of the *Birkenhead*", *Africana Notes and News*, vol. 17 no. 6, June 1967. See Jose Burman's *Great Shipwrecks off the Coast of Southern Africa*, C. Struik, Cape Town, 1967, for a fuller account of the wreck.

Lugubu ka Mangaliso: in C. de B. Webb and J.B. Wright (translators and editors), *The James Stuart Archive*, vol. 1 of 4 vols., Killie Campbell Africana Library manuscript series, University of Natal Press, Pietermaritzburg, from 1976.

M.: See under Eliza.

MacDonald, Henry: *The Times*, January 1 1875. For more on the *Cospatrick*, see Jose Burman's *Shipwreck!*, Human and Rousseau, Cape Town, 1986.

MacKenzie, John: *Ten Years North of the Orange River*, Edmonston and Douglas, Edinburgh, 1871.

Maclear, Thomas: in Brian Warner, "Sir George Grey, Lady Grey and Admiral Sir Henry Keppel", *Quarterly Bulletin of the South African Library*, vol. 33 no. 1, September 1978. For Grey's subsequent vendetta against Keppel, see B.J. Dalton's "Sir George Grey and the Keppel Affair", *Historical Studies*, University of Melbourne, vol. 16, 1974. Whatever Grey's failings, a century and a half later we still owe him gratitude for the magnificent collection of books that he donated to the National Library of South Africa.

Makuza ka Mkomoyi: in C. de B. Webb and J.B. Wright (translators and editors), *The James Stuart Archive*, vol. 2 of 4 vols., Killie Campbell Africana Library manuscript series, University of Natal Press, Pietermaritzburg, from 1976.

Mauch, Carl: *The Journals of Carl Mauch*, edited by E.E. Burke, National Archives of Rhodesia, Salisbury, 1969. For a biography, see F.O. Bernhard's *Karl Mauch, African Explorer*, C. Struik, Cape Town, 1971.

Mesquita Perestrello, Manuel de: "Narrative of the Wreck of the Ship St Benedict", in George McCall Theal (editor), *Records of South-Eastern Africa*, vol. 1 of 9 vols., printed for the government of the Cape Colony, London, 1898-1903.

Methuen, Henry: *Life in the Wilderness*, Richard Bentley, London, 1846.

Mitford, Bertram: *Through the Zulu Country*, Kegan Paul, Trench and Co., London, 1883.

Moffat, Robert: *Missionary Labours and Scenes in Southern Africa*, John Snow, London, 1842.

Mohr, Edward: *To the Victoria Falls of the Zambesi*, Sampson Low, Marston, Searle, and Rivington, London, 1876.

Möller, Peter: *Journey in Africa Through Angola, Ovampoland & Damaraland 1895-1896*, edited by I. and J. Rudner, C. Struik, Cape Town, 1974.

Monclaros, Franciso de: "Account of the Journey made by Fathers of the Company of Jesus", in George McCall Theal (editor), *Records of South-Eastern Africa*, vol. 3 of 9 vols., printed for the government of the Cape Colony, London, 1898-1903.

Morton, William: *South African Diamond Fields*, printed for the American Geographical Society, New York, 1887.

Muller, Willem: "Copie daghregister gehouden bij den corporael Willem Muller ..." in E.C. Godée Molsbergen (editor), *Reizen in Zuid-Afrika in de Hollandse Tijd*, vol. 1 of 4 vols., Martinus Nijhoff, The Hague, 1916-1932.

Muys, Gerrit Ridder: Text described in a margin note as "De tocht van de hoeker De Grundel", in E.C. Godée Molsbergen (editor), *Reizen in Zuid-Afrika in de Hollandse Tijd*, vol. 1 of 4 vols., Martinus Nijhoff, The Hague, 1916-1932.

Ndukwana ka Mbengwana: in C. de B. Webb and J.B. Wright (translators and editors), *The James Stuart Archive*, vol. 4 of 4 vols., Killie Campbell Africana Library manuscript series, University of Natal Press, Pietermaritzburg, from 1976.

Nelson, William: "Some letters by William Nelson, F.R.H.S, L.M.C.A., F.L.Sc.", *Africana Notes and News*, vol. 20 no. 5, March 1973, for "Novelties of interest"; vol. 20 no. 6, June 1973, for "The only white man".

Noah, William: Frank Clune, *Bound for Botany Bay*, Angus and Robertson, London, 1965.

North, Marianne: *Recollections of a Happy Life, Being the Autobiography of Marianne North*, edited by Mrs John Addington Symonds, 2 vols., Macmillan and Co., London, 1892. An abridged version of North's travels, with a wealth of colour illustrations, is in *Marianne North: A Vision of Eden*, published in collaboration with the Royal Botanic Gardens, Kew, by Webb and Bower, Exeter, 1980.

Nzunzu: "Mahaya ka Nongqabana" in C. de B. Webb and J.B. Wright (translators and editors), *The James Stuart Archive*, vol. 2 of 4 vols., Killie Campbell Africana Library manuscript series, University of Natal Press, Pietermaritzburg, from 1976.

Oates, Frank: *Matabele Land and the Victoria Falls*, C. Kegan Paul and Co., London, 1881.

Oswell, William Cotton: William Edward Oswell, *William Cotton Oswell ... The Story of his Life*, 2 vols., William Heinemann, London, 1900.

Owen, Francis: *The Diary of the Reverend Francis Owen*, edited by George Cory, Van Riebeeck Society, Cape Town, 1926.

Owen, William: *Narrative of Voyages to Explore the Shores of Africa, Arabia, and Madagascar*, 2 vols., Richard Bentley, London, 1833. The rest of Msimbithi's extraordinary story can be found in Nathaniel Isaacs' *Travels and Adventures in Eastern Africa* and the "diary" of Henry Francis Fynn, both listed above.

Paravicini di Capelli, Willem: "Journaal en verbaal eener landreyse in den jare 1803 ..." in E.C. Godée Molsbergen (editor), *Reizen in Zuid-Afrika in de Hollandse Tijd*, vol. 4 of 4 vols., Martinus Nijhoff, The Hague, 1916-1932. His personal journal is in W.J. de Kock (editor), *Reize in de Binnen-Landen van Zuid-Africa Gedaan in den Jaare 1803 door W.B.E. Paravicini di Capelli*, Van Riebeeck Society, Cape Town, 1965. For another account of the journey, see W. Blommaert and J.A. Wiid (editors), *Die Joernaal van Dirk Gysbert van Reenen*, Van Riebeeck Society, Cape Town, 1937.

Parkes, Fanny: *Wanderings of a Pilgrim, in Search of the Picturesque*, 2 vols., Pelham Richardson, London, 1850. Parkes is sometimes listed in bibliographies as Fanny Parlby, presumably her married name. Biographies of her and other equally adventurous woman travellers can be found in Jane Robinson's comprehensive *Wayward Women*, Oxford University Press, Oxford, 1990.

Percival, Robert: *An Account of the Cape of Good Hope*, C. and R. Baldwin, London, 1804.

Philipps, Thomas: *Scenes and Occurrences in Albany and Caffer-Land*, William Marsh, London, 1827.

Pump, John (pseudonym): "Mr Pump's Protest Against Railways", *Cape Monthly Magazine*, vol. 2, 1857.

Ramadeen, an Indian: "Indian Immigrants Commission Evidence: Tenth Day" in *The Natal Government Gazette*, vol. 39 no. 2266, Pietermaritzburg, October 18 1887. This is part of the Report of the Indian Immigrants Commission 1885-7, which is consolidated in Y. Meer, *Documents of Indentured Labour*, Institute of Black Research, Durban, 1980.

Renshaw, Richard: *Voyage to the Cape of Good Hope, the Indian Ocean, and up the Red Sea, with Travels into Egypt, through the Desert, &c.*, printed by M. Wilson, Manchester, 1821.

Report of the Select Committee: "Report of the Select Committee appointed to consider the Introduction of Native Labourers from beyond the border of the colony", in The Natal Government Gazette, vol. 24 no. 1386, Pietermaritzburg, November 19 1872.

Ridgill, Richard: "My First Journey", *Cape Monthly Magazine* (new series), vol. 1, 1870.

Roche, Harriet: *On Trek in the Transvaal*, Sampson Low, Marston, Searle and Rivington, London, 1878.

Rose, Cowper: *Four Years in Southern Africa*, Henry Colburn and Richard Bentley, London, 1829.

Rothschild, Ferdinand: *Three Weeks in South Africa*, Hatchard, London, 1895.

Russell, William: *A Voyage to the Cape*, Chatto and Windus, London, 1886.

Sandeman, Edward: *Eight Months in an Ox-waggon*, Griffith and Farran, London, 1880.

Santos, João dos: "Eastern Ethiopia by Friar João dos Santos", in George McCall Theal (editor), *Records of South-Eastern Africa*, vol. 7 of 9 vols., printed for the government of the Cape Colony, London, 1898-1903.

Scherzer, Karl: *Narrative of the Circumnavigation of the Globe by the Austrian Frigate Novara*, 3 vols., Saunders, Otley and Co., London, 1861 to 1863.

Schouten, Wouter: in Roland Raven-Hart, "East Indian Voyage by Wouter Schouten", *Africana Notes and News*, vol. 16 no. 7, September 1965.

Schreyer, Johann: in Roland Raven-Hart, "Johan Schreyer's description of the Hottentots, 1679", *Quarterly Bulletin of the South African Library*, vol. 19 no. 2, December 1964. Raven-Hart has a detailed note on testicle removal.

Schweitzer, Christopher: in Christoph Frick: *A Relation of Two Several Voyages Made into the East-Indies*, printed for D. Brown and others, London, 1700.

Selous, Frederick Courteney: *A Hunter's Wanderings in Africa*, Richard Bentley and Son, London, 1890, for "Kafirs walk in front" and "Torn in three pieces".

— *Travel and Adventure in South-East Africa*, Rowland Ward and Co., London, 1893, for "That's no hymn", "The horrors of that journey" and "As if carved in stone".

Serpa Pinto, Alexandre de: *How I Crossed Africa*, 2 vols., Sampson Low, Marston, Searle and Rivington, London, 1881.

Shelley, Edward: *Diaries of his travels in Africa during the years 1851-54*, typescript in Library of Parliament, Cape Town.

Shipp, John: *Memoirs of the Extraordinary Military Career of John Shipp*, Thomas Tegg, London, 1843.

Silleman, Daniel: *Ongeluckig, of Droevig Verhaal van't Schip de Gouden Buys*, Gijsbert de Groot en Antony van Dam, Amsterdam, 1718.

Slocum, Joshua: *Sailing Alone Around the World*, Sampson Low, Marston and Co., London, 1900.

Smith, Andrew: *The Diary of Dr. Andrew Smith*, edited by Percival Kirby, Van Riebeeck Society, Cape Town, 1939, for "A great quantity of wind" and "A little clay".

— *Andrew Smith's Journal of his Expedition into the Interior of South Africa*, edited by William Lye, published for the South African Museum by A.A. Balkema, Cape Town, 1975, © Swets & Zeitlinger Publishers and used with permission, for "The Man Jackal", "Now you are a man", "And also a large dog" and "Sucking at their clothes".

Soga, John Henderson: *The South-Eastern Bantu*, Witwatersrand University Press, Johannesburg, 1930.

Sparrman, Anders: *A Voyage to the Cape of Good Hope*, edited by V.S. Forbes, 2 vols., Van Riebeeck Society, Cape Town, 1975. For criticism of Sparrman, see Robert Gordon's scathing comments on pages 166-7 of Patrick Cullinan's *Robert Jacob Gordon*, Struik Winchester, Cape Town, 1992.

Steytler, John: "Remembrances from 1832-1900 by John George Steytler", *Quarterly Bulletin of the South African Library*, vol. 25 no. 1, September 1970.

Stout, Benjamin: *Narrative of the Loss of the Ship* Hercules, printed for J. Johnson, London, 1798. Claims that Stout's account was a fiction are dealt with by Percival Kirby in "Sane Hercule", *Africana Notes and News*, vol. 18 no. 1, March 1968.

Stuart, Katie: "Fraserburg to Cape Town twenty years ago", *The Veld*, vol. 3 no. 2, April 1902. See Karel Schoeman's "Katie Stuart, 1862-1925: A public life", *Quarterly Bulletin of the National Library of South Africa*, vol. 56 no. 3, March 2002.

Stubbs, Thomas: *The Reminiscences of Thomas Stubbs*, edited by W.A. Maxwell and R.T. McGeogh, A.A. Balkema, Cape Town, 1978.

Tachard, Gui: *A relation of the voyage to Siam, performed by six Jesuits …*, printed by T.B. for J. Robinson and A. Churchil, London, 1688. A more recent translation of Tachard's visits to the Cape is in Edward Strangman, *Early French Callers at the Cape*, Juta and Co., Cape Town, 1936.

Tappe, David: in Roland Raven-Hart, "The Fifteen-Year Journey of David Tappen", *Quarterly Bulletin of the South African Library*, vol. 21 no. 4, June 1967. The original is in Tappe's *Funffzehen jährige curiöse und denckwürdige auch sehr gefährliche Ost-Indianische Reise-Beschreibung*, Gottfried Freytag, Hanover and Wolffenbüttel, 1704. For a 20th-century perspective on early visitors' fascination with Khoikhoi genitalia, see Yvette Abrahams' paper "The great national insult: science, sexuality and the Khoisan in the eighteenth and early nineteenth century", Grahamstown, 1995.

Teenstra, Marten Douwe: *De Vruchten Mijner Werkzaamheden, Gedurende Mijne Reize Over de Kaap de Goede Hoop*, 3 vols., H. Eekhoff, Groningen, 1830. The Van Riebeeck Society issued a partial reprint with an English précis under the same title in 1943.

Terry, Edward: *A Voyage to East-India*, printed for J. Wilkie, W. Cater, S. Hayes and E. Easton, London, 1777.

Thunberg, Carl: *Travels in Europe, Africa, and Asia*, 3 vols., W. Richardson and J. Egerton, London, 1793.

Transvaal government: in Chamber of Mines of the South African Republic, *Eleventh annual report for the year ending 31st December, 1899*, Argus Printing and Publishing Co., Cape Town, 1900.

Trigardt, Louis: *Die Dagboek van Louis Trigardt*, edited by Prof T.H. le Roux, J.L. van Schaik, Pretoria, 1964. My translation of "Cry the whole night" borrows from the version in Eric Axelson (editor), *South African Explorers*, Oxford University Press, London, 1954.

Trollope, Anthony: *South Africa*, 2 vols., Chapman and Hall, London, 1878.

Van Meerhoff, Pieter: "Journal kept by the junior surgeon Pieter van Meerhoff", in H.B. Thom (editor), *Journal of Jan van Riebeeck*, vol. 3 of 3 vols., A.A. Balkema for the Van Riebeeck Society, Cape Town, 1952-1958.

Van Reenen, Jacob: "A Journal of a Journey from the Cape of Good Hope", in *The Wreck of the Grosvenor*, preface by C. Graham Botha, Van Riebeeck Society, Cape Town, 1927.

Vaz d'Almada, Francisco: "Treatise of the Misfortune that Befell the Great Ship Sao Joao Baptista", in Charles Boxer (editor), *The Tragic History of the Sea*, University Press for the Hakluyt Society, Cambridge, 1959.

Viator (pseudonym): *The Transvaal of To-Day; and How it Struck a Stranger*, printed by Wm. Watson, Pietermaritzburg, 1896.

Wallenberg, Jacob: "The Travels of a Busybody at the Cape", translated by Michael Roberts, *Quarterly Bulletin of the South African Library*, vol. 2 no. 2, December 1947.

Ward, Harriet: *Five Years in Kaffirland*, 2 vols., Henry Colburn, London, 1848.

Wahlberg, Johan: *Johan August Wahlberg: Travel Journals (and some letters)*, edited by A. Craig and C. Hummel, Van Riebeeck Society, Cape Town, 1994.

Webb, William: *A Journal of the Proceedings of the Doddington East-Indiaman*, printed for T. Kinnersly, London, 1758.

Wikar, Hendrik: *The Journal of Hendrik Jacob Wikar*, edited by E.E. Mossop, Van Riebeeck Society, Cape Town, 1935.

Wurmb, Karl von: in O.H. Spohr, "Two letters from the Promontory of the Cape written in March 1775 by Fr. von Wurmb", *Quarterly Bulletin of the South African Library*, vol. 28 no. 2, December 1973.